THE ATLAS OF
GERMAN
W · I · N · E · S
AND TRAVELLER'S GUIDE
TO THE VINEYARDS

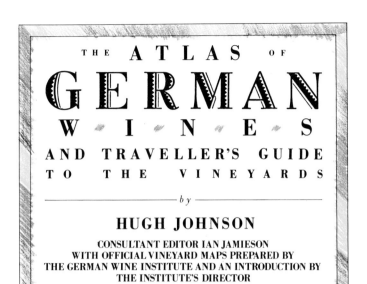

THE ATLAS OF
GERMAN
W · I · N · E · S
AND TRAVELLER'S GUIDE
TO THE VINEYARDS

by

HUGH JOHNSON

CONSULTANT EDITOR IAN JAMIESON
WITH OFFICIAL VINEYARD MAPS PREPARED BY
THE GERMAN WINE INSTITUTE AND AN INTRODUCTION BY
THE INSTITUTE'S DIRECTOR

SIMON AND SCHUSTER
NEW YORK

Editor Anita Wagner
Art Editor Eljay Crompton
Proofreader Alison Franks
Indexer Tom Blott
Researcher Thomas Pawlak
Picture Research Brigitte Arora
Production Philip Collyer

Senior Executive Editor Chris Foulkes
Senior Executive Art Editor Roger Walton
Associate Editor Dian Taylor

The Atlas of German Wines
Edited and designed by Mitchell Beazley International Ltd.,
Artists House, 14–15 Manette Street, London W1V 5LB
Copyright © Mitchell Beazley Publishers 1986
Text copyright © Hugh Johnson and Mitchell Beazley Publishers 1986
Touring maps copyright © Hallwag AG, Bern 1986 and
© Mairs Geographischer Verlag, Stuttgart 1986
Wine maps copyright © Stabilisierungsfonds für Wein 1986
All rights reserved

Published by Simon and Schuster
A Division of Simon & Schuster, Inc.
Simon & Schuster Building
1230 Avenue of the Americas
New York, New York 10020

ISBN 0-672-61102-X

Library of Congress Catalog Card Information upon request

The publishers and the author owe a great debt of gratitude to the German
Wine Institute for providing the wine maps for this Atlas. However, it is
stressed that statements made and opinions expressed in the text are those of
the author, not the Institute.

Some sections of this book update and extend text in *Hugh Johnson's Modern
Encyclopedia of Wine*, published in 1983.

The author and publishers will be grateful for any information which will
assist them in keeping future editions up to date. Although all reasonable care
has been taken in the preparation of this book, neither the publishers nor the
author can accept any liability for any consequences arising from the use
thereof or from the information contained herein.

Filmsetting by Servis Filmsetting Ltd, Manchester, England
Reproduced by Gilchrist Bros. Ltd., Leeds, England
Printed and bound in West Germany by Neue Stalling GmbH & Co KG,
Oldenburg.

FOREWORD

Soil, climate and grape varieties are the three basic factors for growing fine wines, combined by human skill and the dedication of wine growers to centuries of tradition. Soil and climate are the blessed gifts of nature, which give the individual and distinctive character and quality to wines. And nature cannot be changed by man – it is the creation of God, created to last until the end of time. Nature is the reason – not commercial inventions – why the geography of vineyards, with all its elements from soil to climate, is so important for the definition of wine.

This is not the case with other products of human endeavour: in almost any industry, raw materials, equipment and labour can be moved to almost anywhere they may be needed to manufacture a certain product. Agricultural commodities can be produced in many places without much difference in quality or character. A vine, too, can be planted in many places on earth, but the quality and character, the aroma and bouquet, the style and finesse will be different, depending on where the vine is grown. Human intelligence can move almost anything, but never a vineyard. Therefore, there is scarcely any other product in the world for which the birthplace, the place of origin, is as important as it is for noble wines. This is the philosophy behind labelling a wine with its appellation of geographical origin – in contrast to the industrial concept of a trade-mark.

This philosophy is less relevant for winegrowing countries in warm latitudes, where climate and soil may not change over large areas of flat surface; where wine is mostly produced in quantity as a commodity without any individual significance. The appellation of origin is most relevant in countries or regions where individual wines of distinctive character and quality are produced. In Germany, the wine-producing regions along the Rhine and the Mosel are extremely sensitive to geographical designations, because at the latitude of 50 degrees – the same latitude as Labrador – climate and soil often change within a mere hundred metres or so. Germany's winegrowing regions are mostly concentrated in the narrow valleys of the Rhine, Mosel and their tributaries, which twist and turn through mountainous, mainly wooded regions in basin-shaped land areas. The variations in soil structure stem directly from the earth's history: slaty on deep inclines, fertile, alluvial land at the foot of hills; other areas have lime deposits or volcanic rocks. The micro-climate of a vineyard depends on whether it faces south or west, on the steepness of its incline, the intensity of the sun's reflection from the surface of the river, the proximity of sheltering forests or mountain peaks, the altitude and the soil humidity. Therefore, reaching back for centuries in history, every single hill or section of a valley has a different name, is a geographical origin with individual characteristics, is a "Lage" (site) explicitly named on the wine label.

In the 2,000-year-old winegrowing landscapes of Germany, everything is on a small scale. Distances between villages are short. About 90,000 families own mostly small parcels of vineyards in different localities. Most winegrowing communities have several vineyards within their boundaries. Historically, there have been more than 25,000 individual vineyard names in use for centuries; this number was reduced to less than 3,000 in the early 1970s – an important amendment of the wine law. Still this immense variety of natural and historical conditions with so many names makes German wine labels look complicated. But as soon as you understand the philosophy behind such names, labels for German wines tell a fascinating story. As the famous German playwright Carl Zuckmayer said: "Reading a German wine list with imagination is as joyful as having drunk each wine."

The philosophy of German geographical origins is in principle the same as the system of the *Appellation d'Origine Contrôlée* in France. But there is one fundamental difference: in France the appellation of origin simultaneously decides and defines the quality grading. The appellations, for example, *Grand Cru*, *Premier Cru* and *Deuxième Cru*, once determined, are forever kept. The birth-place determines the nobility. If wine is grown in an area without an *appellation d'origine* it cannot be labelled with its birth-place, even if the wine is excellent.

Such a system does not fit for Germany. Here, the geography designates the origin, but not necessarily the quality of a wine. In good years, with special endeavour and dedication, the winegrower can produce the highest classified wines. Under less propitious circumstances his best produce is just a normal quality wine from a specified region. Therefore, German winegrowers even from the most famous vineyards are challenged every year to produce high qualities to justify their reputation. They can never rest on a good name. The "human factor" is still essential for the taste and style of wine. German wines are individuals, as are the men who make them.

God made nature, man makes wine. The cultural history of winegrowing landscapes and their inhabitants is reflected in their wine and its geography. One must travel along the narrow river valleys, through the picturesque historical villages, enjoy the local Gasthaus, see the winegrowers' families, grandparents and children included, working in the vineyard, breathe the incomparable smell of young wine coming from the door of old, vaulted wine cellars, to understand the secret of German wines. What would have been the life-style, art and culture in German wine country without wine? Symphonies from Beethoven, sculptures from Riemenschneider or poems from Goethe have all been inspired by the spirit of German wine.

Germany's legal requirements for wine sound complicated. But they become simpler as you study the labels, or better, when you travel through the wine country. This Atlas, written by an independent and highly respected expert with his own individual judgements, is a complete guide to both. It opens the door to wonderful experiences for the wine connoisseur, for the traveller and for the lover of wine culture.

DR. FRANZ WERNER MICHEL
CO-DIRECTOR OF THE GERMAN WINE INSTITUTE

► C O N T E N T S ◄

C O N T E N T S

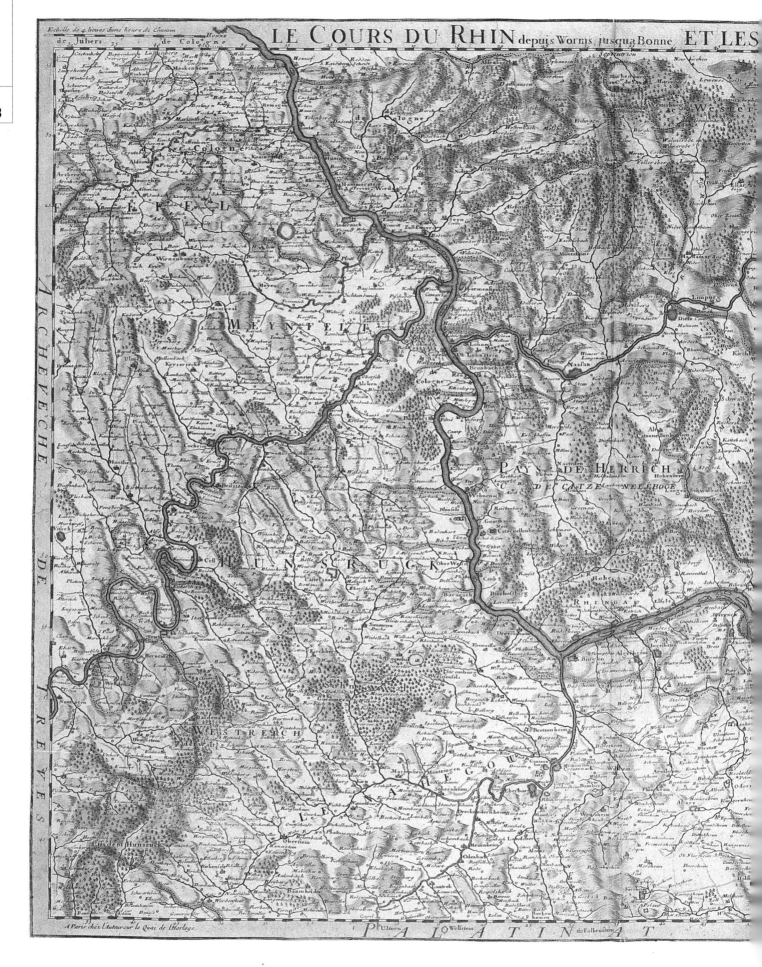

LE COURS DU RHIN depuis Worms jusqu'à Bonne ET LES

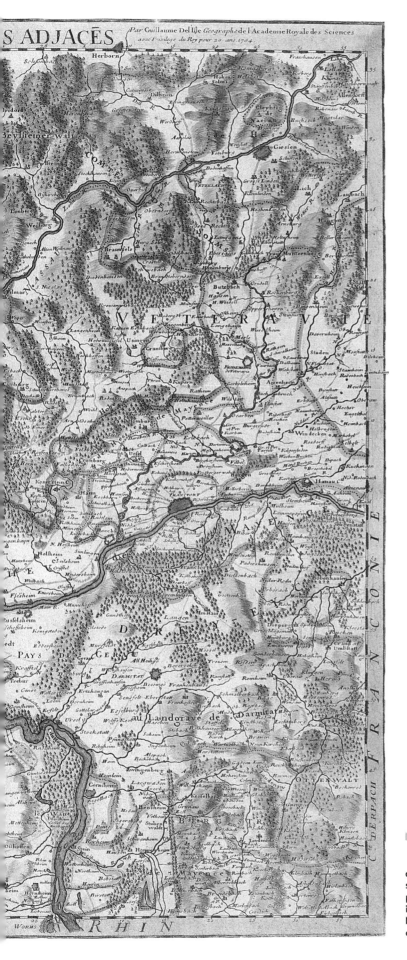

The Rhineland in 1704, as seen by Guillaume Del Lisle, cartographer to the French Academy of Sciences. Like the rest of Germany, the Rhineland was then divided into dozens of princely and ecclesiastical states, and cities such as Frankfurt ("Francfort") still sheltered behind their walls. Many of today's wine villages were in prosperous existence in 1704: the present-day row of Rheingau towns is recognizable in Rüdesheim, Winckel, Estrich, Erbach, Walff (Ob and Nid) and Hochheim. Sadly, though the woods are clearly and delightfully shown, the vines have to be guessed at.

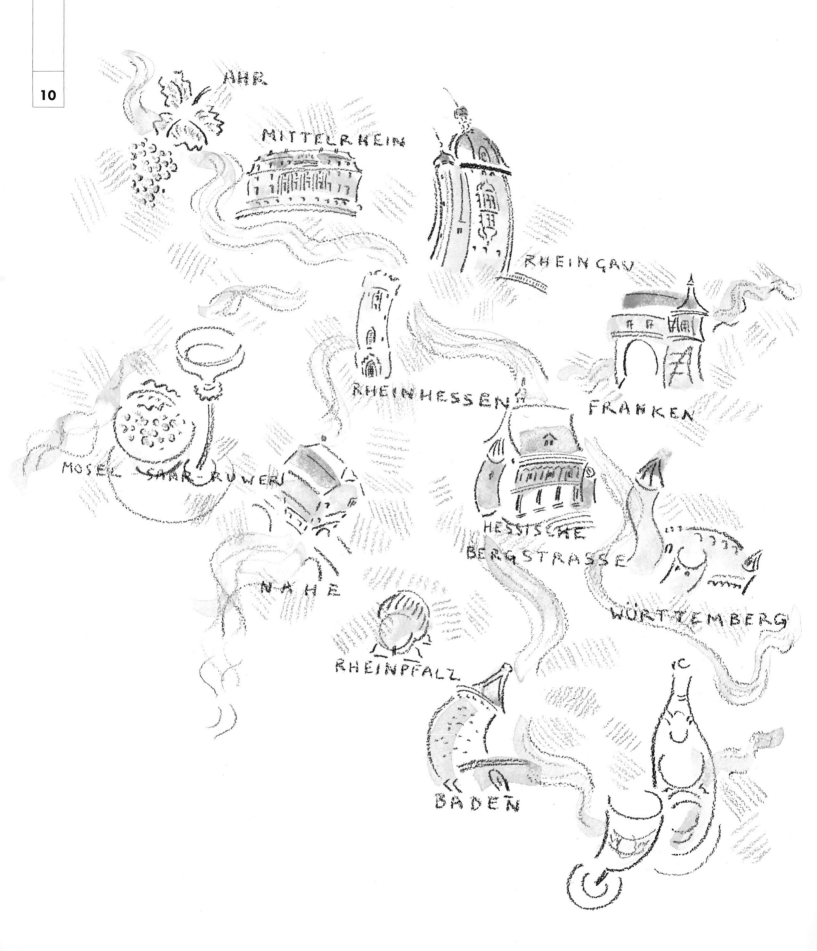

AHR

MITTELRHEIN

RHEINGAU

MOSEL–SAAR–RUWER

RHEINHESSEN

FRANKEN

NAHE

HESSISCHE
BERGSTRASSE

WÜRTTEMBERG

RHEINPFALZ

BADEN

INTRODUCTION

German wine is a category far more distinct and homogeneous than French or Italian: distinct but various in itself as water-colour is among paintings, or woodwind among the sounds of the orchestra.

Its distinctiveness is relatively easy to describe; its variety almost impossible. How does German wine differ from French, or any other within Europe or beyond? Transparency is the word that always comes to my mind first: transparency of texture that makes the intricacies of aroma and flavour more readily discernible than in other wines. A relatively low alcohol content is partly responsible: the sheer winey weight, the warmth in the mouth known as "vinosity", is generally missing. Its place is taken, or should be taken, by a sort of tension between incipient richness and fruity acidity. This tension, or balance, is the hallmark of all the best German wines and is the reason for their astonishing longevity: they continue to mature with benefit for longer than any other white wines except those that are very sweet.

There is another reason, however, for thinking of modern German wines as homogeneous, and that is the powerful tendency of the consumer to settle for a common denominator rather than to exploit the available variety. The tendency is much more pronounced outside Germany, where the German language of the label seems to present a barrier few are prepared to tackle. A regional blend is probably the most characteristic German wine the majority of foreign wine-drinkers have ever tasted. Whether it is labelled Niersteiner or Liebfraumilch it is blended to a predictable formula, mild and slightly sweet, the least quarrelsome of wines, but also the least inspiring. It is as though all France were represented by the Côtes du Rhône, or all Italy by Valpolicella.

Happily, German wine drinkers are more than equal to the challenge, and revel in the variety at their disposal. Nobody knows how, when and where to enjoy their wine better than the Germans – especially the inhabitants of the wine villages themselves. The contrast with France could hardly be more complete. What friendly corner does the Médoc provide for a visitor to sit and sip and discuss Pauillac or Margaux with the locals? But try to find a German wine village without its Weinstube. By definition it is the people who make the wine in Germany who appreciate it most. While there are great estates (and great cooperatives) that specialize in exports, most German growers at least give the impression that they are making wine primarily for themselves, their friends, and the guests at their fireside in winter, and in their flowery courtyard in summer. It is central to the experience of German wine to be guided, barrel by barrel or bottle by bottle, through the range of qualities, of different grape varieties and ages of wine that even a small farmer of the Rhine or Mosel will have in his cellar. Few will have less than a dozen sorts to pour, to justify or criticize or just to enjoy with a craftsman's pride.

The whole family is usually involved. If their taste is not always exquisite, they make up for refinement in appreciation and gratitude for God's gifts. It is hard physical work tending a vineyard and making wine, especially on the steep slopes where all Germany's best wine is made. Yet few people have a more satisfying calling, or a more immediate and tangible return for their labours.

This is the romantic side of German wine. The full picture may contain more steel vats and industrial-looking premises than pretty half-timbered farmhouses. Yet in Germany the romantic imposes itself. It cannot be ignored, any more than the serpentine gorges of the rivers, the eagle's-nest castles, the blackness of the forest or the tender green of spring in the vineyards. The true Germany is here, and not in the airports and autobahns, the city centres and supermarkets. German wines express the essence of these matchless landscapes – at least for their fortunate inhabitants. Happily both are easily accessible for visitors, too.

If sensual enjoyment is the first aim and object of wine, it is followed, qualified and amplified by aesthetic interest. Like any species of thing that is consistent yet alterable, similar yet various, all wines invite analysis and comparison.

With its clear family resemblance, yet its widely various character, German wine appeals to the discriminating mind more than any other, except perhaps claret. It is the most analytically labelled wine on earth, and anyone with the leisure and the capacity could progress logically through each harvest noting and comparing the gradations of quality by categories. Indeed the official government wine-tasting and -approving machinery does just that, systematically controlling every barrel or tank of wine in Germany. Sometimes, it must be said, paper definition seems to take over from definition of flavour. But the system is there, and sets standards that the conscientious achieve and the curious can follow.

The heart of Germany's systematic approach to wine is a simple measurement; a measurement that every winegrower the world over makes before the vintage: the sugar content of the grapes. In warmer climates ripe grapes are taken for granted; in Germany it is only certain privileged sites that reach the necessary sugar-level with any degree of regularity. It could be done more easily, with grape varieties that ripen early in the autumn. But it is a hard fact of life that the best varieties take a long time to reach maturity. Precocious grapes never develop the concentrated fruity acidity that makes wine lively, vigorous and refreshing when young, and gives it the potential to mature; to develop depth and harmony.

The archetypal late grape is the Riesling: with very few exceptions all Germany's best wines are made from it. But it is only worth planting Riesling in warm soils on sheltered south- and east-facing slopes. On flatter, colder land the overwhelming favourite is the early ripening Müller-Thurgau. The two grapes between them account for almost half of the total vineyard of Germany.

The other half is largely composed of such traditional varieties as Silvaner and Ruländer, whose qualities on certain soils, and in certain local climates, ensure their continued use; of the red grapes, led by the Spätburgunder or Pinot Noir, that together make up about ten per cent of Germany's vineyards, and of a dozen or so new vine varieties, led by the Kerner, which have been bred in a continuing effort to achieve Riesling quality without its concomitant drawbacks: uncertain ripening, and (by German standards) less than spectacular crops. (For the grapes of Germany, *see* pages 20–21.)

The German word for vineyard is "Weinberg", literally "winehill". There are flat Weinbergs, even a few very good flat Weinbergs; but the word forcefully expresses the innate superiority of a hill as a place to grow grapes. If it is true on the "Côtes" of France (true even in Italy: it was Vergil who said "vines love an open hill"), it becomes even truer as you go further north. The angle of the sun in the sky gets lower, the shadows longer. With cooler temperatures the grapes start ripening later – so late in the autumn that the vines cast long shadows for most of the day, and mist often wreathes the vineyards all morning long before the sun finds the power to burn it off.

At these latitudes every degree of warmth lasting an hour longer is precious to the ripening fruit. Where everything is marginal the microclimate is crucial – microclimate in the most intimate vine-by-vine detail, as wall or tree or tilt of hill casts shade or gives protection. What is the balance in calories (as the measure of heat) if one vine shades another all morning, but towards dusk prevents accumulated warm air lying in the vine-row from being flushed out by the evening breeze?

One simple rule prevails: a south slope has the edge. A slope at 45 degrees to the sky theoretically (although perhaps not effectively) has the sun straight overhead. Its rays hit the ground perpendicularly, shadows are minimized, and at least one of the consequences of a high latitude is eliminated. The south slope of most German hills is the only one it is worth planting with vines.

In foggy districts a westerly tilt can be an added advantage: there is less fog in the afternoon so the sun has better access. In the majority of districts, though, in Germany as in France (think of Alsace, the Côte d'Or, the Champagne Côte de Blancs), it is better to incline to the east from south for the sake of the early sun that warms the ground, warmth that lingers in a sheltered vineyard even after the afternoon casts shadows between the vines.

The maps in this Atlas make it crystal clear just how far these considerations have shaped the landscapes of Germany. In map after map the vineyards fall exactly as the hill-shadows would if the world were upside down and the sun shining from the north.

Since geology and soil structure is far less consistent and predictable than sunshine it is equally clear that they must be secondary considerations in deciding where to cultivate the vine. Soils change rapidly and often within a district, yet the vines hug each south slope. Certainly there will be differences in fertility, in drainage, in mineral make-up of the soil that will make it yield bigger or smaller crops, ripen them more (or less) regularly, and give hints of flavour to the fruit, and eventually to the wine.

Important though these variations are, the matter for endless earnest discussion over a glass, and certainly the cause of considerable differences in price between one wine and another, in Germany they are not considered central to the question of essential quality. Only the ripeness of the grapes is taken into official account. Theoretically at least any vineyard in Germany can produce top-quality wine: it only needs to conjure the grape-sugar from the elusive sun. Differences between vineyards are officially considered to be questions of style, and therefore in the final analysis subjective.

The German philosophy is thus the precise opposite of the French, which classifies land, and only land. The proprietor of a Burgundy Grand Cru vineyard may add as much sugar as necessary to his wine (within the law) and still sell it as Grand Cru; thus in the highest quality category. Whereas the owner of Germany's noblest plot may find himself, in a year of terrible weather, with nothing but unclassified Tafelwein to sell.

The difference is fundamental, and well worth thinking about. Can both the German and the French philosophies be right in their contexts? It seems to one observer at least that logic and natural justice are truly on the side of the German.

So, in German law, the land is neutral. Quality begins each vintage with the sugar content of the grapes. The vital reading of the "degree Oechsle" – the specific gravity of the must – decides once for all whether the wine will be graded as "quality wine" or not; even more significant, whether it will be allowed as natural quality wine, and if so at what quality level. These distinctions need spelling out in detail. The law is complex and easily misunderstood.

The crop, let us say, is a wash-out. The autumn has turned cold and wet, the grapes are only half-ripened, and with rot beginning and no prospect of better weather the grower is obliged to pick. The specific gravity of the juice from one vineyard is barely enough to convert to 5% of natural alcohol. This is the minimum figure to qualify as even the humblest form of wine, Tafelwein – and to make wine at all it needs a huge addition of non-grape sugar. Whatever the grower does he cannot sell this as his own wine, identified by its vineyard or even district name. He will probably do best to sell it as base-wine to be converted by some big concern into sparkling Sekt.

Three days later in a better-sited vineyard the same grower measures his "must-weight" again, and discovers to his satisfaction that these grapes have a specific gravity of 1.060 (or an "Oechsle-degree" of 60). This means 7.5% potential alcohol, the minimum allowed for a quality wine from a specific region (Qualitätswein bestimmter Anbaugebiete). While the wine still requires the addition of non-grape sugar to increase its alcohol content to a satisfactory level of between 9 and 11 per cent, it is legally acknowledged as the wine of his vineyard. In many cases such "QbA" wines have distinct and satisfying characters – just as their French counterparts from under-ripened grapes helped by chaptalization would do.

It is up to the grower to decide whether the character of the wine emerges best if he leaves it in its natural state after fermentation, which is completely dry, or "trocken", or adds some unfermented (and therefore sweet) must to make it either "halbtrocken" – often a very satisfying compromise – or distinctly sweet. His decision will be influenced by the balance of the wine: if the acidity is very high some "Süßreserve" (the unfermented must) can balance it to make a wine of verve and character. It will also be influenced by his clients' taste; more and more Germans are asking for drier wines to drink with meals. They tend to choose trocken or halbtrocken. Wine with less than 4 grams per litre of sugar can even be labelled as "safe for diabetics".

Another year in the same vineyard the picture is very different. The summer has been glorious, the autumn is golden, and the grapes are fully ripe in early October. The Oechsle reading gives a minimum "must-weight" of 75, which in potential alcohol means 9.8%. In this district (let us say we are in the Rheingau) an Oechsle degree of 73 or over moves the wine into the top category: natural quality wine that needs no additional sugar. The German term, Qualitätswein mit Prädikat, translates clumsily as "quality wine with specific attributes". The "specific attributes" in question are those of Kabinett, Spätlese, Auslese or even later-gathered and more luscious wines.

QmP wines are generally listed as though it was their quality that rose with each step of the ladder of richness; as though Kabinett wines are mere footsoldiers, Spätlesen the non-commissioned officers, while only Auslesen and above are the true officer-class. On the contrary, though, we are talking about style. A Kabinett wine can be as perfect in its way as an Auslese: what is different is the level of natural sugar, therefore strength and impressive flavour.

A week later our grower is picking grapes from different parts of his vineyards at Oechsle degrees ranging from 85 to 95. At 85 degrees the wine has a potential alcohol content of 11.4 per cent; it qualifies as a Spätlese or "Late-Picked". At 95 degrees it qualifies as an Auslese, or "Selection"; its potential alcohol – seldom realized, as the wine will remain sweet to balance its strength – is 13 per cent; the same as an average white burgundy.

In a great vintage as much as half the crop in good sites may be ripe enough to fall into the Auslese category. When this happens the grower gauges his chances of making super-Auslesen; either Beerenauslese by selecting only the ripest berries to achieve an Oechsle degree of 125 or more, or, with patience and good fortune, a Trockenbeerenauslese. The last, a "dry berry selection", depends on the same noble rot as Sauternes to shrivel the bunches into a powder-coated, wizened concentration of sweetness and intense flavour. A good autumn, when morning mists alternate with sunny afternoons, will set off a degree of botrytis, or noble rot, throughout the vineyard. It is at the discretion of the grower whether he seeks it all out to make a quintessence, a Trockenbeerenauslese in a minute quantity, or leaves "nobly rotten" berries and the occasional bunch to give his best Auslesen an extra richness and dimension of flavour. There are miracle vintages, one in a decade or less, when he can do both.

Sometimes at the end of a merely average vintage there are good-looking bunches of grapes left in the vineyard which the grower is reluctant to pick: they give him the sporting chance of making an "Eiswein". The principle of "ice-wine" is that if the grapes can be kept in good condition (which usually means shielding them with plastic sheets) until the first really hard frost, they can be picked at dawn in a deep-frozen state. Pressed while their water content is still solid ice they yield a juice incredibly high in flavour and acidity as well as sugar. (The ice is thrown away.) Eiswein has none of the luscious complexity of a Trockenbeerenauslese made by noble rot. For years it tastes as though it were in suspended animation: stiff and dumb, sweet and acid, scarcely vinous, in fact, at all. Long years of ageing, however, eventually thaw the mastodon. A mature Eiswein can be one of Germany's most spectacular specialities.

All the above categories of ripeness and quality are set forth on all German wine labels in a fashion which, once mastered, leaves no room for doubt.

The other essential label information, the geographic, is unfortunately much more prone to misunderstanding and confusion. Even those who understand German are frequently frustrated by the legal terminology. To foreigners it is a minefield.

How do you explain to someone who is only half-interested that Bernkastel is both a specific village of high renown and a very large district – and that the same is true of Johannisberg? How do you explain that some vineyard names are precisely that, names of specific fields with distinctive attributes, while others are almost brand-names, applicable to wine from any vineyard within a very wide designated area?

To follow how this can be, two concepts must be grasped. Both were introduced by the radical new wine laws of 1971, which swept aside thousands of traditional local names in the cause of simplicity. Unfortunately the same laws muddied the waters by bringing into being the Bereich and the Großlage. They are logically defensible concepts, but they need more explanation than the law permits. (The law is very clear on this point: any information that is not mandatory on a label is forbidden. No glosses, then, to explain the status of a name. One may be forgiven for suspecting that a certain confusion in the public mind is commercially convenient.)

The broadest geographical designation for German wine is the Anbaugebiet: the region. Rheingau is an Anbaugebiet; so is Mosel-Saar-Ruwer. There is no confusion here. Each Gebiet is divided into a number of Bereiche or districts. But these districts commonly bear the name of their most famous wine-town. Those (among foreigners, the vast majority) who do not know that "Bereich" means "district" equally do not know that a wine labelled Bereich Bernkastel is not wine from Bernkastel but from any vineyard in the Middle Mosel. A recent change in the law allows "Bereich" to be translated – but this is rarely done. Johannisberg, Nierstein, Kreuznach, Schloßböckelheim are all Bereich names liable to confuse. It would be a similar case if any wine from the Côte de Beaune could be sold as Beaune, or any Médoc wine as Margaux.

Even more confusing is the concept of the Großlage. A Großlage is a name allowed for use by a group of specific vineyard sites, or Einzellagen. Großlage groupings were made with the idea of simplifying the sales of wines from lesser-known Einzellagen. Notoriety comes more easily with bigger units. But their names are in no way distinguishable from Einzellage names, and the law does not allow any distinction to be made. I have not met a person who claims to remember all the Großlage names in Germany. It follows that even the greatest experts must sometimes resort to a reference book to establish whether a vineyard name is truly a vineyard name – an Einzellage – or the name applicable to any vineyard within quite an extensive area.

As a further confusing factor, in some areas Einzellagen are also groups of separate vineyards deemed to have a common personality. There is then not even the clear-cut distinction I have suggested between the two categories. In the pages that follow the descriptions of some regions follow the pattern of their Großlagen, others, where the local practice suggests it, proceed from one village (Gemeinde) to the next. This Atlas, however, is unique in offering the full official lists of every Gemeinde, Großlage and Einzellage in Germany parallel with the author's commentary. If the answer to any knotty problem of nomenclature is to be found anywhere it is here.

At present the difficulty of recognizing a Großlage name is that it can be preceded by any one of up to a dozen Gemeinde names. One current development that is very much to be welcomed is the statutory linking of each Großlage name with one particular village name, known as its Leitgemeinde.

Großlage names will become more familiar and easier to identify when they are eventually linked officially and unchangeably to a single Gemeinde. Niersteiner Gutes Domtal is the perfect example of a highly successful Leitgemeinde/ Großlage in the public eye and memory. It only seems rather a pity that so little of the wine so named is actually grown in Nierstein.

The true key, inevitably, to the quality and probity of the wine in any bottle, whatever its official status, is the name of the maker. This fact simplifies at a stroke most of the intricacies and ambiguities of any set of wine laws. There are many labels in Germany whose very design, once recognized, gives one the certain hope of an excellently made wine, of whatever category, vineyard, grape or vintage. The descriptions of these establishments occupy a large part of this book, for they are the essential reference points in seeking out true and typical examples of what the maps expound.

How best, then, is the huge range of Germany's production to be explored, and how is it to be enjoyed? The ideal way, without a doubt, is to set off on a leisurely tour, preferably walking, with this Atlas in your pack. The short distances between villages would only lend vigour to the thirst, and zest to the appetite. A month could be spent exploring the Mosel in this way; another month the Rheingau . . . a lifetime of summer holidays could go by without exhausting the variety of every Gemeinde in every Gebiet.

Lacking the leisure to drink in Germany this way, we can quite easily arrange an armchair tour, either in macro-focus, ranging wines of contrasting regions, grapes, categories and ages, or micro-focus, concentrating even on one village, or one producer, and tasting for smaller and more subtle distinctions. Either course will reveal at once how German wine is infinitely various; a unique cultural heritage worth a lifetime of study.

THE GRAPES OF G·E·R·M·A·N·Y

Auxerrois
A shy-bearing white variety with good sugar level but low acidity, grown in very small quantities in Baden. Not to be confused with the red Auxerrois of Cahors, a synonym of Malbec.

Bacchus
A new early-ripening, heavy-yielding cross of (Silvaner × Riesling) × Müller-Thurgau. Spicy, soft, low-acid wines which are best as Auslesen, should be drunk young, and are frequently used as Süßreserve. Rheinhessen, Rheinpfalz, Mosel-Saar-Ruwer, Franken.

Clevner
Synonym for Traminer in Baden, but of Frühburgunder in Württemberg.

Dornfelder
About 400 hectares (1,000 acres) of this successful red grape are planted, most of them in Rheinhessen and Rheinpfalz. It is a crossing of Helfensteiner and Heroldrebe and produces dark wine with good acid.

Ehrenfelser
(Riesling × Silvaner) A good new cross, between Riesling and Müller-Thurgau in quality. Small quantities in Rheinpfalz (280 hectares/690 acres), Rheinhessen (110 hectares/270 acres), Rheingau (82 hectares/200 acres) and Hessische Bergstraße (10 hectares/25 acres).

Elbling
Once the chief grape of the Mosel, said to be named from the Latin Albus (= white). Now mostly grown in the Bereich Obermosel. Neutral but acidic and clean. Good in sparkling wine.

Faber
(Weißburgunder × Müller-Thurgau) An early ripener with better sugar and acidity than Müller-Thurgau. Has a certain following in Rheinhessen (1,710 hectares/4,230 acres), Rheinpfalz (385 hectares/950 acres) and the Nahe (140 hectares/345 acres).

Gewürztraminer (or Traminer)
Pink, spicy grape. Little grown in Germany. Found in Baden and Rheinpfalz, but without the exotic character of its Alsace wine.

Gutedel
South Baden name for the Chasselas (in Switzerland "Fendant"). Light, refreshing but short-lived wine, best *spritzig*.

Huxelrebe
(Gutedel × Courtillier musqué) A prolific new variety, very aromatic, early ripening (an easy Auslese) but tends to over-crop. Popular in Rheinhessen and Rheinpfalz.

Kanzler
(Müller-Thurgau × Silvaner) A rare cross giving a small yield with good ripeness. Rheinhessen, Rheinpfalz.

Kerner
(Riesling × Trollinger) One of the most successful of the new crosses, an early-ripening understudy for Riesling, which it superficially resembles in liveliness and balance. A generous cropper. More than 6,700 hectares (16,500 acres), spread throughout West Germany.

Klingelberger
Synonym for Riesling in Durbach (Baden).

Limberger
Known in Austria as Blaufränkisch. Also known as Lemberger. Late-ripening acidic red grape grown in Württemberg: often blended.

Morio-Muskat
(Silvaner × Weißburgunder) It is hard to believe this early-ripening cross has no muscat blood. The wine it makes (on 2,700 hectares/6,700 acres) in Rheinpfalz and Rheinhessen is good but often too blatant and best blended with something more neutral (e.g., Müller-Thurgau).

Müllerrebe
Alias Schwarzriesling. Alias Pinot Meunier. Makes a little dark red wine in Württemberg and elsewhere.

Müller-Thurgau
Germany's most widely grown grape, on 25,500 hectares (63,000 acres). A Riesling × Riesling cross bred in 1882, the elder brother of many compromises between the ultimate quality of Riesling and such mundane matters as early ripening and heavy crops. Subject to rot and rarely made as Auslese, but occasionally excellent as sweet wine.

Muskat
The highly aromatic Muskat-Ottonel and Gelber Muskateller are grown in small quantities in Baden and Württemberg.

Nobling
(Silvaner × Gutedel) A great improvement on Gutedel, with a fine aroma. 148 hectares (365 acres) in south Baden.

Optima
([Silvaner × Riesling] × Müller-Thurgau) An improvement on Bacchus, delicately spicy. 500 hectares (1,240 acres).

Ortega
(Müller-Thurgau × Siegerrebe) Very early ripening, aromatic and spicy but with lowish acidity. On trial in Mosel-Saar-Ruwer (156 hectares/385 acres) and Franken (51 hectares/126 acres). Also grown in Rheinhessen (610 hectares/1,500 acres) and Rheinpfalz (340 hectares/840 acres).

Perle
(Gewürztraminer × Müller-Thurgau) A very aromatic pink grape on trial in Franken.

Portugieser, Blauer	Germany's second red grape after Spätburgunder. Gives light acidic red wines and good Weißherbst in Rheinpfalz, Rheinhessen, Württemberg and Ahr.
Reichensteiner	(Müller-Thurgau × [Madeleine Angevine × Calabreser Fröhlich]) A Euro-cross, slightly better for both sugar and acidity than Müller-Thurgau. Grown mainly in Rheinhessen and Rheinpfalz. Small planting in Mosel-Saar-Ruwer.
Rieslaner	(Silvaner × Riesling) A rare Franken variety capable of making excellent Auslesen.
Riesling (or Weißer Riesling)	Germany's second most-planted grape, with 19,280 hectares (47,600 acres), but indisputably its first in quality. Gives wines of crisp fruity acidity capable of indefinite ageing, demanding a good site (it ripens late) but repaying with unrivalled character, finesse and "breed". Surely the world's greatest white grape variety.
Rotberger	(Trollinger × Riesling) Makes a minute amount of fine pink wine on the Nahe.
Ruländer	Alias Pinot Gris or Tokay d'Alsace. Blue grapes giving dense, sometimes sticky but very clean and striking white wines; a fine complement to Riesling in Baden and Rheinpfalz.
Scheurebe	(Silvaner × Riesling) The second such cross to become celebrated, now well established in Rheinpfalz and Rheinhessen. Unsubtle, even catty, when under-ripe, but potentially magnificent as Auslese.
Schönburger	A rare pink Spätburgunder cross, making soft wine not unlike low-acid Traminer. Small amounts in Rheinhessen and Rheinpfalz.
Siegerrebe	(Madeleine Angevine × Gewürztraminer) A sweet aromatic variety sometimes useful in blends in Rheinhessen.
Silvaner	Germany's third most popular grape variety, with nearly 9% of the total vineyard. A late ripener like Riesling, also badly affected by drought in light or thin soil, and steadily giving ground to Müller-Thurgau and others. Scarcely noble, but at its best (on chalky clay in Franken, and occasionally in Rheinhessen and on the Kaiserstuhl) the true yeoman; blunt, trustworthy, with unsuspected depths.
Spätburgunder, Blauer	Alias Pinot Noir. There are more than 4,300 hectares (10,600 acres) of the red Burgundy grape in Germany, concentrated in Baden (3,160 hectares/7,800 acres), with a little in Württemberg, Rheinhhessen, Rheinpfalz, Rheingau and Ahr. Its wine is low in tannin and usually colour, often made as Weißherbst or even as a sweet Auslese. Little if any is exported.
Traminer	The usual German name for Gewürztraminer. Not easy to grow. More than 900 hectares (2,200 acres), mainly in Rheinpfalz and Baden.
Trollinger	A popular red grape in Württemberg, although it ripens late to make sharpish wine.
Weißburgunder	Alias Pinot Blanc. Little planted (900 hectares/2,200 acres) in Germany, but giving smooth, rather neutral wine in Baden and on the Nahe.

Other grapes that are currently on trial or grown in extremely small quantities include:

Domina	(Portugieser × Spätburgunder) A good yielder, this red grape is grown in tiny quantities in the Ahr (where red wine is particularly valued) and in Franken.
Findling	Very small amounts of this early-ripening Müller-Thurgau mutation are grown in the Mosel, occasionally elsewhere.
Freisamer	(Silvaner × Ruländer) A local speciality of Freiburg im Breisgau, Baden.
Frühburgunder	An early-ripening form of Spätburgunder, also called Clevner in Württemberg.
Gutenborner	(Müller-Thurgau × Chasselas Napoleon) On trial in Rheingau and the Mosel and seems to be doing well with generous crops.
Helfensteiner	(Frühburgunder × Trollinger) An early-ripening red grape found almost exclusively in Württemberg. More famous as a parent of Dornfelder than in its own right.
Heroldrebe	(Portugieser × Limberger) A late-ripener producing reliable yields, grown mainly in Rheinpfalz and Württemberg.
Noblessa	(Madeleine Angevine × Silvaner Geilweilerhof) Less than 200 hectares (500 acres) are planted, chiefly in Baden. Although an early ripener and tolerant of a variety of soils and aspects, its yields are low.
Regner	(Gamay × Seidentraube) A reliable white-vine variety, early ripening but prone to rot.
Samtrot	A form of Müllerrebe. Low yields. Only a very small amount is grown.
Septimer	(Gewürztraminer × Müller-Thurgau) Developed in Rheinhessen in 1927, where most of its tiny quantities are grown. Prone to disease.
Struwelpeterrebe	Discredited traditional variety; late developer, hirsute and disruptive.
Würzer	(Gewürztraminer × Müller-Thurgau) This grape has inherited the spiciness of Gewürztraminer – witness its name. A good cropper and at its best in clay and loess soils. About 100 hectares (250 acres), the majority in Rheinhessen.

THE ATLAS

HOW TO USE THIS ATLAS

This Atlas is divided into four geographical zones, **Northwest, Central, Eastern** and **Southern**, each identified throughout the book by its own colour (*see* page 27). Each zone is subdivided into the quality-wine regions in that zone. However, for clarity, Baden – the most diffuse of the wine regions – has been divided in this Atlas into north and south, with a general introduction to the area at the beginning of the North Baden section.

German words are used where it is logical to use them: these are explained in the text or in the glossary on page 182. The most commonly used terms and their plurals (usually an additional e, n or en) are:

Auslese (-n)
Beerenauslese (-n)
Bereich (-e)
Einzellage (-n; abbreviated as Einz.)
Großlage (-n)
Ortsteil (-e; abbreviated as Ortst.)
Trockenbeerenauslese (-n)

The German letter ß appears in certain words – it is, quite simply, a double "s".

TOURING MAPS

These are grouped into the four colour-coded geographical zones shown on page 27. The zones are indicated both by name and by the vertical coloured bar at the top of each page. The broad pink bands on the touring maps are the outlines of the vineyard maps, and at the outer edge of each touring map is printed the name of the wine region(s) covered, followed by the page number where the relevant vineyard map can be found.

At the corners of each touring map, directional arrows with page numbers indicate where to find adjacent maps.

Placenames are frequently abbreviated on German maps. The most common of these are, for example:

Veitschöchhm = Veitshöchheim
St. Goarshsn = St. Goarshausen
Idar-Oberstn = Idar-Oberstein
Gr.-Umstadt = Groß-Umstadt.

A key to all the touring maps is on page 26. The map legend is on page 25.

VINEYARD MAPS

The vineyard maps show every registered vineyard (Einzellage) in West Germany, its official number and the Großlage to which it belongs. Each number can be traced from the maps to the lists beside the maps to find the name of the Einzellage as well as the village, Großlage and Bereich under which it is classified (*see* Vineyard Lists). The Großlage names and their boundaries are marked on the map in red. The vineyards within each Großlage are shown in similar colours to make them easily identifiable.

The location map beside every vineyard map cross-refers to the touring maps. It shows the outline of the vineyard map and main towns in the area. The colour of the outline follows the colour-coding of the four zones (*see* page 27), and the strip across the top of the location map gives the touring map page numbers.

VINEYARD LISTS

Beside each vineyard map are listed all the vineyards (Einzellagen) shown on the map, followed by their official numbers. Headings in the list denote the Bereich, Großlage, Gemeinde and (frequently) Ortsteil to which the vineyards belong. (*See* below for an explanation of these terms.)

"P" (for Part) following the number indicates that an Einzellage extends over more than one parish (Ortsteil) or village (Gemeinde).

* An asterisk following the number means that this vineyard lies outside the area covered by the map.

a, b, c, d, e, f or g following the number simply means that a vineyard has been subdivided into two or more separate Einzellagen (using an additional letter instead of renumbering all the vineyards avoids confusion).

Einzellagen

Every vineyard in West Germany (with a very few exceptions) is officially registered as an Einzellage (individual vineyard site), with its own number. It is classified under its village (Gemeinde) name or under an even smaller unit, a parish or a suburb (Ortsteil). Where an Einzellage overlaps into a neighbouring parish or village, it is named under each of these in the vineyard lists.

A handful of wine estates are themselves registered as Ortsteile: these are followed by a letter instead of a number.

A small number of vineyards are registered as einzellagenfrei or großlagenfrei, that is, they are classified under a Bereich only. A few other small vineyards are not registered under this system: these are briefly noted in the vineyard lists but do not appear on the vineyard maps.

The wine from a single Einzellage is labelled with the village name, followed by the Einzellage name. German grammar dictates that "er" must be added to the village name when it is attached in this way. The Einzellage Sackträger in Oppenheim thus becomes Oppenheimer Sackträger on the label.

See also the Introduction on page 10 and the glossary on page 182.

Großlagen

A Großlage ("collective vineyard") consists of a number of Einzellagen whose wines are officially considered to be of similar style. Certain Großlagen cover some of the Einzellagen of one village, others cover all the Einzellagen of several villages. On the wine label the Großlage name must be preceded by the name of one of its Gemeinden, or villages, and "er" must be added to the village name. Wines from Bernkastel in Großlage Badstube, for example, are labelled as Bernkasteler Badstube.

The alphabetical register starting on page 184 lists every Einzellage and Großlage in the country.

See also the Introduction on page 10 and the glossary on page 182.

VILLAGES

The wine villages described in each wine region are arranged in geographical order, usually following the route of the rivers. The Einzellagen mentioned after each of these villages are not a comprehensive list but the author's personal selection. With each Einzellage is given its size in hectares, the direction in which the vineyard faces and its degree of slope.

Total vineyard area is given for many villages. The sizes of most Einzellagen are also listed. Occasionally these add up to more than the village total: this is because an Einzellage may extend across more than one village.

The steepness of German vineyards is indicated according to the German convention. "Steep" means 20° or more (often considerably more) to the horizontal; "sloping" is between 5 and 20°; "flat" between 0 and 5°. A vineyard listed as 90% steep, however, means that 90% of the vineyard is on a slope of 20° or more.

PRODUCERS

The estates described in this Atlas are a purely personal selection, as are their vineyards mentioned. They are arranged in alphabetical order within each region, usually under the last word of their name (unless the name is hyphenated). The word Weingut simply means wine estate. Cooperatives (Winzergenossenschaft or Winzerverein) are listed at the end of each section.

TRAVEL INFORMATION

Because of annual variations, exact dates of many wine events cannot be given, but these – along with much more – can be supplied by the regional wine information offices (addresses below).

REGIONAL WINE INFORMATION OFFICES

Ahr
Gebietsweinwerbung Ahr
Marktplatz 11
5483 Bad Neuenahr-Ahrweiler
Tel: 02641-5555

Baden
Weinwerbezentrale Badischer
Winzergenossenschaften e.G.
Keßlerstraße 5
7500 Karlsruhe 1
Tel: 0721-554300

Franken
Frankenwein-Frankenland e.V.
Juliusspital-Weingut
Postfach 5848
8700 Würzburg
Tel: 0931-12093

Hessische Bergstraße
Weinbauverband Bergstraße
Königsberger Straße 4
6148 Heppenheim/Bergstraße
Tel: 06252-71247

Mittelrhein
Mittelrhein – Burgen und Wein
e.V.
Am Hafen 2
5407 St. Goar
Tel: 06741-7405

Mosel-Saar-Ruwer
Weinwerbung
Mosel-Saar-Ruwer e.V.
Gartenfeldstraße 12a
5500 Trier
Tel: 0651-76621/45967

Nahe
Weinland Nahe e.V.
Brückes 6
6550 Bad Kreuznach
Tel: 0671-27563

Rheingau
Der Rheingau – Der Weingau
Weinwerbung e.V.
Im Alten Rathaus
6225 Johannisberg
Tel: 06722-8117

Rheinhessen
Rheinhessenwein e.V.
An der Brunnenstube 33–35
6500 Mainz
Tel: 06131 681058

Rheinpfalz
Rheinpfalz – Weinpfalz e.V.
Robert-Stolz-Straße 18
6730 Neustadt/Weinstraße
Tel: 06321-7583

Württemberg:
Werbegemeinschaft
Württembergischer
Weingärtnergenossenschaften
Postfach 94
Heilbronner Straße 41
7000 Stuttgart 1
Tel: 0711-20401

TOURING MAP LEGEND

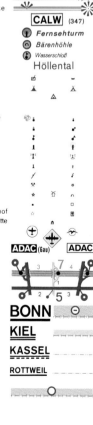
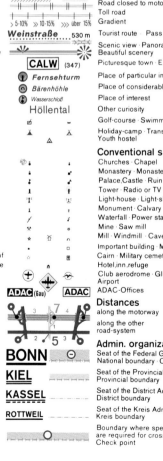

Straßen und Wege	Roads and tracks
Autobahn mit Anschlußstelle und Nummer	Motorway with access point and number
Rasthaus mit Übernachtung	Road house (with night accommod.)
Raststätte · Erfrischungsstelle	Restaurant · Snackbar ·
Tankstelle · Parkplatz mit/ohne WC	Filling station · Parking places ·
Bedarfsumleitung an der Autobahn	By-pass if required
Autobahn in Bau mit baldiger Verkehrsübergabe und Datum	Motorway under construction with early expected completion date
Autobahn in Bau und geplant	Motorway under construction/project.
Zweibahnige Straße (4-spurig)	Dual carriage-way
Sonstige Kfz·Straße	Road for motorvehicles only
Bundesstraße · Straßennummern	Federal road · Road numbers
Wichtige Hauptstraße	Important main road
Hauptstraße · Tunnel · Brücke	Main road · Tunnel · Bridge
Nebenstraße	Minor road
Straßen in Bau	Roads under construction
Straßen in Planung (ohne Farbe und Anschluß)	Roads projected (with out colour and junction)
Fahrweg Fußweg	Carriage-way · Footpath
Bevorzugter Wanderweg (Auswahl)	Footpath (selection)

Bahnen	Railways
Vollspurbahn mit Fernverkehr	Standard gauge,long-distance traffic
Vollspurbahn ohne Fernverkehr	Standard gauge,short-distance traffic
Kleinbahn	Narrow gauge
Bahnhof · Bahnbrücke	Station · Bridge
Tunnel · Niveaukreuzung	Tunnel · Level crossing
Zahnradbahn,Standseilbahn	Rack·railway,Funicular
Kabinenschwebebahn	Aerial railway
Sessellift	Chair-lift

Sonstige Verkehrswege	Other means of communic.
Autofähre	Car ferry
Personenfähre	Passenger ferry
Schiffahrtslinie	Shipping route
Kanal mit Schleuse · Staudamm	Canal with lock · Dam

Touristische Hinweise	Hints for tourists
Naturschutzgebiet · Sperrgebiet	Nature reserve · Milit.training ground
Naturpark · Wald	National park · Forest
Straße für Kfz.gesperrt	Road closed to motor-traffic
Straße für Kfz.gegen Gebühr	Toll road
Steigungen in Pfeilrichtung 5-10% 10-15% über 15%	Gradient
Touristenstraße · Paß Weinstraße 530 m	Tourist route · Pass
Schöner Ausblick · Rundblick	Scenic view · Panoramic view
Landschaftlich bes.schöne Strecke	Beautiful scenery
Malerisches Stadtbild · Ortshöhe CALW (347)	Picturesque town · Elevation
Besonders sehenswertes Objekt Fernsehturm	Place of particular interest
Sehenswertes Objekt Bärenhöhle	Place of considerable interest
Beachtenswertes Objekt Wasserschloß	Place of interest
Sonstige Sehenswürdigkeit Höllental	Other curiosity
Golfplatz · Schwimmbad	Golf-course · Swimming pool
Ferienzeltplatz · Zeltplatz Jugendherberge	Holiday-camp · Transit-camp Youth hostel

Signaturen	Conventional signs
Kirche im Ort,freistehend · Kapelle	Churches · Chapel
Kloster · Klosterruine	Monastery · Monastery ruin
Schloß,Burg · Schloß-,Burgruine	Palace,Castle · Ruin
Turm · Funk-,Fernsehturm	Tower · Radio or TV tower
Leuchtturm · Feuerschiff	Light-house · Light-ship
Denkmal · Feldkreuz	Monument · Calvary
Wasserfall · Kraftwerk	Waterfall · Power station
Bergwerk · Sägewerk	Mine · Saw mill
Mühle · Windmühle · Höhle	Mill · Windmill · Cave
Bauwerk · Marktplatz,Areal	Important building · Market place etc.
Hünen·Hügelgrab · Soldatenfriedhof	Cairn · Military cemetery
Hotel,Wirtshaus,Berggasthaus,-hütte	Hotel,inn,refuge
Landeplatz · Segelfluggelände Verkehrsflughafen	Club aerodrome · Gliding field Airport
ADAC-Geschäftsstellen ADAC (Gau) ADAC	ADAC-Offices

Entfernungen	Distances
auf der Autobahn	along the motorway
auf dem übrigen Straßennetz	along the other road-system

Verwaltung	Admin. organization
Sitz der Bundesregierung Staatsgrenze · Grenzübergang BONN	Seat of the Federal Government National boundary · Custom house
Sitz der Landesregierung Landesgrenze KIEL	Seat of the Provincial Government Provincial boundary
Sitz der Bezirksverwaltung Verwaltungsbezirksgrenze KASSEL	Seat of the District Administration District boundary
Sitz der Kreisverwaltung Kreisgrenze ROTTWEIL	Seat of the Kreis Administration Kreis boundary
Grenze,zu deren Überschreiten besondere Ausweise erforderlich sind,mit Übergang	Boundary where special licences are required for crossing Check point

KEY TO TOURING MAPS

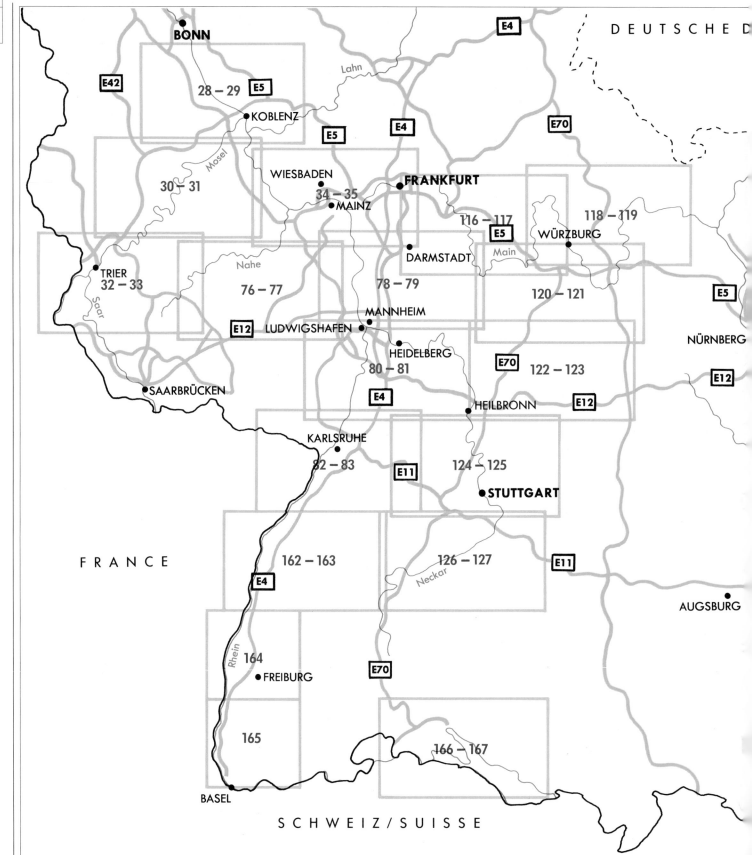

E4   DEUTSCHE D

BONN

E42

28 – 29   E5

Lahn

KOBLENZ

E5   E4   E70

Mosel

WIESBADEN

30 – 31   FRANKFURT

34 – 35
MAINZ

116 – 117   118 – 119

E5   WÜRZBURG

Nahe   DARMSTADT   Main

TRIER
32 – 33   76 – 77   78 – 79   120 – 121   E5

Saar   MANNHEIM

E12   LUDWIGSHAFEN   NÜRNBERG

HEIDELBERG   E70   122 – 123
80 – 81

E12

E4   HEILBRONN   E12

SAARBRÜCKEN

KARLSRUHE

82 – 83   124 – 125

E11   **STUTTGART**

F R A N C E

162 – 163   126 – 127

E4   E11

Neckar

AUGSBURG

Rhein   164

●FREIBURG   E70

165   166 – 167

BASEL

S C H W E I Z / S U I S S E

WINE ZONES

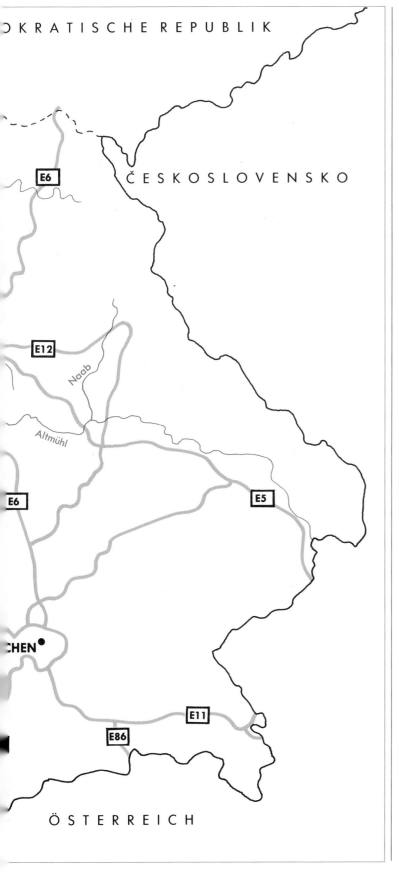

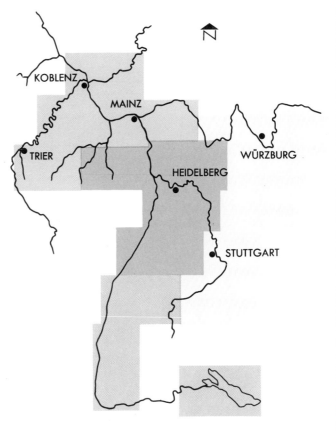

NORTHWEST ZONE:		CENTRAL ZONE:
Ahr		Nahe
Mosel-Saar-Ruwer		Rheinhessen
Mittelrhein		Rheinpfalz
Rheingau		Hessische Bergstraße
EASTERN ZONE:		**SOUTHERN ZONE:**
Franken		South Baden
Württemberg		
North Baden		

166 – 167   Touring Map page number

E11   Motorway (autobahn)

NORTHWEST ZONE

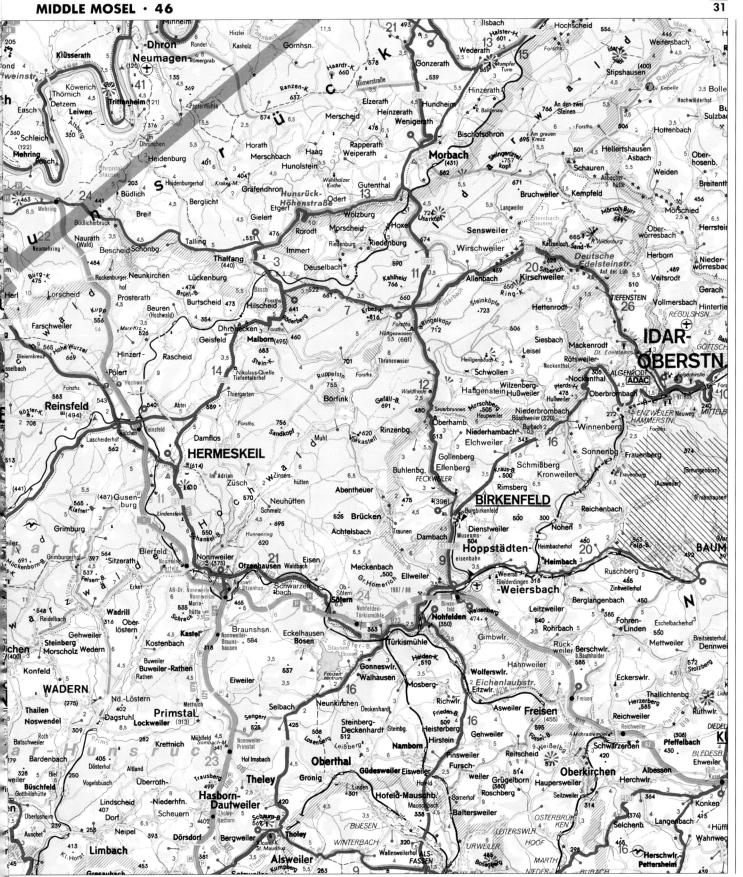

AHR

Red grapes in general need more sunshine and warmth to ripen than white. It seems a piece of perversity that Germany's northernmost wine region should be proudest of its red wine. The countryside is perhaps more remarkable than the wine: the Ahr owes its status as a wine region more to its character and scenery than to any outstanding qualities of flavour in the very light reds it makes. The River Ahr is a western tributary of the Mittelrhein, rising in the Eifel mountains and flowing into the Rhine not far south of Bonn. The steep valley sides are clothed almost continuously in vines for 16 kilometres (10 miles): 400 hectares, of which 30% is Spätburgunder, 30% Portugieser and other red grapes, and 40% Riesling and Müller-Thurgau.

The white wines, when ripe, have a distinct aromatic lilt which is very attractive. Real ripeness for red grapes is almost impossible this far north. The Spätburgunder (much the best) manages only a hollow echo of its Pinot Noir character. The wine is pale and light, often made distinctly sweet, and depends largely for its present prosperity on the beauty of the valley, the nearness of large rich centres of population, and the German fondness for a walk in the vineyard followed by an evening in a snug little restaurant eating country food and drinking the proprietor's wine.

The capital of the Ahr, Bad Neuenahr, is also a spa with healing waters: a useful excuse for tired politicians from nearby Bonn to visit the vineyards with their many inns.

The Ahr vineyards have a long history: winegrowing there goes back to Roman times. The Spätburgunder vine came to the valley in the late 17 or early 18th centuries. Today no less than 900 small growers till the soil, most of them banded into seven cooperatives, but a hundred or so making and selling their own wine. The Ahr growers claim to have founded Germany's first cooperative cellar in 1868. At this time the valley was considered remote, and the area under vine was in decline until quite recently. Very little of the wine they produce leaves the district, and still less is exported.

There is one Bereich and only one Großlage name: Klosterberg, covering the 11 villages and 43 Einzellagen.

▲ Autumn in the Ahr: the vineyard path provides a pleasant and instructive stroll: signs give information about the vineyards. The villages, with their welcoming taverns, are never far away.

TRAVEL INFORMATION

The Ahr Valley is highly organized for wine tourism, with plenty of inns, signposted paths and the benefit of scenic towns. It can get very crowded at weekends, especially in summer.

The north–south autobahn A61 crosses the valley at Heppingen: the autobahn brings the Ahr within 15 minutes' driving time of Bonn. The junction is Bad Neuenahr, with a spur autobahn (A573) running down the valley and rejoining the main A61 at Löhndorf. The B267 runs the length of the valley.

A branch railway leaves the Köln–Frankfurt line at Remagen and runs up the valley, through the wine district and beyond to Adenau.

The *Rotweinwanderweg* – red wine path – runs for 30km between Altenahr and Lohrsdorf through woods and vineyards, with side-paths into the villages, which are conveniently close together. The path is signposted with a symbol of a red grape in a white background. A map is available locally.

The *Rotweinstraße* starts at Sinzig and covers the length of the valley. The signpost is a stylized valley. There are many parking places provided.

Places to visit

Altenahr: romanesque church and ruins of a castle.
Mayschoß: wine cooperative with cellar open for visits at most times, art treasures (such as marble monuments) in the parish church.

Rech: typical wine village with cellars to visit and an ancient bridge.
Dernau: baroque church. Kloster Marienthal State Domain is nearby (*see* producers overleaf).
Bad Neuenahr-Ahrweiler: old town walls, a church (in Heimersheim) with the oldest windows in Germany; castle ruins. Both towns are replete with inns, wine cellars and other amenities.

Food and drink

Specialities include *Rauchfleisch* (smoked meats), mushrooms, *Schinken* (ham) from the Eifel mountains and local trout from the river.

There are more restaurants than hotels – most visitors are day-trippers. Bad Neuenahr, a spa, has the Steigenberger

Kurhotel (tel: 02641-2291); nearby in Walporzheim is the Gourmet im Teufenbach (tel: 02641-34198) with high-class cuisine; also the Romantick-Restaurant Weinhaus St. Peter with its courtyard (tel: 02641-34031). The inns of the valley – *Stuben* – are notoriously *gemütlich*.

VILLAGES

BAD NEUENAHR

The heart of the Ahr Valley, a picturesque town still retaining its medieval walls. A spa with hot alkaline springs, an extra asset in the picturesque little town's bid to attract the visitors from the nearby cities.

Under the Ortsteile Bad Neuenahr-Ahrweiler come the vineyards of the lower half of the valley: Ehlingen, Heimersheim, Lohrsdorf, Heppingen, Neuenahr, Bachem, Ahrweiler, Walporzheim and Marienthal. (The Winzerverein in Marienthal is one of the smallest in Germany, with only 19 members.)

Bachem is known for its Frühburgunder, but all of the vineyards are planted with Spätburgunder and Portugieser.

Vineyards

There are 27 Einzellagen, nearly all with steep slopes.

DERNAU

Site of the central cooperative, well known for red wines. Terraced vineyards are a particular feature. Grapes planted include red-wine varieties plus Müller-Thurgau and Riesling.

Vineyards

Hardtberg, Burggarten, Pfarrwingert, Goldkaul, Schieferlay. All steep, all with southerly exposure, except for Goldkaul, which faces due west.

RECH

A tiny village surrounded by woods, with an 18th century bridge crossing the Ahr. The Hardtberg vineyard is planted with Riesling, the other two Einzellagen mostly with red-wine grapes.

MAYSCHOSS

A ruined 11th century castle, the Saffenburg, stands high above Mayschoß, another picturesque wine village of about 1,000 inhabitants. The wine cooperative set up in 1868 claims to be the first one founded in Germany. 6 Einzellagen, all partly steep or sloping, share the valley with steep cliffs. Riesling predominates.

Vineyards

Mönchberg (43ha, SW, steep) is predominantly Riesling, as are Silberberg, Laacherberg and Lochmühlerley.

ALTENAHR AND AHRBRÜCK

Altenahr, a thousand-year-old village, is the main centre of the upper valley. There are two Einzellagen in this part of the valley: one, Übigberg, is called after the mountain from which there is a panoramic view of the valley and a *Seilbahn* (cable car) down to the village.

◀ Picking in the Schloßgarten vineyard at Kloster Marienthal.

PRODUCERS/VINEYARDS

Weingut J. J. Adeneuer
Max-Planckstraße 8, 5483 Bad Neuenahr-Ahrweiler, tel: 02641-34473. *Owners:* Marc and Frank Adeneuer. 3.8 hectares. *Einzellagen:* Walporzheim: Gärkammer (0.8ha) and Domlay (1); Ahrweiler: Forstberg (1); Heimersheim: Burggarten (1).
A complete red-wine specialist with 500 years of tradition in the family. 76% Spätburgunder, 21% Portugieser, producing wines as stylish as any on the Ahr.

Jakob Sebastian Nachf.
Brückenstraße 111, 5481 Rech, tel: 02643-2025. *Owner:* Bernd Sebastian. 6.6 hectares. *Einzellagen:* Heppingen: Berg (solely owned); Neuenahr: Schieferlay; Ahrweiler: Daubhaus; Walporzheim: Kräuterberg; Dernau: Pfarrwingert; Rech: Hardtberg, Blume and Herrenberg; Mayschoß: Silberberg, Burgberg and Schieferlay.
An old wine-growing family with a complicated little red-wine estate. The Mayschoß vines are rented from Fürst von Arenberg. Heppingen, with heavier soil, produces the "biggest" wines. The wines achieve good results in the national (DLG) competitions, including a Gold Medal for a 1983 Heppinger Berg Spätburgunder Beerenauslese QmP. The vineyards are planted 75% with Spätburgunder, 10% with Riesling, the rest is Müller-Thurgau, Kerner and Portugieser.

Staatliche Weinbaudomäne Kloster Marienthal/Ahr
Klosterstraße, 5481 Marienthal/Ahr. *Director:* Wolfgang Frisch. 18.7 hectares. *Einzellagen:* Marienthal: Klostergarten (9.4ha) and Stiftsberg (6.4) – both solely owned; Walporzheim: Kräuterberg (0.9); Ahrweiler: Rosenthal (1) and Silberberg (0.6); Dernau: Hardtberg (0.4). Großlage: Klosterberg.
Vines are 69% Spätburgunder, 20% Portugieser, 11% mainly experimental red-wine varieties, such as Carmina. An Augustinian convent from the 12th to the 19th century; now the model Ahr estate producing the most prestigious reds, including many Auslesen – a taste which has no equivalent abroad. However, 10% of the produce is exported.

Weingut Jean Stodden
Hauptstraße 114, 5481 Rech/Ahr, tel. 02643-8485.
Owners: Regina and Gerd Stodden. 4.1 hectares. *Einzellagen:* Mayschoß: Mönchberg; Dernau: Burggarten; Rech: Blume, Hardtberg and Herrenberg.
A little estate, merchant-house and distillery for four generations; 40% Portugieser, 40% Spätburgunder, 18% Riesling, 2% Müller-Thurgau. (There are plans to increase the proportion of Portugieser and Spätburgunder to 90% and reduce the Riesling to 10%.) Its Portugieser is very light, Spätburgunder in good years warm and "fiery", Riesling quite sharp and Müller-Thurgau mild. Steep slopes and slate are the secret of the best sites. A little is exported to the USA and the Netherlands.

Vereinigte Ahrwinzergenossenschaften eG Dernau
Heerstraße 91-93, 5483 Bad Neuenahr-Ahrweiler 1, tel: 02641-21022.
A cooperative cellar formed in 1971 from the amalgamation of 7 smaller cellars. The 625 members supply the grapes from 39% (174ha) of the small Ahr valley. All the wines are sold in bottle within West Germany – on average, over 180,000 cases per year passing directly to the consumer. The main vine varieties are Portugieser 38%, Spätburgunder 34% and Müller-Thurgau 16%.

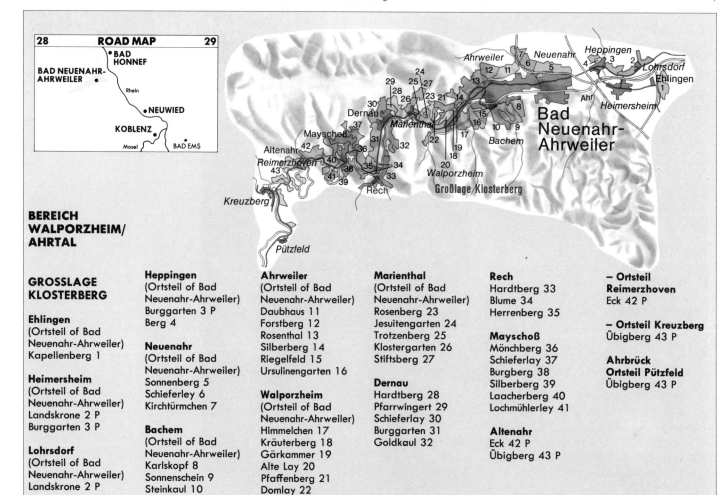

BEREICH WALPORZHEIM/ AHRTAL

GROSSLAGE KLOSTERBERG

Ehlingen
(Ortsteil of Bad Neuenahr-Ahrweiler)
Kapellenberg 1

Heimersheim
(Ortsteil of Bad Neuenahr-Ahrweiler)
Landskrone 2 P
Burggarten 3 P

Lohrsdorf
(Ortsteil of Bad Neuenahr-Ahrweiler)
Landskrone 2 P

Heppingen
(Ortsteil of Bad Neuenahr-Ahrweiler)
Burggarten 3 P
Berg 4

Neuenahr
(Ortsteil of Bad Neuenahr-Ahrweiler)
Sonnenberg 5
Schieferley 6
Kirchtürmchen 7

Bachem
(Ortsteil of Bad Neuenahr-Ahrweiler)
Karlskopf 8
Sonnenschein 9
Steinkaul 10

Ahrweiler
(Ortsteil of Bad Neuenahr-Ahrweiler)
Daubhaus 11
Forstberg 12
Rosenthal 13
Silberberg 14
Riegelfeld 15
Ursulinengarten 16

Walporzheim
(Ortsteil of Bad Neuenahr-Ahrweiler)
Himmelchen 17
Kräuterberg 18
Gärkammer 19
Alte Lay 20
Pfaffenberg 21
Domlay 22

Marienthal
(Ortsteil of Bad Neuenahr-Ahrweiler)
Rosenberg 23
Jesuitengarten 24
Trotzenberg 25
Klostergarten 26
Stiftsberg 27

Dernau
Hardtberg 28
Pfarrwingert 29
Schieferlay 30
Burggarten 31
Goldkaul 32

Rech
Hardtberg 33
Blume 34
Herrenberg 35

Mayschoß
Mönchberg 36
Schieferlay 37
Burgberg 38
Silberberg 39
Laacherberg 40
Lochmühlerley 41

Altenahr
Eck 42 P
Übigberg 43 P

– Ortsteil Reimerzhoven
Eck 42 P

– Ortsteil Kreuzberg
Übigberg 43 P

Ahrbrück
Ortsteil Pützfeld
Übigberg 43 P

MOSEL-SAAR-RUWER

▲ Bernkastel, with its twin town of Kues across the river, seen from the summit of the Doctorberg. Wine from the Doctor is usually the most expensive Mosel.

One regional (Gebiet) name covers the long and tortuous route of the Mosel from Luxembourg to the Rhine and both its winegrowing tributaries. It is justified by the wine. To a surprising degree the wines of the Mosel (Upper, Middle and Lower), of the Saar and the Ruwer are homogenous in style, however widely they vary in quality. They are the brightest, briskest, most aromatic and yet most hauntingly subtle of all the fruits of the Riesling. This is essentially Riesling country, and no soil or situation brings out the thrilling harmony of the finest of all white grapes to better effect.

Low-priced Mosels, sold under such popular regional names as Moselblümchen (the regional equivalent of Liebfraumilch), Zeller Schwarze Katz or Kröver Nacktarsch, or under the generously wide Bereich name of Bernkastel, are usually not Riesling but Müller-Thurgau. The finer sites all grow Riesling, and all go to great pains to identify themselves precisely. The complications of nomenclature can become excruciating but the rewards are sublime.

The river is described and mapped here in three sections, corresponding to the Bereiche of Zell or Untermosel (Lower Mosel); Bernkastel or Mittelmosel (Middle Mosel); and Saar-Ruwer, Obermosel and Moseltor (Upper Mosel). The text goes into the greatest detail on the vineyards of the Mittelmosel, Saar and Ruwer, where the growing conditions are most favourable and the wines are most individual.

LOWER MOSEL

▲ The dramatic bend of the Mosel at Bremm encircles the ruins of a medieval convent. The almost flat vineyards around it are the Abtei Kloster Stuben and Stubener Klostersegen Einzellagen. On the near side of the river is the very steep south-facing Calmont (first documented in 1373), which is divided between Bremm and the village of Eller, further round the river bend.

The Mosel region is, in wine terms, entirely a product of the river. Few of the vineyards are out of sight of the water. The valley sides, more or less steep, form the vineyard sites. For a variety of reasons the steepest slopes make the best wine – but also cost most to farm. The cost of working a steep Mosel vineyard is amongst the highest per hectare in Germany.

The meandering course of the Mosel in its deeply-cut valley covers double the direct distance between Koblenz and Luxembourg. Roads and a railway run along its banks for much of the distance, linking a string of villages and towns of considerable charm. The Mosel is ideally adapted to vinous tourism.

The determinants of wine quality are the soil – slate is best, and occurs most frequently in the Middle Mosel – and microclimate. In this northern region, the angle and exposure of each slope makes a difference to the amount of sun it receives, and the consequent ripeness of the grapes it produces. The Lower Mosel begins – or rather ends – at Koblenz, where the river makes a majestic confluence with the Rhine. The Mosel follows a fairly straight northeasterly course for the last few kilometres before Koblenz, with most of the vineyards, consequently, on the southeast-facing left bank. But above Cochem the characteristic swinging bends begin. It is this tortuous course that is responsible for the creation of so many of the steep, south-facing vineyard sites of the Mosel – and, of course, for very many less favoured north-facing ones.

It is generally accepted that none of the Lower Mosel villages have sites of the standard of the best of the Middle Mosel, but there are exceptions, places where exposure and slope combine to ripen Riesling properly. Slate soil is rarer here than further up the river; much of the area is composed of sandstone.

The Mosel vineyards start within the Koblenz city boundaries, with two small sites at Metternich and Güls. Once outside the city, the river valley soon takes on its characteristic steepness, with well-placed vineyards in villages such as Winningen. If favoured sites are rare here compared with higher upstream, they are just as highly prized. Despite this, Riesling is very much in the majority – many villages grow nothing else.

The Bereich is divided into five Großlagen, of which Schwarze Katz ("black cat") is the best-known. Few great estates own land here: the small grower, usually working part-time, is paramount, often taking his grapes or wine to the local cooperatives. The cooperative at Gondorf dates back to 1896 and is the oldest in the valley. Large merchants also buy quantities of Lower Mosel wine for blending.

TRAVEL INFORMATION

The Lower Mosel is easily accessible from Koblenz and makes a fascinating side-trip to a journey along the Rhine. Unlike the Rhine Valley, however, the Mosel is relatively undiscovered by tourists.

The north–south A61 autobahn crosses the Mosel southwest of Koblenz. There is a junction (Koblenz/Dieblich) on the south side with a spur road leading down into the valley. This gives access to the south bank: to reach the Moselweinstraße on the north bank, leave the autobahn at the A61/A48 junction and head for Koblenz or (to the west) Kobern.

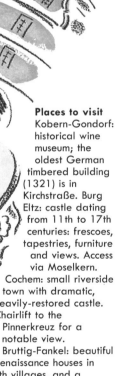

Bridges are scarce on the Mosel: there is one at Koblenz, another at Löf and a third at Kerden, where the south bank road is interrupted by steep slopes.

A railway runs along the north bank as far as Cochem, where it tunnels through the neck of the Cochemer Krampen – a great 24km-bend – in the Kaiser Wilhelm tunnel. River boats of the KD Line run from Koblenz to Cochem, with a train connection to the start of the upper Mosel service at Bernkastel.

Southeast from the river, the wooded Hunsrück hills offer walking, hunting and peaceful villages. The Eifel hills to the northwest have spectacular volcanic lakes.

Places to visit
Kobern-Gondorf: historical wine museum; the oldest German timbered building (1321) is in Kirchstraße. Burg Eltz: castle dating from 11th to 17th centuries: frescoes, tapestries, furniture and views. Access via Moselkern.
Cochem: small riverside town with dramatic, heavily-restored castle. Chairlift to the Pinnerkreuz for a notable view.
Bruttig-Fankel: beautiful Renaissance houses in both villages, and a splendid parish church in Fankel.
Beilstein: picturesque half-timbered town, less busy than Cochem.

▶ Merl, near Zell, a village on the right bank which the twists and turns of the river gives an unusual southerly exposure.

Bad Bertrich: spa in a side valley 10km from the river, 1780 Kurhaus, castle.
Zell: busy wine centre with Roman origins.

Wine roads
The Moselweinstraße runs the length of the river, switching banks periodically. Well signposted: look for the stylized "M".

Wine festivals
Cochem (mid-June), Ellenz (Jul & Aug), Ediger (Jul, Aug & Oct), Mesenich (1st w/e in Aug), Winningen (last w/e in Aug to 1st in Sept), Moselkern (1st w/e in Sept).

Wine trails
Wine trails at Mesenich, Senheim-Senhals, Valwig & Winningen, Wine tasting everywhere in grower's cellars, wine centres at Bruttig-Fankel, Ellenz-Poltersdorf, Kobern-Gondorf. One-day seminars in Senheim every Mon (Jul–Oct).

Food and drink
Mosel specialities include pork marinated in local wine, snails cooked with grapes, *Weincräwes* – rib of pork with sauerkraut, pickled pork tongues with cream and mustard sauce, and "vintner's breakfast": liver sausage, mustard and onion rings on wholemeal bread.

The tourist office in Koblenz (tel: 0261-31304) opposite the main station will book rooms, as will the information office by the bridge in Cochem (tel: 02671-39710). All the historic towns have characterful restaurants & hotels: Zell's Schloß Zell

MOSEL WEIN STRASSE

restaurant (tel: 06542-4084) has a garden; Weingut Haus Lippman in Beilstein offers fish specialities, own wines and a baronial hall. (tel: 02673-15730); the Alte Thorschenke in Cochem dates from 1332 (hotel, tel: 02671-7059).

VILLAGES

ZELL

This is the best-known wine community of the Lower Mosel, due in some measure to its memorable Großlage name Schwarze Katz and the inevitable black cat on the label. Zell and Zell-Merl, immediately downstream, both have steep slopes with slaty soil, planted largely in Riesling and capable of very tempting, light but aromatic and flowery wines.

Vineyards

All in Großlage Schwarze Katz with *Einzellagen:* Merl: Sonneck, 6ha, SW, 100% sloping; Adler, 20ha, S-SSW, 80% steep; Königslay-Terrassen, 10ha, S, 100% steep; Stephansberg, 50ha, SSE, 70% steep; Fettgarten, 21ha, SSE, 90% steep; Klosterberg, 83ha, SE, 95% steep. Zell: Nußberg, 13ha, SSW, 80% steep; Burglay-Felsen, 50ha, SSW-SW, 70% steep; Petersborn-Kabertchen, 31ha, WSW, 90% steep; Pomerell, 22ha, WSW, 90% steep; Kreuzlay, 28ha, SSE, 90% steep; Domherrenberg, 74ha, SE, 75% steep.

BULLAY

A small community, little known to the outside world, with limited but very worthwhile steep slaty slopes producing fine light Riesling. Kronenberg, sheltered in a side valley, gives particularly satisfying wine.

Vineyards

In Großlage Grafschaft with *Einzellagen:* Graf Beyßel-Herrenberg, 17ha, S-W, 100% steep. Brautrock, 10ha, S-W, 60% steep. Kronenberg, 6ha, SSE, 100% steep. Kirchweingarten, 10ha, SSE, 100% steep. Sonneck, 9.5ha, SW, 60% steep.

ALF

Alf, on the opposite bank to Bullay, has some well-placed sites on the slopes of the main river and in a side-valley. The prime sites are 100% Riesling.

Vineyards

38ha in Großlage Grafschaft with *Einzellagen:* Kapellenberg, 15ha, E-SE, 70% steep, Katzenkopf, 5.3ha, SE, 70% steep. Herrenberg, 10ha, SSE, 80% steep. Burggraf, 17.5ha, S-SSW, 70% steep.

NEEF

Little Neef, on the right bank at the next bend below Bullay, rejoices in one very fine steep slope in the classic Mosel style: the Frauenberg.

Vineyards

In Großlage Grafschaft with *Einzellage:* Frauenberg, 39.5ha, SSW-WSW, 100% steep.

ST ALDEGUND

Three sites on the left bank opposite Neef provide promising conditions for Riesling.

Vineyards

74ha in Großlage Grafschaft with *Einzellagen:* Himmelreich, 17ha, SSE, steep. Palmberg-Terrassen, 13ha, SE, steep. Klosterkammer, 40ha, E-SSE, 35% steep.

Similar favoured sites occur less and less frequently as the Mosel flows tortuously on down past Cochem, then takes a straighter course north through Karden and Löf towards Koblenz, vines still hugging its immediate banks. The Großlage names for this lower section are Grafschaft, Rosenhang, Goldbäumchen and finally Weinhex.

EDIGER-ELLER

The river bends sharply at Bremm to provide the two villages of Ediger and Eller with a fine southwest-facing slope. Eller has some venerable wine cellars. Parts of the Calmont site, on the outside of the tight river bend, are reckoned to be the steepest vineyards in Europe.

Vineyards

195ha in Großlage Grafschaft with *Einzellagen:* Ediger: Osterlämmchen, 58ha, SW, 40% steep; Hasensprung, 5ha, SE-SW, steep; Elzhofberg, 20ha, SW, 70% steep; Pfaffenberg, 11ha, SSW, 70% steep; Feuerberg, 11.5ha, SSW, 70% steep; Pfirsichgarten, 35ha, S-WSW, 20% steep; Calmont, 5ha, SSE-S, 60% steep. Eller: Höll, 10ha, SE, 70% steep; Schützenlay, 5ha, SE, 100% steep.

ELLENZ-POLTERSDORF

Ellenz, on the north bank, is well-placed on a big bend of the river. Opposite is the showpiece village of Beilstein. Ellenz has two large gently sloping sites growing Riesling, Müller-Thurgau and (unusually at this end of the river) Elbling.

Vineyards

152ha in Großlage Goldbäumchen with *Einzellagen:* Altarberg, 50ha, S, 30% steep. Kurfürst, 84ha, SE, sloping.

COCHEM

Another village – or rather town – gaining from a side valley which provides a south-facing slope for its Pinnerkreuzberg site.

Vineyards

43ha in Großlage Goldbäumchen with *Einzellagen:* Pinnerkreuzberg, 18ha, S-SW, steep. Herrenberg, 7ha, SE, steep. Both are Riesling.

WINNINGEN

This last wine village of the Mosel is just below the autobahn bridge and almost within sound of the bells of Koblenz. Riesling predominates.

Vineyards

148ha in Großlage Weinhex with *Einzellagen:* Uhlen, 17.5ha, SW, steep. Hamm, 16ha, S-SW, steep. Domgarten, 121ha, SE-S, 25% steep.

BEREICH ZELL/MOSEL

GROSSLAGE WEINHEX

Metternich
(Ortsteil of Koblenz)
Marienberg 1 P

Güls
(Ortsteil of Koblenz)
Marienberg 1 P
Bienengarten 2
Königsfels 3
Im Röttgen 4 P

Moselweiß
(Ortsteil of Koblenz)
Hamm 5 P

Lay
(Ortsteil of Koblenz)
Hamm 5 P
Hubertusborn 6

Winningen
Im Röttgen 4 P
Brückstück 8
Domgarten 9
Hamm 10
Uhlen 11

Kobern-Gondorf
Ortsteil Kobern
Uhlen 11 a
Fahrberg 12
Weißenberg 13
Schloßberg 14 P

– Ortsteil Gondorf
Schloßberg 14 P
Gäns 15
Fuchshöhle 16
Kehrberg 17

Dieblich
Heilgraben 18

Niederfell
Fächern 19
Kahllay 20
Goldlay 21

Lehmen
Lay 22
Klosterberg 23
Würzlay 24
Ausoniusstein 25

Oberfell
Goldlay 26
Brauneberg 27
Rosenberg 28

Moselsürsch
(Ortsteil of Lehmen)
Fahrberg 29 P

Kattenes
(Ortsteil of Löf)
Fahrberg 29 T
Steinchen 30

Alken
Bleidenberg 31
Burgberg 32
Hunnenstein 33

Brodenbach
Neuwingert 34

Löf
Goldblume 35
Sonnenring 36

Hatzenport
(Ortsteil of Löf)
Stolzenberg 37
Kirchberg 38
Burg Bischofstein 39

Burgen
Bischofstein 40

GROSSLAGE GOLDBÄUMCHEN

Moselkern
Rosenberg 41
Kirchberg 42
Übereltzer 43

Müden
Funkenberg 44
Leckmauer 45
Sonnenring 46
St. Castorhöhle 47
Großlay 48

Treis-Karden
Ortsteil Karden
Dechantsberg 49
Münsterberg 50
Juffermauer 51

Pommern
Zeisel 52
Goldberg 53
Sonnenuhr 54
Rosenberg 55

Klotten
Rosenberg 55 a
Burg Coreidelsteiner 56
Sonnengold 57
Brauneberg 58

Cochem
Herrenberg 59
Pinnerkreuzberg 60
Schloßberg 61

Cochem
Ortsteil Sehl
Hochlay 62
Klostergarten 63
(Ebernach)

VINEYARDS

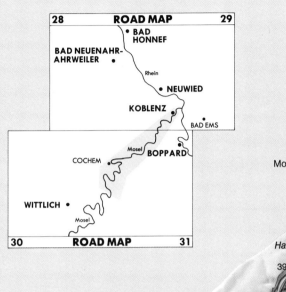

ROAD MAP 28 | 29

BAD HONNEF
BAD NEUENAHR-AHRWEILER
Rhein
NEUWIED
KOBLENZ
BAD EMS
COCHEM
Mosel
BOPPARD
WITTLICH
Mosel

ROAD MAP 30 | 31

Sonnenberg 64
(Ebernach)
Bischofstuhl 65
(Ebernach)

Ernst
Feuerberg 66
Kirchlay 67

Bruttig-Fankel
Götterlay 68

Ellenz-Poltersdorf
Kurfürst 69
Altarberg 70
Rüberberger Dom-
herrenberg 71 P

Briedern
Rüberberger Dom-
herrenberg 71 P

Senheim
Ortsteil Senhals
Rüberberger Dom-
herrenberg 71 P
Römerberg 73

Ellenz-Poltersdorf
Woogberg 89
Silberberg 90

Beilstein
Schloßberg 91

Briedern
Herrenberg 92
Kapellenberg 93
Servatiusberg 94
Römergarten 95

Mesenich
Abteiberg 96
Goldgrübchen 97
Deuslay 98

Senheim
Wahrsager 99
Bienengarten 100
Vogteiberg 101
Rosenberg 102

Bremm
Abtei Kloster
Stuben 103

Ediger-Eller
Ortsteil Eller
Stubener
Klostersegen 104

GROSSLAGE ROSENHANG

Treis-Karden
Ortsteil Treis
Kapellenberg 74
Greth 75
Treppchen 76

Cochem
Ortsteil Cond
Arzlay 77
Rosenberg 78
Nikolausberg 79

Valwig
Schwarzenberg 80
Palmberg 81
Herrenberg 82

Bruttig-Fankel
Ortsteil Bruttig
Pfarrgarten 83
Rathausberg 84
Kapellenberg 85 P

– Ortsteil Fankel
Kapellenberg 85 P
Martinsborn 86
Layenberg 87
Rosenberg 88

GROSSLAGENFREI

Senheim
Lay 105

GROSSLAGE GRAFSCHAFT

Nehren
Römerberg 106

Ediger-Eller
Ortsteil Ediger
Osterlämmchen 107
Hasensprung 108
Elzhofberg 109
Pfaffenberg 110
Feuerberg 111

– Ortsteil Eller
Pfirsichgarten 112
Kapplay 113
Bienenlay 114
Höll 115
Engelströpfchen 116
Schützenlay 117
Calmont 118

Bremm
Calmont 118 a
Schlemmertröpfchen 119
Laurentiusberg 120
Frauenberg 121 P

Neef
Frauenberg 121 P
Petersberg 122
Rosenberg 123

St. Aldegund
Himmelreich 124
Palmberg Terrassen 125
Klosterkammer 126

Alf
Kapellenberg 127
Katzenkopf 128
Herrenberg 129
Burggraf 130
Kronenberg 131
Arrasberg-
Schloßberg 132
Hölle 133

Beuren
Pelzerberger 133 a*

Bullay
Graf Beyßel-
Herrenberg 134
Brautrock 135
Kroneberg 136
Kirchweingarten 137
Sonneck 138

Also vineyards not
registered as Einz. in
Zell, Ortsteil Merl

GROSSLAGE SCHWARZE KATZ

Zell
Ortsteil Merl
Sonneck 139
Adler 140
Königslay-Terrassen 141
Stephansberg 142
Fettgarten 143
Klosterberg 144

Zell
Nußberg 145
Burglay-Felsen 146
Petersborn-
Kabertchen 147
Pommerell 148
Kreuzlay 149
Domherrenberg 150
Geisberg 151

Zell
Ortsteil Kaimt
Marienburger 153
Rosenborn 154
Römerquelle 155

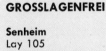

MIDDLE MOSEL

The Bereich Bernkastel, still known to old-timers by its pre-1971 name of Mittelmosel (Middle Mosel), contains all the best vineyard sites of the main stream, now slowed and broadened by locks to make it a noble river, winding in matchless beauty through alternating cliffs of vineyard to the right and left. Whichever side confronts the river with a high hill and makes it bend, offers vines the inclination they need towards the sun.

The river's banks here would be better called cliffs: in many places they rise, almost sheer, in 200-metre (700-feet) precipices. The geology gives the Middle Mosel a structure and a soil of pure slate, which is both highly porous and an efficient reflector of heat. The porosity allows the rain to run straight through the soil, keeping it stable on the steep slopes. The heat reflecting from the slate lets the Riesling make the most of every ray of sun.

Here, as throughout the length of the Mosel, the exposure of the slope is central to the quality of its wine. The river bends provide perfect south- and southeast-facing vineyards and also half-shaded northerly ones. Many of the villages own land on both sides of the river. Some, like Brauneberg, restrict themselves to the south bank, leaving the sun-facing north bank entirely to the vines. The practice of using village – and sometimes Einzellage – titles for land on both banks means that some names have to be treated with caution.

Bernkastel is the natural centre of the region; a major crossing point, an irresistible architectural museum in its huddle of tall timbered houses, and the producer of its most celebrated wine.

Authors differ on where the villages of noteworthy quality upstream and downstream begin and end. The conservative view limits the classic Middle Mosel to the stretch from Trittenheim to Ürzig. But excellent estates extend much farther upstream and downstream in the best sites. Those on the extremities are more dependent, like the Saar and Ruwer, on exceptional seasons. But lovely, lively, classic Riesling is within their grasp and they should be remembered along with Piesport, Bernkastel and Wehlen.

The first villages below Trier to present good south-facing slopes to the Mosel are Longuich and (across its bridge) Schweich, then the hamlets of Longen and Lörsch. No particularly distinguished growers have illuminated their names, but in the first-class vintages they can make notable wine. The majority of the vines here are Riesling, the first essential for fine Mosel. Mehring (see entry opposite) has some well-known sites. Just downstream at Pölich the river makes a dramatic bend to the north, the first of a series of sweeping oxbows which continue for the length of the Middle Mosel. Pölich has a notable vineyard in the Einzellage Held. From here on the north bank downstream to Klüsserath is the Großlage St. Michael – not to be confused with Michelsberg around Piesport.

TRAVEL INFORMATION

The Middle Mosel has the greatest vineyards and many of the most well-known estates. Many growers accept visitors, and there are plenty of opportunities to taste the wines.

Places to visit
Bernkastel, with its spectacular site and old buildings, is a well-known tourist town, so much so that it is hard to find a photograph without a row of coaches along the edge of the Mosel. The town is worth a visit, however, for the wine museum and for the view from the nearby Burg Landshut. Bernkastel apart, Piesport, Wintrich, Graach and the other villages familiar from wine lists provide tasting cellars and superb views of the vineyards. It is worth following side-roads such as those above Trarbach and Graach in order to enjoy the dramatic prospects along the river.

Wine roads
The *Moselweinstraße* follows the river. There are vineyard paths in Ensch, Enkirch, Kröv, Leiwen, Reil, Schleich, Schweich and Trittenheim.

Wine seminars
Weekend wine courses are held in Traben-Trarbach, Senheim and Bernkastel.

Wine festivals
Alf (1st Sunday in Aug), Bernkastel-Kues (1st w/e in Sept), Burg (Sept), Enkirch (Whitsun and Aug), Kröv (1st w/e in Oct), Traben-Trarbach (end of June & last w/e in July), Zeltingen-Rachtig (Aug).

Food and drink
Bernkastel and its suburb Kues have several hotels, and guest houses and private rooms are numerous – consult the tourist office beside the river (tel: 06531-4023). Traben-Trarbach's tourist office will also find rooms (Bahnhofstraße 22). In Traben-Trarbach, the Gasthof Altes Moseltor (tel: 06541-6551) has rooms and a famous restaurant. Wehlen has the quiet Mosel-Hotel (tel: 06531-8527) and the encouragingly-named Sonnenlay (tel: 06531-6496) and Sonnenuhr (tel: 06531-8423) hotels. Dreis, in the countryside 8 km (5 miles) from Wittlich, has the Waldhotel Sonnora (tel: 06578-406), a peaceful place with good food. The Robertmühle hotel in Büdlicherbrück is similarly placed in the Dhron valley near Trittenheim (tel: 06509-515), on the road south to Reinsfeld.

▼ The village of Piesport huddles round its white church tower at the foot of the Goldtröpfchen, a five-kilometre (three-mile) amphitheatre of vines 150 metres (500 feet) high, with ideal southerly exposure.

VILLAGES

MEHRING

Mehring is somewhat better known, partly because of its size, no doubt partly because the famous Friedrich-Wilhelm-Gymnasium is among the owners of its south slope. Here the Großlage St. Michael applies to the better sites. Those facing northeast round the river bend have the Großlage name Probstberg again.

Vineyards
290ha with *Einzellagen* in Großlage St. Michael: Zellerberg, 185ha, SSW, 50% steep. Blattenberg, 12ha, S–SW, 100% steep. Goldkupp, 160ha, S–SSW, 40% steep. Probstberg, 50ha, NE, 100% steep.

KLÜSSERATH

The Einzellage Bruderschaft (brotherhood) not only has a pleasant name; its 250-odd hectares are planted with 90% Riesling.

Vineyards
353.5ha in Großlage St. Michael with *Einzellagen:* Bruderschaft, 250ha, SSE–S–SW, 80% steep. Königsberg, 100ha, SE and SW, 30% steep, 40% flat.

KÖWERICH

Köwerich lies on the south bank of the river, facing the steep and narrow Einzellage Laurentiuslay (100% Riesling) across the water. Its other vineyards are not in the same class.

Vineyards
Großlage St. Michael with *Einzellagen:* Laurentiuslay, 23ha, SW–WSW, 100% steep. Held, 140ha, NE, 80% sloping.

LEIWEN

Leiwen also lies on the south bank and shares the name of Laurentiuslay with Köwerich, but for a detached fragment of vineyard on the opposite side of the river with a different exposure. Leiwen's other vineyards are not so privileged.

Vineyards
449ha in Großlage St. Michael with *Einzellage:* Laurentiuslay, 19ha, WSW and WNW, 100% steep.

TRITTENHEIM

Trittenheim occupies the centre of a splendid oxbow bend, with equally fine sites on both sides of the river. Although its vines seldom if ever produce wine of great body, they achieve classic Riesling finesse in a more delicate style. Poor vintages find them thin. From Trittenheim north the Großlage is (Piesporter) Michelsberg.

Vineyards
326ha in Großlage Michelsberg with *Einzellagen:* Altärchen, 245ha, SSE–W, 60% steep. Apotheke, 55ha, SW–W (on the right of Mosel), ESE–WSW (on the left of Mosel), 65% steep.

NEUMAGEN-DHRON

Neumagen lies on a straight south-north stretch of the river; Dhron in the valley of the tributary Dhron behind the hill. There are good but not outstanding sites in both villages, on both sides of the river, the best being the Hofberger, steep and sheltered in the Dhron valley. Rosengärtchen and the tiny Sonnenuhr are the best-placed sites in Neumagen.

Vineyards
315ha in Großlage Michelsberg with *Einzellagen:* Neumagen: Laudamusberg, 38ha, SSW–W, 95% steep; Rosengärtchen, 37.8ha, SW–W, 100% steep; Sonnenuhr, 0.9ha, SW, 100% steep. Dhron: Hofberger, 17.5ha, E–ESE, 100% steep; Roterd, 125ha, W, 50% steep.

PIESPORT

The village lies in the middle of the biggest south-facing horseshoe of the steepest vineyards on the river. All the north-bank vineyards are fine, although Goldtröpfchen is much the most famous. These Piesporters are the most succulently pleasing of all Mosels, uniting ripeness and a touch of spice with the underlying "nerve" that gives lasting power and style. They are seldom very full-bodied, even by Mosel standards, yet they leave a glowing impression.

Vineyards
387ha in Großlage Michelsberg with *Einzellagen:* Treppchen, 250ha, E–N–W, 20% steep, 30% flat. Falkenberg, 30ha, SE–S, 80% steep. Goldtröpfchen, 122ha, SE–S–SW, 100% steep. Günterslay, 40ha, S–W, 100% steep.

MINHEIM

Minheim lies on an oxbow bend, a replica of Trittenheim but without its good fortune in the steepness or orientation of its slopes.

Vineyards
155ha in Großlage Michelsberg with *Einzellagen:* Burglay, 30ha, E, 80% steep. Rosenberg, 60ha, SE, 40% steep.

WINTRICH

Wintrich echoes the geography of Neumagen, its best site, Ohligsberg, lying by the river to the south of the village. Here the Bernkastel Großlage Kurfürstlay takes over from (Piesporter) Michelsberg.

Vineyards
272.7ha in Großlage Kurfürstlay with *Einzellagen:* Stefanslay, 82.8ha, WNW, 30% sloping, 70% flat. Großer Herrgott, 97.6ha, S–W–NW, 40% steep. Ohligsberg, 9.7ha, SW–W, 70% steep.

KESTEN

Kesten has vineyards on the north bank of the Mosel as it turns again to flow east, but only one outstanding site, Paulinshofberger, facing south across the river.

Vineyards
121ha in Großlage Kurfürstlay with *Einzellage:* Paulinshofberger, 9ha, SSE, 100% steep.

MONZEL AND OSANN

These two villages lie behind Kesten in the hills with no remarkable sites but some fair ones. Their wine is as likely to be sold as Bernkasteler Kurfürstlay as by their own little-known names.

Vineyards
In Großlage Kurfürstlay with *Einzellagen:* Monzel: Paulinslay, 25ha, NW, 90% sloping. Kätzchen, 100ha, S, 60% steep. Osann: Kirchlay, 25ha, S–SSW, 30% steep; Rosenberg, 120ha, S–WSW, 35% steep.

BRAUNEBERG

Brauneberg, on the south bank, faces its proudest possession, the Juffer, across the water. Before the Doktorberg in Bernkastel rose to fame, this was the highest-priced Mosel; robust wine of body and full of fruit which aged admirably, in the style of the time, to amber pungency. The name of Brauneberg's hamlet, Filzen, is sometimes seen on good-value bottles.

Vineyards
306.2ha in Großlage Kurfürstlay with *Einzellagen:* Mandelgraben, 11ha, SE, 100% steep. Klostergarten, 93ha, WNW, 100% steep. Juffer, 31ha, SSE, 100% steep. Juffer Sonnenuhr, 10ha, SSE, 100% steep. Kammer, 1ha, SSE, 80% steep. Hasenläufer, 12ha, SSE, 100% steep.

MARING-NOVIAND

Lying in a side valley north of the river opposite Brauneberg, Maring-Noviand has some well-sheltered if not ideally exposed sites, the Honigberg forming a southwest-facing arc in imitation of a river bend but unfortunately one hill back from the all-important river.

VINEYARDS

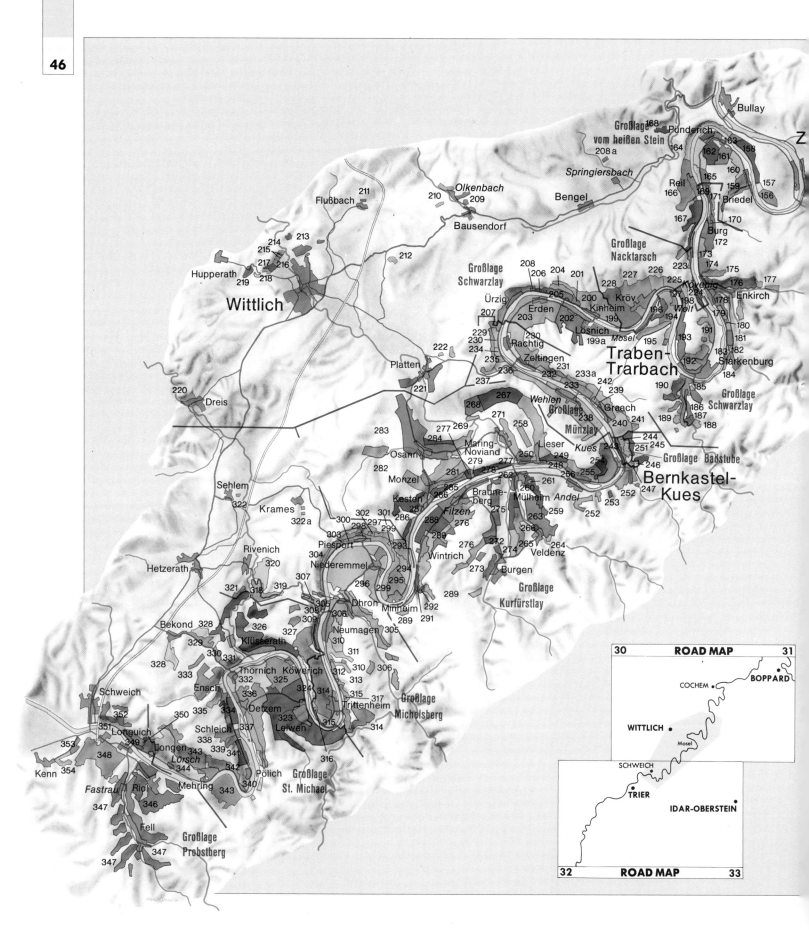

BEREICH BERNKASTEL

GROSSLAGE VOM HEISSEN STEIN

Briedel
Weisserberg 156
Schäferlay 157
Herzchen 158
Nonnengarten 159
Schelm 160

Pünderich
Goldlay 161
Rosenberg 162
Nonnengarten 163
Marienburg 164

Reil
Goldlay 165
Falklay 166
Moullay-Hofberg 167
Sorentberg 168

GROSSLAGE SCHWARZLAY

Burg
Wendelstück 169
Hahnenschrittchen 170
Thomasberg 171
Falklay 172
Schloßberg 173

Enkirch
Edelberg 174
Monteneubel 175
Steffensberg 176
Weinkammer 177
Herrenberg 178
Zeppwingert 179
Batterieberg 180
Ellergrub 181

Starkenburg
Rosengarten 182

Traben-Trarbach Ortsteil Traben
Gaispfad 183
Zollturm 184
Königsberg 191
Kräuterhaus 192
Würzgarten 193

– Ortsteil Trarbach
Burgberg 185
Schloßberg 186
Ungsberg 187
Hühnerberg 188
Kreuzberg 189
Taubenhaus 190

Wolf
(Ortsteil of Traben-Trarbach)
Schatzgarten 194

Sonnenlay 195
Klosterberg 196
Goldgrube 197
Auf der Heide 198

Kinheim
Rosenberg 199
Römerhang 199 a
Hubertuslay 200

Lösnich
Försterlay 201
Burgberg 202

Erden
Busslay 203
Herrenberg 204
Treppchen 205
Prälat 206

Ürzig
Würzgarten 207
Goldwingert 208

Bengel Ortsteil Springiersbach
Klosterberg 208 a

Bausendorf Ortsteil Olkenbach
Herzlay 209
Hubertuslay 210

Flußbach
Reichelberg 211

Wittlich
Kupp 212
Lay 213
Bottchen 214
Felsentreppchen 215
Rosenberg 216
Portnersberg 217
Klosterweg 218
Klosterweg 219 P

Hupperath
Klosterweg 219 P

Dreis
Johannisberg 220

Platten
Klosterberg 221
Rotlay 222

GROSSLAGE NACKTARSCH

Kröv
Steffensberg 225
Letterlay 226
Kirchlay 227
Paradies 228

– Ortsteil Kövenig
Burglay 223
Herrenberg 224

GROSSLAGE MÜNZLAY

Zeltingen-Rachtig (Zeltingen)
Deutschherrenberg 229
Himmelreich 230
Schloßberg 231
Sonnenuhr 232

Wehlen
(Ortsteil of Bernkastel-Kues)
Sonnenuhr 233
Rosenberg 233 a
Hofberg 234
Abtei 235
Klosterhofgut 236
Klosterberg 237
Nonnenberg 238

Graach
Domprobst 239
Himmelreich 240
Abtsberg 241
Josephshöfer 242

GROSSLAGE BADSTUBE

Bernkastel-Kues Ortsteil Bernkastel
Lay 243
Matheisbildchen 244
Bratenhöfchen 245
Graben 246
Doctor 247

Lieser
Süßenberg 248
Niederberg-Helden 249
Rosenlay 250
Schloßberg 252 P

GROSSLAGE KURFÜRSTLAY

Bernkastel-Kues Ortsteil Bernkastel
Johannisbrünnchen 251
Schloßberg 252 P
Stephanus-Rosengärtchen 253

Andel
(Ortsteil of Bernkastel-Kues)
Schloßberg 252 P

Bernkastel-Kues Ortsteil Kues
Rosenberg 254
Kardinalsberg 255
Weisenstein 256

Mülheim
Elisenberg 259 P

Sonnenlay 260
Helenenkloster 261
Amtgarten 262

Veldenz
Elisenberg 259 P
Kirchberg 263
Mühlberg 264
Grafschafter Sonnenberg 265
Carlsberg 266

Maring-Noviand
Honigberg 267
Klosterberg 268
Römerpfad 269
Sonnenuhr 271

Burgen
Römerberg 272
Kirchberg 273
Hasenläufer 274

Brauneberg
Mandelgraben 275 P
Klostergarten 276
Juffer 277
Juffer Sonnenuhr 278
Kammer 279

– Ortsteil Filzen
Mandelgraben 275 P

Osann-Monzel Ortsteil Monzel
Paulinslay 281
Kätzchen 282

– Ortsteil Osann
Kirchlay 283
Rosengarten 284

Kesten
Paulinshofberger 285
Herrenberg 286
Paulinsberg 287

Wintrich
Stefanslay 288
Großer Herrgott 289
Ohligsberg 291
Geierslay 292

GROSSLAGE MICHELSBERG

Minheim
Burglay 293
Kapellchen 294
Rosenberg 295
Günterslay 299 P

Piesport
Treppchen 296 P
Falkenberg 297
Goldtröpfchen 298 P
Günterslay 299 P
Domherr 300
Schubertslay 303

Grafenberg 304 P

– Ortsteil Niederemmel
Treppchen 296 P
Goldtröpfchen 298 P
Gärtchen 301
Kreuzwingert 302
Hofberger 305 P

Neumagen-Dhron Ortsteil Dhron
Goldtröpfchen 298 P
Grafenberg 304 P
Hofberger 305 P
Roterd 306
Großer Hengelberg 307
Häs'chen 308

– Ortsteil Neumagen
Nußwingert 309
Engelgrube 310
Laudamusberg 311
Rosengärtchen 312
Sonnenuhr 313

Trittenheim
Altärchen 314
Apotheke 315
Felsenkopf 316
Leiterchen 317

Rivenich
Niederberg 318
Geisberg 319
Rosenberg 320
Brauneberg 321 P

Hetzerath
Brauneberg 321 P

Sehlem
Rotlay 322

Klausen Ortsteil Krames
Vineyard not registered as Einz. 322 a

GROSSLAGE ST. MICHAEL

Leiwen
Klostergarten 323
Laurentiuslay 324

Köwerich
Laurentiuslay 324 a
Held 325

Klüsserath
Bruderschaft 326
Königsberg 327

Bekond
Schloßberg 328
Brauneberg 329

Thornich
Enggaß 330
Ritsch 331
Schießlay 332

Ensch
Mühlenberg 333
St. Martin 334
Sonnenlay 335

Detzem
Würzgarten 336
Maximiner Klosterlay 337

Schleich
Sonnenberg 338
Klosterberg 339

Pölich
Held 340
Südlay 341

Mehring
Blattenberg 342
Goldkupp 343
Zellerberg 344 P

Lörsch
(Ortsteil of Mehring)
Zellerberg 344 P

Longen
Zellerberg 344 P

GROSSLAGE PROBSTBERG

Riol
Römerberg 346

Fell
(incl. Ortsteil Fastrau)
Maximiner Burgberg 347

Longuich
Hirschlay 348
Maximiner Herrenberg 349
Herrenberg 350 P

Schweich
Herrenberg 350 P
Annaberg 351
Burgmauer 352

Kenn
Held 353
Maximiner Hofgarten 354

LIESER

Lieser has a position as prime as Brauneberg's Juffer, without its great reputation. The soil seems to mark it with a stony tang of its own. Confusingly, most of Lieser, although next door to Bernkastel, has the Großlage name of Beerenlay, peculiar to itself.

Vineyards

149ha with *Einzellagen* in Großlage Kurfürstlay: Schloßberg, 143ha, SW (117.6ha) and ENE and S (21ha), 40% steep. Großlage Beerenlay: Niederberg-Helden, 24ha, SSW, 100% steep.

BERNKASTEL-KUES

This is the hub of the Middle Mosel: Kues, the larger town, on flat land on the left bank; Bernkastel across the bridge, crammed up against its precipitous vineyards, with the most famous of them, the Doctor, apparently on the point of sliding straight into its streets. Bernkastel's best wines bring together all the qualities of the Mosel: delicacy and drive, force and grace, honey and earth. Riesling, in other words, and pure grey slate. A suggestion of a flinty edge and some say a hint of smoke often distinguishes them from their neighbours.

The vineyards are divided into two Großlagen: Kurfürstlay for the herd (which includes many vineyards upstream from the town boundaries) and Badstube for the select few sites that share a hill with the Doctor.

Vineyards

356ha with *Einzellagen* in Großlage Badstube: Doctor, 3.3ha, S-SSW, 100% steep; Lay, 7.9ha, WSW, 100% steep; Bratenhöfchen, 18.4ha, WSW, 50% steep; Matheisbildchen, 11.4ha, WSW, 90% steep; Graben, 12.8ha, S-SW, 95% steep. Großlage Kurfürstlay: Johannisbrünnchen, 33ha, WSW-W, 100% steep; Schloßberg, 50.6ha, SW-W, 50% steep; Stephanus-Rosengärtchen, 2ha, SW, 100% steep; Kardinalsberg, 73ha, SSE-SSW, 60% steep; Rosenberg, 8.6ha, ESW, 90% steep; Weisenstein, 7.1ha, SSW, 50% steep.

GRAACH

Bernkastel melts into Graach, Graach into Wehlen and Wehlen into Zeltingen along the 8-kilometre (five-mile) hill of uninterrupted vines that starts with the Doctorberg. It rises over 200m above the river, hardly deviating from its ideal vertiginous tilt or its steady orientation south-southwest. It may well be the largest vineyard of sustained superlative quality in the world.

Graach has a major share of this treasure: all its vines are sandwiched between Bernkastel and Wehlen's greatest site, the Sonnenuhr. Its wines can achieve similar intensity and richness; they belong firmly in the top flight of the Mosel.

Vineyards

98ha in Großlage Münzlay with *Einzellagen*: Domprobst, 28.5ha, SW, 100% steep. Himmelreich, 86.9ha, SW, 100% steep. Josephshöfer, 5.8ha, SSW, 90% steep.

WEHLEN

Another of the villages whose growers have the pleasure of admiring their best vineyard across the river. The Sonnenuhr, with the sundial that gives the vineyard its name conspicuous among the vines, lies directly opposite the village centre. The other Wehlen vineyards are on the south bank and have less to offer. (Klosterberg is the best.) The fame of Wehlen hangs entirely on its one great site and the honeyed quintessence of Riesling it can produce.

Vineyards

154ha in Großlage Münzlay with *Einzellage*: Sonnenuhr, 65ha, SSW, 100% steep.

ZELTINGEN

The village is called Zeltingen-Rachtig, being a union of two small settlements, again with land on both sides of the river. Its Sonnenuhr vineyard is only slightly less renowned than Wehlen's, and the excellent Schloßberg above it gives powerful, beautifully balanced, rather earthy wines. The famous name of Himmelreich is one of those which has been extended to embrace sites of very uneven quality, facing several points of the compass. On the opposite shore, Deutschherrenberg tends to less ripeness but foreshadows the famous spicy flavour of its neighbour, Ürzig.

Vineyards

178ha in Großlage Münzlay with *Einzellagen*: Deutschherrenberg, 20ha, ENE-ESE, 100% steep. Himmelreich, 130ha, SW-WNW and E, 70% steep. Schloßberg, 60ha, SW, 100% steep. Sonnenuhr, 40ha, SSW, 100% steep.

ÜRZIG

Ürzig tucks all its modest parcel of vineyards into a sheltered bend of the river facing south-east, on deep slaty soil mixed with red clay in snug crannies where the Riesling ripens to a high level of spicy intensity. Würzgarten means "spice garden". Its wines have strong character and should be among the most identifiable of the great Middle Mosels. From Ürzig downstream to just above Kröv the Großlage is Schwarzlay.

Vineyards

60.6ha in Großlage Schwarzlay with *Einzellage*: Würzgarten, 56ha, ESE-S, 80% steep.

ERDEN

The village lies opposite Ürzig, surrounded by the broad, gentle slopes of its Einzellage Busslay, a Müller-Thurgau rather than a Riesling site, comparable to Piesport's Treppchen. Erden's fine vineyards lie on the opposite bank next to Ürzig. The tiny Prälat is the best, and the last of the truly great vineyards of the Mosel on this downstream route.

Vineyards

100ha in Großlage Schwarzlay with *Einzellagen*: Busslay, 110ha, WNW-NW, 100% sloping. Herrenberg, 20ha, SSE-SSW, 65% steep. Treppchen, 45ha, S, 90% steep. Prälat, 2.2ha, S, 100% steep.

KINHEIM

Kinheim, on the north bank, has one fine site, Hubertuslay, but here the soil starts to change to a less outrageously slaty mixture and the chance of superlative wine to diminish.

Vineyards

115ha in Großlage Schwarzlay with *Einzellagen*: Rosenberg, 49ha, SE-SSW, 25% steep. Hubertuslay, 105ha, SSE-SSW, 60% steep.

KRÖV

Kröv makes its reputation and its fortune more on its Großlage name Nacktarsch (and the accompanying label showing a little boy being spanked with his pants down) than on its Einzellagen, good though their wine can be in a freshly fruity style.

Vineyards

341ha in Großlage Nacktarsch with *Einzellagen*: Burglay, 16ha, E, 100% steep. Herrenberg, 22ha, E, 95% steep. Steffensberg, 43ha, S-SSW, 90% steep. Letterlay, 6ha, SSE-SSW, 100% steep. Kirchlay, 72ha, SE, 70% steep. Paradies, 242ha, SE, 50% steep.

TRABEN-TRARBACH

The next across-the-river pair of settlements, these share yet another mighty oxbow bend. But here the riverside slopes have moderated and the best steep sites are back in a side-valley.

Vineyards

200ha in Großlage Schwarzlay with *Einzellagen*: Schloßberg, 31.6ha, SW-W and S, 90% steep. Ungsberg, 9.1ha, SW, 100% steep. Hühnerberg, 9.3ha, SSW, 100% steep.

ENKIRCH

As the river recovers its northward course, Enkirch has a site that recalls Neumagen and Dhron, with the steep riverfront facing west and a side-valley (Steffensberg) facing south. Riesling here makes wines of balanced, deft lightness and spiciness which deserve a higher reputation.

Vineyards

162ha in Großlage Schwarzlay with *Einzellagen*: Steffensberg, 82ha, SSE-SSW, 100% steep. Batterieberg, 1ha, WSW, 100% steep. Herrenberg, 15ha, WSW, 100% steep. Monteneubel, 27ha, SSE-WSW, 100% steep. Zeppwingert, 17ha, WSW, steep.

REIL

The next major left-bank centre, Reil has good sheltered slopes for Riesling. The best are Goldlay, across the river, and Sorentberg, in a side-valley. These produce light wines, capable of gulpable fruitiness in good vintages.

Vineyards

In Großlage Vom heißen Stein with *Einzellagen*: Falklay, 85ha, E, 60% steep. Moullay-Hofberg, 75ha, ENE-SE, 65% steep. Goldlay, 25ha, W, 90% steep. Sorentberg, 12ha, S, 100% steep.

PÜNDERICH

Both sides of the river at the next right-hand bend are in Pünderich. The steep slopes are dying away here, and Riesling sites are limited. Nonnengarten makes softly fruity Rieslings; the Marienburg lighter and more flowery wine.

Vineyards

In Großlage Vom heißen Stein with *Einzellagen*: Goldlay, 55ha, NE, 30% sloping. Rosenberg, 58ha, W, 30% sloping. Nonnengarten, 10ha, SSW, 20% steep. Marienburg, 96ha, E-S-SW (left side of the river), W (right side), 70% steep.

UPPER MOSEL

The Mosel wears its first tentative vineyards in France, flows through the little Grand-Duchy of Luxembourg festooned with them, then enters Germany near the ancient Roman capital of Trier to be joined by the rivers Saar and Ruwer. It is their side-valleys, rather than the main stream, that boast the first great Mosel vineyards. Upper Mosel ("Obermosel") wines at their best are gentle. A good deal of the pleasantly neutral, often rather sharp Elbling grape is grown on sites where the noble Riesling fails to ripen, but where its junior cousin has apparently given yeoman service since the Roman origins of the vineyard. Vines were well established here by the first century.

Germany's first vineyards face those of Luxembourg across the still-narrow river. Schloß Thorn at Perl still operates a 16th-century press, said to be the oldest in Germany still to be doing its annual duty. The little town of Wincheringen is the busiest centre in the district, with a press-house out-station of the giant Mosel-Saar-Ruwer cooperative (whose headquarters is at Kues, opposite Bernkastel).

Two Großlage names cover the Obermosel: Gipfel, for the bulk of the district on the east bank of the river, opposite Luxembourg, and Königsberg for the few vineyards round Mesenich on the west bank, clustered near the confluence of the Mosel and the Saar.

In the Saar valley the Riesling takes a giant stride to greatness. It still has difficulty ripening in the great majority of vintages. But when it does, on the best slopes here and the neighbouring valley of the Ruwer, the results are unsurpassable anywhere on earth: quintessential Riesling, clean as steel, haunting with the qualities of remembered scents or distant music.

A scattering of sites in these two pleasantly pastoral valleys must be listed among the very greatest in Germany, or in the world, for white wines of the greatest finesse, "breed", and, curiously enough, longevity. It seems strange that such pale and apparently insubstantial wines should share this quality with, for example, vintage port. But this is the magic of the Riesling: equilibrium which seems everlasting.

The uppermost vineyards of the Mosel are within the Bereich Moseltor, which has one Großlage: Schloß Bübinger. Just north of the village of Palzem the Bereich Obermosel takes over with its two Großlagen Gipfel and Königsberg.

The vineyards of the Saar and Ruwer, plus one or two on the main river around Konz and Trier, belong in the Bereich Saar-Ruwer, with its two Großlagen Scharzberg (Saar) and Römerlay (Ruwer). Usefully for the student, there is a short gap between the Ruwer vineyards and the first sites of the Middle Mosel around Schweich.

TRAVEL INFORMATION

▲ Steep slopes and slippery slate make the picker's job a hard one. A glass is always welcome.

The gentle landscape of the Upper Mosel is not obvious tourist country and is hence uncrowded.

Places to visit
Trier: a Roman town with many relics surviving, also many Renaissance and baroque buildings. Information at the Porta Nigra Roman gate (tel: 0651-75440).
Konz: town at Mosel-Saar confluence, baroque *Karthause* – monastery
Saarburg: pretty small town, one of the oldest in Germany. Medieval buildings include castle, town walls, church. A wine centre for the Saar (see festivals).
The Ruwer: Kasel, Waldrach and Eitelsbach are small, old and charming wine villages.

Wine festivals
Ockfen (1st w/e in June), Trier (3rd w/e in June), Saarburg (1st w/e in July), Serrig (last w/e in July), Wiltingen (last w/e in July), Olewig-Trier (1st w/e in Aug), Saarburg (2nd w/e in Aug), Ayl (3rd w/e in Aug), Saarburg: Saar Wine Festival (1st w/e in Sept).
Food and drink: see page 41.

► Saarburg, the capital of the Saar, is hardly a metropolis. With its castle, church and setting of woods and meadows it epitomizes the gentle charm of the region.

VILLAGES

SERRIG
The uppermost wine village of the Saar (still higher up are steelworks). Steel is also the appropriate metaphor; Serrig has problems ripening Riesling and makes much excellent acid base-wine for Sekt. The State Domain is its principal estate. In exceptionally warm autumns its wines ripen to become legends.

Vineyards
84ha, *Einzellagen:* Antoniusberg, 12ha, S-W, 60% steep. Schloß Saarsteiner, 8.3ha, W-SW, 80% steep, Schloß Saarfelser Schloßberg, 5.2ha, SW, 60% steep. Kupp, 12ha, S, 100% sloping. Vogelsang, 22ha, SE-SW, 100% steep. Heiligenborn, 7ha, SSW, 100% steep. Würtzberg, 6.5ha, S, 100% steep. Herrenberg, 6.5ha, SE-SSW, 100% steep.

IRSCH
In a side valley to the north is Irsch, a minor wine village with the same problems as Serrig.

Vineyards
61ha. *Einzellagen:* Sonnenberg, 47ha, S-WSW, 70% steep. Hubertusberg, 34ha, S-SW, 100% steep. Vogelsang, 22ha, SE-SW, 100% steep.

SAARBURG
The principal town of the area, with several good growers on slopes that are capable of great finesse in good years.

Vineyards
56ha. *Einzellagen:* Antoniusbrunnen, 10ha, S, 100% steep. Bergschlößchen, 8ha, SE-S-SW, 100% steep. Fuchs, 16.5ha, SE, 100% steep. Klosterberg, 5ha, SW, 80% steep. Schloßberg, 9ha, E, 100% steep. Rausch, 12ha, SE-S, 100% steep.

OCKFEN
The first of the noble Saar vineyards is the great hump of the Bockstein in Ockfen, owned by the State Domain and many others. Again, a dry autumn is needed for balanced wines but such vintages can last almost indefinitely.

Vineyards
101ha. *Einzellagen:* Kupp, 7ha, S-W, 90% steep. Herrenberg, 7.5ha, S, 30% steep. Heppenstein, 6.6ha, SSW, 100% steep. Bockstein, 52ha, S-SW, 60% steep. Neuwies, 3ha, S, 90% steep. Geisberg, 1ha, E-ESE, 60% steep.

AYL
The village faces the whale-like ridge of its Kupp vineyard. Thrillingly honey-and-flint sweet-and-sour wines at their best.

Vineyards
64ha. *Einzellagen:* Kupp, 81ha, E-W, 100% steep. Herrenberger, 6.8ha, SW, 100% steep.

WAWERN
A small village with no famous site name to conjure with, but fine wines in true Saar style.

Vineyards
21ha. *Einzellagen:* Herrenberger, 7.7ha, S, 30% steep. Goldberg, 16ha, S-SW, 60% steep.

WILTINGEN
The hub of the Saar region, surrounded by major vineyards and giving its name to most Saar Großlage wines ("Wiltinger Scharzberg").

Its best site, Scharzhofberg – remember the essential "hof" – is considered so important that it dispenses with the name of Wiltingen on its label. A galaxy of the top producers own land in the dozen first-rate vineyards, which often produce some of Germany's more delectably elegant, balanced, age-worthy wines and noblest Auslesen.

Vineyards
192ha. *Einzellagen:* Scharzhofberg, 27ha, SE-S, 80% steep. Braune Kupp, 5.8ha, SSW, 90% steep. Rosenberg, 61.7ha, S-W, 40% steep. Hölle, 2.3ha, SSE, 90% steep. Kupp, 7.3ha, S, 60% steep. Klosterberg, 71.3ha, S-W, 50% steep. Schlangengraben, 54.4ha, ESE-S, 20% steep. Schloßberg, 18ha, E, 90% steep. Sandberg, 2.2ha, SE, 100% steep. Gottesfuß, 4.4ha, WSW, 100% steep. Braunfels, 58.5ha, SW and W, 90% steep.

KANZEM
Just downstream from Wiltingen, Kanzem evokes only slightly less superlatives for its much smaller area of steep vineyards dropping to the river. Wines with teasing hints of earth and perhaps spice.

Vineyards
57ha. *Einzellagen:* Altenberg, 31ha, SE, 90% steep. Hörecker, 0.73ha, SE, 100% steep. Schloßberg, 4.3ha, E, 90% steep. Sonnenberg, 25ha, SW-WNW, 70% steep.

KONZ
The town at the meeting place of the Saar and Mosel includes in its boundaries the place names Falkenstein (known for its 18-hectare Hofberg), Filzen, Mennig and Oberemmel.

OBEREMMEL
In a side valley east of Wiltingen, Oberemmel has some superb sites, including Hütte and Rosenberg, and considerable land of rather less distinction.

Vineyards
211ha. *Einzellagen:* Karlsberg, 42ha, S-W, 65% steep. Altenberg, 75ha, S-SE, 80% steep. Hütte, 5ha, S-SE, 40% steep. Raul, 2.4ha, S-SE, 80% steep. Agritiusberg, 5.3ha, SE, 100% steep. Rosenberg, 81ha, SE-S-W, 40% steep.

FILZEN
Towards the mouth of the Saar, Filzen has a smaller reputation but some good growers.

Vineyards
52ha. *Einzellagen:* Pulchen, 4.8ha, W, 70% steep. Urbelt, 12ha, SW, 100% steep.

TRIER
Trier's own vineyards and those of the tiny river Ruwer (pronounced Roover) together make up only a drop in the ocean, yet one of the most precious drops of all. Ruwer wines are feather-light, often *spritzig*; on the face of it scarcely more serious than *vinho verde*. Yet if quintessential Riesling is made anywhere it is here; frail but tenacious, even the dry wines poised in balance for years and the sweet ones growing subtly harmonious for decades.

The boundaries of Trier now include the vineyards of Avelsbach, brilliantly exploited by the State Domain and the Cathedral estates (Hohe Domkirche) to make the most of their perfume, despite a tartness that dogs them in all but the ripest years.

Vineyards
Trier: *Einzellagen:* Sonnenberg, 4ha, SSW, 45% steep; Marienholz, 55ha, SW-W, 30% steep; Thiergarten Unterm Kreuz, 3.4ha, S-SW, 100% steep.
Avelsbach: *Einzellagen:* Herrenberg, 12ha, SW, 50% steep; Altenberg, 10.2ha, S-SW, 100% steep; Hammerstein, 11.9ha, SSW-S, 70% steep; Rotlei, 9.4ha, S-W, 80% steep.

WALDRACH
The first Ruwer wine village coming downstream, Waldrach is the least celebrated, though its wines have almost the potential of Kasel. Growers include the Bischöflichen Weingüter.

Vineyards
121.2ha. *Einzellagen:* Krone, 65ha, SW, 80% steep. Jesuitengarten, 2.4ha, SW, 100% steep. Laurentiusberg, 5.9ha, S, 90% steep. Hubertusberg, 4ha, SW, 100% steep. Sonnenberg, 4ha, SW, 100% steep.

KASEL
The "capital", tiny as it is, of the Ruwer. Its best site, Nies'chen, performs wonders of delicacy, perfume and utter charm.

Vineyards
42ha. *Einzellagen:* Herrenberg, 8.8ha, SSW-W, 50% steep. Dominikanerberg, 6ha, S-SW, 100% steep. Kehrnagel, 22.2ha, S-SW, 90% steep. Hitzlay, 22ha, SE-SW, 70% steep. Nies'chen, 16.8ha, SSW, 80% steep. Paulinsberg, 10.2ha, E-SE, 100% steep. Timpert, 3.4ha, SE, 100% steep.

MERTESDORF
Known entirely for the one magnificent estate, von Schubert, that faces it across the valley.

Vineyards
Einzellagen: Maximin Grünhäuser Bruderberg, 4ha, SE, 100% steep. Maximin Grünhäuser Abtsberg, 11ha, S-SW, 65% steep. Maximin Grünhäuser Herrenberg, 18ha, WSW–S-SW, 80% steep.

EITELSBACH
Almost equally identified with one estate, the Karthäuserhofberg. These last two in their different styles are the "first-growths" of the Ruwer, and hold that rank in comparison with any properties in Germany.

Vineyards
74.5ha. *Einzellagen:* Karthäuserhofberg Burgberg, 5.8ha SE-SW, 30% steep. Karthäuserhofberg Kronenberg, 5.2ha, SSE, SSW, 80% steep. Karthäuserhofberg Sang, 3ha, SSE–SSW, 30% steep.

Bereich Obermosel
Above Konz the Großlagen Königsberg and Gipfel encompass some 26 Einzellagen plus scattered plots.

Bereich Moseltor
Frontier vineyards in Nenning, Sehndorf and Perl.

VINEYARDS

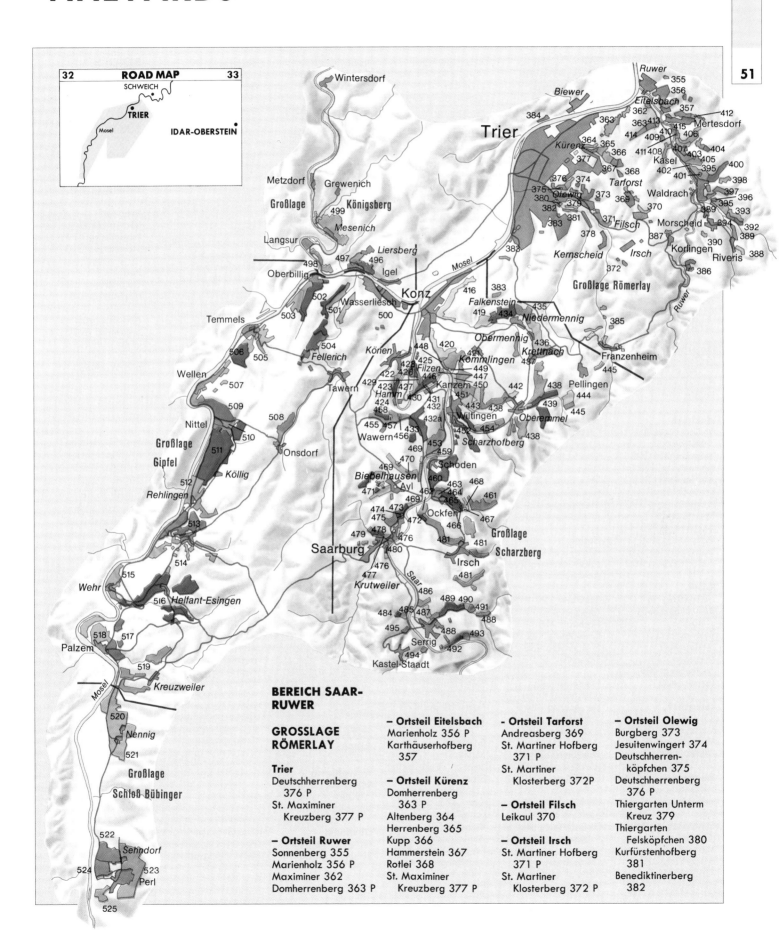

ROAD MAP
32 · 33
SCHWEICH
TRIER
Mosel
IDAR-OBERSTEIN

Wintersdorf
Ruwer 355
Biewer 356
Eitelsbach 357
384 362
Trier 363 412
Kürenz 363 413 415 Mertesdorf
364 365 414 409 410 406
366 411 408 407 404
377 Kasel 403 405
367 368 402 401 400
376 374 398
Metzdorf Grewenich 375 Tarforst 373 369 397 395
Großlage 380 Olewig 370 Waldrach 389 393
Königsberg 499 382 379 371 394 392
Mesenich 383 381 Filsch 387 389
378 390
Langsur 383 Kernscheid 372 Morscheid 388
Liersberg Irsch Korlingen Riveris
498 497 496 Igel Großlage Römerlay 386
Oberbillig Mosel
502 Wasserliesch 416 383
501 Konz Falkenstein 435
Temmels 503 500 419 434 Niedermennig
504 Königen 448 420 Obermennig 436 385
506 505 Fellerich 425 421 Krettnach Franzenheim
Wellen 422 426 Filzen 446 449 437 445
507 429 423 427 Kanzem 447 450 438 Pellingen
Tawern Hamm 430 451 442 444
509 508 424 431 432 443 438 439 445
458 Wiltingen 438
Nittel 455 457 432a Oberemmel
510 Wawern 456 433 452 454
Großlage 511 469 453 459 438
Gipfel 470 Scharzhofberg
512 Köllig 469 Schöden
Rehlingen Biebelhausen 460 463 468
471 Ayl 462 464 461
513 469 465
474 473 Ockfen 467
475 472 466
514 479 478 476 481 Großlage
515 Saarburg 480 481 Scharzberg
Wehr 476 Irsch
516 Helfant-Esingen 477 481
Krutweiler 486
518 517 484 485 487 489 490 491
Palzem 495 488 488 493
519 Serrig 492
494
Kreuzweiler Kastel-Staadt
Mosel
520
Nennig
521
Großlage
Schloß Bübinger
522
Sehndorf
524 523
Perl
525

BEREICH SAAR-RUWER

GROSSLAGE RÖMERLAY

Trier
Deutschherrenberg 376 P
St. Maximiner Kreuzberg 377 P

– Ortsteil Ruwer
Sonnenberg 355
Marienholz 356 P
Maximiner 362
Domherrenberg 363 P

– Ortsteil Eitelsbach
Marienholz 356 P
Karthäuserhofberg 357

– Ortsteil Kürenz
Domherrenberg 363 P
Altenberg 364
Herrenberg 365
Kupp 366
Hammerstein 367
Rotlei 368
St. Maximiner Kreuzberg 377 P

- Ortsteil Tarforst
Andreasberg 369
St. Martiner Hofberg 371 P
St. Martiner Klosterberg 372P

– Ortsteil Filsch
Leikaul 370

– Ortsteil Irsch
St. Martiner Hofberg 371 P
St. Martiner Klosterberg 372 P

– Ortsteil Olewig
Burgberg 373
Jesuitenwingert 374
Deutschherren-köpfchen 375
Deutschherrenberg 376 P
Thiergarten Unterm Kreuz 379
Thiergarten Felsköpfchen 380
Kurfürstenhofberg 381
Benediktinerberg 382

Carl Aug. Immich-Batterieberg

5585 Enkirch, tel: 06541-9376. *Owner:* Georg and Ingrid Immich. About 6 hectares. *Einzellagen:* Enkirch: Ellergrub, Zeppwingert, Steffensberg and Batterieberg
(solely owned).

The Immichs have been growers in Enkirch since 1425. Georg Immich qualified at the Geisenheim Wine School and stoutly defends the Mosel traditions of Riesling and oak.

Weingut Kanzemer Berg

Maximilian v. Othegraven, 5511 Kanzem.
5 hectares, including a holding in the modernized Kanzemer Altenberg.

Small high-quality estate, already established in the 16th century. Vines are 95% Riesling, producing superb wines that last for years in bottle. The '76 vintage included two different Trockenbeerenauslesen.

Weingut Christian Karp-Schreiber

5551 Brauneberg, tel: 06534-236. *Owner:* Günter Karp. 3 hectares. *Einzellagen:* Brauneberg: Juffer, Juffer Sonnenuhr and Mandelgraben.

A family property since 1664. Günter Karp and his son Alwin make prize-winning Rieslings and (in Mandelgraben) Müller-Thurgau and Kerner, mostly sold to private customers.

Gutsverwaltung Karthäuserhof

(Formerly H. W. Rautenstrauch), Karthäuserhof 1, 5500 Trier-Eitelsbach. *Owners:* the Tyrell family. 20 hectares. *Einzellage:* Eitelsbach: Karthäuserhofberg.

A beautiful old manor of the Carthusian monks in a side valley of the Ruwer, bought by the ancestor of the present owners when Napoleon secularized church land. The long hill of Karthäuserhofberg is divided into Kronenberg (one half), Burgberg, Sang and the tiny Orthsberg and Stirn; all belong to the estate, which also breeds Prussian Trakehner horses. The vines are 90% Riesling and the wines can be fabulous in great vintages, but tend to have harsher acidity (and are usually made drier) than the only comparable Ruwer estate, Maximin Grünhaus (*see* C. von Schubert'sche Gutsverwaltung). The bottle is unmistakable, with only a narrow label on the neck, none on the body.

Weingut Reichsgraf von Kesselstatt

Liebfrauenstraße 10, 5500 Trier, tel: 0651-75101. *Owners:* Günther and Käthi Reh. 96 hectares in most of the best villages.

This was the greatest private estate of the Mosel-Saar-Ruwer, with about 60 hectares, when it was bought in 1978 by Günther Reh, son of Carl Reh of Leiwen. Since then the empire has expanded with the addition of several more high-quality estates (see below), either bought, leased or part-owned. Each has its own character but the general standard is very high and the entire estate is planted with Riesling. Between 60 and 70 percent of the wines are trocken or halbtrocken. The estate makes a point of guar-anteeing that its wines will last 10 years; if they don't, they will refund customers.

The splendid baroque Kesselstatt palace in Trier, from which the Counts promulgated the planting of Riesling in the 18th century, is the headquarters. The estate is in 4 parts, each with its own press house and cellars. The most famous is the Josephshof at Graach, which owns the whole Josephshöfer Einzellage of 6 hectares at the foot of the hill between the greatest vineyards of Bernkastel and Wehlen.

The following 4 Weingüter were bought around 1820 and constitute the main estate.

Weingut Domklausenhof Piesport/ Mosel. *Einzellagen:* Piesport: Domherr (2ha), Goldtröpfchen (5.3) and Treppchen (4.2); Neumagen: Rosengärtchen (1.3); Leiwen: Laurentiuslay (2.2); Brauneberg: Juffer (1.1).
Weingut Der Josephshof Graach/Mosel. *Einzellagen:* Graach: Josephshöfer (6ha), Himmelreich (2); Bernkastel: Stephanus-Rosengärtchen (1); Zeltingen: Sonnenuhr (4).
Weingut Oberemmeler Abteihof Oberemmel/Saar. *Einzellagen:* Niedermennig: Herrenberg (4.4ha) and Euchariusberg (1.9); Oberemmel: Karlsberg (8.5), Rosenberg (3.4) and Agritiusberg (3.7); Wiltingen: Braunfels (3.1), Klosterberg (2.9); Scharzhofberg (5.8).
Weingut St. Irminenhof Kasel/Ruwer. *Einzellagen:* Kasel: Nies'chen (3.8ha), Herrenberg (2), Kehrnagel (1.5) and Hitzlay (2.6); Waldrach: Heiligenhäuschen (5.8).

These estates are relatively recent aquisitions:

Weingut Geschwister Ehses-Berres Zeltingen/Mosel. 1 hectare including Zeltingen: Sonnenuhr and Schloßberg.
Weingut Dr. J. B. Hain Neumagen-Dhron/Mosel. 3 hectares including *Einzellagen:* Dhron: Häschen; Piesport: Goldtröpfchen; Neumagen: Rosengärtchen.
Apollinar Joseph Koch Wiltingen/Saar. *Einzellagen:* Scharzhofberg (2ha); Wiltingen: Gottesfuß (2). One of the great Saar names.
Felix Müller Wiltingen/Saar. *Einzellagen:* Scharzhofberg (1ha); Wiltingen: Rosenberg (1.2). Classic Saar production makes wines of elegance and ripeness.
Staatsminister a.D. Otto van Volxem Oberemmel/Saar. 3ha including Scharzhofberg (2ha).

Weingut Kies-Kieren

Hauptstraße 22, 5551 Graach, tel: 06531-3428. *Owner:* Ernst Kies. 3.7 hectares. *Einzellagen:* Kinheim: Hubertuslay and Rosenberg: Graach: Himmelreich and Domprobst; also at Lösnich, Erden and Kesten.

The Kies family has been growing vines since the 17th century. The concentration today is on Rieslings which have brought the estate the highest awards at national competitions.

Weingut Rudolf Kochems

5591 Mesenich, tel: 0263-4524. *Einzellagen:* Mesenich: Deuslay, Goldgrübchen, Abteiberg.

Estate producing quality wines from Riesling, Müller-Thurgau, Ehrenfelser and Kerner, including a Riesling/Kerner halbtrocken Spätlese. Deuslay Rieslings and an Ehrenfelser Abteiberg Auslese have been prizewinners.

Weingut Schloßkellerei Freiherr von Landenberg

Am Kriegerdenkmal, Moselweinstraße 60, 5591 Ediger-Eller, tel: 2675-277. *Owners:* Baroness Nelly von Landenberg and family. 9.8 hectares. *Einzellagen:* Eller: Bienenlay, Engelströpfchen, Höll, Pfirsichgarten and Calmont; Ediger: Elzhofberg and Osterlämmchen.

An award-winning estate with vineyards on steep slopes planted 95% with Riesling.

Weingut J. Lauerburg

Graacherstraße 24, 5550 Bernkastel, tel. 06542-2481. *Owners:* Karl-Heinz Jacob and Karl Patrik Lauerburg. *Einzellagen:* Bernkastel: Schloßberg, Johannisbrünnchen, Matheisbildchen, Lay, Bratenhöfchen and Doctor: Graach: Himmelreich.

A small but very prestigious family estate founded in 1700 (when the cellars were dug under the vineyards). The oldest owner in the Doctor site. 100% Riesling, making wines intended for bottle-ageing. No cellar visits: "it might impair the quality of the wine!"

Weingut Alfred Lex

Laurentiusstraße 4, 5559 Leiwen. *Einzellagen:* Leiwen: Klostergarten and Laurentiuslay; Pölich: Held; Klüsserath: Bruderschaft.

A family estate dating back more than 400 years with holdings in some excellent sites, producing quality wines to Auslese level.

Weingut P. Licht-Bergweiler Erben

Bernkastelerstraße 33, 5551 Brauneberg. *Owners:* Leo and Ria Licht (father and daughter). About 12 hectares. *Einzellagen:* Brauneberg: Juffer, Hasenläufer, Mandelgraben and Klostergarten; Wehlen: Sonnenuhr; Graach: Domprobst; Bernkastel: Johannisbrünnchen.

The Licht family inherited this 200-year-old property with traditional methods and cellars. Their finest wines are from the Juffer.

Weingut Karl Loewen

Matthiasstraße 30, 5559 Leiwen. *Owner:* Karl Loewen. 5 hectares. *Einzellagen:* Leiwen: Laurentiuslay and Klostergarten; Detzem: Würzgarten, Maximiner Klosterlay; Pölich: Held.

The Loewens bought the once monastic land when it was secularized by Napoleon. It includes a very steep slope in the Laurentiuslay where Riesling ripens magnificently. The house speciality is really full, dry Riesling made in the style of centuries ago.

Weingut Benedict Loosen-Erben
Würzgartenstraße 1, 5564 Ürzig. *Owners:* Hanni Müller and family. 2.4 hectares. *Einzellagen:* Ürzig: Würzgarten (1.7ha); Erden: Treppchen (0.6) and Prälat; Lösnich: Försterlay.
Small growers with 100% Riesling plots in the best sites of Erden and Ürzig (they own Ürzig's sundial, set in the Würzgarten). No Süßreserve, oak maturation. They also own a Weinstube-Pension, the Klosterhof, in Ürzig.

Weingut J. Matheus-Lehnert
In der Zeil 1, 5559 Neumagen-Dhron, tel. 06507-2237. *Owner:* Ferdinand and Dorothea Krebs-Matheus. 5.5 hectares. *Einzellagen:* Piesport: Goldtröpfchen; Neumagen: Rosengärtchen; Trittenheim: Altärchen; Dhron: Hofberger and Roterd.
A fine small property: 90% Riesling and 90% steep slopes. Wood-aged Auslesen from his old vaulted cellar win gold medals.

Weingut Milz Laurentiushof
5559 Trittenheim, tel: 06507-2300. *Owner:* Karl Josef Milz. About 8 hectares. *Einzellagen:* Neumagen: Laudamusberg (1ha), Rosengärtchen (0.5) and Nußwingert (0.8); Dhron and Piesport: Hofberger; Trittenheim: Altärchen (2), Apotheke (1.5), Felsenkopf (0.5) and Leiterchen (0.5) (last two solely owned): Ockfen: Geisberg (0.5).
A family house by the church, Milz property since the 17th century. The vines are all Riesling and the wines well-balanced towards dryness.

Weingut Egon Müller-Scharzhof
5511 Scharzhof-Wiltingen, tel: 06501-17232. *Owner:* Egon Müller. 8.5 hectares. Ortsteil: Scharzhofberg.
Five generations of Müllers have farmed the Scharzhofberg, formerly church land secularized under Napoleon. The steep grey schist slope is planted with 95% Riesling. Only QmP wines use the estate name: Spätlese wines and above are often bottled in individual cask lots: there may be five or six different Auslese as each day's ripening intensifies the honeyed sweetness of the latest wines. Wines above Auslese level are rare here in the Saar, but a Scharzhof Auslese has as much penetrating perfume, vitality and "breeding" as any wine in Germany.

Rudolf Müller GmbH & Co. KG
Postfach 20, 5586 Reil, tel: 06532-3004. *Owners:* Walter and Richard Müller, and Margrit Müller-Burggraef who owns 50% of Weingut Wwe. Dr. H. Thanisch. 14.5 hectares. *Einzellagen:* Ockfen: Bockstein, Herrenberg and Geisberg; Kanzem: Sonnenberg; Saarburg: Antoniusbrunnen and Scharzhof; Reil: Sorentberg, Mullay-Hofberg, Goldlay, Falklay; Ürzig: Würzgarten.
The trocken and halbtrocken Saar wines have been much in demand in recent years. The estate also operates as a merchant with its internationally known brand, "The Bishop of Riesling". Exports to the USA, UK, Japan, Norway, Canada and The Netherlands. Riesling is planted 98% in the Saar and 80% in the Mosel.

Weingut Peter Nicolay, C.H. Berres Erben
Gestade 15, 5550 Bernkastel-Kues, tel: 06531-2063. *Owner:* Helga Pauly-Berres. 15.1 hectares. *Einzellagen:* Ürzig: Würzgarten and Goldwingert (solely owned); Erden: Treppchen, Herrenberg and Prälat; Zeltingen: Himmelreich and Deutschherrenberg; Wehlen: Klosterberg; Kinheim: Hubertuslay, Rosenberg.
Peter Nicolay was a famous innkeeper of a century ago. The Berres family are his descendants, now connected by marriage to the Paulys who own Dr. Pauly Bergweiler of Bernkastel. 60% of the estate is on steep slopes; 92% is Riesling. The wines are matured as individuals in oak and offer the full spectrum of styles that come from the bend in the Mosel from Wehlen to Kinheim.

Weingut Paulinshof
Paulinstraße 14, 5561 Kesten b. Bernkastel, tel: 06535-544. *Owner:* Klaus Jungling. *Einzellagen:* Kesten: Paulinsberg, Paulins-Hofberg, Herrenberg; Brauneberg: Juffer, Juffer-Sonnenuhr.
Small one-time monastic estate planted with 90% Riesling. Light, *spritzig* wines, built to last.

Weingut Otto Pauly KG
Bernkastelerstraße 5-7, 5550 Graach, tel: 06531-6641. *Owners:* Otto-Ulrich and Axel Pauly. 3 hectares. *Einzellagen:* Graach: Domprobst, Himmelreich; Wehlen: Sonnenuhr; Bernkastel: Lay, Johannisbrünnchen.
The vineyards lie on steep slopes, planted 95% with Riesling, in the heart of the Middle Mosel. The wines, full in character, racy and elegant, are sold exclusively via the estate's own merchant company, Weinkellerei Otto Pauly GmbH. The Paulys, growers since 1620, also own the small but well sited estate Weingut Abteihof in the Mosel.

Weingut Dr. Pauly-Bergweiler Zach. Bergweiler-Prüm Erben
Gestade 15, 5550 Bernkastel-Kues, tel: 06531-3002. *Owner:* Dr. Peter Pauly. 11.3 hectares. *Einzellagen:* Bernkastel: Graben (1ha), Lay (0.5), Bratenhöfchen, Matheisbildchen (0.6), Schloßberg (1.9) and Johannisbrünnchen (0.4); Graach: Himmelreich (1.8) and Domprobst (0.5); Wehlen: Sonnenuhr (1.3), Nonnenberg (0.1) and Rosenberg (0.2); Zeltingen: Himmelreich (1.8); Erden: Busslay (0.5); Brauneberg: Juffer-Sonnenuhr (0.2) and Juffer (0.3).
Inheritors of a fine part of the Prüm properties. 50% of the estate is on the steepest slopes, 25% on moderate slopes and 25% on level ground. The wide range of wines is made in both stainless steel and oak, emphasizing vineyard character as far as possible. The estate prefers to use physics rather than chemistry in its winemaking. Süßreserve is not used and no blue fining takes place. The wines have a "breath of carbon dioxide" – naturally, I assume. The owner's wife belongs to the Berres family, who own Nicolay of Ürzig. 97% is Riesling.

Weingut der Pfarrkirche
Bernkastel, 5559 Longuich. *Owner:* Kath. Kirchengemeinde. About 10.5 hectares. *Einzellagen:* Bernkastel: Graben, Lay, Bratenhöfchen, Schloßberg and Johannisbrünnchen; Graach: Himmelreich.
The old estate of the parish church, now run by Schmitt Söhne of Longuich. The vines are on the steep slaty slopes which give a particular smack of the soil to good Bernkastel.

Weingut Ökonomierat Piedmont
Saartal 1, 5503 Konz-Filzen, tel: 06501-16801. *Owner:* Max-G. Piedmont. 6 hectares. *Einzellagen:* Filzen: Pulchen, Urbelt and Steinberg.
A fourth-generation family estate in the narrow valley of the lower Saar. 90% is Riesling, 10% Müller-Thurgau; stylish dry wines aged in oak.

Weingut S.A. Prüm Erben
Uferallee 25-36, 5550 Bernkastel-Wehlen, tel: 06531-3110. *Owners:* Raimund and Erika Prüm. 5.5 hectares. *Einzellagen:* Wehlen: Sonnenuhr, Klosterberg, Rosenberg (0.2) and Nonnenberg; Bernkastel: Lay, Schloßberg and Johannisbrünnchen; Graach: Himmelreich and Domprobst; Zeltingen: Schloßberg.
Part of the great Prüm estate which became separate in 1911, was divided into 6 parts in 1964 but has since been partially reconstituted and recently enlarged. The third generation since 1911 took over in 1981. The wines are made with great emphasis on the character of each cask; no Süßreserve is used. The biggest holding (1.5ha) is Wehlener Sonnenuhr. 100% Riesling.

Weingut J. J. Prüm
Uferalee 19, 5550 Bernkastel-Wehlen, tel: 06531-3091. 14.2 hectares. *Owners:* Dr. Manfred and Wolfgang Prüm. *Einzellagen:* Wehlen: Sonnenuhr (4ha), Klosterberg (1.2) and Nonnenberg (2); Graach: Himmelreich (3) and Domprobst (0.2); Zeltingen: Sonnenuhr (1); Bernkastel: Bratenhöfchen, Graben, Matheisbildchen and Lay.
The most famous family of growers of the Middle Mosel, with records going back to the 12th century. Johann Josef Prüm (d. 1944) developed the present estate; his son Sebastian (d. 1969) was an equally renowned grower. Sebastian's son Manfred is now in charge. The estate house, down by the river, looks up to the great Sonnenuhr vineyard, of which it has one of the largest holdings, across the water. The huge sundials among the vines here and in Zeltingen were built by an earlier Prüm. The estate's signature is wine of glorious honeyed ripeness, setting off the raciness of Riesling grown on slate with deep notes of spice and honey. Its reputation was at its zenith in the 1950s and 1960s.

Weingut Edmund Reverchon
Saartalstraße 3, 5503 Konz, tel: 06501-17319. *Owner:* Eddie and Nicole Reverchon. 27.3 hectares. *Einzellagen:* Filzen: Steinberger, Urbelt and Herrenberg (solely owned); Wiltingen: Gottesfuß and Klosterberg; Ockfen: Bockstein and Geisberg; Kanzem: Altenberg; Konz: Karthäuser, Klosterberg and Euchariusberg; Oberemmel: Altenberg.

MITTELRHEIN

A more logical name for this spectacular but dwindling wine region would be the Lower Rhine. It is exactly analogous to the Lower Mosel – the part of the river downstream from the classic sites, where custom (and extraordinary effort) maintain a narrow necklace of vineyards on the immediate riverside slopes – and sometimes cliffs. The very steep valley sides provide pockets of slaty soil with the crucial south or southwest exposure.

There are 760 hectares of vines – a declining total – along some 100 kilometres (60 miles) of river. Moving from north to south, the vines start on the east bank at Königswinter, opposite Bonn. From Koblenz southward the vineyards line both banks, ending at Trechtingshausen on the left bank, almost opposite Assmannshausen, the last of the Rheingau. The most northerly vineyards are in decline, but the rest of the valley benefits, as does the Ahr, from its scenic beauty. The chief towns are Bacharach, St. Goarshausen, Boppard, Koblenz, Neuwied, Bad Honningen and Unkel. The great sights are the Rhine gorge, the Loreley rock and dozens of perching medieval castles, and the confluence with the Mosel at Koblenz. The entire valley reverberates with the legends of the German past: the Nibelung treasure is said to be in the keeping of "Father Rhine".

Another little tributary, the Lahn, flowing from the east through the spa town of Bad Ems, also has a few vines which are included in the Mittelrhein region.

Riesling is the principal grape of the morsels of vineyard that cling to the hills. It makes good, even very good, but usually austere and even sharp wine, used in good vintages in the Weinstuben of its growers and in poor ones for processing as Sekt. Bacharach is the centre of the wine trade, such as it is. It was once an important entrepot for all Rhine wines; a good harbour just downstream of the treacherous rapids at Bingen.

▶ Rhine towns like Boppard and Bacharach boast pleasantly tree-lined riverside promenades to set off the steep, vine-clad hills. The Rhine gorge has castles both romantic and forbidding, ruined and inhabited. Many can be visited. Some (see p 74) are hotels.

TRAVEL INFORMATION

Though its wine is not quite in the top rank, the Mittelrhein makes up with some of Europe's most spectacular scenery.

The federal capital, Bonn, marks the northern limit of the region. It is also a university town and a musical centre: Beethoven's birthplace at Bonngasse 20 is now a museum, and Schumann lived and died in the city.

The Rhine gorge begins at Bonn, with the most spectacular section starting south of Koblenz. At Bingen the river's abrupt bend marks the southern limit of the Mittelrhein.

The gorge is a great north–south route, with major roads and railways on each bank. There is much river traffic, both cargo barges and passenger steamers.

▲ Timbered houses in Braubach. The sign is for a farmer's tavern.

The many villages are well used to tourists, and are amply equipped with taverns, restaurants and tasting cellars.

Autobahns run parallel to the Rhine on both banks, but at some distance. For the best view of the river, follow the B9 on the right bank, or take the quieter B42 on the other shore. Note that there are no bridges between Koblenz and Mainz, but several ferries. The railway offers fine views, but to see the Rhine Gorge at its best, take a steamer. Many services start at Koblenz. Combined train/steamer tickets can be had.

Places to visit
Bonn: see above.
Bad Ems: spa in the pretty side-valley of the Lahn.
Braubach: fine well-preserved medieval castle.
Boppard: old houses, castle, several hotels.
St. Goarhausen: close by is the Loreley rock, a giant cliff over the Rhine. The *Loreleyburgstraße* runs from the village to the summit and on, past imposing castles, back to the river at Kaub.
St. Goar: ferry from its twin across the river. Fine view of the Loreley.
Bacharach: the steep, scenic *Rheingoldstraße* runs from here to St. Goar through hill villages and past castles. The town has good shops – antiques especially. Tourist information: Heerstraße 120 (tel: 06741-383).
Die Pfalz: island castle in the river, a medieval customs post for extracting river tolls. Open for visits.

Wine festivals
Kaub (1st week in Sept), Rhens (2nd w/e in Sept), Boppard (last week in Sept), Koblenz (last w/e in Sept), Dattenberg (1st week in Oct), Leubsdorf (2nd w/e in Oct).

Food and drink: see p 74.

VILLAGES

The vineyards of the Mittelrhein are split into three Bereiche and 11 Großlagen. The Bereich Siebengebirge – Seven Mountains – consists of just one Großlage, Petersberg. Bereich Rheinburgengau takes in everything from Großlage Burg Hammerstein south of Königswinter to Großlage Herrenberg, opposite the town of Bacharach. Bereich Bacharach includes two Großlagen: Schloß Stahleck and Schloß Reichenstein.

GROSSLAGE PETERSBERG
The most northerly vineyards in Germany: 23 hectares on the slopes of the Siebengebirge, with only a handful of growers, most part-time.

GROSSLAGE BURG HAMMERSTEIN
South of Königswinter an intermittent string of vineyards, 15 sites in all, lines the east bank until just north of Koblenz. Riesling predominates in the increasingly steep and stony sites.

GROSSLAGE LAHNTAL
The scattered vineyards of the beautiful Lahn Valley, around the spa of Bad Ems and the ancient town of Nassau. There are five Einzellagen, making up only just over 30 hectares of Riesling and Müller-Thurgau.

GROSSLAGE MARKSBURG
Right-bank vineyards north and south of Koblenz, including the first really steep sites around Braubach and Osterspai.

GROSSLAGE GEDEONSECK
The vineyards of Boppard, Spay and their neighbours on the left bank. The Boppard sites – including Engelstein, Feuerley, Mandelstein and Ohlenberg – face due south thanks to a sharp bend in the river.

GROSSLAGE LORELEYFELSEN
A collection of right-bank vineyards which includes one (Loreley Edel) below the famous Loreley rock. All are Riesling except Teufelstein at Patersberg, which grows a little red Spätburgunder: a foretaste of the red-wine vineyards of Assmannshausen in the Rheingau to the south.

GROSSLAGE BURG RHEINFELS
Four small sites around St. Goar on the left bank.

GROSSLAGE SCHLOSS SCHÖNBURG
Side valleys give southerly slopes for a dozen small vineyards, all growing Riesling.

GROSSLAGE SCHLOSS STAHLECK
Once again, the side-valley sites have the best aspect here. The Rhine gorge vineyards face east, even a little north. All are steep, all grow Riesling.

GROSSLAGE HERRENBERG
Right-bank vineyards around Kaub, with an advantageous southwesterly outlook as the river northwestwards.

GROSSLAGE SCHLOSS REICHENSTEIN
The southernmost sites of the Mittelrhein: those opposite on the right bank are in the Rheingau. A side-valley behind Niederheimbach gives some well-placed sites.

PRODUCERS

Weingut Toni Jost
"Hahnenhof", Oberstraße 14, 6533 Bacharach, tel: 06743-1216. *Owner:* Peter Jost. 6.5 hectares in Bacharach, including 4.4ha in the steep, slaty Hahn Einzellage. Also 3.5ha in the Großlage Rauenthaler Steinmächer in the Rheingau.
Riesling 70%, Müller-Thurgau 10%, Spätburgunder 8%, etc. 1983 Spätlese and 1985 Kabinett wines, with excellent acidity, will develop well in bottle.

August Perll
Oberstraße 81, 5407 Boppard, tel: 06742-3906. 3.8 hectares. *Einzellagen:* Boppard: Feuerley, Ohlenberg and Fässerlay.
A small grower of 68% Riesling on the vertiginous slopes of the Boppard bend of the Rhine. Dry wines of character. Wins many prizes at national competitions.

Weingut Heinrich Weiler
Mainzerstraße 2-3, 6532 Oberwesel am Rhein, tel: 06744-323. *Owner:* Heinrich Wilhelm Weiler. 6.5 hectares. *Einzellagen:* Oberwesel: Römerkrug and St. Martinsberg; Engehöll: Goldemund; Kaub: Backofen and Roßstein (solely owned).
Perhaps the best-known property of this lovely part of the Rhine valley, with steeply terraced slaty vineyards capable of full-flavoured, even fruity Riesling. The Weiler family has been growing vines in Oberwesel since 1607 and has holdings on both sides of the Rhine.

Winzergenossenschaft Loreley eG
Rheinstraße 14, 5421 Bornich.
A small cooperative cellar dating from 1934, in the most romantic part of the Rheinland near the Loreley rock. Each year, it sells 90% of the wine of its 47 members (some 10,000 cases) in bottle to private customers, restaurants and the retail trade. The vineyards are 80% Riesling.

▼ Burg Gutenfels, near Kaub, and the Pfalz tower, one of several on islands in the river. They were once used as customs posts to extract tolls from shipping.

Schloß Neuwied

VINEYARDS

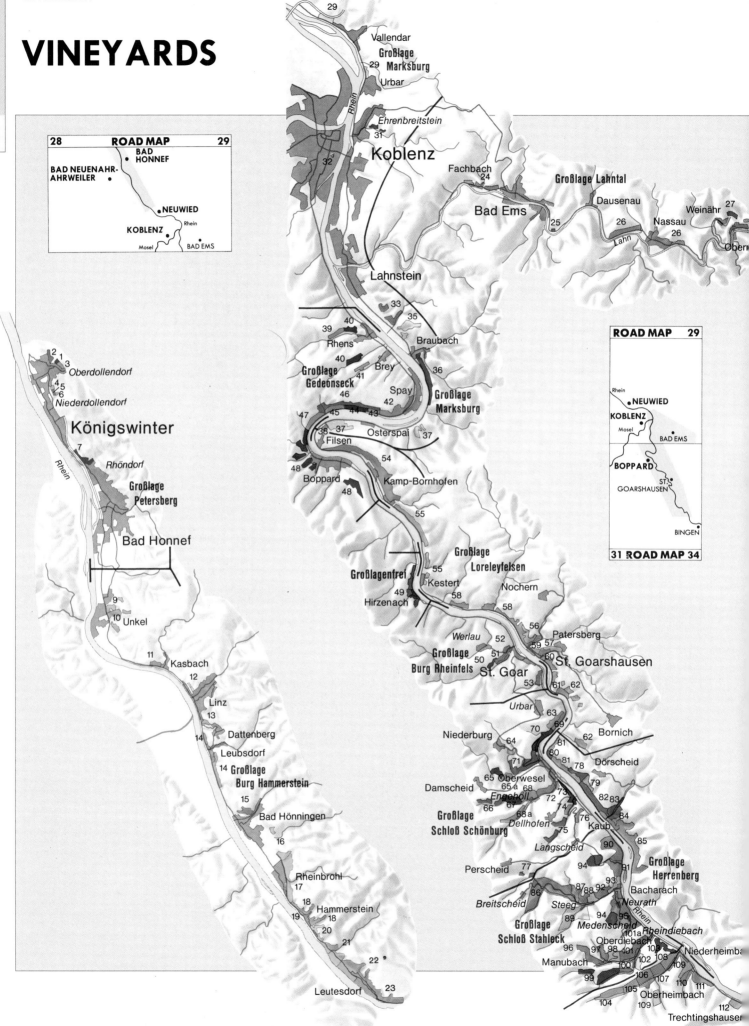

ROAD MAP

28   29

BAD NEUENAHR-
AHRWEILER

BAD
HONNEF

NEUWIED

KOBLENZ

Rhein

Mosel

BAD EMS

ROAD MAP   29

Rhein

NEUWIED

KOBLENZ

Mosel

BAD EMS

BOPPARD

ST.
GOARSHAUSEN

BINGEN

31 ROAD MAP 34

29

Vallendar

Großlage
Marksburg

Urbar

Ehrenbreitstein

Koblenz

Fachbach   24

Bad Ems

Großlage Lahntal

Dausenau

Weinähr   27

Nassau

Lahn

Ober

Lahnstein

33

35

40
39

Rhens

Braubach

40

Brey

36

Großlage
Gedeonseck

41

Spay

Großlage
Marksburg

46

42

47

45 44 43

38 37

Osterspai

37

Filsen

54

48

Boppard

Kamp-Bornhofen

48

55

Großlage
Loreleyfelsen

Großlagenfrei

55

Kestert

Nochern

49

58

Hirzenach

58

56

Werlau

52

Patersberg

Großlage
Burg Rheinfels

50 51

59 57

60

St. Goarshausen

53

St. Goar

61 62

Urbar

63

Bornich

70

69

62

Niederburg

64

81

80

71

81 78

Dörscheid

65 Oberwesel

79

Damscheid

65 a 68

Engehöll

72

73

82 83

66

67

74

76

84

68 a

Dellhofen

75

Kaub

Großlage
Schloß Schönburg

90

85

Langscheid

Großlage
Herrenberg

Perscheid

77

94

91

Bacharach

87 88 92

93

Breitscheid

Steeg

86

Neurath

89

94

95

Medenscheid

Rheindiebach

Großlage
Schloß Stahleck

101a

Oberdiebach

96

97 98 101 102 108

Manubach

100

106 107

Niederheimba

99

105

109 110 111

104

107

Oberheimbach

109

112

Trechtingshauser

2 1
3   Oberdollendorf

4 5
6   Niederdollendorf

Königswinter

7

Rhöndorf

Rhein

Großlage
Petersberg

Bad Honnef

9

10 Unkel

11

Kasbach

12

Linz

13

14

Dattenberg

Leubsdorf

14 Großlage
Burg Hammerstein

15

Bad Hönningen

16

Rheinbrohl

17

18

Hammerstein

19   18

20

21

22

23   Leutesdorf

Großlage Schloß Reichenstein

BEREICH SIEBENGEBIRGE

GROSSLAGE PETERSBERG

Oberdollendorf
(Ortsteil of Königswinter)
Rosenhügel 1
Laurentiusberg 2
Sülzenberg 3

Niederdollendorf
(Ortsteil of Königswinter)
Goldfüßchen 4
Longenburgerberg 5
Heisterberg 6

Königswinter
Drachenfels 7 P

Rhöndorf
(Ortsteil of Bad Honnef)
Drachenfels 7 P

BEREICH RHEINBURGEN-GAU

GROSSLAGE BURG HAMMERSTEIN

Unkel
Berg 9
Sonnenberg 10

Kasbach
(Ortsteil of Kasbach-Ohlenberg)
Stehlerberg 11

Linz
Rheinhöller 12

Dattenberg
Gertrudenberg 13

Leubsdorf
Weißes Kreuz 14

Bad Hönnigen
Schloßberg 15

Rheinbrohl
Monte Jup 16
Römerberg 17

Hammerstein
In den Layfelsen 18
Hölle 19
Schloßberg 20

Leutesdorf
Forstberg 21
Gartenlay 22
Rosenberg 23

GROSSLAGE LAHNTAL

Fachbach
Vineyard not registered as Einz.

Bad Ems
Hasenberg 25 P

Dausenau
Hasenberg 25 P

Nassau
Schloßberg 26

Weinähr
Giebelhöll 27

Obernhof
Goetheberg 28

GROSSLAGE MARKSBURG

Vallendar
Rheinnieder 29 P

Urbar
Rheinnieder 29 P

Koblenz
Ortsteil Ehrenbreitstein
Kreuzberg 31

Koblenz
Schnorbach
Brückstück 32

Lahnstein
Koppelstein 33 P

Braubach
Koppelstein 33 P
Mühlberg 35
Marmorberg 36

Osterspai
Liebeneck-Sonnenlay 37

Filsen
Pfarrgarten 38

GROSSLAGE GEDEONSECK

Rhens
König Wenzel 39
Sonnenlay 40

Brey
Hämmchen 41

Spay
Engelstein 42 P

Boppard

Ortsteil Bopparder Hamm
Engelstein 42 P
Ohlenberg 43
Feuerley 44
Mandelstein 45
Weingrube 46
Fässerlay 47
Elfenley 48

GROSSLAGENFREI

Hirzenach
(Ortsteil of Boppard)
Probsteiberg 49

GROSSLAGE BURG RHEINFELS

St. Goar
Ortsteil Werlau
Rosenberg 50
Frohwingert 51 P
Ameisenberg 52 T

St. Goar
Frohwingert 51 P
Ameisenberg 52 P
Kuhstall 53

GROSSLAGE LORELEYFELSEN

Kamp-Bornhofen
Pilgerpfad 54
Liebenstein-Sterrenberg 55 P

Kestert
Liebenstein-Sterrenberg 55 P

Nochern
Brünnchen 56

Patersberg
Teufelstein 57

St. Goarshausen
Ortsteile Wellmich & Ehrental
Burg Maus 58

St. Goarshausen
Hessern 59
Burg Katz 60
Loreley Edel 61

Bornich
Rothenack 62

GROSSLAGE SCHLOSS SCHÖNBURG

Urbar
(Ortsteil of Oberwesel)
Beulsberg 63

Niederburg
Rheingoldberg 64
Bienenberg 65

Damscheid
Frankenhell 66
Sonnenstock 67
Goldemund 68

Oberwesel
Bienenberg 65 a
Goldemund 68 a
Sieben Jungfrauen 69
Ölsberg 70
St. Martinsberg 71
Römerkrug 73

– Ortsteil Engehöll
Bernstein 72

Dellhofen
(Ortsteil of Oberwesel)
Römerkrug 74
St. Werner-Berg 75

Langsheid
(Ortsteil of Oberwesel)
Hundert 76

Perscheid
Rosental 77

GROSSLAGE HERRENBERG

Dörscheid
Wolfsnack 78
Kupferflöz 79

Kaub
Roßstein 80
Backofen 81
Rauschelay 82
Blüchertal 83
Burg Gutenfels 84
Pfalzgrafenstein 85

BEREICH BACHARACH

GROSSLAGE SCHLOSS STAHLECK

Bacharach
Ortsteil Breitscheid
Schloß Stahlberg 86 P

– Ortsteil Steeg
Schloß Stahlberg 86 P
Lennenborn 87
St. Jost 88
Hambusch 89

Bacharach
Hahn 90
Insel Heylesen Werth 91
Wolfshöhle 92
Posten 93

– Ortsteile Medenscheid & Neurath
Mathias Weingarten 94
Kloster Fürstental 95

Manubach
Langgarten 96
St. Oswald 97
Mönchwingert 98
Heilgarten 99

Oberdiebach
Bischofshub 100
Fürstenberg 101 P
Kräuterberg 102

Rheindiebach
(Ortsteil of Oberdiebach)
Fürstenberg 101 P
Rheinberg 103

Vineyards not registered as Einzellagen

Schloß Fürstenberg
(Ortsteil of Oberheimbach)
Rebflächen 101 a

GROSSLAGE SCHLOSS REICHENSTEIN

Oberheimbach
Römerberg 104
Klosterberg 105
Wahrheit 106
Sonne 107

Niederheimbach
Froher Weingarten 108
Schloß Hohneck 109
Reifersley 110
Soonecker Schloßberg 111

Trechtingshausen
Morgenbachtaler 112

RHEINGAU

The winegrowing Rhine reaches its undisputed climax where the broad body of its waters, hurrying northwards in a perpetual turmoil of eddies and islands, barge-traffic and wheeling birds, meets the bulk of the Taunus mountains, rising to their forested heights three or four kilometres (two or three miles) back from the river.

These three or four kilometres are given entirely to the vine. The river, balked by the rising ground, turns and dashes westward below the vineyards for a space of thirty kilometres (twenty miles) – thirty kilometres of monoculture that link the words Rheingau and Riesling like a rallying cry.

The English name for all Rhine wine comes from the Rheingau: specifically the village of Hochheim that extends the scope of the Rheingau eastward towards Frankfurt. Hochheim's vineyard hill looks down on the tributary river Main, with the broad bend of the Rhine dim in the distance to the south. From Hochheim came the original "hock": wine of a soft vigorous earthiness that could mature as long as claret, the other English favourite.

It is 50-odd kilometres (30 miles) from Hochheim to Rüdesheim, the western end of the Rheingau. Sixteen of these kilometres (10 miles) are occupied by the sprawl of Wiesbaden, but where the vineyards start again at Niederwalluf they start in earnest, and fill every unurbanized cranny through the succession of a dozen riverside and hillside villages that constitute the heart of the Rheingau.

Riesling is the predominant grape in area as well as quality, planted over three-quarters of the whole vineyard and almost without exception in all the best sites. The soils of the Rheingau vary widely with the altitude and exposure of the vineyards; in general lighter, more recently weathered soils on the higher ground grading to heavier loess, loam and finally clay in the valleylands. The steeper and higher the vineyards the more sunshine they enjoy (as mists form closer to the river), but higher, more exposed sites are also subject to cooling winds. The soil/sunshine/shelter equation is never simple, and the best sites of the Rheingau seem to be scattered almost at random, from the surprisingly low-lying suntrap of Marcobrunn to the extremely exposed, almost cliff-like south slopes of the Rüdesheimer Berg. All, however, are said to benefit from the effect of the Rhine flowing by, 800 metres wide (875 yards), as both a stabilizing factor for temperature and, as it were, a vast mirror for solar radiation.

These conditions allow the Riesling to achieve wine with all the force, the cut, the drive and follow-through that makes its finest Rheingau wines the best of the Rhine.

To some the purest magic is when all this vitality is captured in the relative delicacy and miniature scale of a Kabinett wine. It is not so difficult to be impressive with forceful late-gathered Spätlesen and Auslesen. It is when the region is judged on what it can pack into the lightest category of top quality wine that the Rheingau asserts its supremacy.

The entire region has only one Bereich name: Johannisberg, a name that should therefore be regarded with caution. It is divided into ten Großlagen: Daubhaus (for the Hochheim extension), Steinmächer for the eastern vineyards as far west as Kiedrich (which also has a small Großlage, Heiligenstock), Deutelsberg for Erbach and Hattenheim, Mehrhölzchen (and also the smaller Gottesthal) for Hallgarten and Oestrich, Erntebringer (and also Honigberg) for Mittelheim, Winkel, Johannisberg and

▲ The Rhine, with the Mäuseturm (Mouse Tower Island), from the Rüdesheimer Berg Schloßberg.

Geisenheim. Rüdesheim, part of Geisenheim, Lorch and Lorchhausen have the Großlage name of Burgweg, and Großlage Steil takes in Assmannshausen and Aulhausen.

Officially the Rheingau rounds the river bend past Rüdesheim to include the red-winegrowing village of Assmannshausen and the Riesling village of Lorch. Assmannshausen is a special case, hotly defended by the State Domain. Lorch and Lorchhausen are more realistically classed with the other good Riesling sites of the Mittelrhein.

▼ Below: Lorch is in the Rheingau, but the west bank opposite (the Rheinberg, in Großlage Schloß Stahleck) is in the Mittelrhein.

TRAVEL INFORMATION

The landscape of the Rheingau is more gentle than the Rhine gorge, but the wine is of far greater stature. Many and ancient villages, castles and wine estates provide interest.

The Rheingau officially begins at Lorch, well into the gorge.

Wine roads
The *Rheingauer Riesling Route* follows the right bank of the river from Lorch through Assmannshausen, opposite Bingen, and then weaves east through the undulating vineyard country to Hochheim and Wicker, close to the River Main. The signposts are green and white, showing a large goblet. A footpath follows a similar route.

Places to visit
Lorch: wine village, painted medieval houses.
Assmannshausen: red wines are the local speciality.
Rüdesheim: dozens of wine taverns, especially in the famous Drosselgasse. Wine museum in the ancient Brömsersburg, west of the town. Tourist office: Rheinstraße 16 (tel: 06722-2962).
Geisenheim: home of the famous wine teaching and research college, also the Rheingauer Dom (cathedral).
Schloß Johannisberg: former Benedictine monastery, now a great wine estate.
Winkel: the Graues Haus is the oldest wine tavern in Germany. Nearby is Schloß Vollrads.
Kloster Eberbach: 12th C. church, ancient monastery, now base of the Rheingau State Domain and the German Wine Academy, which runs wine courses. The famous Steinberg is a monastic walled vineyard, first planted in the 12th C. and still part of the Eberbach estate. The Steinberg wines are stored in the monastery cellars.
Kiedrich: wine village with a Gothic church and especially fine timbered houses.
Eltville: the Prince Elector's castle, the church and the old mansions of the wine estates are worth a visit.
Wiesbaden: major spa, casino, many sports facilities and a cultural festival in May.

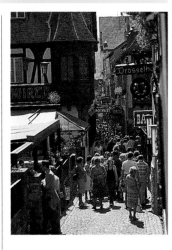

▲ Wine taverns line Rüdesheim's Drosselgasse.

Hochheim: at the eastern end of the Rheingau, isolated among busy towns, an island of Riesling.
The Taunus: wooded hills that bound the Rheingau to the north. Nature reserves, walks, hunting, scenic farms and villages.

Wine festivals
Wicker, near Winkel, has cellar open days (end Apr), Assmannshausen, red-wine festival (early May), Niederwalluf & Kiedrich (3rd w/e in June), Eltville, sparkling wine festival (last w/e in June), Hochheim (1st w/e in July), Flörsheim, winetasting festival (end July), Hallgarten (1st w/e in Aug), Wiesbaden, Rheingau Wine Week (2nd week in Aug), Rüdesheim & Rauenthal (3rd w/e in Aug), Hattenheim (4th w/e in Aug), Martinsthal & Aulhausen (last w/e in Aug), Oestrich (1st w/e in Sept), Oberwalluf (2nd w/e in Sept), Johannisberg, cellar open day (last w/e in Sept).

Wine tasting
There are plenty of opportunities to buy local wine in taverns and cafés. Many wine estates offer tasting facilities: see the list of producers. At many estates it is possible to buy bottles of the wine made there. Some such as Schloß Johannisberg, have a Weinstube on the premises. Kloster Eberbach (see above) offers tastings.
Food and drink: see p 74.

WEINSTADT
HOCHHEIM
AM MAIN

Auf Wiedersehen

VINEYARDS

BEREICH JOHANNISBERG

Lorchhausen
(Ortsteil of Lorch)
Rosenberg 1
Seligmacher 2

Lorch
Schloßberg 3
Kapellenberg 4
Krone 5
Pfaffenwies 6
Bodental-Steinberg 7

GROSSLAGE STEIL
Einzellagen 8–10

Assmannshausen
(Ortsteil of Rüdesheim)
Frankenthal 8
Höllenberg 9 P
Hinterkirch 10

Aulhausen
(Ortsteil of Rüdesheim)
Höllenberg 9 P

GROSSLAGE BURGWEG
Einzellagen 1–7,
11–22, 24, 26, 27

Rüdesheim
Berg Kaisersteinfels 11
Berg Roseneck 12
Berg Rottland 13
Berg Schloßberg 14
Bischofsberg 15
Drachenstein 16
Kirchenpfad 17
Klosterberg 18
Klosterlay 19
Magdalenenkreuz 20
Rosengarten 21

Geisenheim
Rothenberg 22
Kläuserweg 23 P
Fuchsberg 24
Kilzberg 25 P
Mäuerchen 26
Mönchspfad 27
Schloßgarten 28
Klaus 29 P

GROSSLAGE ERNTEBRINGER
Einzellagen 23, 25,
30–35, 37, 44; A,
28, 29, 42, 43
(part)

Johannisberg
(Ortsteil of Geisenheim)
Kläuserweg 23 P
Kilzberg 25 P
Klaus 29 P
Schwarzenstein 30
Vogelsang 31
Hölle 32
Hansenberg 33
Goldatzel 34
Mittelhölle 35
Schloß Johannisberg
  (Ortsteil) A

GROSSLAGE HONIGBERG
Einz. 36, 38–40, B,
29, 42, 43, A

Winkel
(Ortsteil of Oestrich-Winkel)
Klaus 29 P
Gutenberg 36 P
Dachsberg 37
Schloßberg 38
Jesuitengarten 39
Hasensprung 40
Schloß Vollrads
  (Ortsteil) B

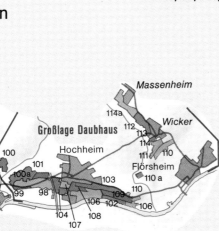

Wiesbaden

Massenheim

114a

Großlage Daubhaus

112

113

Wicker

114

100

Hochheim

111

110

Kostheim

101

Flörsheim

100a

110 a

103

99 98

110

106 109

104 102 106

108

107

Mittelheim
(Ortsteil of Oestrich-Winkel)
Gutenberg 36 P
St. Nikolaus 42
Edelmann 43
Goldberg 44

GROSSLAGE GOTTESTHAL
Einzellagen 46, 47, C; 45 (part)

Oestrich
(Ortsteil of Oestrich-Winkel)
Klosterberg 45
Lenchen 46
Doosberg 47
Schloß
    Reichhartshausen
    (Ortsteil) C

GROSSLAGE DEUTELSBERG
Einzellagen 48–55 a, 60–65, 67, D; 58, 59, 66 (part)

Hattenheim
(Ortsteil of Eltville)
Mannberg 48
Nußbrunnen 49
Wisselbrunnen 50
Hassel 51
Heiligenberg 52
Schützenhaus 53
Engelmannsberg 54
Pfaffenberg 55
Rheingarten 55 a P
Jungfer 58 P
Hendelberg 59 P
Marcobrunn 60 P
Steinberg (Ortsteil) D

GROSSLAGE MEHRHÖLZCHEN
Einzellagen 56–57; 45, 58, 59 (part)

Hallgarten
(Ortsteil of Oestrich-Winkel)
Schönhell 56
Würzgarten 57
Jungfer 58 P
Hendelberg 59 P

Erbach
(Ortsteil of Eltville)
Rheingarten 55 a P
Marcobrunn 60 P
Schloßberg 61
Siegelsberg 62
Honigberg 63
Michelmark 64
Hohenrain 65
Steinmorgen 66 P
Rheinhell 67

GROSSLAGE HEILIGENSTOCK
Einzellagen 68–70; 66, 71 (part)

Kiedrich
Klosterberg 68
Gräfenberg 69
Wasseros 70
Sandgrub 71 P

GROSSLAGE STEINMÄCHER
Einzellagen 72–90, 92–97; 66, 71 (part)

Eltville
Steinmorgen 66 P
Sandgrub 71 P
Taubenberg 72
Langenstück 73
Sonnenberg 74
Rheinberg 75
Kalbspflicht 76

Rauenthal
(Ortsteil of Eltville)
Baiken 77
Gehm 78

Wülfen 79
Rothenberg 80
Langenstück 81
Nonnenberg 82

Martinsthal
(Ortsteil of Eltville)
Wildsau 83
Langenberg 84
Rödchen 85

Walluf
Ortsteil
Niederwalluf
Berg-Bildstock 86
Walkenberg 87
Oberberg 88
Gottesacker 88 a

– Ortsteil
Oberwalluf
Vitusberg 89
Langenstück 90

Wiesbaden
Neroberg 91
    (independent Einz.)

Schierstein
(Ortsteil of Wiesbaden)
Dachsberg 92
Hölle 93
Herrnberg 96 P

Frauenstein
(Ortsteil of Wiesbaden)
Marschall 94
Homberg 95
Herrnberg 96 P

Dotzheim
(Ortsteil of Wiesbaden)
Judenkirch 97

GROSSLAGE DAUBHAUS
Einzellagen 98–114 a

Kostheim
(Ortsteil of Mainz)
Reichesthal 98 P
Weiß Erd 99
Steig 100
St. Kiliansberg 100 a
Berg 101 P

Hochheim
Reichesthal 98 P
Berg 101 P
Kön. Victoriaberg 102
Hofmeister 103
Stielweg 104
Hölle 106
Domdechaney 107
Kirchenstuck 108
Stein 109
Herrnberg 110 P

Flörsheim
Herrnberg 110 P
St. Anna Kapelle 110 a

Wicker
(Ortsteil of Flörsheim)
Stein 111
Mönchsgewann 112
König-Wilhelmsberg 113
Nonnberg 114

Massenheim
(Ortsteil of Hochheim)
Schloßgarten 114 a

Frankfurt
Lohrberger Hang 115*

Böddiger
(Ortsteil of Felsberg/Schwalm-Eder-Kreis)
Berg 116*

Einz. Lohrberger Hanz in Frankfurt and Berg in Böddiger are not part of the Großlage or Bereich

VILLAGES

HOCHHEIM

The vineyards are separated from the main Rheingau by Wiesbaden and many an autobahn. The isolated hillside owes its survival to the quality and strength of character of the wines: full-bodied almost to the point of coarseness (and immensely long-lived) in hot years, but generally combining Riesling finesse with a soft earthiness of their own. The English term "hock", meaning any Rhine wine, is a contraction of "hockamore" – an early attempt at pronouncing Hochheimer. Its early fame is amply justified by the highly individual, occasionally superlative, wines made there today.

Vineyards

241.2ha in Großlage Daubhaus with *Einzellagen:* Berg, 35.3ha, S-SW, flat. Reichesthal, 26.5ha, S, flat. Stielweg, 5.3ha, flat. Domdechaney, 10.5ha, S, flat. Kirchenstück, 14.9ha, S, flat. Sommerheil, 21.9ha, S, flat. Hofmeister, 33.9ha, S, flat. Hölle, 35.9ha, S, sloping. Stein, 26.9ha, S, flat. Königin Victoriaberg, 5ha, S, sloping. Herrnberg, 4ha, S, flat.

FLÖRSHEIM AND WICKER

East of Hochheim, in a little rural valley surrounded by suburbs, are a string of vineyards around the villages of Flörsheim, Wicker and Massenheim. Riesling predominates in these flat or gently sloping vineyards.

Vineyards

All in Großlage Daubhaus. *Einzellagen:* Flörsheim: Herrnberg, 20ha, SE, flat and St. Anna Kapelle. Wicker: Mönchsgewann, 18ha, SW, flat; König-Wilhelmsberg, 2.4ha, SW, flat; Nonnberg, 2.1ha, SW, flat; Stein, 20ha, SSW, flat.

WIESBADEN

Wiesbaden is not normally seen as a wine name except on the labels of its 4.4ha Neroberg. The wines of the rest of its 150ha are normally bottled under the Großlage name: Rauenthaler Steinmächer.

Vineyards

Großlage Steinmächer with *Einzellagen:* Frauenstein: Herrnberg, 58.6ha, S,SW, sloping; Marschall, 8.5ha, SSW, sloping; Homberg, 8.3ha, SSW, sloping. Schierstein: Hölle, 32.6ha, S, sloping; Dachsberg, 27.3ha, SSW, sloping. Dotzheim: Judenkirch, 10.3ha, SW, sloping. Neroberg (no Großlage), 4.4ha, S, sloping.

MARTINSTHAL

The altitude, soil, shelter and orientation of Martinsthal, 180 metres (600 feet) up and a good kilometre and a half (a mile) from the river, facing south, are very similar to those of its more famous neighbour Rauenthal. Rauenthal's best sites are steeper, but Martinsthal also makes wines of full, spicy flavour in good vintages. The Großlage name Steinmächer has not overwhelmed its identity.

Vineyards

78ha in Großlage Steinmächer with *Einzellagen:* Langenberg, 19ha, SW, sloping. Wildsau, 30.9ha, S,SW, sloping. Rödchen, 28.1ha, SSW, flat.

WALLUF

The little-known village stretches back from the river front up the valley of its stream. Most of its wines, which can be full-flavoured and keep excellently, take advantage of the Großlage name Rauenthaler Steinmächer.

Vineyards

Niederwalluf and Oberwalluf. 103.8ha. Großlage Steinmächer with *Einzellagen:* Langenstück, 13ha, SSE, flat. Vitusberg, 13.9ha, SSE, flat. Oberberg, 12.9ha, SSE, sloping. Berg-Bildstock, 30.4ha, SSE, sloping. Walkenberg, 29.4ha, SW, sloping. Hof Nußberg, 3ha, S, flat.

RAUENTHAL

The Leitgemeinde of the Großlage Steinmächer lies high on the hill above its skirt of highly prized vineyards. From Baiken and Gehrn the State Domain and others coax bottles of smoothly measured, spicy, notably firm yet almost low-key Auslesen. Drier wines, including Kabinetts, are less distinctive than a Rauenthaler of a very ripe vintage.

Vineyards

98ha in Großlage Steinmächer with *Einzellagen:* Langenstück, 25.8ha, SW-SE, flat. Gehrn, 18ha, S, sloping. Baiken, 14.9ha, S, sloping. Wülfen, 13.9ha, S, sloping. Rothenberg, 20ha, S, sloping. Nonnenberg, 5ha, S, sloping.

ELTVILLE

The most substantial town of the Rheingau waterfront, the headquarters of the State Domain and several other important estates, with ample gently sloping vineyards just below the first class in soil and situation, and correspondingly often a better bargain than more exclusive names.

Vineyards

240.3ha in Großlage Steinmächer with *Einzellagen:* Taubenberg, 79.8ha, S, flat. Langenstück, 63ha, SW, sloping. Sonnenberg, 67.9ha, S, flat. Rheinberg, 29.9ha, S, flat. Sandgrub, 57.8ha, SW,S, flat.

KIEDRICH

The atmospheric old village lies just over 3 kilometres (2 miles) up a little valley from Eltville and the river. Thanks to a Victorian English benefactor, its Gothic church of rosy stone is still resplendent with Gregorian sounds. Vinously, Kiedrich occupies a place just behind Rauenthal, also needing the ripeness of a good vintage to give the ultimate vitality to its flavour.

Vineyards

171.5ha in Großlage Heiligenstock with *Einzellagen:* Klosterberg, 66.6ha, SW-SE, sloping. Wasseros, 36.3ha, SW, sloping. Gräfenberg, 10.9ha, SW, sloping. Sandgrub, 57.8ha, SW, S, flat.

ERBACH

The town is like a western continuation of Eltville, but lapped round with vineyards on every side. Strangely, here it is not the apparently best-sited vineyards tilting up behind the town that produce the best wine but a low-lying strip by the river (and the railway) with deep, fat, marly soil, suggesting by its position that it is both a frost trap and a swamp after rain. It is neither, but bears the name of Marcobrunn: for centuries a synonym for luxuriously full and high-flavoured hock. In fact, the drainage is excellent, the 5-degree slope sufficient and the whole of this stretch of riverbank a suntrap.

Vineyards

269.2ha in Großlage Deutelsberg with *Einzellagen:* Honigberg, 99.8ha, SW-SE, flat. Michelmark, 74.8ha, SW-S, flat. Siegelsberg, 15.6ha, S, sloping. Marcobrunn, 5.2ha, S, flat. Hohenrain, 18ha, SE-SW, flat. Steinmorgen, 31.9ha, SE-S, flat. Schloßberg, 5.7ha, S, sloping. Rheinhell, 18ha, SE-S, flat.

HATTENHEIM

The name of Hattenheim is not as celebrated as its great vineyards deserve. Down by the river, round the lovely little timbered town, Mannberg, Wisselbrunnen and Nußbrunnen share the suntrap qualities of Marcobrunn. High on the hill behind is perhaps the most famous vineyard in Germany, the Steinberg. (As an Ortsteil, it omits the Gemeinde name.) Behind the Steinberg, up the wooded coomb of the purling Erbach, lies Kloster Eberbach, the great Cistercian monastery belonging to the State Domain, now effectively the ceremonial headquarters of the German wine industry.

The wines of Hattenheim thus range from the sensuous, smooth and subtly spicy products of the riverside to the martial harmonies of the Steinberg. The great walled vineyard was chosen 700 years ago by the monks for its exposure high on the flank of the hill on stony ground. They were looking for power and concentration, which with Riesling means steel as well as scent. The State Domain has recently been testing some of the new grape varieties in the Steinberg, producing wines of almost outrageous perfume. Steinberger Riesling needs time. Its harshness sometimes fights with sweetness for years before the harmonies emerge.

Vineyards

229.3ha in Großlage Deutelsberg with *Einzellagen:* Heiligenberg, 35.6ha, S, sloping. Schützenhaus, 65.8ha, SW, flat. Engelmannsberg, 20ha, SW, flat. Pfaffenberg, 6ha, S, flat. Hassel, 29.9ha, S, flat. Nußbrunnen, 10.3ha, SSE, sloping. Wisselbrunnen, 18ha, S, incline. Mannberg, 11.2ha, SSE, sloping. Steinberg (Ortsteil), 31.9ha, S,SW, sloping.

HALLGARTEN

Hallgarten continues the succession of upland villages from Rauenthal and Kiedrich, here rising to the Rheingau's highest point: vines in the Hendelberg are more than 200 metres (700 feet) above sea level. With less mist and less frost than below, cooler nights, more sunshine and wind, combined with alkaline clay in the soil, Hallgarten wines are big-bodied and slow to develop – certainly below the first rank in charm but with some of the attack of Steinbergers. The Großlage name for these 209 hectares of vineyards is Mehrhölzchen (though the Hendelberg vineyard is also in Großlage Deutelsberg).

Vineyards
Großlage Mehrhölzchen with *Einzellagen:* Würzgarten, 42.4ha, S, flat. Schönhell, 58.4ha, S, flat. Hendelberg (also in Großlage Deutelsberg), 53.3ha, S, SE, sloping. Jungfer, 54.5ha, SSE, flat.

OESTRICH
Nestling snugly along its wharves, Oestrich is the biggest vineyard commune and one of the most reliable names of the middle rank, rising to star quality in Auslesen from the best growers in the Lenchen; wines of sinful, almost oily lusciousness.

Vineyards
442ha in Großlagen Gottesthal and Mehrhölzchen with *Einzellagen:* Klosterberg, 141.7ha, SSE, flat (Gottesthal and Mehrhölzchen). Lenchen, 145ha, S, flat (Gottesthal). Doosberg, 152.7ha, S, flat (Gottesthal). Schloß Reichhartshausen (registered as an Ortsteil), 3ha, S, flat (Gottesthal).

MITTELHEIM
Mittelheim is squeezed between Oestrich and Winkel, while its wines are half in the Winkel Großlage of Honigberg and half in Erntebringer, going to market as Johannisbergers. Its reputation thus dispersed, wines that proudly bear the name Mittelheim are likely to have character ·at a reasonable price.

Vineyards
166.6ha in Großlagen Erntebringer and Honigberg with *Einzellagen:* Goldberg, 24ha, S, flat (Erntebringer). Edelmann, 93ha, S, flat (Erntebringer and Honigberg). St. Nikolaus, 50ha, S, flat (Erntebringer and Honigberg).

WINKEL
Winkel continues to line the river road with a huggermugger blend of buildings and vineyards at the foot of the slopes that lead up to two of the greatest sites on the Rhine: Schloß Johannisberg, obvious on the skyline, and Schloß Vollrads, sheltering discreetly in a fold of the hill at the back of the parish. Schloß Vollrads is the great name of Winkel, but an Ortsteil which sheds no reflected glory on its neighbours. The flag-carrying vineyard for Winkel is its Hasensprung (Hare leap), the eastern flank of the hill of Schloß Johannisberg. It gives very lovely, perfumed and almost delicate wines of infinite nuance and distinction.

Vineyards
262.6ha in Großlagen Erntebringer and Honigberg with *Einzellagen:* Dachsberg, 52ha, SSE, flat (Erntebringer). Hasensprung, 100ha, SSE, flat (Honigberg). Gutenberg, 51ha, SSW, flat (Honigberg). Jesuitengarten, 26ha, S, flat (Honigberg). Bienengarten, 1ha, S, flat (Honigberg). Schloß Vollrads (Ortsteil), 33.1ha, S, flat (Honigberg).

JOHANNISBERG
Johannisberg is the village behind the famous Schloß. It is also the Bereich name for the entire Rheingau. California vintners call their Rieslings after it. In fact, it must be the most borrowed name in Germany. What is its special quality? The situation of Schloß Johannisberg,

dominating the river from a sort of saluting base of its own, explains itself.

The wines of Schloß Johannisberg inevitably have a hard time living up to their reputation. The competition from the neighbours, moreover, could hardly be fiercer in this area where ancient and noble estates are the rule rather than the exception. There is considerable justice in looking on Johannisberg as the epitome of the Rheingau; the place where all its qualities of vitality, spice, delicacy and grace, with length of flavour (and life) come together.

Vineyards
117.4ha mainly in Großlage Erntebringer with *Einzellagen:* Goldatzel, 24ha, S,SW, sloping. Hölle, 27ha, S,SW, sloping. Mittelhölle, 6.5ha, SSW, sloping. Klaus (also in Großlage Honigberg), 2ha, S, flat. Hansenberg, 3.8ha, S, sloping. Schwarzenstein, 5.5ha, S, flat. Vogelsang, 14ha, S,SE, flat. Schloß Johannisberg (Ortsteil), 35ha, S, sloping.

GEISENHEIM
The riverside town below Johannisberg is known by name as much for its research and teaching institute, the H.Q. of German viticulture, grape breeding and oenology, as for its excellent vineyards, only a little, if at all, below the best in potential. The Rothenberg, a modest mountain above the centre of the town, has produced Rieslings whose perfume has driven me almost to ecstasy. Fuchsberg (where the experimental plots of the Institute are) and Mäuerchen, higher on the hill on the way to Rüdesheim, have ideal situations and soil – though Fuchsberg can be struck by untimely frosts.

Vineyards
427ha in Großlagen Burgweg and Erntebringer with *Einzellagen:* Mönchspfad, 160ha, S, flat (Burgweg). Mäuerchen, 33ha, SSE, flat (Burgweg). Fuchsberg, 68ha, S, flat (Burgweg). Rothenberg, 36ha, S, sloping (Burgweg). Schloßgarten, 18ha, S, flat (Erntebringer). Kilzberg, 56ha, SSE, flat (Erntebringer). Kläuserweg, 57ha, S, sloping (Erntebringer).

RÜDESHEIM
Rüdesheim brings the main block of the Rheingau to a triumphant close. Here the crest of the Taunus mountains closes in on the river and squeezes the vineyards into steeper and steeper formation. The town is the tourist centre of the Rheingau, with a summer population it is pleasanter to avoid (but with a very useful car ferry to Bingen).

The vineyards west of the town become steeper and narrower as they approach the river bend. The best carry the distinctive name of Berg after Rüdesheimer and before their individual names. Until recently they were terraced in tortuous steps and ramps, impossible to work except by hand. An astonishingly bold Flurbereinigung relandscaped the whole hillside. For a while bulldozers looked as if they would roll into the river. Now all is orderly again and the Berg wines once more the ripest, strongest, most concentrated (if not the subtlest) of the Rhine.

Vineyards
327ha in Großlage Burgweg with *Einzellagen:* Berg Schloßberg, 29.1ha, S, steep. Drachenstein, 48.5ha, S, sloping. Berg Roseneck, 28.9ha, S, sloping. Berg Rottland, 37ha, S, sloping. Rosengarten, 3.7ha, S, flat. Klosterberg, 39.4ha, S-SE, sloping. Klosterlay, 37.8ha, SSE, sloping. Kirchenpfad, 20ha, S, sloping. Magdalenenkreuz, 48.9ha, S, flat. Bischofsberg, 39.4ha, S, sloping.

ASSMANNSHAUSEN
Everything changes at the Rüdesheim bend – even the colour of the wine. The village of Assmannshausen, with its sheltered valley of vines giving west on to the river, is two thirds planted with Spätburgunder to produce a red which at best is pallid and at worst pink. It has little appeal to most foreigners, but the German cognoscenti dote on it.

The State Domain (at Eltville) is the principal producer, obtaining remarkable prices for sweet Auslesen of a disconcerting colour. The sweetness helps to mask the lack of a kernel of real Pinot Noir flavour which is common to all German reds.

Vineyards
174ha in Großlagen Steil and Burgweg with *Einzellagen:* Hinterkirch, 59ha, S-SW, steep (Steil). Höllenberg, 55ha, S-SW, steep (Steil). Frankenthal, 45ha, S-SW, steep (Steil). Berg Kaisersteinfels, 15ha, S, sloping (Burgweg).

LORCH AND LORCHHAUSEN
These villages are the transition from Rheingau to Mittelrhein – though still within the Rüdesheim Großlage, Burgweg. The best growers produce very creditable Riesling even without the natural advantages of the Rheingau.

Vineyards
Lorch, 181.3ha in Großlage Burgweg with *Einzellagen:* Schloßberg, 53ha, SW, sloping; Kapellenberg, 58ha, S, sloping; Krone, 13ha, SW, sloping; Pfaffenwies, 35ha, SW, sloping; Bodental-Steinberg, 23ha, SW, steep. Lorchhausen, 89.8ha in Großlage Burgweg with *Einzellagen:* Rosenberg, 40ha, SW, steep; Seligmacher, 50ha, SW, sloping.

Schloß Groenesteyn

Suttonstraße 22, Postfach 1180, 6229 Kiedrich, tel: 06123-2492. *Owner:* Baron von Ritter zu Groenesteyn. 32 hectares. *Einzellagen:* Kiedrich: Gräfenberg, Wasseros, Sandgrub, Klosterberg; Rüdesheim: Berg Rottland, Berg Roseneck, Berg Schloßberg, Bischofsberg, Kirchenpfad, Klosterlay and Magdalenenkreuz.

Another of the lordly estates of the Rheingau, dating from 1400, held by the Barons von Ritter zu Groenesteyn since 1640 and based at their great baroque mansion (the Schloß) in Kiedrich, with its cellars in Rüdesheim. Vines are 92% Riesling, the rest Spätburgunder and Müller-Thurgau. The wines are kept in the old way in individual barrels to encourage variety and nuance, the Kiedrichers delicate and scented; the Rüdesheimers (especially from the Berg sites) fruity and spicy. A wide variety of wines is available from the cellars.

Weingut Hupfeld Erben

Rheingaustraße 113, Mittelheim, 6227 Oestrich-Winkel, tel: 06723-3307. *Owner:* Arndt-Richard Hupfeld. 5 hectares. *Einzellagen:* Mittelheim: Edelmann and St. Nikolaus; Oestrich: Lenchen and Klosterberg; Winkel: Jesuitengarten and Hasensprung; Johannisberg: Hölle and Vogelsang. Wine growers since 1907 and merchants before that, since the 1940s the Hupfelds have established themselves as a top-quality small estate, aiming for medium-dry balance, and winning regular medals. This estate is planted with 85% Riesling; the rest consists of Ehrenfelser, Kerner and Gewürztraminer.

Schloß Johannisberg

Fürst von Metternich-Winneburg'sche Domaine. 6222 Geisenheim-Johannisberg, tel: 06722-8027. *Owner:* Paul Alfons Fürst von Metternich. 35 hectares.

The most famous estate of the Rhine, whose name is often used to designate the true Riesling vine. Its first planting is credited to Charlemagne; the first monastery was built on its hilltop commanding the Rhine in 1100; full flowering came in the 18th century under the Prince-Abbot of Fulda. Its vintage of 1775 was the first to be gathered overripe (the Abbot's messenger having arrived late with permission to pick): the term Spätlese and the appreciation of noble rot are said to have started with this incident.

The estate was secularized under Napoleon and presented in 1816, after the Treaty of Vienna, by the Austrian Emperor to his Chancellor, Prince Metternich, for his diplomatic services. His descendant Prince Paul Alfons von Metternich-Winneburg is still nominally the owner, although the estate is now part of a group controlled by the food tycoon Rudolf August Oetker of Bielefeld, together with the neighbouring von Mumm estate.

In 1942 the monastery-castle (but not its cellar) was destroyed in an air raid. It is now totally rebuilt. The vineyard, in one block on the ideally sloping skirts of the castle hill, is planted entirely in Riesling. Technically it is an Ortsteil – a local entity which needs no Einzellage name. Average production is 70 hl/ha, a potential total of some 25,000 cases. The varying qualities within this mass of wine are designated by two different labels and 10 coloured capsules as well as the usual terminology. Standard wines are labelled with the Metternich coat of arms with capsules ranging from yellow (for QbA) to red (Kabinett), green (Spätlese), pink (Auslese) and pink-gold (Beerenauslese). The other label, with a picture of the estate, has an orange capsule for Kabinett, white for Spätlese, sky-blue for Auslese, blue-gold for Beerenauslese and gold for Trockenbeerenauslese. A third label (in Germany only) carries a landscape and a portrait of the great Prince Metternich. The capsules were originally wax – in German, *Lack*; thus Rotlack equals red seal, Grünlack, green seal, etc. (Coincidentally, the characteristic bouquet of mature Johannisberg is said to be a smell of burning sealing wax.)

At their best Schloß Johannisberg's wines are extraordinarily firm in structure, concentrated and long-lived, with every quality of classic Riesling grown on an exceptional site. I have drunk an 1870 which at a century old was still vigorous and bore traces of its original flavour. Recent wines, like those of several of the great lordly estates, have shown signs of commercialization: lightness and lack of "grip". The defence is that few people intend to keep them for maturing.

The majority of Schloß Johannisberg is now drunk abroad and, I fear, by people who have no yardstick to judge it by. Auslesen of 1971 and 1976 were quite properly superb, but this is only as it should be.

Weingut Johannishof, Eser

6222 Johannisberg, tel: 06722-8216. *Owner:* Hans Hermann Eser. 18 hectares. *Einzellagen:* Johannisberg: Hölle, Klaus, Vogelsang, Schwarzenstein and Goldatzel; Winkel: Jesuitengarten, Hasensprung and Gutenberg; Geisenheim: Kläuserweg and Kilzberg.

The estate (dating from 1685) is conspicuous on the road up to Johannisberg for its huge 18th-century wine press by the door. The Esers both come from old growers' families and have made a reputation for powerful and full-flavoured wines. *Flurbereinigung* has recently remodelled the vineyards into areas that can be worked by tractor, but the deep cellars, 10 metres under the hill, are traditional; cold and damp with dark oval casks for maturing wine of character.

Weingut Graf von Kanitz

Rheinstraße 49, 6223 Lorch, tel: 06726-346. *Owner:* Count Carl Albrecht von Kanitz. 17 hectares. *Einzellagen:* Lorch: Schloßberg, Kapellenberg, Krone, Pfaffenwies and Bodental-Steinberg.

An ancient family property on steep slopes of varying soils, from slaty to sandy loam, giving fine but milder, softer wines than the main Rheingau. The grapes are all organically grown. The inheritance, dating from the 13th century, includes the earliest Renaissance building of the area, the Hilchenhaus in Lorch, now a Weinstube. 91% is Riesling, 5% Müller-Thurgau, 2% Gewürztraminer and the rest new varieties (Kanzler, Kerner, Ehrenfelser).

Weingut Freiherr zu Knyphausen

Klosterhof Drais, 6228 Eltville, tel: 06123-62177. *Owner:* Gerko, Baron zu Innhausen und Knyphausen. 20 hectares. *Einzellagen:* Erbach: Marcobrunn, Siegelsberg, Hohenrain, Steinmorgen and Michelmark; Hattenheim: Wisselbrunnen; Kiedrich: Sandgrub; Eltville: Taubenberg.

A former monastic estate of the Cistercians of Kloster Eberbach, bought in 1818 by the Baron's forebears. 90% is Riesling, 4% Spätburgunder, 3% Ehrenfelser, 2% Kerner and 1% Gewürztraminer. The property is run on traditional and personal lines, making full-flavoured wines.

Weingut Königin Victoria Berg

Rheinstraße 2, 6203 Hochheim, tel: 06723-3307. *Owner:* Irmgard Hupfeld. 5 hectares. *Einzellage:* Hochheim: Königin Victoria Berg (solely owned).

Queen Victoria stopped to watch the vintage in this fortunate vineyard on the lower slopes of Hochheim in 1850. The then owners, the Pabstmann family, were not slow to commemorate the visit, getting the Queen's permission to rename the vineyard after her, erecting a Gothic monument and designing the most tinselly (now quite irresistible) label. Deinhards, who sell the wine abroad, go to great lengths to maximize its quality. It is not Hochheim's finest, but full, soft, flowery and just what Queen Victoria might well have enjoyed. The label is printed in black and white for QbA wines, yellow and gold for Trocken wines and glorious Technicolor for QmP wines.

Weinbau Heinrich Kühn

Beinerstraße 14, 6227 Oestrich-Winkel, tel: 06723-2106. *Owner:* Karl-Heinz Kühn. 1.5 hectares. *Einzellagen:* Oestrich: Lenchen and Doosberg; Mittelheim: Edelmann and St. Nikolaus.

A tiny part-time business, but a maker of serious prize-winning wines (100% Riesling) specifically for long bottle-ageing.

Weingut Lamm-Jung

Eberbacherstraße 50, 6229 Erbach, tel: 06123-62148. *Owner:* Josef Jung. 7.8 hectares. *Einzellagen:* Erbach: Honigberg, Hohenrain, Steinmorgen and Michelmark; Kiedrich: Sandgrub.

The vineyards are planted with 73% Riesling, followed by Spätburgunder, small parcels of Ruländer and Gewürztraminer, and various new crossings. In the wine bar there are 25 different vintages to be tasted, including the rosé (Weißherbst) and the increasingly popular red wine from Spätburgunder.

Weingut Hans Lang
Rheinallee 6, 6228 Eltville-Hattenheim, tel: 06723-2475. 12 hectares. *Einzellagen:* Hattenheim: Nußbrunnen (0.2ha), Schützenhaus (5), Heiligenberg (0.5), Wisselbrunnen (1) and Rheingarten (0.2); Kiedrich: Sandgrub
A nurseryman, merchant and (since 1959) grower who has expanded rapidly. His style is robust with plenty of character and acidity. 80% Riesling, 10% Spätburgunder, 10% Müller-Thurgau and other varieties.

Weingut Langehof
Martinsthalerstraße 4, 6228 Eltville-Rauenthal, tel: 06123-71638. *Owners:* Josef and Marianne Klein. 1.9 hectares. *Einzellagen:* Rauenthal: Langenstück, Wülfen, Rothenberg and Baiken.
Small but very keen grower with 80% Riesling and 20% Gutenborner on good slopes. The main building dates from 1566, with a well in the cellar. Wines mainly halbtrocken and trocken. His 1976 Rothenberg Beerenauslese was a considerable medal winner.

G. H. von Mumm'sches Weingut
Schulstraße 32, 6222 Geisenheim, tel: 06722-8012. *Owner:* Rudolf August Oetker. 70 hectares. The Weingut is sole owner of (in Johannisberg): Hansenberg (4ha) and Schwarzenstein (4). Other *Einzellagen:* Johannisberg: Vogelsang (5), Hölle (3), Mittelhölle (6) and Klaus (1); Rüdesheim: Bischofsberg, Berg Rottland (1), Berg Schoßberg (0.4) and Berg Roseneck (3); Assmannshausen: Höllenberg, Hinterkirch and Frankenthal; Geisenheim: Mönchspfad, Mäuerchen, Kilzberg and Kläuserweg; Winkel: Dachsberg.
An estate founded on the profits of the legendary 1811 "Comet" vintage, when the banker Peter Mumm of Frankfurt bought the whole crop of Schloß Johannisberg (which was temporarily in the hands of one of Napoleon's marshals, Kellermann). Mumm bought land in Johannisberg and the neighbourhood. In 1957 Rudolf August Oetker of Bielefeld, famous for his grocery products, bought the property and has much enlarged it to its present 70 hectares. 8 hectares are planted with Spätburgunder in Assmannshausen; the balance of vines is 86% Riesling.
Oetker also controls Schloß Johannisberg. The technical wine-making side of both properties is now handled at the Mumm cellars; the administration at Schloß Johannisberg.
The Mumm wines have evolved in a modern style with the emphasis on trocken and halbtrocken categories. The better qualities are still wood-matured and well balanced to age moderately. The estate owns a restaurant at Burg Schwarzenstein, high above Johannisberg, where its wide range of wines is on offer.

Weingut Dr. Heinrich Nägler
Friedrichstraße 22, 6220 Rüdesheim, tel: 06722-2835. *Owner:* Dr. Heinrich Nägler. A distinguished small estate specializing in fine Rüdesheimer since the 19th century. 6.5 hectares. *Einzellagen:* Rüdesheim: Berg Rottland (0.7ha), Berg Schloßberg (0.8), Berg Roseneck (1.0), Bischofsberg (0.9), Drachenstein (3.1), Klosterlay (3.1) and Magdalenenkreuz (3.1).
Nägler goes to great lengths to achieve concentrated wines of character, thinning the grapes and nursing small individual lots. He likes rather dry wines to accompany food, but makes some luxurious polished Spätlesen and Auslesen. 86% is Riesling, 9% Ehrenfelser, 5% Spätburgunder (latest plans are to increase the proportion of the latter).

Weingut Heinz Nikolai
Ringstraße 14, 6229 Erbach. 7 hectares. *Einzellagen:* Erbach: Steinmorgen, Hohenrain, Michelmark and Honigberg; Kiedrich: Sandgrub; Hallgarten: Jungfer.
A fourth generation grower with 85% Riesling, 10% Scheurebe, 5% Ruländer. His aromatic Scheurebe and soft fat Ruländer are popular. Three quarters of his output are sweet, or at least "mellow", wines.

Weingut Nonnenberg
6229 Martinsthal, tel: 06721-13311. *Owners:* Ludwig Edmund Ebling and Heinrich Schwarz of the Weigand family. 7 hectares. *Einzellage:* Rauenthal: Nonnenberg (solely owned).
The management and 90% of the sales of this mainly Riesling Rheingau estate are in the hands of the Bingen wine merchants, A. Weigand. Half the crop is made into dry/medium-dry wine. A dry Riesling Sekt is also produced.

Robert von Oetinger'sches Weingut
Rheinallee 1–3, 6228 Eltville-Erbach, tel: 06123-62528. *Owner:* Baron Detlev von Oetinger. 7.5 hectares. *Einzellagen:* Erbach: Hohenrain, Steinmorgen, Honigberg, Michelmark, Siegelsberg and Marcobrunn; Kiedrich: Sandgrub.
An old Erbach family in new premises (since 1966) by the Rhine, with Weinstube and garden. Their speciality is dry wines with pronounced acidity and powerful flavour, mainly drunk in the neighbourhood.

Schloß Reinhartshausen
6229 Erbach, tel: 06123-4009. *Owners:* The Princes of Prussia. 67 hectares between Erbach and Hattenheim. *Einzellagen:* Erbach: Marcobrunn, Schloßberg (solely owned), Siegelsberg, Rheinhell (solely owned), Hohenrain, Steinmorgen, Michelmark and Honigberg; Hattenheim: Wisselbrunnen and Nußbrunnen; Kiedrich: Sandgrub; Rauenthal: Wülfen; Rüdesheim: Bischofsberg.
The riverside estate of the Prussian royal family; the mansion is now a luxury hotel facing the tranquil green island of Mariannenaue (Rheinhell) across the busy waters of the Rhine. 80% of the estate is Riesling; the rest is divided between Weißburgunder for full-bodied dry wine, Spätburgunder for light red and Weißherbst (rosé), and Gewürztraminer and Kerner (aromatic wines for the table).
The rich loam of Erbach, especially Marcobrunn, gives notably full-bodied wines.

The island's wine is also soft and rich. The estate uses traditional casks and maintains a balance between top-quality wines (recently particularly good) and commercial lines, some sold under the subsidiary name "Prinz von Preußen".

Balthasar Ress
Rheinallee 7–11, 6220 Rüdesheim am Rhein, tel: 06723-3011. *Owner:* Stefan B. Ress. Some 20.4 hectares scattered among good sites. *Einzellagen:* Rüdesheim: Berg Rottland, Berg Schloßberg, Bischofsberg, Kirchenpfad, Klosterlay and Magdalenenkreuz (2.8); Geisenheim: Kläuserweg (2.6); Hattenheim: Wisselbrunnen, Nußbrunnen, Hassel, Heiligenberg, Schützenhaus, Engelmannsberg and Rheingarten (7); and small sites in Johannisberg, Hallgarten, Winkel, Oestrich, Erbach, Kiedrich and Hochheim.
A century-old family firm of growers and merchants (under the name Stefan B. Ress). Vines are 83% Riesling, 5% Spätburgunder. In 1978 Ress rented the 4-hectare Schloß Reichartshausen, originally Cistercian property but latterly neglected. Ress wines are cleanly made, bottled very early for freshness, balanced in sweetness for modern taste. Each year a modern artist is commissioned to paint a label for a selected Auslese of top quality (e.g. Hattenheimer Wisselbrunnen, Oestricher Doosberg).

Weingut Richter-Boltendahl
Walluferstraße 25, 6228 Eltville, tel: 06123-2504. 15 hectares. *Einzellagen:* Eltville: Taubenberg (0.8ha), Langenstück (1.6), Sonnenberg (2.2) and Rheinberg (4.5); Erbach: Honigberg (1.3) and Steinmorgen (1.1); Kiedrich: Sandgrub (0.6).
A century-old family estate. The buildings are an old barge-horse stable by the Rhine. The wines are fresh and fruity, with Eltville Rheinberg, Riesling and Scheurebe Kabinett, and Weißherbst (rosé) as specialities. 86% Riesling, 7% Müller-Thurgau, 5% Spätburgunder, 2% Scheurebe.

Weingut J. Riedel
Taunusstraße 1, 6227 Hallgarten, tel: 06723-3511. *Owners:* Christine and Wolfgang Riedel. 3.5 hectares. *Einzellagen:* Hallgarten: Jungfer, Hendelberg, Schönhell and Würzgarten.
A 17th-century property making full-bodied, heavy wines, bottled very young and intended for long maturing. 100% Riesling.

Weingut Valentin Schlotter
Lorcherstraße 13, 6220 Rüdesheim, tel: 06722-4427. *Owner:* Karl-Heinz Runck. 9.5 hectares. *Einzellagen:* Rüdesheim: Berg Rottland, Berg Schloßberg, Berg Roseneck, Bischofsberg, Kirchenpfad, Klosterlay, Klosterberg, Drachenstein and Magdalenenkreuz (5.5ha); Assmannshausen: Höllenberg and Hinterkirch (4ha).
A well-established grower of both white and red wines. The cellars are next door to the famous inn Zur Krone in Assmannshausen. His red wines are light and flowery with a hint of almonds; his Rüdesheimer 50% trocken or halbtrocken, particularly good in "off" vintages.

Domänenweingut Schloß Schönborn

Hauptstraße 53, Hattenheim, 6228 Eltville, tel:
06723-2007. *Owner:* Count Dr. Karl von
Schönborn-Wiesentheid. 75 hectares. *Einzellagen:*
Hattenheim: Pfaffenberg (6, sole owner),
Nußbrunnen (2), Wisselbrunnen (1),
Engelmannsberg, Schützenhaus; Erbach:
Marcobrunn (2.2); Rauenthal: Baiken; Oestrich:
Doosberg (13); Winkel: Gutenberg (2) and
Hasensprung (3); Johannisberg: Klaus (4);
Geisenheim: Schloßgarten (2), Mäuerchen (1),
Rothenberg and Kläuserweg; Rüdesheim: Berg
Schloßberg (2), Berg Rottland (1.5) and
Bischofsberg; Hochheim: Domdechaney (1.5),
Kirchenstück (2.5), Hölle (3), Stielweg, Reichesthal
and Sommerheil.

The biggest privately owned estate in the
Rheingau, since 1349 in the hands of a family of
great political and cultural influence. The present owner lives in his Franconian castles of
Pommersfelden and Wiesentheid. The same
director, Domänenrat Robert Englert, has run
the wine estates for more than 20 years and his
signature appears on the labels.

Critics are divided over the recent perform-
ance of Schönborn wines. Some find them
beautifully balanced – the ultimate in finesse.
Others have described them as the "Rubens of
the Rheingau", while others have found them
heavy and oversweetened. They come in vast
variety from the central Marcobrunn to
Rüdesheim in the west and Hochheim at the
extreme east of the region. 86% of the estate is
Riesling, 6% Spätburgunder, 2%
Weißburgunder (made into a fully dry wine),
1% Müller-Thurgau and 5% others. All the
wines are stored in small casks and should repay
keeping in bottle.

Commercialism may have affected parts of
the range, but the best Schönborn wines are
undoubted Rheingau classics.

Weingut Schumann-Nägler

Nothgottesstraße 29, 6222 Geisenheim, tel: 06722-
5214. *Owners:* Karl and Fred Schumann. 18
hectares. *Einzellagen:* Rüdesheim:
Magdalenenkreuz; Geisenheim: Mäuerchen,
Mönchspfad, Kilzberg, Kläuserweg; Winkel:
Dachsberg.

A high proportion (97%) of Riesling, planted on
sloping sites is the characteristic of this estate.
The owners have been making Rheingau wine
since 1438, and are at present increasing the size
of their holdings. The wines are typical of the
region – good acidity and fruit. All are matured
with individual attention in wood.

Freiherrlich Langwerth von Simmern'sches Rentamt

Langwerther Hof, Kirchgasse, 6228 Eltville, tel:
06123-3007. The present Baron Friedrich owns a
property held by his family since 1464, now
amounting to 45 hectares (87% Riesling) in the
best sites of Erbach, Hattenheim, Rauenthal and
Eltville, including Erbach: Marcobrunn (1.7ha);
Hattenheim: Nußbrunnen (4.8), Mannberg (6.3)
and Rheingarten (14.8); Rauenthal: Baiken (1.5)
and Rothenberg (0.8); Eltville: Sonnenberg (6.3).

The Gutshaus is the beautiful Renaissance
Langwerther Hof in the ancient riverside centre
of Eltville – one of the loveliest spots in the
Rheingau. The richly heraldic (if scarcely leg-
ible) red label is one of the most reliable in
Germany for classic Riesling, whether dry or
sweet, balanced to age for years.

Weingut Georg Sohlbach

Oberstraße 15, 6229 Kiedrich, tel: 06123-2281.
Owner: Georg Sohlbach. 4.6 hectares. *Einzellagen:*
Kiedrich: Sandgrub, Wasseros, Klosterberg and
Gräfenberg.

An old estate, originally called Bibo, with an
ancient cask cellar in the centre of Kiedrich.
60% is QbA wine, mainly trocken or
halbtrocken, as fresh and flowery as possible.
Red wine from Spätburgunder grapes has been
made since 1983.

Weingut Sturm & Sohn

Hauptstraße 31, 6228 Eltville 5, tel: 06123-71514.
Owner: Walter Sturm. 2.6 hectares. *Einzellagen:*
Rauenthal: Baiken, Wülfen, Langenstück and
Gehrn.

Growers in Rauenthal since 1653 and much
respected for their typically spicy, cask-matured
wines with a long life. The largest holding is
Wülfen and the best Baiken. Sturm's 1976
Trockenbeerenauslese won the top German
prize for that great vintage. 70% is Riesling, the
rest consists of Kerner, Ehrenfels and
Portugieser.

Weingutsverwaltung H. Tillmanns Erben

Hauptstraße 2, 6228 Eltville 2 – Erbach, tel: 06123-
4014. *Owner:* Wolf Jasper Musyal. 14.2 hectares.
Einzellagen: Erbach: Hohenrain, Michelmark,
Honigberg, Steinmorgen; Kiedrich: Sandgrub;
Hattenheim: Wisselbrunnen.

Ancient cellars once owned by Kloster
Eberbach. Herr Musyal believes strongly in
natural methods: no herbicides, etc., and as little
filtering as possible. 91% is Riesling. Three-
quarters of production is trocken or
halbtrocken. Erbacher Hohenrain is his
speciality.

Weingut Adam Vollmer

Winkelerstraße 93, 6222 Geisenheim, tel: 06722-
8388. *Owner:* Rainer Vollmer. 4.5 hectares.
Einzellagen: Geisenheim: Fuchsberg, Mäuerchen,
Mönchspfad, Rothenberg, Kläuserweg and
Kilzberg.

Old established estate, planted exclusively with
Riesling in the best sites in Geisenheim. Classic,
fresh and fruity wines are produced and matured in the vaulted cellar.

Weingut Schloß Vollrads

6227 Oestrich-Winkel, tel: 06723-5056. *Owner:*
Graf Matuschka-Greiffenclau.

Erwein Matuschka-Greiffenclau, an impres-
sively involved young man who presides over
this magnificent old estate in the hills a mile
above Winkel, is the 29th in a line of
Greiffenclaus who have owned estates in Winkel
since at least 1210. Their original "Grey House"
in Winkel, one of the oldest in Germany, is now a
wine-restaurant. In about 1300 the family built
the castle, whose great stone tower symbolizes
their estate, accepted as an Ortsteil, a separate
entity which uses no commune or Einzellage
name. The 50 hectares are 98% Riesling, 2%
Ehrenfelser, of the old Rheingau strain that
gives the "raciest", relatively light but very
long-lived wines. Schloß Vollrads specializes in
dry wines with as little residual sugar as possible.
On average about half the production of some
33,300 cases is QmP wine, Kabinett or better
(34% Kabinett, 10% Spätlese, 2% Auslese and
very sweet wines).

Since 1979 the estate has rented the Weingut
Fürst Löwenstein, a 20-hectare neighbouring
princely estate in Hallgarten (Einzellagen
Jungfer, Schönhell and Hendelberg), which
produces relatively riper, mellower and more
aromatic wines than the austere Vollrads style.
Georg Senft, the cellar-master at Vollrads,
makes both. The Löwenstein wines are more
immediately pleasing: the Vollrads need several
years' bottle-age.

The estate has technical and commercial
connections with the excellent Bürklin-Wolf
estate in the Rheinpfalz; also an informal link
with the Suntory winery in Japan, where
Vollrads is well known. Visitors to Vollrads can
taste a wide range and by booking can take part
in sumptuous "Lukullische" tastings with appropriate meals from a well-known Mainz
restaurant. Count Matuschka leads this gastronomic match-making personally.

Different qualities of the estate's wines are
distinguished by an elaborate system of coloured
capsules: green for QbA, blue for Kabinett, pink
for Spätlese, white for Auslese, gold for
Beerenauslese and Trockenbeerenauslese, with
a code of silver bands for dry wines and gold for
sweeter wines.

Gutsverwaltung Wegeler-Deinhard

Friedensplatz 9, 6227 Oestrich-Winkel, tel: 06723-
3071. *Owner:* Deinhard & Co. KGaA. 55 hectares.
Einzellagen: Oestrich: Lenchen, Doosberg and
Klosterberg (16.4ha); Hallgarten: Schönhell (1);
Mittelheim: Edelmann and St. Nikolaus (7.6);
Winkel: Hasensprung and Jesuitengarten (4.5);
Johannisberg: Hölle and Vogelsang (0.9);
Geisenheim: Rothenberg, Kläuserweg and
Schloßgarten (15.1); Rüdesheim: Magdalenenkreuz,
Bischofsberg, Berg Rottland, Berg Schloßberg and
Berg Roseneck (9.5).

The very substantial Rheingau estate of the
Koblenz merchant house of Deinhard, assem-
bled by Geheimer Rat (Counsellor) Wegeler, a

Deinhard partner and cousin, a century ago. 95% is Riesling, 2% Scheurebe, 1% Müller-Thurgau and 2% others. 30% of the estate is on steep slopes. The average production is 37,500 cases.

Deinhards are known for their old-fashioned devotion to quality. Their wines are true individuals; the best (especially from Oestricher Lenchen, Winkeler Hasensprung, Geisenheimer Rothenberg and the vineyards on the Rüdesheimer Berg) are often long-lived classics. Since 1970 Eiswein has been a house speciality.

Altogether one of the biggest and most reliable Rheingau producers. On the export market the wines are sold as "estate-bottled" Deinhard.

Weingut Dr. R. Weil
Mühlberg 5, 6229 Kiedrich, tel. 06123-2308. *Owner:* Dr. Robert Weil. 17.8 hectares. *Einzellagen:* Kiedrich: Sandgrub (6), Wasseros (7), Klosterberg (1) and Gräfenberg (3.8).
The leading estate of Kiedrich with a fine old reputation for Kiedrich's characteristically spicy delicacy of flavour. The Weils bought the property in 1868, partly from an Englishman, Sir John Sutton, still remembered as a benefactor by the village where he restored the splendid Gothic church and its famous organ. Dr. Weil plans to increase the proportion of recently planted Spätburgunder to 10% (the estate is almost entirely Riesling).

Weingut Wagner-Weritz
Eberbacherstraße 86-88, 6229 Erbach, tel: 6123-63263. *Owner:* Jakob Weritz. 7.5 hectares. *Einzellagen:* Erbach: Michelmark, Honigberg, Hohenrain, Siegelsberg and Steinmorgen; Hattenheim: Hassel; Kiedrich: Sandgrub.
The old Wagner property has been enlarged by the present owner, who also bought the "Erbacher Hof" in 1971. Substantial and firm wines. Over 85% Riesling, particularly from the Steinmorgen vineyard.

Domdechant Werner'sches Weingut
Rathausstraße 30, 6203 Hochheim, tel: 06146-2008. *Owner:* Dr Franz Werner Michel. 13.5 hectares. *Einzellagen:* Hochheim: Domdechaney, Kirchenstück, Hölle, Stielweg, Stein and Reichestal.
The Werner family bought this superbly sited manor, overlooking the junction of the Rhine and Main, from the Duke of York in 1780. The buyer's son, Dr. Franz Werner, was the famous Dean (Domdechant) of Mainz who saved the cathedral from destruction by the French. The seventh generation of the same family (now called Werner Michel) still owns and runs the estate, making some of the most serious, full-flavoured Hochheimers from the mingled soils of the old river terraces, sloping fully south. Traditional barrel-ageing makes essentially dry but long-flavoured and long-lived wines. 95% are Riesling.

Weingut Freiherr von Zwierlein
Schloß Kosakenberg, Bahnstraße 1, 6222 Geisenheim, tel: 06722-8307. *Owner:* Frau Gisela Wegeler. 23.5 hectares. *Einzellagen:* Geisenheim: Kläuserweg (7.5ha), Mäuerchen (1.5), Fuchsberg (2.5), Rothenberg (7) and Schloßgarten (4); Winkel: Jesuitengarten (1)
The Schloß, built by the Prince-Bishop of Mainz, took its name from a Cossack regiment in Napoleon's time. The finest wines are from the Kläuserweg, made rather dry, slightly tannic and intended to last a good 10 years. 100% Riesling.

Winzergenossenschaft Hallgarten eG
Hattenheimerstraße 15, 6227 Oestrich-Winkel-Hallgarten. 191 members. 63 hectares in the excellent *Einzellagen:* Hallgarten: Schönhell, Jungfer, Würzgarten, Hendelberg; Oestrich: Lenchen and Doosberg. The Großlage names used are Mehrhölzchen and Deutelsberg.
The substantial local growers' cooperative of Hallgarten. Vines are 85% Riesling, 13% Müller-Thurgau. All the wine is sold in Germany.

Vereinigte Weingutsbesitzer Hallgarten eG
Hallgartener Platz 3, 6227 Hallgarten. 95 members. 60 hectares. *Einzellagen:* Hallgarten: Jungfer, Schönhell, Würzgarten and Hendelberg; Oestrich: Lenchen and Doosberg; Hattenheim: Deutelsberg; Mittelheim: Endelmann.
One of two growers' cooperatives (founded 1902) in Hallgarten, popularly dubbed "The Englishman" because it excluded growers with less than 3 "Morgen" (i.e. about 0.8 hectares, which made them plutocrats, like Edwardian Englishmen). 90% Riesling, 8% Müller-Thurgau, 2% new crossings. The standard of wine-making is excellent.

Winzergenossenschaft Kiedrich eG
6229 Kiedrich im Rheingau. *Einzellagen:* Kiedrich: Gräfenberg, Wasseros, Sandgrub and Klosterberg.
Small co-operative cellar, founded in 1893, of 87 members with holdings exclusively at Kiedrich. About 75% of the crop, the equivalent of some 35,000 cases, is sold each year, mainly directly to the consumer. The balance is taken in bulk by the wine trade. Riesling occupies 95% of the vineyards – a high proportion, even for the Rheingau.

Gebietswinzergenossenschaft Rheingau eG
Erbacherstraße 31, 6228 Eltville, 330 members. 150 hectares scattered through the whole region.
The major cooperative of the Rheingau. 80% of their vines are Riesling, 8% Müller-Thurgau, 10% new white varieties, 2% Spätburgunder. Total production averages 1.3 million litres over 144,000 cases. 10% sold abroad via export houses.

Other Rheingau estates
Among other reputable producers in the Rheingau are the following, details on which were not available at the time of going to press:

Erbslöh'sches Weingut
Erbslöhstraße 1, 6222 Geisenheim, tel: 06722-8065

Weingut-Weinkellerei Graf von Francken-Sierstorpff
Rheinstraße 7, 6222 Geisenheim, tel: 06722-8042

Frankhof Kellerei
Burgeffstraße 19, 6203 Hochheim, tel: 06146-4052

Geromont'sches Weingut
Hauptstraße 80, 6227 Oestrich-Winkel, tel: 06723-2078

Weingut Jakob Hamm
Hauptstraße 60, 6227 Oestrich-Winkel, tel: 06723-2432

Weingut Franz Künstler
Freiherr-vom-Stein-Ring 3, 6203 Hochheim, tel: 06146-5666

Weingut Rentmeister Egon Mauer a.D.
Friedrichstraße 54, 6228 Eltville, tel: 06123-2639

Weingut Troitzsch, Haus Schöneck
Bächergrund 12, 6223 Lorch, tel: 06726-9481

Weingut der Landeshauptstadt Wiesbaden
Kapellenstraße 99, 6200 Wiesbaden, tel: 06121-313588

For exporting houses see p181.

FOOD AND DRINK IN THE RHEINGAU AND MITTELRHEIN

The superlative wines of the Rheingau are well complemented by the local cuisine. This is a prosperous region, as it has been for centuries, and in contrast to less sophisticated regions of Germany the gastronomic traditions are well developed.

Both the Rheingau and the Mittelrhein have some excellent hotels, many in romantic locations.

Recently there has been a well-publicized attempt to develop a cuisine to match the qualities of the Rheingau wines. The man behind this is Erwein, Count Matuschka-Greiffenclau of Schloß Vollrads. Vollrads specializes in dry wines, which are matched with carefully-chosen dishes at banquets at the Schloß (booking essential).

At the other end of the scale, countless Weinstuben offer local wine by the 200ml glass with simple food to match.

Hotels range from the simple to the elaborate. Those listed here are only a selection: for a wider choice consult the official lists and guidebooks.

Historic hotels
It is possible to stay in some very ancient buildings such as castles and monasteries which have been converted into hotels. Contact the Gast im Schloß (guests in castles) organization at Postfach 40, Vor der Burg, D 3526 Trendelburg 1.

Historic hotels in the Rhine valley include the Hotel Klostergut Jakobsburg, a monastery founded in the year 1157. The hotel occupies a superb site above the Rhine between Boppard and Rhens (tel: 06742-3061). Just up-river at Oberwesel is the Hotel Römerkrug, a half-timbered building in the village with a 500-year-old wine cellar (tel: 06744-8176). Close by is the Burghotel Auf Schönburg, a castle above the Rhine with 1,000 years of history and romantic tower bedrooms (tel: 06744-7027). The Jagdschloß Niederwald is set above the Rhine behind Rüdesheim: the cuisine emphasizes game (tel: 06722-1004).

At Lahnstein, at the entrance to the beautiful Lahn valley, is the Historisches Wirtshaus an der Lahn, a restaurant with noted cuisine (tel: 02621-7270). The famous Graues Haus in Winkel in the Rheingau describes itself as "a modern restaurant in a historic house" (tel: 06723-2619).

Mittelrhein hotels and restaurants
Königswinter, close to Bonn at the northern end of the Mittelrhein, is a river and forest resort. Information: tel: 02223-21048. Boppard in the Rhine gorge has the Bellevue Rheinhotel, well-placed on the riverside promenade. A medium-sized hotel with two restaurants and a swimming pool (tel: 06742-1020).

Bad Ems, a spa in the Lahn valley, has many hotels including the Staatliches Kurhaus, with a thermal swimming pool and sauna (tel: 02603-3016).

St. Goar's Schloßhotel auf Burg Rheinfels is a quiet, well-equipped hotel with fine views (tel: 06741-7455). Four km from St. Goarhausen on the other bank, the Auf dem Loreleyfelsen restaurant at the famous Loreley rock has rooms (tel: 06771-4011).

Rheingau hotels and restaurants
Close to Winkel, in Oestrich, is the Romantik-Hotel Schwan, which has its own vineyard, a historic wine cellar and high standards of cuisine (tel: 06723-3001).

Eltville's Schloß Reinhartshausen, once the riverside retreat of the Prussian royal family, is now a hotel as well as the HQ of a wine estate (see producers). Beautiful outlook over the Rhine and a good restaurant (tel: 06123-4081).

In Eltville, the Schänke Altes Holztor is a typical Rheingau inn with a good winelist and local cuisine.

Hattenheim, near Oestrich, has Zum Krug, a wine restaurant in the heart of the village (tel: 06723-2812).

Rüdesheim has many hotels and restaurants, among the most attractive being the Jagdschloß Niederwald (see above under historic hotels). Less grand is the Gasthof Trapp in the village itself (tel: 06722-3640).

Assmannshausen's Alte Bauernschänke dates from 1408. It offers entertainment daily and a "true Rhineland atmosphere".

Specialities
Fruit other than grapes thrives in the gentle Rheingau climate: almonds are grown, figs and even lemons can be coaxed to crop in warm corners. Fruit finds its way into several savoury dishes on the sweet-and-sour principle. But forest game and the produce of the farmlands form the solid basis of Rhine cuisine.

Sausages are legion in Germany, but only the Frankfurt sort has gained world fame. At one time just those made in the old part of Frankfurt, "the Sausage Quarter" with its 150 butchers, were allowed the name. But the monopoly was broken and the frankfurter is now universal. Real ones are made from lean pork and spices and are smoked, thus the yellowish colour of the skins.

Game – *Wild* – is a likely component of Rhineland menus. The adjoining woods are no more generous than those further south, but the local gastronomy is that bit more sophisticated. You are likely to come across *Fasan* – pheasant, *Hase* – hare, and *Reh* – venison in various forms.

The Rhineland is the home of the *Rheinischer Sauerbraten*, a pot roast of marinated beef which, typically, is often served with stewed dried fruit. Cheese, such as the Harzer from the Harz mountains, is often good – Harzer is eaten with bread and goose dripping.

Rheingau wines, especially the Kabinetts and drier Spätlesen, complement food well. Mittelrheins are more delicate and work best as apéritifs or on their own.

◀ Schloß Vollrads, one of the great estates of the Rheingau, seen from its Schloßberg vineyard. The labels carry no Einzellage or village name: the estate is accepted as an Ortsteil.

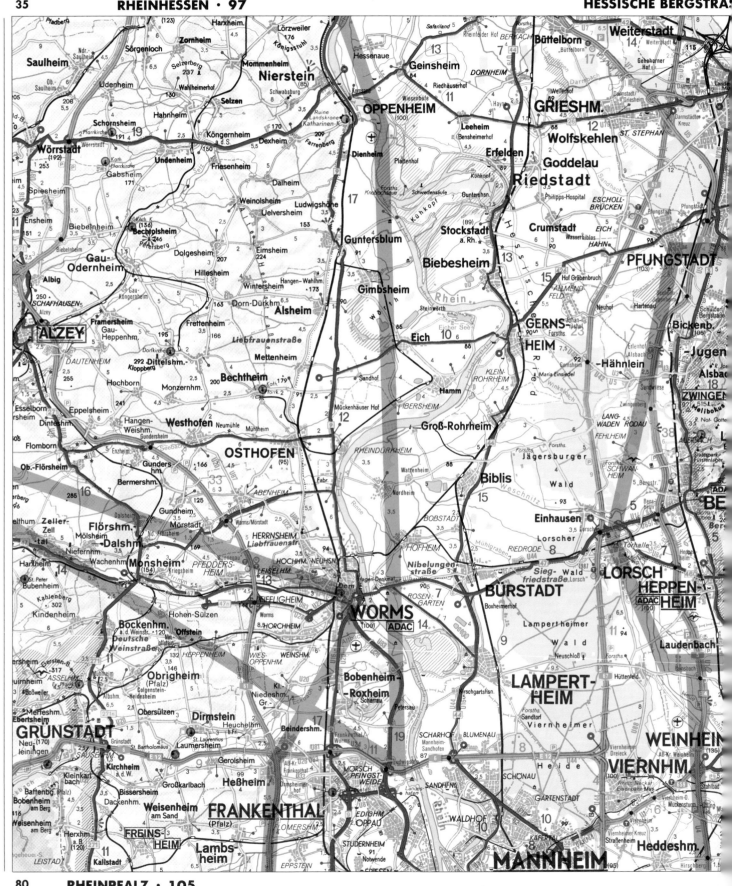

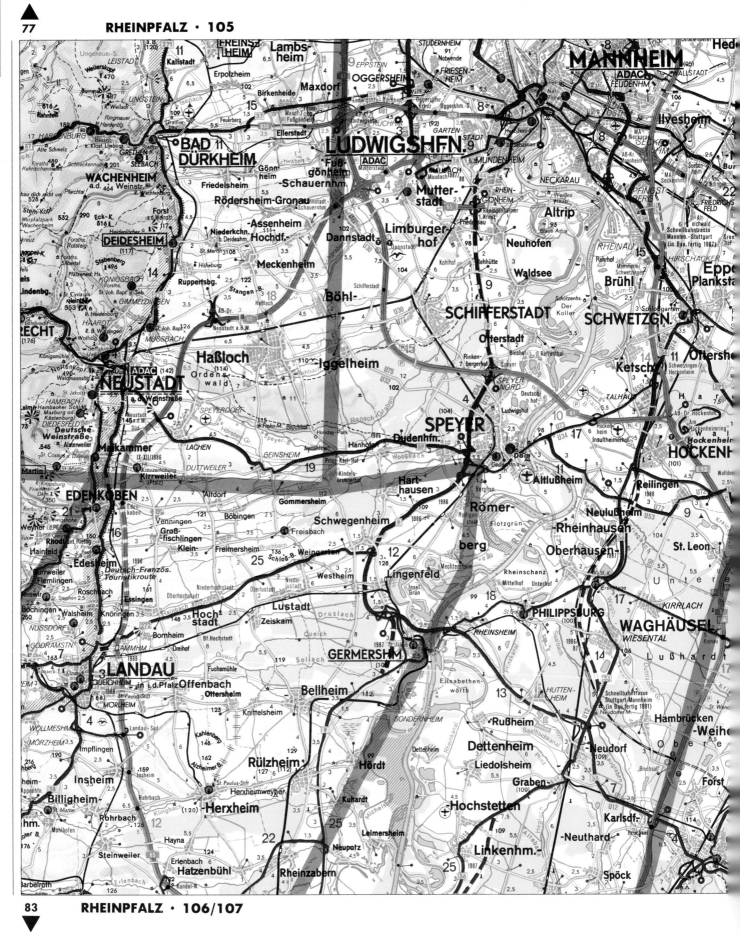

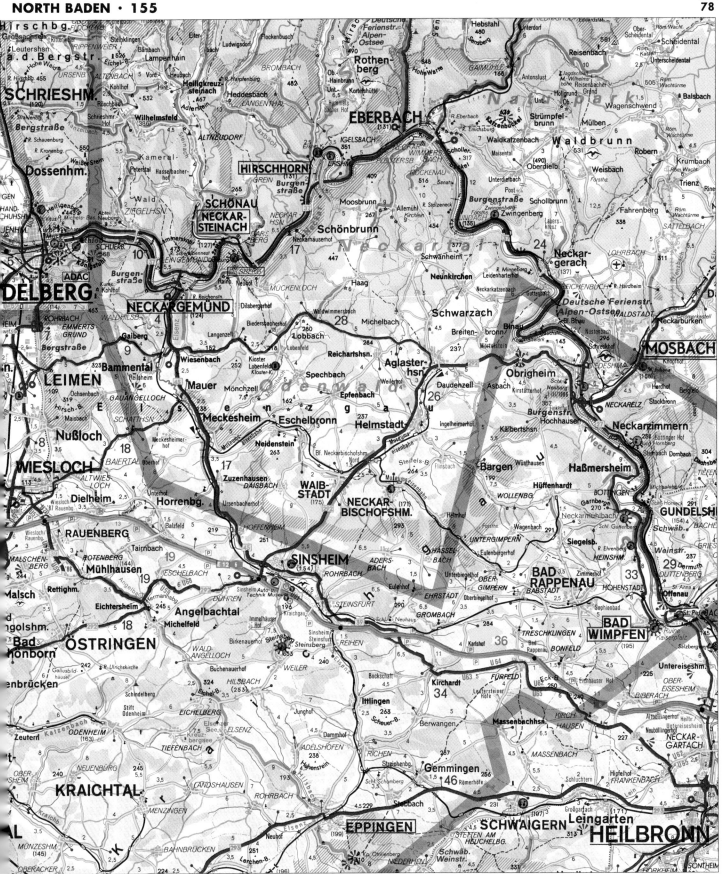

122

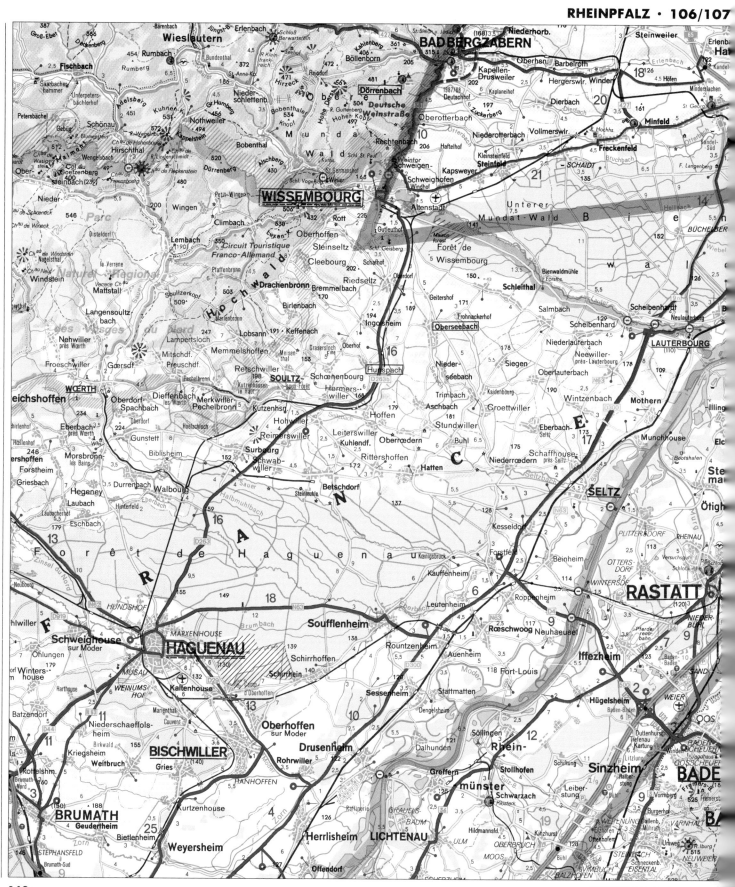

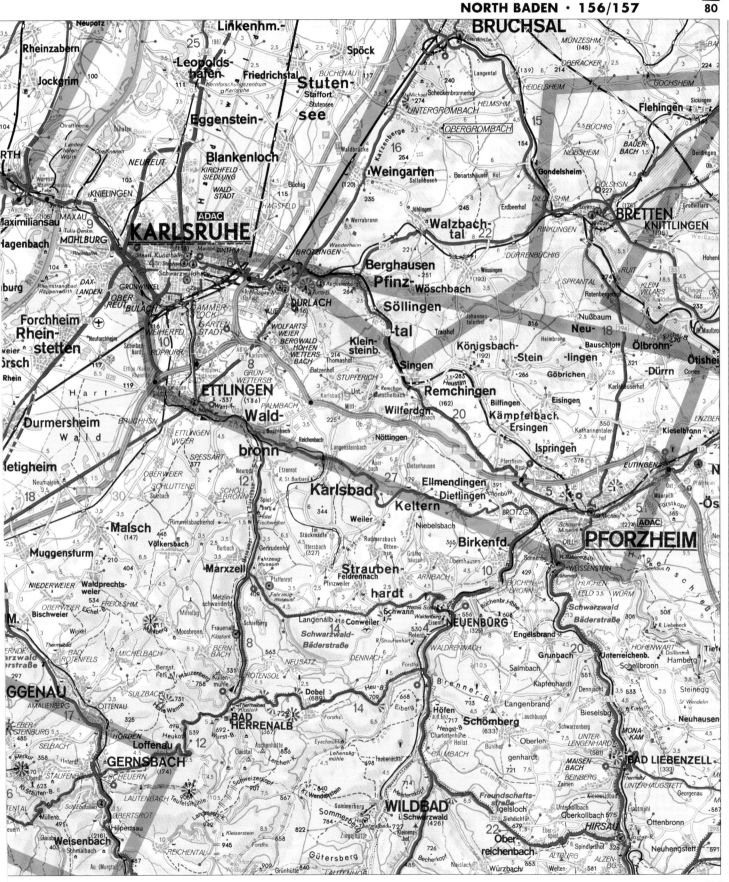

TRAISEN

Traisen is equally variable, from the sloping Nonnengarten, largely Müller-Thurgau, to the supreme Bastei, an extraordinary little ramp of Riesling at the foot of the immense red porphyry cliff of the Rotenfels. The Einzellage Rotenfels, also entirely Riesling, makes almost equally distinguished wine. The words "race" or "breeding" are quite unequal to its balance of finesse and fire.

Vineyards
Großlage Burgweg with *Einzellagen:* Bastei, 2ha, S, 95% steep. Rotenfels, 16ha, S, 95% steep.

BAD MÜNSTER

The Nahe turns the corner northward at the town of Bad Münster. Its vineyards, though excellent, are infinitesimal compared with those of Münster-Sarmsheim farther downstream. Münsterer Felseneck and Steigerdell, though rarely seen, produce exceptional Rieslings worth searching for. Ebernburg, with its ancient castle over the river, also has three fine steep south slopes: Schloßberg, Erzgrube and Feuerberg.

ALTENBAMBERG

Altenbamberg lies in a side-valley 3km (2 miles) south of the Bad Münster bend. The hills around offer several steep and sheltered slopes, largely planted with Riesling, here lighter and tauter than on the classic riverside sites, but also some notable Müller-Thurgau and Silvaner.

Vineyards
Großlage Burgweg with *Einzellagen:* Treuenfels, 6ha, SW-S, 75% steep. Kehrenberg, 16ha, S, 85% steep. Schloßberg, 20ha, S-SE, 50% steep. Rotenberg, 17ha, SW-S, 85% steep.

BAD KREUZNACH

The hub of the Nahe is the little spa-cum-commercial city of Kreuznach. Its name is known all over the wine world for its Seitzwerke, the factory where filter technology has reached perfection. The spa section of the town is quietly pretty, made interesting (and presumably salubrious) by an ambitious system of creating ozone by pouring salt water on to vast frames of birch twigs; a bizarre feature of the road into town.

Kreuznach gives its name to the lower Nahe Bereich. It also musters the enormous total of 1,000 hectares of vineyards – approaching a quarter of the entire Nahe region. They lie almost all round the town, the best of them coming close to the centre on the northwest. Kahlenberg, Steinweg, Krötenpfuhl and Brückes are considered the top sites, but several others, including Steinberg, Narrenkappe, Forst and Kauzenberg are excellent vineyards for Riesling.

On a more modest level, and with other grape varieties, the Einzellage wines of Kreuznach are generally a safe bet and often a very pleasant surprise.

Vineyards
Großlage Kronenberg with *Einzellagen:* Bad Kreuznach: Himmelgarten, 16.3ha, SW, 50% sloping. Tilgesbrunnen, 89.8ha, SW, 20% sloping. Osterhöll, 39.4ha, S, 60% sloping. Mollenbrunnen, 24.8ha, SW-S, 15% steep. Hinkelstein, 34ha, SW-S, 20% sloping. Hofgarten, 20.5ha, S, 40% sloping. Kahlenberg, 13.6ha, S, 90% sloping. Steinweg, 9.9ha, SW-S, 60% sloping. Forst, 20.4ha, S-SE, 100% sloping. Vogelsang, 25.1ha, S-SE, 50% sloping. Monhard, 7.9ha, S, 50% sloping. Kapellenpfad, 25.9ha, S-SE, 100% flat. Krötenpfuhl, 9.7ha, S, 50% sloping. Brückes, 19.1ha, SE, 90% sloping. St. Martin, 37.4ha, 30% sloping. Gutental, 21.2ha, S-SE, 50% sloping. Mönchberg, 29.9ha, SE-S, 60% sloping. Narrenkappe, 30.1ha, SW-S, 90% sloping. Steinberg, 3ha, SW-S, 100% flat. Hungriger Wolf, 26.3ha, SW-S, 20% sloping. In den Siebzehn Morgen, 1.9ha, SW, 100% flat. Rosenheck (Winzenheim), 14.4ha, SE, 90% sloping. Honigberg (Winzenheim), 20.4ha, S-SE, 50% sloping. Berg (Winzenheim), 29.7ha, SW-S-SE, 100% sloping.

WINZENHEIM

Winzenheim continues the left-bank vineyards of the Nahe without a break from Kreuznach. Its Einzellagen Rosenheck, Honigberg and Berg are all slopes with good potential, now included with Bad Kreuznach.

BRETZENHEIM

The vineyards flow on from Winzenheim with increasingly loamy, fertile soil, Silvaner and Müller-Thurgau becoming more prominent than Riesling.

Vineyards
Großlage Kronenberg with *Einzellagen:* Felsenköpfchen, 33.7ha, S, 90% sloping. Vogelsang, 40.5ha, SW-W-SE, 80% steep. Hofgut, 48.3ha, S-SE, 20% sloping. Pastorei, 35.2ha, SE, 60% steep.

LANGENLONSHEIM

The next community of the northward-flowing Nahe has another huge vineyard area taking advantage of a south slope of sandy loam at right angles to the river. The Steinchen is largely planted with Müller-Thurgau and Silvaner, which give fairly full-bodied and aromatic wines, but a far cry from the upstream classics. The best site is the Rothenberg. Langenlonsheim is in the Großlage Sonnenborn.

Vineyards
Großlage Sonnenborn with *Einzellagen:* Löhrer Berg, 50ha, S, 60% steep. Bergborn, 26ha, SE-S, 100% sloping. Lauerweg, 42ha, SE-S, 100% sloping. Königsschild, 23ha, S-SE, 20% steep. Rothenberg, 16ha, S, 100% steep. Steinchen, 139.7ha, S, 30% sloping. St. Antoniusweg, 49.9ha, S, 30% sloping.

LAUBENHEIM

Laubenheim, again on the river, has loamy slopes similar to those in Langenlonsheim; none of outstanding reputation.

Vineyards
Großlage Schloßkapelle with *Einzellagen:* Karthäuser, 27ha, SE-S, 20% steep. St. Remigiusberg, 5.2ha, S-SE, 60% steep. Krone, 26ha, S-SE, 5% steep.

DORSHEIM

Dorsheim lies immediately west of Laubenheim, facing the community of Burg Layen and the Rümmelsheim across a little valley. Its best sites lie on the Burg Layen side, stonier and steeper than Laubenheim, with a high proportion of Riesling of real style. Goldloch and Pittermännchen are the best slopes.

Vineyards
Großlage Schloßkapelle with *Einzellagen:* Burgberg, 6ha, S-SE, 100% steep. Honigberg, 15ha, S, 10% sloping. Goldloch, 15ha, S, 95% steep. Pittermännchen, 8ha, S, 100% steep. Trollberg, 15ha, SW-S, 80% steep. Klosterpfad, 65ha, SE-S, 80% sloping.

BURG LAYEN AND RÜMMELSHEIM

Burg Layen and Rümmelsheim are effectively one village, with vineyard conditions similar to Dorsheim, reaching their best, for notable Silvaner and Müller-Thurgau as well as Riesling, in the Schloßberg, Hölle and Steinköpfchen Einzellagen.

Vineyards
Großlage Schloßkapelle with *Einzellagen:* Steinköpfchen, 15.7ha, S, 70% steep. Schloßberg, 20.9ha, S, 30% steep. Hölle, 27.8ha, S, 20% steep. Rothenberg, 68.9ha, S, 40% sloping. Johannisberg, 66.8ha, S, 70% steep.

MÜNSTER SARMSHEIM

Münster Sarmsheim brings the Nahe vineyards to an end just before Bingen, with slopes angled southeast away from the river. The Nahe State Domain has demonstrated that these gentle inclines of stony loam are capable of ripening magnificent Riesling, more full-bodied and robust than their beautiful wines from Schloßböckelheim and Niederhausen. Dautenpflänzer is the best of the Einzellagen.

Vineyards
Großlage Schloßkapelle with *Einzellagen:* Kapellenberg, 38ha, SE-S, 50% steep. Dautenpflänzer, 6ha, S, 100% sloping. Pittersberg, 12ha, SW-S, 100% sloping. Königsschloß, 100ha, S-SE, 50% sloping. Steinkopf, 12ha, SW-S, 70% steep.

A number of villages west of the river contribute worthy wines to the Nahe contingent. Weinsheim, Sponheim, Roxheim, Wallhausen, Dalberg and Guldental all have above-average sites. These wines come into the Großlagen Pfarrgarten and Rosengarten, which respectively cover the side-valleys of the Gräfenbach and Ellerbach streams.

PRODUCERS

Weingut Ökonomierat August E. Anheuser

Brückes 53, 6550 Bad Kreuznach, tel: 0671-2077. *Owner:* August E. Anheuser. 52 hectares. *Einzellagen:* Kreuznach: Brückes, Hinkelstein, Hofgarten, Kahlenberg, Krötenpfuhl, Mönchberg, St. Martin, Narrenkappe, Steinberg (solely owned); Winzenheim: Rosenheck; Norheim: Kafels and Dellchen; Niederhausen: Hermannshöhle; Schloßböckelheim: Königsfels.

The Anheuser family dominates the best sections of the Kreuznacher vineyards, with roots going back to the 17th century. This company (founded 1869) also owns Anheuser and Fehrs, who are merchants, not growers. Vines are 74% Riesling and 13% Müller-Thurgau, the rest being Scheurebe, Ruländer, Silvaner and Weißburgunder. The heroic rock-cut cellars are a treasure house of old vintages. The Anheuser family is also famous in American brewing for Anheuser-Busch and Budweiser beers.

Weingut Paul Anheuser

Strombergerstraße 15–19, 6550 Bad Kreuznach, tel: 0671-28748. *Owners:* Peter and Dorothee Anheuser. The present estate consists of 76 hectares. *Einzellagen:* Kreuznach: Brückes, Forst, Hinkelstein (7ha), Kahlenberg, Kapellenpfad, Krötenpfuhl (4.5), Mönchberg, Mollenbrunnen, Narrenkappe (4), Osterhöll, St. Martin (6) and Tilgesbrunnen; Schloßböckelheim: Felsenberg, Heimberg, In den Felsen (6.5), Königsfels (10) and Mühlberg; Niederhausen: Felsensteyer (3.5) and Pfingstweide (4); Altenbamberg: Kehrenberg, Rotenberg, Schloßberg; Norheim: Dellchen and Kafels; Roxheim: Berg and Höllenpfad; Monzingen: Halenberg

This house has the same origins as the previous entry, but in 1888 became a separate estate under Rudolf Anheuser, who was the first to introduce the Riesling to the Nahe. The name Rudolf still appears on some labels, adding to the general confusion. 70% is Riesling, 7% each Müller-Thurgau, Ruländer, Kerner and 2% Weißburgunder (with some others, but not Silvaner). The speciality of the house is Riesling Kabinett halbtrocken with the singular Nahe character.

Weinkellereien Anheuser & Fehrs

Brückes 41, 6550 Bad Kreuznach, tel: 0671-2077. Wine merchants (*see* August Anheuser).

Weingut Hans Crusius & Sohn

Hauptstraße 2, 6551 Traisen, tel: 0671-33953. *Owners:* Hans and Dr. Peter Crusius. *Einzellagen:* Traisen: Bastei (0.5), Rotenfels (5), Kickelskopf (0.2), Nonnengarten (3.4); Norheim: Kirchheck (0.2), Klosterberg (0.5); Schloßböckelheim: Felsenberg (1.5).

Hans Crusius of Traisen in the middle Nahe is the type of German grower who quietly achieves perfection, without apparent ambition to do more than till the land that his family has owned since the 16th century.

The Crusius property is 11.5 hectares, 5 of them in the Einzellage Traiser Rotenfels, with small parcels in Norheim, Niederhäuser Rosen-berg, Schloßböckelheimer Felsenberg and a precious half hectare in the sandstone suntrap of Traiser Bastei. 72% is Riesling, 12.5% Müller-Thurgau, 7.5% Weißburgunder, 5% Kerner and 3% Spätburgunder.

Hans and his son Peter work in their traditional vaulted cask-cellar to produce wines of extraordinary quality and character, to my taste among the best in Germany. Each vineyard has its own character. They ascribe the remarkable delicacy of their Felsenberg and Rosenberg to the rare "melaphyr" soil. Bastei is pungent; the steep Norheimer Kirschheck powerfully scented. Rotenfels is more scattered and variable – yet always firm with a racy clarity of flavour that is never neutral.

Schloßgut Diel auf Burg Layen

6531 Burg Layen, tel: 06721-45045. *Owners:* Dr. Ingo Diel and Armin Diel. 10 hectares. *Einzellagen:* Rümmelsheim (Ortsteil Burg Layen): Schloßberg, Rothenberg and Hölle; Dorsheim: Goldloch, Honigberg, Pittermännchen and Klosterpfad.

The Diel family has farmed the manor surrounding the ruins of Burg Layen castle for 200 years. Radical changes have recently been made: previously an enthusiast for new varieties and unusual wines, Dr. Diel is now digging up his new crossings, has increased his Riesling to 45% and is maturing some of his wines in new oak. The barrique wines are sold as Tafelwein, although they come from Spätlese musts. All the wines are now trocken, except for the Beerenauslesen and Eiswein. He is not interested in expanding the 5% exported, as his wines are easily sold on the home market. The range is well made as well as wide: Dorsheimer Auslesen can be splendid.

Weingut Carl Finkenauer

Salinenstraße 60, 6550 Bad Kreuznach, tel: 0671-28771. *Owner:* Frau Lisl Finkenauer-Trummert. 33 hectares. *Einzellagen:* Kreuznach: Brückes, St. Martin, Gutental, Narrenkappe; Winzenheim: Rosenheck; Roxheim: Mühlenberg.

The sixth generation of the family runs this estate in the attractive spa area of Bad Kreuznach. 50% is Riesling, 14.5% Müller-Thurgau, 10.5% Silvaner, 7.5% Scheurebe, 5.5% Spätburgunder and 12% others (Kerner, Ruländer, Weißburgunder and Dornfelder). Good tasty and vigorous Nahe wines, particularly in the dry range – even extending to an unusual dry Auslese.

Kirschheck 82
Höllenpfad 83
Hasensprung 84
Pastorenberg 85
Backöfchen 86
Sonnenweg 87
Laurentiusberg 88

Sommerloch
Birkenberg 89
Steinrossel 90
Sonnenberg 91
Ratsgrund 92

Gutenberg
St. Ruppertsberg 93
Römerberg 94
Schloßberg 95
Schloß Gutenburg 96
Sonnenlauf 97
Felseneck 98

**GROSSLAGE
KRONENBERG**

Bad Kreuznach
Galgenberg 100 P
Tilgesbrunnen 101
Rosenberg 102
Kauzenberg-
    Oranienberg 103
Kauzenberg-
    Rosenhügel 104
Kauzenberg in den
    Mauern 105
Osterhöll 106
Hofgarten 107
Kahlenberg 108
Mollenbrunnen 110
Hinkelstein 111
Forst 112
Vogelsang 113
Kapellenpfad 115
Krötenpfuhl 116
Brückes 117
St. Martin 118
Gutental 120
Mönchberg 121
Narrenkappe 122
Steinberg 123
Hungriger Wolf 124

**– Ortsteil
Winzenheim**
In den siebzehn
    Morgen 125
Honigberg 126
Berg 127
Rosenheck 128

**– Ortsteil
Bosenheim**
Höllenbrand 99 P
Galgenberg 100 P
Hirtenhain 133
Paradies 135

– Ortsteil Ippesheim
Himmelgarten 129
Junker 130

– Ortsteil Planig
Höllenbrand 99 P
Römerhalde 131
Katzenhölle 132
Nonnengarten 134

Bretzenheim
Felsenköpfchen 137
Vogelsang 138
Hofgut 139
Pastorei 140
Schloßgarten 141

Hargesheim
Straußberg 142
Mollenbrunnen 143

**BEREICH
SCHLOSS
BÖCKELHEIM**

**GROSSLAGE
ROSENGARTEN**

Braunweiler
Michaeliskapelle 144
Wetterkreuz 145
Hellenpfad 146
Schloßberg 147

St. Katharinen
Fels 148
Klostergarten 149
Steinkreuz 150

Mandel
Alte Römerstraße 151
Schloßberg 152
Delichen 153
Palmengarten 154
Becherbrunnen 155

Roxheim
Berg 156
Hüttenberg 157
Sonnenberg 158
Höllenpfad 159
Mühlenberg 160
Birkenberg 161

Rüdesheim
Wiesberg 162
Goldgrube 163

Weinsheim
Katergrube 165
Kellerberg 166
Steinkaut 167

Sponheim
Mühlberg 168
Abtei 169
Grafenberg 170
Klostergarten 171
Schloßberg 172 P

Burgsponheim
Schloßberg 172 P
Höllenpfad 173
Pfaffenberg 174

Bockenau
Geisberg 175
Stromberg 176
Im Neuberg 177
Im Felseneck 178

Hüffelsheim
Mönchberg 179
Steyer 180
Gutenhölle 181

**GROSSLAGE
PARADIES-
GARTEN**

Auen
Kaulenberg 182
Römerstich 183

Martinstein
Schloßberg 184

Weller/Monzingen
Herrenzehntel 185
Heiligenberg 186

Merxheim
Vogelsang 187
Römerberg 188
Hunolsteiner 189

Monzingen
Frühlingsplätzchen
    190
Rosenberg 191
Halenberg 192

Nußbaum
Sonnenberg 193
Höllenberg 194
Rotfeld 195

Kirschroth
Wildgrafenberg 196
Lump 197

Meddersheim
Liebfrauenberg 198
Rheingrafenberg 199
Präsent 200
Altenberg 201
Edelberg 202

Lauschied
Edelberg 203

Sobernheim
Marbach 204
Domberg 205

**Sobernheim
Ortsteil Steinhard**
Spitalberg 206
Johannesberg 207 P

Waldböckelheim
Johannesberg 207 P
Kastell 208 P

Oberstreit
Auf dem Zimmerberg
    209

Boos
Kastell 208 P
Herrenberg 210 P

Staudernheim
Herrenberg 210 P
Goldgrube 211

Odernheim am Glan
Kloster Disi-
    bodenberg 212
Heßweg 213
Montfort 214
Weinsack 215
Kapellenberg 216
Langenberg 216 a

Rehborn
Herrenberg 217
Schikanenbuckel 218
Hahn 219

Raumbach/Glan
Schwalbennest 220
Schloßberg 221
Allenberg 222

Desloch
Vor der Hölle 223
Hengstberg 224

Meisenheim
Obere Heimbach 225

Lettweiler
Rheingasse 226
Inkelhöll 227

Unkenbach
Würzhölle 228
Römerpfad 229

Obermoschel
Sonnenplätzchen 230
Schloßberg 231
Langhölle 232
Geißenkopf 233 P
Silberberg 234 P

Niedermoschel
Geißenkopf 233 P
Silberberg 234 P
Hahnhölle 235
Layenberg 236

Feilbingert
Feuerberg 237
Königsgarten 238
Bocksberg 239
Kahlenberg 240
Höchstes Kreuz 241

Hochstätten
Liebesbrunnen 242

Kalkofen
Graukatz 243

Alsenz
Elkersberg 244
Pfaffenpfad 245
Falkenberg 246
Hölle 247

Oberndorf
Weißenstein 248
Feuersteinrossel 249
Aspenberg 250
Beutelstein 251

Mannweiler-Cölln
Weißenstein 248 a
Schloß Randeck 252
Seidenbach 253
Rosenberg 254

**Bayerfeld-
Steckweiler**
Adelsberg 255
Schloß Stolzenberg
    256
Aspenberg 257
Mittelberg 258

Gaugrehweiler
Graukatz 259

Oberhausen/Appel
Graukatz 259 a

Münsterappel
Graukatz 259 b

Niederhausen/Appel
Graukatz 259 c

Winterborn
Graukatz 260

**GROSSLAGE
BURGWEG**

Altenbamberg
Laurentiusberg 261
Treuenfels 262
Kehrenberg 263
Schloßberg 264
Rotenberg 265

**Bad Münster am
Stein-Ebernburg
Ortsteil Ebernburg**
Schloßberg 266
Erzgrube 267
Köhler-Köpfchen 268
Stephansberg 269
Feuerberg 270
Luisengarten 271
Götzenfels 272
Königsgarten 273

**– Ortsteil
Münster am Stein**
Steigerdell 274
Höll 275

**Rotenfelser im
    Winkel 276**
Felseneck 277

Traisen
Bastei 278
Kickelskopf 279
Rotenfels 280
Nonnengarten 281

Norheim
Götzenfels 282
Sonnenberg 283
Onkelchen 284
Oberberg 285
Kirschheck 286
Dellchen 287
Klosterberg 288
Kafels 289

Niederhausen/Nahe
Pfingstweide 290
Felsensteyer 291
Rosenberg 292
Rosenheck 293
Pfaffenstein 294
Steinwingert 295
Stollenberg 296
Kertz 297
Klamm 298

Hermannshöhle 299
Hermannsberg 300
Steinberg 301

Schloßböckelheim
Kupfergrube 302
Felsenberg 303
Mühlberg 304
In den Felsen 305
Heimberg 306
Königsfels 307 P

Waldböckelheim
Königsfels 307 P
Mühlberg 308
Muckerhölle 309
Kirchberg 310
Romerberg 311
Hamm 312
Kronenfels 313
Drachenbrunnen 314
Marienpforter
    Klosterberg 315

Weiler
186
184
185
Martinstein
Merxheim
187
188
189
196
Kirschroth

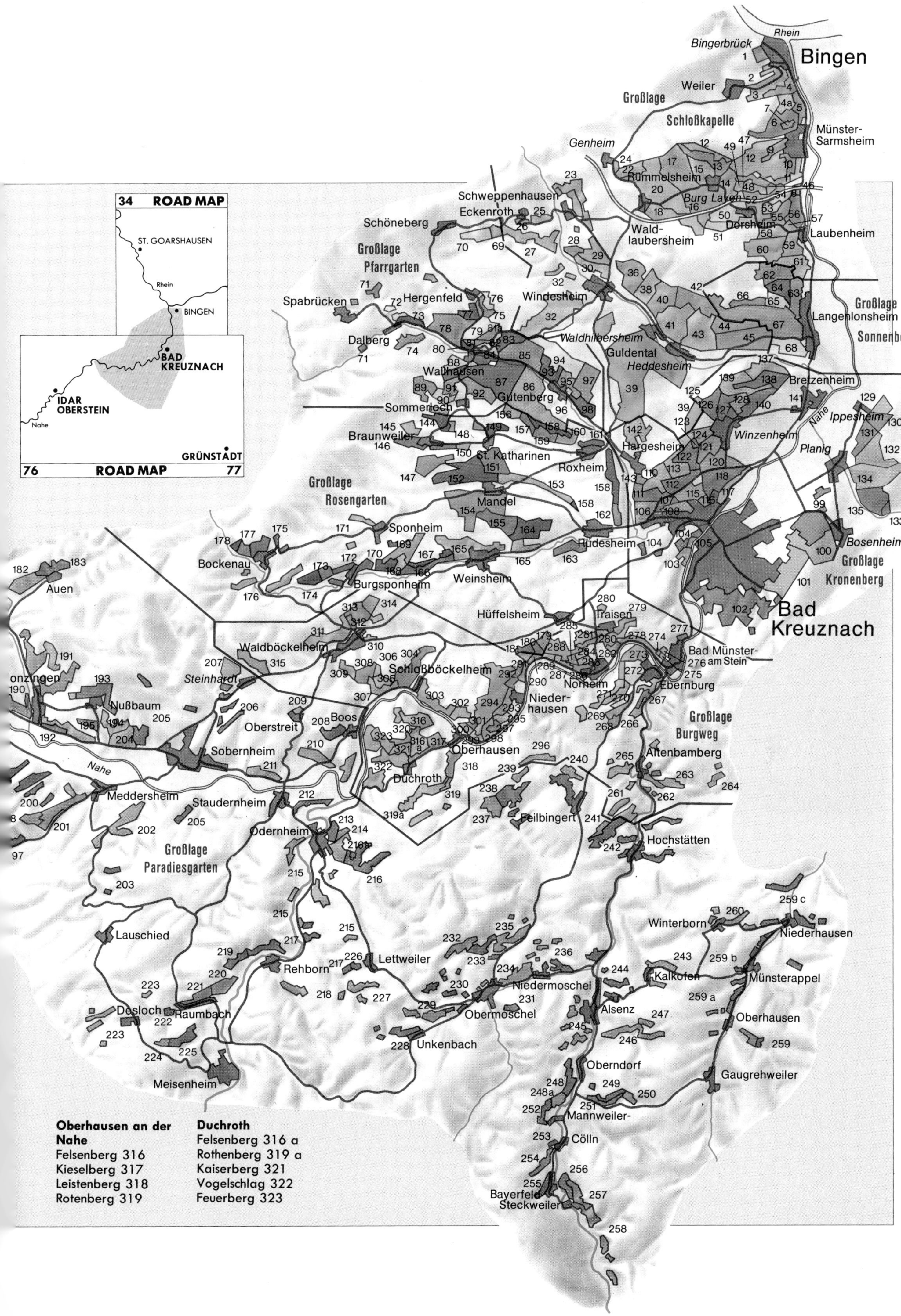

Rhein

Bingerbrück

Bingen

Weiler

Großlage
Schloßkapelle

Genheim

Münster-
Sarmsheim

Rümmelsheim

Burg Layen

Dorsheim

Laubenheim

Schweppenhausen
Eckenroth

Schöneberg

Waldlaubersheim

Großlage
Pfarrgarten

Spabrücken

Hergenfeld

Windesheim

Großlage
Langenlonsheim
Sonnenborn

Dalberg

Waldhilbersheim

Guldental
Heddesheim

Bretzenheim

Wallhausen

Gutenberg

Ippesheim

Planig

Winzenheim

Sommerloch

Braunweiler

St. Katharinen

Roxheim

Hargesheim

Bosenheim

Großlage
Kronenberg

Mandel

Rüdesheim

Bad
Kreuznach

Großlage
Rosengarten

Sponheim

Bockenau

Weinsheim

Auen

Burgsponheim

Hüffelsheim

Traisen

Waldböckelheim

Steinhardt

Schloßböckelheim

Bad Münster-
am Stein

Ebernburg

Großlage
Burgweg

Nußbaum

Oberstreit

Boos

Niederhausen

Altenbamberg

Sobernheim

Duchroth

Oberhausen

Meddersheim

Staudernheim

Feilbingert

Hochstätten

Odernheim

Großlage
Paradiesgarten

Lauschied

Winterborn

Niederhausen

Lettweiler

Kalkofen

Münsterappel

Rehborn

Oberhausen

Desloch

Raumbach

Niedermoschel

Alsenz

Obermoschel

Unkenbach

Oberndorf

Gaugrehweiler

Meisenheim

Mannweiler-
Cölln

Bayerfeld
Steckweiler

Oberhausen an der Nahe
Felsenberg 316
Kieselberg 317
Leistenberg 318
Rotenberg 319

Duchroth
Felsenberg 316 a
Rothenberg 319 a
Kaiserberg 321
Vogelschlag 322
Feuerberg 323

34 ROAD MAP
ST. GOARSHAUSEN
Rhein
BINGEN
BAD KREUZNACH
IDAR OBERSTEIN
Nahe
GRÜNSTADT
76 ROAD MAP 77

RHEINHESSEN

Not even the local tourist board rates the Rheinhessen as the place for an exciting holiday. "Restful" is their favourite adjective. This is farm country, vineyards as far as the eye can see, dotted with unspectacular villages.

Places to visit
Mainz, the capital, is one of the great cities of Germany, and the cathedral and Gutenberg museum – printing began here – are well worth seeing. Nierstein and Oppenheim, twin centres of the Rheinterrasse district, are rewarding places to taste wine and visit cellars. Bingen, in the far northwest of the region, is at the mouth of the Rhine gorge and a stopping-place for river steamers. The Rheingau is paradoxically best seen from the Rheinhessen bank between Bingen and Mainz. The Hessische Schweiz is a wooded, hilly region to the west of the wine districts, with the usual amenities of forest paths and inns. Worms, apart from the vineyard which gave birth to Liebfraumilch, is an ancient city with a fine cathedral.

Wine tasting
In Mainz-Mombach the Rheinhessen wine office (address on p25) has a tasting cellar which offers many Rheinhessen wines (open by prior arrangement only). Worms has a similar cellar at Neumarkt 14 (tel: 06241-25045). Tastings, with a winegrower's supper, can be organized for groups of 10 or more in the Schloß at Alzey (tel: 06731-2061).

Wine seminars and trails
In Mainz, wine weekends; in Oppenheim, daily seminars in

◀ The Rheinterrasse at Nierstein, looking south to the north-flowing Rhine. Nierstein hides behind the ridge of its best site, the Großlage Rehbach.
▶ Modern stained glass in Heinrich Seip's cellars captures an ageless vintage scene.

Anonymity behind the *nom de verre* of Liebfraumilch is the fate of much Rheinhessen wine. The heart of the winegrowing Rhineland specializes in soft, sufficiently flowery Müller-Thurgau, blunt, often rather mild Silvaner, and (increasing rapidly) the aromatic new varieties that offer the thrills of flowery bouquet with the chance of a better balance (and a better crop) than the Müller-Thurgau. Only six per cent of its 24,000-odd hectares is planted with Riesling, concentrated in its few outstanding sites. Of these by far the most important is the "Rheinterrasse", the riverside communities from Mettenheim to Bodenheim, with Nierstein as their centre.

Frank Schoonmaker points out in his classic book *The Wines of Germany* that of the 160-odd villages producing wine in Rheinhessen no less than 120 have names ending in "heim" – home. They are scarcely a rarity anywhere in Germany, but this stress on domesticity seems especially fitting for Rheinhessen, an area of bland, fertile farmland. The Rhine curls protectingly around its eastern and northern boundaries; the Nahe guards its western limits. The cities of Worms (in the south), Mainz, Bingen and Kreuznach mark its corners.

Nierstein is the wine capital of Rheinhessen; its most famous name both for quality and quantity. Unfortunately the wine-laws

completely obscure the fact that the two aspects of Nierstein are unrelated: high-quality Niersteiner is a scarce commodity, produced only in the narrow strip of vineyards fronting the Rhine, whereas the famous name is available, either as a Bereich name or attached to its notorious Großlage Gutes Domtal, to almost one-third of the total production of Rheinhessen.

Indeed, Rheinhessen is divided into only three Bereiche: Nierstein for the eastern and south-central part, Bingen for the western and north-central, and the less important Wonnegau for the so-called "happy-land" around Worms.

Traditional regional divisions are more specific. They distinguish the Bingen area, which grows some good Riesling, from the Ingelheim area to the west, whose tradition is for light red Spätburgunder. It was at Ingelheim that Charlemagne had a manor, from which legend says he looked north across the Rhine in winter and noticed how the snow thawed first on the slope he caused to be planted as the Johannisberg. The western villages neighbouring the Nahe, close to Bad Kreuznach, are locally known as the Rheinhessen Switzerland: a hilly corner producing fruity light wines. The river-villages north and south of Nierstein are the Rheinterrasse: the aristocrats of the Rheinhessen with the region's only world-class wine. The important central district

September; in Ingelheim, a "Wein-Kolleg". Details from the state's tourist board (Postfach 1420, D-5400 Koblenz). Vineyard trails in Bingen, Flonheim, Alsheim and elsewhere.

Wine festivals
Gau-Odernheim (last w/e in May), Alsheim (2nd w/e in June), Nackenheim (last w/e in July or 1st in Aug), Nierstein (1st w/e in Aug), Oppenheim (2nd w/e in Aug), Guntersblum (2nd to last w/e in Aug), Worms fried fish festival (last w/e in Aug), Bingen (1st to 2nd w/e in Sept), Alzey (3rd w/e in Sept), Ingelheim red wine festival (last w/e in Sept and 1st in Oct).

Food and drink
The nearby Rheingau may have grander – and older – hotels, but the Rheinhessen has plenty of small restaurants and inns, serving country specialities such as potato soup and dumplings, asparagus, ham – and plenty of wine. One local dish is simply described in dialect: "Weck, Worscht, Woi" – meaning bread roll, sausage and wine. More sophisticated pleasures are offered by the hotels and restaurants of Mainz and the Frankfurt conurbation, just across the river and a world away.

▶ The heraldic carving of massive oak barrel-heads is still a living art-form. German barrels, unlike those of Bordeaux and Burgundy, are permanent fixtures in the cellar.

round Alzey is called the Hügelland, the hill country: cooperatives here make some very pleasant fresh and balanced wines. The Wonnegau and the region of Worms in the south are on balance the least interesting with the weightiest, least inspiring wines.

Throughout Rheinhessen the units of small-holding are very small, and most of the wine is made by cooperatives. A few, such as Weinheim and Armsheim, have made international reputations. By the nature of the cooperative system, however, it tends to be the Großlage name if any that comes to prominence. Discouragingly, such wines sell better in the anonymous blend of a Liebfraumilch, so there is little incentive to concentrate on quality and build even a Großlage name into a matter for local pride.

Müller-Thurgau is the most popular grape variety, with over 6,200 out of a total of 24,000 hectares; but not by an overwhelming margin. Silvaner comes second with nearly 3,400 hectares. But more strikingly, perhaps, six of the "new" varieties between them account for over 8,000 hectares. This, more even than Rheinpfalz, is the land of the Scheurebe, Bacchus, Faberrebe, Kerner, Morio-Muskat and Huxelrebe. These aromatic grapes make up a large proportion of the Bereich Nierstein wines, but they are not allowed in Liebfraumilch.

LIEBFRAUMILCH

The official definition of a Liebfraumilch is a wine "of pleasant character" and medium sweetness (technically more than 18 grams per litre of sugar, the upper limit of "halbtrocken" wines). It must be made predominantly from Riesling, Müller-Thurgau, Silvaner and/or Kerner and must have the essential fruit flavour of one or more of these grapes (although it may not bear a grape name). It must be white, of QbA quality, and be grown in the Rheinhessen, or the Rheinpfalz. It can come from the Nahe and even the Rheingau, but this is rare.

In practice Liebfraumilchs range in quality from the skilfully-blended, utterly reliable famous international brands to some very dubious, flat-tasting, scarcely palatable wines at half the price. By definition no Liebfraumilch is a wine of individuality. The vast amount sold is depressing witness to the sheepishness of the Anglo-Saxons when confronted with a choice between an individual and a mass-produced product. Safety first is a motto that has nothing to do with wine.

Needless to say, Liebfraumilch is almost unknown to the German consumer.

VINEYARDS

Büdesheim
Dietersheim

Sponshei
Großla
Grolsheir

St. Rochuskapell

Gensing

**BEREICH
BINGEN**

**GROSSLAGE
SANKT
ROCHUSKAPELLE**

**Bingen
Ortsteil Kempten**
Schloßberg-
 Schwätzerchen 1 P
Kirchberg 2
Kapellenberg 3
Pfarrgarten 4 P

– Ortsteil Gaulsheim
Pfarrgarten 4 P

**– Ortsteil
Büdesheim**
Schloßberg-
 Schwärtzerchen
 1 P
Bubenstück 5
Osterberg 6
Rosengarten 7
Scharlachberg 8
Schelmenstück 9 P
Schwarzenberg 10

**– Ortsteil
Dietersheim**
Schelmenstück 9 P

**– Ortsteil
Sponsheim**
Palmenstein 11

Grolsheim
Ölberg 12

Gensingen
Goldberg 13

Horrweiler
Goldberg 13 a
Gewürzgärtchen 14

Welgesheim
Kirchgärtchen 15

Biebelsheim
Honigberg 16
Kieselberg 17

**Pfaffen-
Schwabenheim**
Hölle 18
Mandelbaum 19
Sonnenberg 20

Zotzenheim
Johannisberg 21
Klostergarten 22

Badenheim
Galgenberg 23
Römerberg 24

Aspisheim
Johannisberg 25
Sonnenberg 26

**Bingen
Ortsteil Dromersheim**
Honigberg 27
Klosterweg 29
Mainzerweg 30

Ockenheim
Laberstall 31
Hockenmühle 32
St. Jakobsberg 33
Klosterweg 34
Kreuz 35
Schönhölle 36

**GROSSLAGE
ABTEY**

Gau-Algesheim
Steinert 37
Johannisberg 38
Goldberg 39
Rothenberg 40

**– Ortsteil
Laurenziberg**
St. Laurenzikapelle
 41

Appenheim
Daubhaus 42
Hundertgulden 43
Eselspfad 44
Drosselborn 45

Nieder-Hilbersheim
Honigberg 46
Steinacker 47
Mönchspforte 48 P

Ober-Hilbersheim
Mönchspforte 48 P

Sprendlingen
Klostergarten 49
Honigberg 50
Hölle 51
Sonnenberg 52
Wißberg 53

Sankt Johann
Klostergarten 54
Steinberg 55
Geyersberg 56

Wolfsheim
Götzenborn 57
Osterberg 58
Sankt Kathrin 59

Partenheim
Sankt Georgen 60
Steinberg 61

**GROSSLAGE
RHEINGRAFEN-
STEIN**

Pleitersheim
Sternberg 62

Volxheim
Mönchberg 63
Alte Römerstraße
 64 P
Liebfrau 65

Hackenheim
Klostergarten 66
Sonnenberg 67
Galgenberg 68
Gewürzgarten 69
Kirchberg 70

Freilaubersheim
Alte Römerstraße
 64 P
Kirchberg 70 a
Fels 71
Rheingrafenberg 72
Reichskeller 73

Tiefenthal
Graukatz 74

Fürfeld
Kapellenberg 75
Eichelberg 76
Steige 77

Stein-Bockenheim
Sonnenberg 78

Wonsheim
Sonnenberg 78 a
Hölle 79
Martinsberg 85 P

Neu-Bamberg
Eichelberg 76 a
Kletterberg 80
Kirschwingert 81
Heerkretz 82

Siefersheim
Heerkretz 82 a
Goldenes Horn 83
Höllberg 84
Martinsberg 85 P

Wöllstein
Haarberg-
 Katzensteg 86
Ölberg 87
Äffchen 88
Hölle 89

Eckelsheim
Kirchberg 90
Eselstreiber 91
Sonnenköpfchen 92

**GROSSLAGE
ADELBERG**

Neider-Wiesen
Wingertsberg 93

Nack
Ahrenberg 94

Wendelsheim
Heiligenpfad 95
Steigerberg 96

Flonheim
Bingerberg 98 P
Rotenpfad 100
Klostergarten 101
Geisterberg 102 P

– Ortsteil Uffhofen
Pfaffenberg 97
Bingerberg 98 P
La Roche 99
Geisterberg 102 P

Erbes-Büdesheim
Bingerberg 98 P
Geisterberg 102 P
Vogelsang 103

Bornheim
Hähnchen 104
Hütte-Terrassen 105
Kirchenstück 106
Schönberg 107 P

Lonsheim
Schönberg 107 P
Mandelberg 108

**Bermersheim
v. d. H.**
Klostergarten 109
Hildegardisberg 110

Armsheim
Goldstückchen 111
Geiersberg 112

**– Ortsteil
Schimsheim**
Leckerberg 113

Ensheim
Kachelberg 114 a

Wörrstadt
Rheingrafenberg 115

**– Ortsteil
Rommersheim**
Kachelberg 114

Sulzheim
Greifenberg 116
Honigberg 117
Schildberg 118

**GROSSLAGE
KURFÜRSTEN-
STÜCK**

Gumbsheim
Schloßhölle 119 P

Gau-Bickelheim
Bockshaut 120 P
Saukopf 121
Kapelle 122

Wallertheim
Vogelsang 123
Heil 124

Wöllstein
Schloßhölle 119 P
Bockshaut 120 P

Gau-Weinheim
Wißberg 125
Kaisergarten 126
Geyersberg 127

Vendersheim
Sonnenberg 128
Goldberg 129

**GROSSLAGE
KAISERPFALZ**

Jugenheim
St. Georgenberg
 130
Goldberg 131
Hasensprung 132
Heiligenhäuschen
 133

Engelstadt
Adelpfad 134
Römerberg 135

Bubenheim
Kallenberg 136
Honigberg 137

Schwabenheim
Sonnenberg 138
Schloßberg 139 a
Klostergarten 140

Ingelheim
Schloß Westerhaus
 144 P

**– Ortsteil Groß-
Winternheim**
Schloßberg 139
Klosterbruder 141
Bockstein 142
Heilighäuschen 143
Schloß Westerhaus
 144 P
Sonnenhang 145
Rheinhöhe 146
Sonnenberg 147
Burgberg 148
Kirchenstück 149

Bad
Kreuznac

67

68
Hackenheim 70
69 71
Frei- 72
Laubersheim
73 Bamb

Großlage
Rheingrafenstein
77 76

Fürfeld 7

75 74
Tiefentha

Rhein

Kempten
Gaulsheim

Heidesheim

162
160
155
154
152
157
156
158
161
159

Mainz

Ingelheim
Gau-Algesheim
146
147
151 150
149
148
153

157a Wackernheim

163

Hechtsheim

164
165

Laubenheim

166

Großlage
St. Alban

170
173
171
174
172

Bodenheim

Ober-Olm
Klein-Winternheim
190
193
192
191

179
181
184
183 182
176 175
180
177

Nackenheim

Großlage
Kaiserpfalz
142

Groß-Winternheim
145
143
144
139
141
140

Schwabenheim
138
197

Essenheim
194
196
195
198
194

Ebersheim

186
185
167
169
168
187

Gau-Bischofsheim
188
189
220

244 245

Ockenheim
35
37
39
38 39
36
40
41
42
44
45
43
46
137
136
134

Stadecken-Elsheim
199

Nieder-Olm
216
217
218
Zornheim
241
243
289 234a
242
238 240
237
236a 236 235
234
233

Harxheim
Lörzweiler
219
Spiegel
249
Mommenheim
248
250

246
247
268
259
261 262
260
263
255

Großlage Rehbach
257

Großlage
Auflangen
Nierstein
269 272
279

Laurenziberg
31
30
29
28
Dromersheim
27
26
25
Nieder-Hilbersheim
47
135
133
132
131
130

Engelstadt
Jugenheim
Großlage
Domherr

Sörgenloch
205
Saulheim

208
Hahnheim

Selzen
232
221

Schwabsburg
251
252
253
254
280

282
270
271
274
281
273
275
Dienheim

Horrweiler
13a
14
15
Welgesheim
21
49
23
50
55
Großlage
Abtey
59
56
Wolfsheim
60
Partenheim
202
203
201
Domherr
204
206
207
Udenheim
209
210
Schornsheim
211
Königernheim
231
225a
228
225
Friesenheim
222
223
224
Dalheim
301
285
300
299
286
284
Oppenheim
268
277
276
280
283
302
303
304
305
306
307
Großlage
Guldenmorgen
Ludwigshöhe
Großlage
Vogelsgärten
Guntersblum
288

Biebelsheim
16
17
Zotzenheim
St. Johann
54
57
58
Vendersheim
124
128
129
118
117
Sulzheim
116
Wörrstadt
212
213
214
215
Gabsheim
230
Undenheim
228
227
Weinolsheim
226
Uelversheim
296
295
Dolgesheim
298
297
Eimsheim
Krötenbrunnen
292
294
330
327
Wintersheim
331

Pfaffen-
Schwabenheim
18
19
20
52
Sprendlingen
53
122
121
Gau-Weinheim
127
126
125
123
Wallertheim
Rommersheim
114
113
112
Spießheim
326
324
325
Ensheim
308
309
310
311
312
Bechtolsheim
Biebelnheim
313
293
Gau-Odernheim
Hillesheim
Dorn-Dürkheim
332
Gau-Königernheim
316
314
372
373
Frettenheim
329
328
334
Großlage
Rheinblick
333
390
Mettenheim
Alsheim
290
291
Krötenbrunnen
Eich

Pleitersheim
Badenheim
24
Gau-Bickelheim
Großlage
Kurfürstenstück
120
119
Wokstein
Gumbsheim
92
Armsheim
111
114a
Großlage
Adelberg
106
Bornheim
110
Lonsheim
108
109
107
105
Bermersheim
322
323
315
Albig
321
317
316
Framersheim
318
Gau-Heppenheim
374
375
Dittelsheim
Hebloch
377
378
379
380
381
382
Bechtheim
383
389
391
Großlage
Pilgerpfad
384
385
387
386
388
Großlage
Gottesilfe
392
Osthofen
393
393a
394

Volxheim
65
63
88
89
Siefersheim
86
87
84
82
83
82a
85
Eckelsheim
98
Flonheim
Wonsheim
78a
Uffhofen
97
96
99
100
101
104
102
103
Wendelsheim
345
Heimersheim
348
Schafhausen
347
Alzey
320
319
Dautenheim
351
350
352
Wahlheim
Esselborn
Dintesheim
354
357
Freimersheim
353
355
356
Monzernheim
358
Hangen-Weisheim
370
369
368
367
366
365
Großlage
Bergkloster
359
Westhofen
371
364
363
362
Abenheim
415
412
416
417
418
419
Großlage
Liebfrauenmorgen
Herrnsheim

Stein-Bockenheim
95
78
Nack
341
342
343
344
338
340
Weinheim
Bechenheim
337
93
Nieder-Wiesen
339
Offenheim
Mauchenheim
Großlage
Sybillenstein
Flomborn
Ober-Flörsheim
395
396
Gundersheim
360
398
397
399
400
Bermersheim
361
Gundheim
405
Mörstadt
424
423
425
428
Leiselheim
429
420
421
Hochheim

ROAD MAP 34 35
ST. GOARSHAUSEN
Rhein
WIESBADEN
MAINZ
BINGEN
Nahe
Rhein
WORMS
FRANKENTHAL
ROAD MAP 77 78

Großlage
Burg Rodenstein
Flörsheim-Dalsheim
401
402
400
Mölsheim
406
407
403
404
400
426
410
427
Wachenheim
408
407a
409
Monsheim
407a
Kriegsheim
Pfeddersheim
Pfiffligheim
Worms

Hohen-Sülzen
412
Großlage
Domblick
411
Offstein
414
413
Heppenheim
433
Wies-
Oppenheim
432
431
Weinsheim
434
430
422

Täuscherspfad 150
Horn 151
Pares 152
Steinacker 153
Höllenweg 154
Rotes Kreuz 155
Lottenstück 156
Rabenkopf 157

Wackernheim
Rabenkopf 157 a
Schwalben 158
Steinberg 159

Heidesheim
Geißberg 160
Steinacker 161
Höllenberg 162

**BEREICH
NIERSTEIN**

**GROSSLAGE
SANKT ALBAN**

**Mainz
Ortsteil
Hechtsheim**
Kirchenstück 163

**– Ortsteil
Laubenheim**
Johannisberg 164
Edelmann 165
Klosterberg 166

– Ortsteil Ebersheim
Sand 167
Hüttberg 168
Weinkeller 169

Bodenheim
Mönchspfad 170
Burgweg 171
Ebersberg 172
Heitersbrünnchen 173
Reichsritterstift 174
Westrum 175
Hoch 176
Kapelle 177
Leidhecke 178
Silberberg 179
Kreuzberg 180

Gau-Bischofsheim
Glockenberg 181
Pfaffenweg 182
Kellersberg 183
Herrnberg 184

Harxheim
Börnchen 185
Schloßberg 186
Lieth 187

Lörzweiler
Ölgild 188
Hohberg 189

**GROSSLAGE
DOMHERR**

Klein-Winternheim
Geiershöll 190
Villenkeller 191
Herrgottshaus 192

Ober-Olm
Kapellenberg 193

Essenheim
Teufelspfad 194
Römerberg 195

**Stadecken-Elsheim
Ortsteil Elsheim**
Bockstein 196
Tempelchen 197
Blume 198

– Ortsteil Stadecken
Lenchen 199
Spitzberg 200

Saulheim
Probstey 201
Schloßberg 202
Hölle 203
Haubenberg 204
Pfaffengarten 205
Heiligenhaus 206

Udenheim
Goldberg 207
Sonnenberg 208
Kirchberg 209

Schornsheim
Mönchspfad 210
Ritterberg 211
Sonnenhang 212

Gabsheim
Dornpfad 213
Kirchberg 214
Rosengarten 215

Also vineyards not
registered as Einz.
in the parishes of
Budenheim,
Mainz-Finthen and
Mainz-Drais

**GROSSLAGE
GUTES DOMTAL**

Nieder-Olm
Klosterberg 216
Sonnenberg 217
Goldberg 218

Lörzweiler
Königstuhl 219

Nackenheim
Schmittskapellchen
220

**Nierstein
Ortsteil Schwabsburg**
Pfaffenkappe 221

Dexheim
Doktor 222

Dalheim
Steinberg 223
Kranzberg 224
Altdörr 225

Weinolsheim
Hohberg 226
Kehr 227

Friesenheim
Altdörr 225 a
Bergpfad 228
Knopf 229

Undenheim
Goldberg 230

Köngernheim
Goldgrube 231

Selzen
Rheinpforte 232
Gottesgarten 233
Osterberg 234

Hahnheim
Knopf 235
Moosberg 236

Sörgenloch
Moosberg 236 a

Zornheim
Vogelsang 237
Guldenmorgen 238
Mönchbäumchen 239
Dachgewann 240
Pilgerweg 241

Mommenheim
Osterberg 234 a
Silbergrube 242
Kloppenberg 243

**GROSSLAGE
SPIEGELBERG**

Nackenheim
Engelsberg 244
Rothenberg 245

Nierstein
Rosenberg 246
Klostergarten 247
Findling 248
Kirchplatte 249
Schloß Hohenrechen
250
Ebersberg 251 P
Bildstock 252
Brückchen 253
Paterberg 254
Hölle 255

**– Ortsteil
Schwabsburg**
Ebersberg 251 P

**GROSSLAGE
REHBACH**

Nierstein
Pettenthal 256
Brudersberg 257
Hipping 258
Goldene Luft 259

**GROSSLAGE
AUFLANGEN**

Nierstein
Kranzberg 260
Zehnmorgen 261
Bergkirche 262
Glöck 263
Ölberg 264
Heiligenbaum 265
Orbel 266
Schloß Schwabsburg
267 P

**– Ortsteil
Schwabsburg**
Schloß Schwabsburg
267 P

**GROSSLAGE
GÜLDENMORGEN**

Oppenheim
Daubhaus 268
Zuckerberg 269
Herrenberg 270 P
Sackträger 271
Schützenhütte 272
Kreuz 273 P
Gutleuthaus 274

Dienheim
Herrenberg 270 P
Kreuz 273 P
Falkenberg 275
Siliusbrunnen 276
Höhlchen 277
Tafelstein 278 P

Uelversheim
Tafelstein 278 P

**GROSSLAGE
KRÖTEN-
BRUNNEN**

Oppenheim
Schloßberg 279
Schloß 280 P
Paterhof 281 P
Herrengarten 282 P

Dienheim
Schloß 280 P
Paterhof 281 P
Herrengarten 282 P

Ludwigshöhe
Honigberg 283

Guntersblum
Steinberg 284
Sonnenhang 285
Sonnenberg 286
Eiserne Hand 287
Sankt Julianen-
brunnen 288

Gimbsheim
Sonnenweg 289
Liebfrauenthal 290

Alsheim
Goldberg 291 P

Eich
Goldberg 291 P

Mettenheim
Goldberg 291 P

Hillesheim
Altenberg 292
Sonnheil 293

Wintersheim
Frauengarten 294

Dolgesheim
Kreuzberg 295
Schützenhütte 296

Eimsheim
Hexelberg 297
Sonnenhang 298
Römerschanze 299

Uelversheim
Aulenberg 300
Schloß 301

**GROSSLAGE
VOGELSGÄRTEN**

Ludwigshöhe
Teufelskopf 302

Guntersblum
Kreuzkapelle 303
Steig-Terrassen 304
Bornpfad 305
Authental 306
Himmelthal 307

**GROSSLAGE
PETERSBERG**

Bechtolsheim
Wingertstor 308
Sonnenberg 309
Homberg 310
Klosterberg 311

Gau-Odernheim
Herrgottspfad 312
Ölberg 313
Fuchsloch 314

Vogelsang 315

Framersheim
Zechberg 316
Kreuzweg 317
Hornberg 318

Gau-Heppenheim
Schloßberg 319
Pfarrgarten 320

Albig
Schloß Hammerstein
321 P
Hundskopf 322
Homberg 323

Alzey
Schloß Hammerstein
321 P

Biebelnheim
Pilgerstein 324
Rosenberg 325

Spiesheim
Osterberg 326

**GROSSLAGE
RHEINBLICK**

Alsheim
Fischerpfad 327
Frühmesse 328
Römerberg 329
Sonnenberg 330

Dorn-Dürkheim
Hasensprung 331
Römerberg 332

Mettenheim
Michelsberg 333
Schloßberg 334

**BEREICH
WONNEGAU**

**GROSSLAGE
SYBILLENSTEIN**

Bechenheim
Fröhlich 337

Offenheim
Mandelberg 338

Mauchenheim
Sioner Klosterberg
339

Weinheim
(Ortsteil of Alzey)
Mandelberg 340
Hölle 341
Kirchenstück 342
Kapellenberg 343 P
Heiliger Blutberg
344

Heimersheim
(Ortsteil of Alzey)
Sonnenberg 345
Rotenfels 347 P

Alzey
Kapellenberg 343 P
Rotenfels 347 P
Römerberg 348
Wartberg 350

**– Ortsteil
Schafhausen**
Pfaffenhalde 349

Dautenheim
(Ortsteil of Alzey)
Himmelacker 351

Wahlheim
Schelmen 352

Freimersheim
Frankenstein 353

**GROSSLAGE
BERGKLOSTER**

Esselborn
Goldberg 354

Flomborn
Feuerberg 355
Goldberg 356

Eppelsheim
Felsen 357

Hangen-Weisheim
Sommerwende 358

Gundersheim
Höllenbrand 359
Königstuhl 360

Gundheim
Sonnenberg 361
Mandelbrunnen 362
Hungerbiene 363

Bermersheim
Hasenlauf 364

Westhofen
Rotenstein 365
Steingrube 366
Benn 367
Morstein 368
Brunnenhäuschen 369
Kirchspiel 370
Aulerde 371

**GROSSLAGE
PILGERPFAD**

Frettenheim
Heil 372

**Dittelsheim-Heßloch
Ortsteil Dittelsheim**
Leckerberg 373
Pfaffenmütze 374
Mönchhube 375
Kloppberg 376
Geiersberg 377

– Ortsteil Heßloch
Liebfrauenberg 378
Edle Weingärten
379
Mondschein 380

Monzernheim
Goldberg 381
Steinhöhl 382

Bechtheim
Hasensprung 383
Heiligkreuz 384

Osthofen
Rheinberg 385
Klosterberg 386
Liebenberg 387
Kirchberg 388

**GROSSLAGE
GOTTESHILFE**

Bechtheim
Rosengarten 389
Geyersberg 390
Stein 391

Osthofen
Hasenbiß 392
Neuberg 393
Leckzapfen 393 a
Goldberg 394

**GROSSLAGE
BURG
RODENSTEIN**

Ober-Flörsheim
Blücherpfad 395
Deutschherrenberg
396

Bermersheim
Seilgarten 397

**Flörsheim-Dalsheim
Ortsteil Dalsheim**
Hubacker 398
Sauloch 399
Steig 400 P
Bürgel 401

**– Ortsteil
Niederflörsheim**
Steig 400 P
Goldberg 402
Frauenberg 403

Mörstadt
Nonnengarten 404
Katzenbuckel 405

**GROSSLAGE
DOMBLICK**

Mölsheim
Zellerweg am
schwarzen Herr-
gott 406
Silberberg 407

Wachenheim
Rotenberg 408
Horn 409

Monsheim
Silberberg 407 a

**– Ortsteil
Kriegsheim**
Rosengarten 410

Hohen-Sülzen
Sonnenberg 411
Kirchenstück 412

Offstein
Engelsberg 413
Schloßgarten 414

**GROSSLAGE
LIEBFRAUEN-
MORGEN**

Worms
St. Cyriakusstift 420
Liebfrauenstift-
Kirchenstück 421
Remeyerhof 422

– Ortsteil Abenheim
Goldapfel 415
Klausenberg 416
Kapellenstück 417
Bildstock 418

**– Ortsteil
Herrnsheim**
Rheinberg 419
Lerchelsberg 423
Sankt Annaberg 424
Hochberg 425 P
Römersteg 428

**– Ortsteil
Pfeddersheim**
Hochberg 425 P
St. Georgenberg
426
Kreuzblick 427
Nonnenwingert
429 P

**– Ortsteil Wies-
Oppenheim**
Am Heiligen
Häuschen 432

– Ortsteil Leiselheim
Nonnenwingert
429 P

– Ortsteil Hochheim
Nonnenwingert
429 P

**– Ortsteil
Pfiffligheim**
Nonnenwingert
429 P

– Ortsteil Horchheim
Goldberg 430

**– Ortsteil
Weinsheim**
Burgweg 431

**– Ortsteil
Heppenheim**
Affenberg 433
Schneckenberg 434

"AP" NUMBERS

Before being sold in bottle all quality wines (QbA and QmP), and quality sparkling wines (Sekt), must receive an official control number (Amtliche Prüfungsnummer or "AP" number), which must later appear on the bottle label. To obtain an AP number, the bottler sends three samples of the wine to the local control centre. There are nine of these centres, each dealing with an area. With the samples the bottler must send a chemical analysis issued by an officially recognized laboratory. This shows the amount of alcohol, sugar, extract, acid and sulphur dioxide in the wine. Other basic information such as the date and size of the bottling must also be given to the control centre. One sample is tasted by a panel of between three and five experts. The other samples are kept by the AP authorities for at least two years in case a query should arise about the wine.

The tasting panel examines up to sixty wines or so in one session, probably tasting a new wine every two or three minutes. The panel is not to be given the name of the bottler or supplier, but only that of the wine itself. Marks are awarded on a scale of points from 1.5 to 5, individually for the bouquet, taste and balance, the total mark being divided by three to give a maximum of 5 points. There is a formal procedure for appealing against a refusal by a control centre to grant an AP number, but less than 3% of wines fail the test.

The AP number consists of a series of digits identifying the control centre, the village or town of the bottler, the bottler's reference number, the application number of the bottling, and the year of application for the AP number. Although these figures can be broken down into their individual sections, there may be local variations which make this somewhat difficult.

The immediate purpose of the AP system is to maintain the quality of German wine. It also generates useful statistics about the styles of wine being bottled, particularly in respect of sugar content (the amount of dry or medium-dry wines), and indirectly produces marketing information of much interest to the wine trade. Criticism has been made that the standard set by the AP system is too low. Nevertheless, it has contributed to the high level of technical excellence of the majority of German wines that reach the consumer.

PRODUCERS

Weingut der Stadt Alzey

Schloßgasse 14, 6508 Alzey. *Director:* U. Kaufmann. 18 hectares. *Einzellagen:* Rotenfels, Kapellenberg, Kirchenstück, Mandelberg, Römerberg and Wartberg, all in the Großlage Sybillenstein.

The town of Alzey in central Rheinhessen is unusual in possessing (since 1916) its own wine estate, planted with one sixth each of Riesling, Müller-Thurgau and Silvaner; the remaining half with a score of other varieties. The wines are well made, estate bottled and among the best of their district.

Weingut Bürgermeister Anton Balbach Erben

Mainzerstraße 64, 6505 Nierstein, tel: 06133-5585. *Owner:* Frau Charlotte Bohn. 18 hectares. 58% in Großlagen Rehbach and Auflangen, the rest in Spiegelberg. *Einzellagen:* Nierstein: Hipping, Pettenthal, Ölberg, Kranzberg, Klostergarten, Rosenberg and Bildstock.

The best known of several Balbachs who were Bürgermasters of Nierstein since the 17th century was Anton, who cleared woods from what is now the famous Pettenthal vineyard. The estate, down by the Rhine, with Victorian cellars now full of stainless steel, is planted with 80% Riesling, 7% Müller-Thurgau, 8% Kerner, 5% Silvaner. It produces some of the finest, raciest Rieslings of Rheinhessen and specializes in Auslesen, Beerenauslesen and Trockenbeerenauslesen.

Weingut Friedrich Baumann

Friedrich-Ebert-Straße 55, 6504 Oppenheim, tel: 06133-2312. *Owner:* Friedrich Baumann. About 8 hectares. *Einzellagen:* Oppenheim: Sackträger (1.7ha), Herrenberg (0.5), Kreuz (1.4), Paterhof (1.3), Daubhaus (0.2) and Herrengarten (2.4); Nierstein: Pettenthal (0.2) and Findling (0.3); Dienheim: Falkenberg (0.4) and Tafelstein (0.2).

A long-established family business remodelled in the 1970s but still using barrels and aiming for fresh, sprightly wines which win prizes. A quarter of the property is in the excellent Einzellage Oppenheimer Sackträger, from which a brut Riesling Sekt is now also being made. 40% Riesling, 22% Silvaner, 17% Müller-Thurgau and 21% others.

Brenner'sches Weingut

Pfandturmstraße 20, 6521 Bechtheim, tel: 06242-894. *Owner:* Bürgermeister Christian Brenner. About 24 hectares. *Einzellagen* all in Bechtheim: Geyersberg (2ha), Rosengarten (2), Hasensprung (2), Heiligkreuz (2.5), Stein (1).

A family estate since 1877 and the principal grower of Bechtheim, using old methods: wooden casks in spacious cellars with an emphasis on substantial dry wines. 80% of the vineyards are on sloping sites. 20% is Silvaner, 25% Müller-Thurgau, 15% Riesling, 25% Weißburgunder, 10% Spätburgunder. Weißburgunder, Riesling and red wines are made absolutely dry – even Auslesen. Also dry Riesling Sekt.

Sanitätsrat Dr. Dahlem Erben KG

Rathofstraße 21–25, 6504 Oppenheim, tel: 06133-2003. *Owners:* The Dahlem family. 25 hectares. *Einzellagen:* Oppenheim: Sackträger (1.5ha), Herrenberg (3), Schloß (3.8), Kreuz (3) and Herrengarten (6); Dienheim: Tafelstein (4.3), Paterhof (2.3) and Falkenberg (1.1); Guntersblum: Kreuzkapelle (0.6).

An old family estate (since 1702) among the most reliable for traditional Rheinhessen wines. The vineyards are 60% on slopes; the vines 25% Riesling, 20% each Silvaner and Müller-Thurgau, 8% Bacchus and 27% others, including new varieties. The wines are barrel-aged.

Weingut Louis Guntrum

Wörrstädterstraße 6, 6505 Nierstein, tel: 06133-59746. *Directors:* Lorenz and Hanns-Joachim Guntrum. 67 hectares. In the Großlagen Rehbach, Auflangen and Spiegelberg. *Einzellagen:* Nackenheim: Rothenberg; Nierstein: Pettenthal, Rosenberg, Klostergarten, Hölle, Ölberg, Heiligenbaum, Orbel and Paterberg; Oppenheim: Schloß, Herrenberg, Sackträger, Schützenhütte, Kreuz; Dienheim: Tafelstein.

The family business was started in 1824 in the present buildings, lying right on the Rhine. About 20% of the business is in estate-bottled wines; the vines are 30% Riesling, 25% Müller-Thurgau, 14% Silvaner, 9% Scheurebe, 7% Kerner, 4% Ruländer, 3% Gewürztraminer, 3% Bacchus and 5% new crossings under trial. The estate wines are particularly ripe and lively with a wide range of flavours, each variety and site being made individually. The 4th and 5th Guntrum generations now direct the estate and a merchant house with many bread-and-butter lines such as Liebfraumilch Seagull, Bereich Nierstein Goldgrape and a catalogue of other growers' wines from Rheinhessen and elsewhere.

Weingut Freiherr Heyl zu Herrnsheim

Mathildenhof, Langgasse 3, 6505 Nierstein, tel: 06133-5120. *Owners:* The von Weymarn family. 28.1 hectares. *Einzellagen:* many, including the solely owned Brudersberg (1.3ha) in Großlagen Rehbach, Spiegelberg, Auflangen, Gutes Domtal, Güldenmorgen and Krötenbrunnen.

A dignified manor, its gardens full of experimental vine plots, in the heart of Nierstein. The estate has been inherited for 5 generations. 60% is Riesling, particularly fine in the Rehbach and Auflangen vineyards; 16% is Silvaner, which in Ölberg makes a powerful dry wine; 20% is Müller-Thurgau, very popular from Spiegelberg. The wines are matured in cask and often need a couple of years before they are ready to drink. Ecological vine-growing methods are increasingly being used.

Weingut Kurfürstenhof

See Heinrich Seip.

Bürgermeister Carl Koch Erben

6504 Oppenheim. *Owner:* Klaus Stieh-Koch. 11 hectares. *Einzellagen:* Oppenheim: Sackträger, Kreuz, Herrenberg, Schloß, Paterhof and Herrengarten; Dienheim: Tafelstein.

In the family since 1824, concentrating on Oppenheimer Sackträger, from dry to Trockenbeerenauslese. 35% Riesling, 15% Müller-Thurgau, 15% Silvaner, 10% Kerner, 8% Scheurebe, 6% Bacchus, 5% Faber, etc. The estate offers 10-year-old wines.

Weingut Koehler-Weidmann

Hindenburgring 2, 6509 Bornheim, tel: 06734-224. *Owner:* Wilhelm Gustav Weidmann. 18.6 hectares. *Einzellagen:* Bornheim: Hähnchen (12.3ha), Hütte-Terrassen (0.8), Schönberg (0.8) and Kirchenstück (2.4); Flonheim: Klostergarten (1.2), La Roche (1.2).

Both traditional grapes and new crossings/ experimental grapes figure in the wide range of vines grown on this estate, now in its 9th generation. The Riesling, however, sells out first of the dozen varieties offered. The list includes 2 Beerenauslesen and, unusually, a 1984 Silvaner Eiswein. Modest cropping makes intense wines.

Weingut Köster-Wolf

Langgasse 62, 6509 Albig, tel: 06731-2538. *Owners:* Werner Köster and Manfred Wolf. 24 hectares. *Einzellagen:* Albig: Hundskopf and Schloß Hammerstein; Flonheim: Rotenpfad and Klostergarten; Heimersheim: Sonnenberg.

A 400-year-old vintner family. Their best Riesling is from one hectare of steep slope in Flonheim; a particular pride is dry Silvaner, "though most customers prefer soft, spicy wines". Other grapes grown are Müller-Thurgau and a variety of new crossings.

Weingut Müller-Dr. Becker

Vordergasse 16, 6523 Flörsheim-Dalsheim, tel: 06243-5524. *Owner:* Dr. Klaus Becker. 22.5 hectares. *Einzellagen:* in Flörsheim-Dalsheim: Hubacker, Steig, Sauloch and Bürgel.

Very varied and differentiated "varietals", two-thirds trocken or halbtrocken, made as fruity and flavoury as possible. 20% Müller-Thurgau, 20% Riesling, 10% each of Silvaner, Kerner, Weißburgunder, Spätburgunder, Faber; plus others. Sauloch in particular makes good Riesling Kabinett.

Kommerzienrat P.A. Ohler'sches Weingut

Gaustraße 10, 6530 Bingen. *Owner:* Bernhard Becker. 7 hectares. *Einzellagen:* Bingen: Schloßberg-Schwätzerchen, Rosengarten and Scharlachberg; Münster-Sarmsheim: Kapellenberg and Dautenpflänzer; Ockenheim: Klosterweg and St. Jakobsberg.

Since the 17th century a small estate in the centre of Bingen with parcels of the best surrounding vineyards, aiming for racy, spicy, aromatic Kabinetts and Spätlese, especially from Riesling, Kerner and similar vines.

Weingut Rappenhof
Bachstraße 47–49, 6526 Alsheim, tel: 06249-4015.
Owner: Dr. Reinhard Muth. 36 hectares.
Einzellagen: Alsheim: Fischerpfad, Frühmesse,
Sonnenberg and Goldberg; Guntersblum:
Bornpfad, Himmelthal, Kreuzkapelle, Steinberg
and Eiserne Hand; Dienheim: Siliusbrunnen;
Nierstein: Rosenberg.
A very old family estate, among the best of its
district, well known particularly for dry wines
(half of production). 41% is Riesling, 14%
Weißburgunder, Ruländer and Blauburgunder,
11% Silvaner, 12% Müller-Thurgau, 4%
Gewürztraminer. Riesling and the neutral
varieties (Pinots) are to be increased. A dry
Alsheimer Rheinblick (Großlage) Spätlese is the
house speciality.

Weingut Schales
Alzeyerstraße 160, 6523 Flörsheim-Dalsheim, tel:
06243-7003. *Owners:* The Schales family. 35
hectares. *Einzellagen:* Flörsheim-Dalsheim:
Hubacker, Steig, Bürgel, Sauloch and Goldberg.
Großlage: Burg Rodenstein.
A 7th generation family with a private wine
museum, making the usual wide range of
aromatic wines from the limestone soil of
Dalsheim, which it finds gives even the QbA and
Kabinett wines a 5-10-year life span. 20%
Müller-Thurgau, 11% Siegerrebe, 15% Ries-
ling, 8% Huxelrebe, 7% Bacchus, 6% Kerner,
4% Gewürztraminer, 5% Faber, 5%
Scheurebe, etc. More Riesling, Silvaner and
Weißburgunder is to be planted.

Weingut Schmitt-Dr. Ohnacker
Neustraße 6, 6524 Guntersblum, tel: 06249-1221.
Owner: Walter Ohnacker. 9 hectares in Großlage
Vogelsgärten (on slopes) with *Einzellagen* all in
Guntersblum: Himmelthal, Authental, Bornpfad,
Steig-Terrassen and Kreuzkapelle; 4ha in Großlage
Krötenbrunnen (on the flat) with *Einzellagen:*
Eiserne Hand, St. Julianenbrunnen and Steinberg.
150 years of family ownership; now one of the
best specialists in the village, with wines ranging
from Himmelthal Riesling (full-bodied and slow
to develop) to light-drinking Müller-Thurgau,
largely aged in cask, in cellars cut into the hill out
of reach of Rhine floods. The yield from about a
quarter of the vineyards is sent to a cooperative.
The vines are 37% Müller-Thurgau, 22%
Riesling, 10% Silvaner, 2% each of Scheurebe,
Ruländer, Gewürztraminer, Kerner and Bacchus, 5% Portugieser. The first 3 are to be
increased at the expense of the new crossings.

Gustav Adolf Schmitt'sches Weingut
Wilhelmstraße 2–6, 6505 Nierstein, tel: 06133-5151.
Owner: Georg Ottmar Schmitt. About 100 hectares
including *Einzellagen:* Nierstein: Pettenthal,
Ölberg, Hipping and Kranzberg; Dienheim:
Falkenberg; Oppenheim: Herrenberg and Kreuz;
Dexheim: Doktor.
Growers since 1618, merchants since about
1920. 75% of the very big estate is planted in
standard vine varieties with an emphasis on the
Riesling, and about 25% in crossings such as

Scheurebe, Kerner, Ehrenfelser and Bacchus.
The range of wines is wide, including very fine
intense and full-bodied QmP from the best sites.
Two-thirds of turnover is in such commercial
lines as Liebfraumilch "Gloria", Bereich
Nierstein "Fisherman", Bereich Bernkastel
"Silver Bell".

Weingut Geschwister Schuch
Oberdorfstraße 22, 6505 Nierstein, tel: 06133-5652.
Owners: Diether and Michael Günther. 16 hectares.
Einzellagen: Nierstein: Ölberg, Pettenthal,
Findling, Orbel, Hipping, Heiligenbaum,
Rosenberg and Klostergarten; Oppenheim:
Sackträger; Dienheim: Falkenberg.
One of the most respected old family estates of
Nierstein, founded by the Schuchs in 1817.
Planted with 50% Riesling, 15% Scheurebe,
10% red-wine varieties; 25% other varieties,
such as Müller-Thurgau, Silvaner and Kerner.
The wines are models of the gentle but distinc-
tive "Rheinterrasse" style, particularly in
trocken and halbtrocken Riesling.

Heinrich Seip, Kurfürstenhof
6505 Nierstein. *Owner:* Heinrich Seip. 35 hectares
in Nierstein. *Einzellagen:* Nierstein: Paterberg,
Bildstock, Kirchplatte, Findling, Rosenberg,
Klostergarten, Pettenthal, Hipping, Kranzberg,
Ölberg, Heiligenbaum, Orbel, Schloß Schwabsburg
and Goldene Luft (sole owner); Oppenheim:
Schloß; Dienheim: Tafelstein, Kreuz and
Falkenberg; Nackenheim: Engelsberg.
An ancient royal estate bought by the Seip
family in 1950 and now regarded as a leader in
wines from the new grape varieties. One of the
specialities, a grape called Jubiläum, ripens so
early that it rarely fails to make Auslese and
Beerenauslese, in the rather low-acid Ruländer
style. Seip's cellar techniques combine old casks
with modern ideas, aiming at aromatic sweet
wines of real quality and character.

Weingüter Carl Sittmann
Wormserstraße 61, 6504 Oppenheim, tel: 06133-
2021. *Owner:* Dr. Liselotte Sittmann. Nearly 80
hectares. *Einzellagen:* Alsheim: Goldberg,
Frühmesse, Römerberg; Oppenheim: Herrenberg,
Sackträger; Dienheim: Falkenberg, Paterhof.
Einzellagen also in Nierstein.
The biggest private estate in the district, inherit-
ed by the granddaughter of the founder, who
also runs a big merchant house under the name
Dr. Itschner. The vines are 20% Müller-
Thurgau, 16% Silvaner, 14% Kerner, 12%
Riesling. Wines from the best sites are matured
in casks: Oppenheimer Sackträger makes splen-
did Auslesen. Weißherbst (rosé) under the name
Alsheimer Rheinblick is a speciality.

Staatsweingut der Landes-Lehr- und Versuchsanstalt
Zuckerberg 19, 6504 Oppenheim, tel: 06133-2098.
Director: Dr. Finger. 40 hectares. *Einzellagen:*
Oppenheim: Sackträger, Kreuz, Herrenberg and
Zuckerberg; Nierstein: Paterberg, Ölberg and
Pettenthal; Dienheim: Tafelstein.

The regional wine school, founded in 1885 by
the Duke of Hessen and now considered an
exemplary college for winemakers, using the
most modern methods. In 1980 the school
opened a new German wine museum in the heart
of Oppenheim. 40% of the estate is on steep
slopes and nearly half is Riesling, but only
Niersteiner Pettenthal is 100% Riesling. Among
the many other varieties planted, a large proportion are experimental vines.

Weingut J. & H. A. Strub
Rheinstraße 42, 6505 Nierstein, tel: 06133-5649.
Owners: Reinhard and Walter Strub. 17 hectares in
Großlagen Rehbach, Auflangen, Güldenmorgen
and Spiegelberg. *Einzellagen:* Nierstein; Hipping,
Ölberg, Heiligenbaum, Orbel, Brückchen,
Paterberg, Findling and Bildstock; Dienheim:
Falkenberg.
An old family estate with a good name for gentle,
mellow wines from the best parts of the
"Rheinterrasse". Early bottling (end of March).
Vines are 30% Riesling, 30% Silvaner, 30%
Müller-Thurgau, 10% Ruländer.

Weingut Villa Sachsen
Mainzerstraße 184, 6530 Bingen, tel: 06721-10985.
27 hectares. *Einzellagen:* Bingen: Scharlachberg
(11ha), Kirchberg (7), Schloßberg-Schwätzerchen
(4), Osterberg (2), Kapellenberg, Rosengarten and
Bubenstück (each 0.4).
The Victorian villa starred in a bestseller of
1869, *The Country House on the Rhine*, was
bought by a prince of Hessen in 1879, became a
model wine estate and in 1963 was bought by
St. Ursula, the big wine merchants of Bingen.
Over 50% is Riesling; also Müller-Thurgau,
Silvaner, Kerner, Weißburgunder, Ruländer
and others. The Scharlachberg is the best site,
producing stylish, manly Rieslings, particularly
trocken and halbtrocken types.

Weingut Eugen Wehrheim
Mühlgasse 30, 6505 Nierstein, tel: 06133-58125.
Owner: Klaus Wehrheim. 10.3 hectares.
Einzellagen Nierstein: Orbel, Ölberg, Hipping,
Paterberg, Pettenthal, Klostergarten, Brückchen
and Findling.
Specialists in Nierstein since 1693; 40% Ries-
ling, 21% Silvaner, 15% Müller-Thurgau, 24%
other varieties. The Rieslings are light and
sprightly; more serious wines are sweet,
aromatic and heavy, for example Ruländer and
Huxelrebe Beerenauslese.

Zentralkellerei Rhein. Winzergen. eG
Wöllsteinerstraße 16, 6551 Gau-Bickelheim.
Central cooperative cellars, established in 1946,
receiving the crop from 3000 hectares of the
Rheinhessen and Rheingau, covering no less
than 622 Einzellagen. 32 different vine varieties
are grown, of which the most significant are
Müller-Thurgau (25%), Silvaner (20%),
Scheurebe (15%), and Bacchus (10%). All the
wines are sold as "estate bottlings" – as the law
permits.

RHEINPFALZ

Germany's most fertile, sunniest and most productive wine region takes its English name, the Palatinate, from the former Counts Palatine of the Holy Roman Empire. The wine district takes its bearings not from a river but from a range of forested hills. It stretches in a narrow 80-kilometre (50-mile) band along the eastern flank of the Haardt mountains, from the southern edge of Rheinhessen to the French frontier where the Haardt become the Vosges. At the border, in an extraordinary sudden switch, the wines change from the flowery sweetness and lively attack of Germany to the savoury vinosity of Alsace.

With 21,900 hectares of vines, Rheinpfalz is marginally second in vineyard area to Rheinhessen – though regularly a bigger producer. The southern half of the region, from Neustadt south, known as the Bereich Südliche Weinstraße, is Germany's most up-to-date and intensive vineyard. The last two decades have seen formidable progress – in vine varieties, reorganization of vineyards and cellar technology.

Natural conditions are so favourable here that the city of Landau was once Germany's biggest wine market. Sadly, because it was almost entirely a Jewish enterprise, it was destroyed in 1935 by the Nazis, who then invented the Deutsche Weinstraße and obliged each German city to adopt a wine village as its supplier of bulk wine. More than half was shipped in tanks to the Mosel for blending – a practice that continued until 1971. Little wine was bottled in the region until after World War II. Judgements based on its history and reputation are therefore likely to be wide of the mark. The Südliche Weinstraße has no history as a producer of great wine, no great estates, yet its potential is formidable and its wines at present some of the best value in Germany – indeed in Europe.

Although Müller-Thurgau is the most-planted grape, here as in Rheinhessen, it is outplanted both by the new vine varieties (totalling over 6,075 hectares against 5,300 hectares of Müller-Thurgau) and by the combined totals of Riesling and Silvaner. Riesling firmly holds its own in the best vineyards and accounts for one in seven hectares in the whole region. Of the new varieties Kerner with 1,900 hectares and Morio-Muskat with 1,800 hectares are the most popular, Scheurebe rather less so. Here, as in Baden, the noble old secondary variety, the Ruländer or Pinot Gris, makes a respectable showing.

To characterize Rheinpfalz wines as a whole is much more difficult than, for example, the generally mild products of Rheinhessen or the widely homogeneous styles of the Rheingau or Mosel. The finest Rheinpfalz wines – almost all Riesling – add to the classic Riesling character a generosity of ripeness that marks them as wines from a sunnier climate. They vary in finesse, in lively acidity and honeyed depths. Yet many regularly approach the ideal of what well-ripened Riesling can achieve. The same can be said for each other variety: its character is distinctly articulated by the favourable conditions – in the case of some of the aromatic varieties too much so; the aromas become overwhelming. All the prestige of Rheinpfalz is centred on the half-dozen villages at the centre of its northern half, known as the Mittelhaardt. The 1971 wine law divided the entire region into only two Bereiche: Südliche Weinstraße for the south and Mittelhaardt/Deutsche Weinstraße for the north, with the city of Neustadt approximately between them. It thus gave the prestige of the Mittelhaardt to a wide range of vineyards in the north of the region which have nothing in common with it. There should be a third Bereich name

▲ The Südliche Weinstraße is a sea of vines for over 80 kilometres (50 miles). Maikammer, in Großlage Mandelhöhe, lies at its northern (and generally better) end.

for what was formerly called the Unterhaardt. (The Südliche Weinstraße was formerly called the Oberhaardt, making a logical trio which might well have been preserved.)

The Rheinpfalz vineyards are divided into 25 Großlagen. Some are the usual large tracts of country, others more specific and thus more useful. Großlage names are widely used on labels, especially in the south. Only a few Mittelhardt Einzellagen have any notoriety. The geographical listing that follows is organized by Großlage rather than by village.

TRAVEL INFORMATION

The wine country of the Rheinpfalz is strung together by a wine road so special it is known as the *Deutsche Weinstraße* – the German Wine Road. In its succession of half-timbered villages, inns and vineyards it indeed epitomizes them all. Walking in the forests – the Pfälzerwald nature park covers the entire Haardt Mountains – and eating in the taverns are the other recreations, apart from wine.

Wine festivals
Bad Dürkheim's sausage fair in September leads a score or more festivals, including a radish fair in Schifferstadt each May. Wine festivals include: Wachenheim (July), Deidesheim (Aug), Speyer & Obermoschel (Sept), Bockenheim & Landau (Oct).

Wine tasting and trails
Every village has well-signposted tasting cellars, and vineyard educational trails are found in Deidesheim, Edenkoben, Großkarlbach, Schweigen-Rechtenbach and Wachenheim.

Food and drink
Pfalzer Saumagen, inadequately translated as Palatinate haggis, typifies local food: hearty foundations for local wine and plenty of it. A Pfalz recipe for a pork stew begins "take as large

a pot as possible . . ." Deidesheim, a well-preserved old town, has fine inns such as the Deidesheimer Hof in the marketplace (tel: 06326-1811) and Zum Reichsrat (tel: 06326-6011). All the wine towns have their taverns and hotels, and there are country hotels such as the Königsmühle in the

▼ The Forster Kirchenstück vineyard changed hands four centuries ago, and the new owners erected a plaque to mark their purchase.

Kaltenbrunner valley (tel: 06321-83031) and the Haardter Schloß near Neustadt (tel: 06321-32625). The Krone restaurant at Münchweiler has a high reputation (tel: 06395-1681; booking recommended). Its specialities include marinated salmon.

◄▼ The ancient city of Neustadt is the pivot of the Palatinate, between the Mittelhaardt and the Südliche Weinstraße. Its wine-school has been a great producer of new grape varieties.

◄ Spätlese Riesling grapes are collected in the famous Gerümpel vineyard, with the little Mittelhaardt village of Wachenheim in the background. Late-picked wines from this region are some of Germany's most luscious.

GROSSLAGE REBSTÖCKEL (NEUSTADT AN DER WEINSTRASSE ORTSTEIL DIEDESFELD)

Neustadt an der Weinstraße
Grain 200
Erkenbrecht 201

Hambach an der Weinstraße
(Ortsteil of Neustadt an der Weinstraße)
Kaiserstuhl 202
Kirchberg 203
Feuer 204
Schloßberg 205

Diedesfeld an der Weinstraße
(Ortsteil of Neustadt an der Weinstraße)
Ölgässel 206
Johanniskirchel 207
Paradies 208

GROSSLAGE PFAFFENGRUND (NEUSTADT AN DER WEINSTRASSE, ORTSTEIL DIEDESFELD)

Diedesfeld
(Ortsteil of Neustadt an der Weinstraße)
Berg 209

Hambach/Weinstraße
(Ortsteil of Neustadt)
Römerbrunnen 210

Lachen-Speyerdorf
(Ortsteil of Neustadt an der Weinstraße)
Langenstein 211
Lerchenböhl 212
Kroatenpfad 213

Duttweiler
(Ortsteil of Neustadt an der Weinstraße)
Kreuzberg 214
Mandelberg 215
Kalkberg 216

Geinsheim
(Ortsteil of Neustadt an der Weinstraße)
Gässel 217

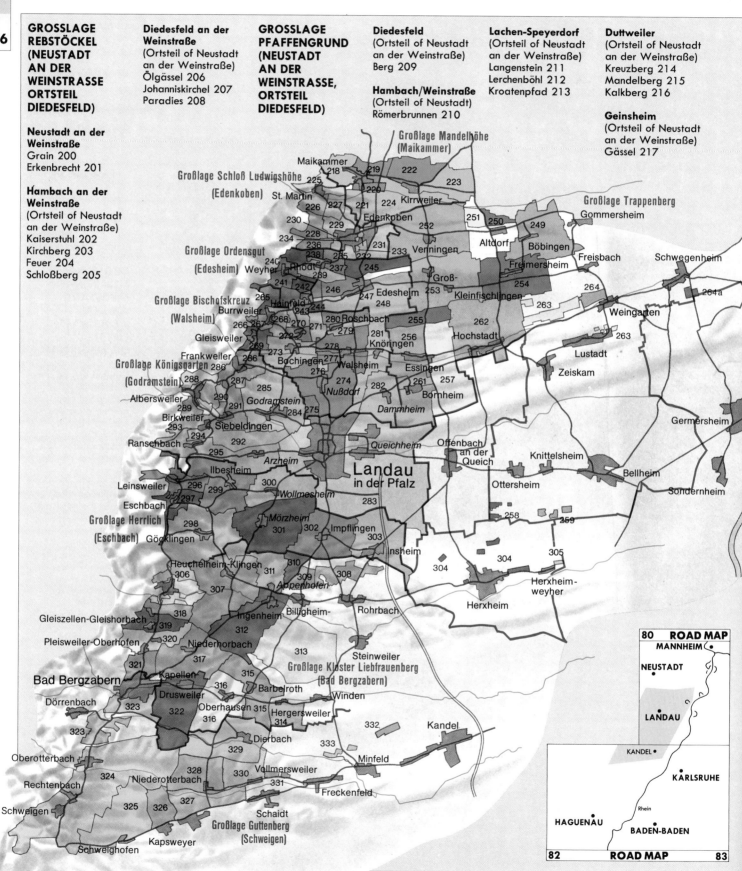

80 ROAD MAP

82 ROAD MAP 83

**BEREICH
SÜDLICHE
WEINSTRASSE**

**GROSSLAGE
MANDELHÖHE
(MAIKAMMER)**

Maikammer
Alsterweiler
Kapellenberg 218
Kirchenstück 219
Immengarten 220
Heiligenberg 221

Kirrweiler
Römerweg 222
Mandelberg 223 .
Oberschloß 224

**GROSSLAGE
SCHLOSS
LUDWIGSHÖHE
(EDENKOBEN)**

St. Martin
Kirchberg 225
Baron 226
Zitadelle 227

Edenkoben
Bergel 228
Heilig Kreuz 229
Klostergarten 230
Heidegarten 231
Kirchberg 232
Blücherhöhe 233
Mühlberg 234
Schwarzer Letten
235
Kastaniengarten 236

**GROSSLAGE
ORDENSGUT
(EDESHEIM)**

Rhodt unter Rietburg
Klosterpfad 237
Schloßberg 238
Rosengarten 239

Weyher in der Pfalz
Michelsberg 240
Heide 241

Hainfeld
Letten 242
Kapelle 243
Kirchenstück 244

Edesheim
Forst 245
Mandelhang 246
Schloß 247
Rosengarten 248

**GROSSLAGE
TRAPPENBERG
(HOCHSTADT)**

Böbingen
Ortelberg 249

Altdorf
Gottesacker 250
Hochgericht 251

Venningen
Doktor 252

**Groß- und
Kleinfischlingen**
Kirchberg 253

Freimersheim
Bildberg 254

Essingen
Roßberg 255
Sonnenberg 256
Osterberg 257

Ottersheim
Kahlenberg 258

Knittelsheim
Gollenberg 259 P

Bellheim
Gollenberg 259 P

Bornheim
Neuberg 261

Hochstadt
Roter Berg 262

Zeiskam
Klostergarten 263 P

Lustadt
Klostergarten 263 P

Weingarten
Schloßberg 264

Schwegenheim
Bründelsberg 264 a

**Römerberg (bei
Speyer)**
Ortsteil
Mechtersheim
Schlittberg 264 b
Alter Berg 264 c P

**– Ortsteil
Heiligenstein**
Alter Berg 264 c P
Narrenberg 264 d P

**– Ortsteil
Berghausen**
Narrenberg 264 d P

Also vineyards
without site-names
in the parishes of
Gommersheim (22ha)
and Offenbach
(0.6ha)

**GROSSLAGE
BISCHOFSKREUZ
(WALSHEIM)**

Burrweiler
Altenforst 265
St. Annaberg 266
Schäwer 267
Schloßgarten 268

Gleisweiler
Hölle 269

Flemlingen
Herrenbuckel 270
Vogelsprung 271
Zechpeter 272

Böchingen
Rosenkranz 273

Nußdorf
(Ortsteil of Landau in
der Pfalz)
Herrenberg 274
Kaiserberg 275
Kirchenstück 276

Walsheim
Forstweg 277
Silberberg 278

Roschbach
Simonsgarten 279
Rosenkränzel 280

Knöringen
Hohenrain 281

Dammheim
(Ortsteil of Landau in
der Pfalz)
Höhe 282

**GROSSLAGE
KÖNIGSGARTEN
(GODRAMSTEIN)**

Landau in der Pfalz
incl. Queichheim and
Mörlheim
Altes Löhl 283

Godramstein
(Ortsteil of Landau in
der Pfalz)
Klostergarten 284
Münzberg 285

Frankweiler
Kalkgrube 286
Biengarten 287

Albersweiler
Latt 288
(St. Johann)
Kirchberg 289

Siebeldingen
Mönchspfad 290
Im Sonnenschein 291
Rosenberg 292 P

Birkweiler
Rosenberg 292 P
Kastanienbusch 293
Mandelberg 294

Ranschbach
Seligmacher 295 P

Arzheim
(Ortsteil of Landau in
der Pfalz)
Rosenberg 292 P
Seligmacher 295 P

Vineyard (6ha) not
registered as Einz. in
the parish of
Gräfenhausen.

**GROSSLAGE
HERRLICH
(ESCHBACH)**

Leinsweiler
Sonnenberg 296 P

Eschbach
Hasen 297

Göcklingen
Kaiserberg 298

Ilbesheim
Sonnenberg 296 P
Rittersberg 299

Wollmesheim
(Ortsteil of Landau in
der Pfalz)
Mütterie 300

Mörzheim
(Ortsteil of Landau in
der Pfalz)
Pfaffenberg 301

Impflingen
Abtsberg 302

Insheim
Schäfergarten 303 P

Rohrbach
Schäfergarten 303 P

**Herxheim bei
Landau in der Pfalz**
Engelsberg 304

Herxheimweyher
Am Gaisberg 305

**GROSSLAGE
KLOSTER
LIEBFRAUENBERG
(BAD
BERGZABERN)**

Klingenmünster
Maria Magdalena
306

Göcklingen
Herrenpfad 307 P

**Heuchelheim-
Klingen**
Herrenpfad 307 P

Rohrbach
Mandelpfad 308 P

**Billigheim-
Ingenheim**
Mandelpfad 308 P
(Billigheim)
Venusbuckel 309
(Billigheim)
Sauschwänzel 310
(Billigheim)
Steingebiß 311
(Appenhofen)
Pfaffenberg 312
(Ingenheim)
Rosenberg 313 P
(Mühlhofen and
Billigheim)

Steinweiler
Rosenberg 313 P

Winden
Narrenberg 314 P

Hergersweiler
Narrenberg 314 P

Barbelroth
Kirchberg 315

Oberhausen
Frohnwingert 316

Niederhorbach
Silberberg 317

**Gleiszellen-
Gleishorbach**
Kirchberg 318
Frühmess 319

**Pleisweiler-
Oberhofen**
Schloßberg 320

Bad Bergzabern
Altenberg 321

Kapellen-Drusweiler
Rosengartan 322

**GROSSLAGE
GUTTENBERG
(SCHWEIGEN)**

Bad Bergzabern
Wonneberg 323 P

Dörrenbach
Wonneberg 323 P

Oberotterbach
Sonnenberg 324 P

**Schweigen-
Rechtenbach**
Sonnenberg 324 P

Schweighofen
Sonnenberg 324 P
Wolfsberg 325

Kapsweyer
Lerchenberg 326

Steinfeld
Herrenwingert 327

Niederotterbach
Eselsbuckel 328

Dierbach
Kirchhöh 329

Vollmersweiler
Krapfenberg 330

Freckenfeld
Gräfenberg 331

Kandel
Galgenberg 332

Minfeld
Herrenberg 333

PRODUCERS

Weingut Dr. von Bassermann-Jordan
Kirchstraße 10, 6705 Deidesheim, tel: 06326-6006. *Owner:* Dr. Ludwig von Bassermann-Jordan. 40 hectares. *Einzellagen:* Deidesheim: Hohenmorgen, Grainhübel, Kieselberg, Kalkofen, Leinhöhle, Herrgottsacker, Paradiesgarten, Mäushöhle, Langenmorgen; Forst: Jesuitengarten, Kirchenstück, Ungeheuer, Pechstein, Freundstück, Stift, Musenhang; Ruppertsberg: Reiterpfad, Hoheburg, Spieß, Nußbien, Linsenbusch; Dürkheim: Michelsberg and Spielberg; Ungstein: Herrenberg. Großlagen: Hofstück, Mariengarten, Schnepfenflug and Honigsäckel.
A historic house, perhaps the first to make top-quality wines in the region, under its 18th-century founder Andreas Jordan. His grandson-in-law, Dr. Friedrich von Bassermann-Jordan, was in turn a legislator of great influence and a famous historian of wine who started an important wine museum in his medieval cellars. The present owner, his son, maintains impeccable, entirely traditional standards and methods, with Rieslings more delicate than many in the Rheinpfalz but no less long-lived. 99% of the estate is Riesling.

F. & G. Bergdolt
Klostergut St. Lamprecht, 6730 Neustadt-Duttweiler, tel: 06327-5027. *Owner:* Rainer Bergdolt. 15 hectares. *Einzellagen:* Kirrweiler: Mandelberg; Duttweiler: Mandelberg, Kalkberg and Kreuzberg.
First mentioned in 1290 when it became church property, the estate has been owned by the Bergdolt family for over 230 years. The

winemaking aims to retain freshness and good acidity. In particular the dry wines from Riesling and Weißburgunder, that cover 30% and 10% respectively of the vineyards, have been much in demand. Other varieties grown include Kerner (15%), Müller-Thurgau (12%), Silvaner (10%) and Gewürztraminer (5%).

Weingut Josef Biffar
Niederkirchenerstraße 13, 6705 Deidesheim, tel: 06326-5028. *Owner:* Gerhard Biffar. 12 hectares. *Einzellagen:* Deidesheim: Nonnenstück, Herrgottsacker, Mäushöhle, Kieselberg, Leinhöhle, Grainhübel and Kalkofen; Ruppertsberg: Nußbien, Linsenbusch and Reiterpfad. Großlagen: Hofstück and Mariengarten.
A well-regarded estate for traditional cask-aged wines of good balance. 80% is Riesling, 10% Müller-Thurgau, 6% Weißburgunder and 4% Scheurebe and Gewürztraminer. A rare Herrgottsacker Spätlese was made in 1984.

Weingut Alfred Bonnet
6701 Friedelsheim, tel: 06322-2162. *Owners:* Alfred and Philipp Bonnet. 24.5 hectares. *Einzellagen:* Herxheim: Honigsack; Kallstadt: Steinacker; Dürkheim: Hochbenn and Nonnengarten; Wachenheim: Mandelgarten; Deidesheim: Letten; Forst: Bischofsgarten; Friedelsheim: Kreuz; and others.
A family estate of Huguenot origins, now in its 10th generation. Red wines are matured in cask, but the whites are stored in stainless steel to avoid oxidation. Ageing is in bottle, rather than in bulk and the wine from scented grapes is

fermented at a low temperature to retain the bouquet. Unusually, the estate produces its own sparkling wine, and does not have it made by a contract Sekt manufacturer. Many vine varieties are grown, including Riesling (53%), Heroldrebe (6%), Portugieser (6%) and Müller-Thurgau (6%).

Weingut Reichsrat von Buhl
Weinstraße 16, 6705 Deidesheim, tel: 06326-1851. *Owner:* Georg Enoch, Reichsfreiherr von und zu Guttenberg. *Director:* Michael Hiller. 95.5 hectares. *Einzellagen:* Forst: Bischofsgarten, Ungeheuer, Pechstein, Kirchenstück, Freundstück and Jesuitengarten; Deidesheim: Nonnenstück, Paradiesgarten, Kieselberg and Leinhöhle; Ruppertsberg; Linsenbusch, Hoheburg and Reiterpfad; Wachenheim: Luginsland; Königsbach: Idig and Jesuitengarten. Großlagen: Mariengarten, Schnepfenflug, Hofstück and Meerspinne.
One of the biggest and most illustrious wine estates in Germany, founded in 1849 and still in the same family. 80% is Riesling, 15% Müller-Thurgau, 3% Gewürztraminer, 2% Scheurebe, all on flat or gently sloping fertile land. Silvaner and Riesling are increasingly planted here (the latter is to rise to 90%) and Chardonnay is being tested. The wines are barrel-aged, powerful and full-bodied, and range from dry, even severe, café wines to Trockenbeerenauslesen. Resisting the trend, this estate harvests and bottles early.

Weingut Dr. Bürklin-Wolf
Weinstraße 65, 6706 Wachenheim, tel: 06322-8955. *Owner:* Bettina Bürklin. *Director:* Georg Racquet. 110 hectares. *Einzellagen:* Wachenheim: Gerümpel, Goldbächel, Altenburg, Böhlig, Luginsland, Bischofsgarten, Mandelgarten, Königswingert and Rechbächel (sole owner); Forst: Kirchenstück, Ungeheuer, Jesuitengarten, Pechstein, Bischofsgarten; Deidesheim: Hohenmorgen, Langenmorgen, Kalkofen, Herrgottsacker; Ruppertsberg: Hoheburg, Reiterpfad, Nußbien, Linsenbusch and Gaisböhl (sole owner). Großlagen: Schnepfenflug, Mariengarten, Schenkenböhl and Hofstück.
A magnificent estate in all the best vineyards of the Mittelhaardt, generally acknowledged as the finest in the region and one of the best in Germany. It has been in the family for 400 years and the cask cellar goes back to the 16th century. Dr. Albert Bürklin, one of his country's greatest wine men, died in October 1979 and his daughter inherited the estate. The Director, formerly at the great Nahe State Domain (the Verwaltung der Staatlichen Weinbaudomänen) at Niederhausen, is supremely qualified to continue the tradition.
The vines are Riesling, Müller-Thurgau, Ehrenfelser, Weißburgunder, with some Gewürztraminer, Scheurebe, Spätburgunder (for red wine) and experimental varieties. The style of wine is the most "racy", deft and harmonious in the Rheinpfalz, from light-vintage halbtrocken Riesling Kabinetts, so pure and refreshing that you could drink them for breakfast, to great orange-tinted late-picked

wines of amazing spice and expressiveness. Recently some superb Eiswein (including in 1979 a very rare Trockenbeerenauslese Eiswein) has been made. Technology includes the most modern ideas; many young winemakers have learned their art here.

Gutsverwaltung Wegeler-Deinhard

Weinstraße 10, 6705 Deidesheim, tel: 06326-221. *Owner:* Deinhard & Co. KGaA. 18 hectares. *Einzellagen:* Deidesheim: Herrgottsacker (5.5ha) and Paradiesgarten (0.6); Ruppertsberg: Linsenbusch (8.1); Forst: Ungeheuer (3.8).

The Koblenz merchants Deinhard rented this section of the old Dr. Deinhard estate in 1973. There are said to be old family connections and the two estates are run by the same Director – Heinz Bauer – from the same fine sandstone Gutshaus in Deidesheim (*see* next entry), but their wines are made apart and labelled differently. Deinhard's wines, like those of their estates in the Rheingau and Mosel, are models of correct and characterful winemaking. Linsenbusch is a relatively light wine from flat land; the others are on slopes, riper and more "Pfalzy" – Ungeheuer best of all, rarely producing less than Spätlesen. 74% is Riesling, 17% Müller-Thurgau, 4% Scheurebe, 3% Gewürztraminer and 2% others.

Weingut Dr. Deinhard

Weinstraße 10, 6705 Deidesheim, tel: 06326-221. *Owner:* Frau Renate Hoch. *Director:* Heinz Bauer. *Einzellagen:* Deidesheim: Leinhöhle, Grainhübel, Kieselberg, Kalkofen, Paradiesgarten, Mäushöhle and Nonnenstück; Ruppertsberg: Reiterpfad and Nußbien; Forst, Neustadt, Gimmeldingen and Mußbach.

A well-known estate built up in the 19th century by Dr. Andreas Deinhard, a founder of the German Winegrowers' Association and an influential legislator. His handsome Gutshaus (built 1848) now houses both this and the estate rented to Deinhards (*see* previous entry). Vines are Riesling, Müller-Thurgau, Scheurebe, Gewürztraminer, Ehrenfelser, Kerner and others. The wines are mainly trocken and halbtrocken, and emphasis is on Kabinett wines with good acidity.

Weingut K. Fitz-Ritter

Weinstraße Nord 51, 6702 Bad Dürkheim, tel: 06322-5389. *Owner:* Konrad Fitz. 23.3 hectares. 4ha in Großlage Schenkenböhl: *Einzellagen* in Dürkheim: Abtsfronhof (sole owner), Fronhof and Fuchsmantel; in Wachenheim: Mandelgarten. 7.5ha in Großlage Hochmess: *Einzellagen* in Dürkheim: Michelsberg, Spielberg, Rittergarten and Hochbenn. 5ha in Großlage Feuerberg: *Einzellagen* in Dürkheim: Nonnengarten and Steinberg; in Ellerstadt: Bubeneck and Sonnenberg; in Kallstadt: Annaberg. 1.4ha in Großlage Honigsäckel: *Einzellage* in Ungstein: Herrenberg. 2.1ha in Großlage Hofstück: *Einzellage* in Ellerstadt: Kirchenstück.

A family estate with a fine classical 18th-century mansion (1785) whose park contains the largest

maidenhair tree (*Ginkgo biloba*) in Germany, along with other noble trees. The Fitz family also started (in 1837) one of the oldest Sekt businesses in Germany. 65% of their vines are Riesling, 3% Gewürztraminer, 6% Spätburgunder, 26% others. Most of their wines are QmP (Kabinett or better) with a high reputation for individuality.

Emil Hammel & Cie

Weinstraße Süd 4, 6719 Kirchheim, tel: 06359-3003. *Owners:* Rudolf and Martin Hammel. 21 hectares. *Einzellagen:* Bissersheim: Goldberg and Held; Kirchheim: Kreuz, Römerstraße, Steinacker and Geißkopf; Neuleiningen: Sonnenberg; Kleinkarlbach: Herrenberg; Dirmstein: Mandelpfad. Großlagen: Schwarzerde and Höllenpfad.

Growers and merchants with a total production of some 75,000 cases – five times their own production, which is supplemented by buying grapes locally. The company is known for very good carafe wines, mainly halbtrocken with the stress on Müller-Thurgau, Riesling and (red) Portugieser (but plenty of alternatives, including the excellent St-Emilion, Château Soutard).

Weingut Kloster Heilsbruck

Klosterstraße 170, 6732 Edenkoben, tel: 06323-2883. *Owners:* Karl Ueberle Erben. *Manager:* Rudolf Nagel. 12 hectares. *Einzellagen:* Edenkoben: Klostergarten, Heilig Kreuz and Bergel; Ruppertsberg: Reiterpfad.

Old monastic buildings with the rustic atmosphere of a century ago shelter an enormous range of old oak casks with a total capacity of 450,000 litres. The oak-aged wines keep remarkably: although not particularly fine they are fascinating in representing an almost-lost tradition. The minimum storage in oak is one year, the maximum three years. 70% is Riesling.

Weingut Johannes Karst & Söhne

Burgstraße 15, 6702 Bad Dürkheim. *Owner:* Heinz Karst. 10 hectares. *Einzellagen:* Dürkheim: Fuchsmantel, Spielberg, Hochbenn and Michelsberg. Großlagen: Feuerberg, Schenkenböhl and Hochmess.

A family firm of growers and merchants. 80% of their own vines are Riesling, 10% Scheurebe. Scheurebe has recently become something of a speciality; and Huxelrebe is being made into Auslesen, Beerenauslesen and Trockenbeerenauslesen.

Weingut Dr. Kern

Schloß Deidesheim, 6705 Deidesheim, tel: 06326-260. *Owner:* Gottfried Kern. 5.8 hectares. *Einzellagen:* Deidesheim: Herrgottsacker, Kieselberg, Leinhöhle, Langenmorgen, Paradiesgarten, Grainhübel and Nonnenstück; Forst: Ungeheuer; Ruppertsberg: Linsenbusch, Reiterpfad; Niederkirchen: Klostergarten.

Relatively small but well-known estate with holdings in some of the best vineyards of the Mittelhaardt. The plantation of Riesling (69%) is high, and other vines grown are Kerner

(10%), Müller-Thurgau (4%), Gewürztraminer (8%) and Spätburgunder (9%). The estate is very proud of its dry Rieslings, deliberately bottled late to allow the maximum development in bulk. The result can be tasted in the wine bar.

Weingut Koehler-Ruprecht

Weinstraße 84, 6701 Kallstadt, tel: 06322-1829. *Owners:* The Philippi family. *President:* Otto Philippi. 8.25 hectares. *Einzellagen:* Kallstadt: Saumagen, Steinacker and Kronenberg. Großlagen: Kobnert and Feuerberg.

A family property going back centuries, including the charming hotel "Weincastell" – all typical antiques and local food. Vines are 68% Riesling, with red Spätburgunder as another speciality (their 1983 Kallstadter Feuerberg is a great rarity). The vineyards ripen grapes remarkably: Herr Philippi reports that he can always make an Auslese. Cellar methods are traditional, the wines full of flavour.

Weingut Karl & Hermann Lingenfelder

Hauptstraße 27, 6711 Großkarlbach, tel: 06238-754. *Owners:* the Lingenfelder family. 10 hectares. *Einzellagen:* Großkarlbach: Burgweg and Osterberg (7.6); Friensheim: Goldberg, Musikantenbuckel (2.4).

This family estate – in its 13th generation – produces wines high in extract, of considerable individuality and character, that are increasingly successful in international competitions. The vineyards are planted with 22% Riesling, 15% Scheurebe, 14% Spätburgunder, 17% Müller-Thurgau and 12% Kerner. The Spätburgunder, made like a Burgundy, is matured in French oak. Rainer Karl Lingenfelder is the Chief Oenologist of the wine shippers H. Sichel Söhne.

Weingut Georg Mosbacher

Weinstraße 27, 6701 Forst, tel: 06326-329. *Owner:* Richard Mosbacher. 9.3 hectares. *Einzellagen:* Forst: Ungeheuer, Pechstein, Elster, Freundstück, Musenhang and Stift; Deidesheim: Herrgottsacker; Wachenheim: Altenburg. Großlagen: Mariengarten and Schnepfenflug.

The Mosbachers have steadily improved this small estate in the centre of Forst since they first bottled their wine in 1920. 80% is Riesling, 9% Müller-Thurgau, 3% each of Scheurebe, Kerner and Spätburgunder, and 2% Gewürztraminer. (Riesling is to be increased to 90%.) They regularly win prizes with freshly flowery wines, particularly dry Riesling Kabinett from Forster Pechstein and Stift. Wines are sold direct or at their own Weinstube.

Weingut K. Neckerauer

Ritter von Geißlerstraße 9, 6714 Weisenheim am Sand, tel: 06353-8059. *Owners:* Klaus and Arnd Neckerauer. 16 hectares. *Einzellagen* all in Weisenheim am Sand: Hahnen, Hasenzeile, Goldberg, Altenberg, Halde and Burgweg. 16% of the property is only under the Großlage names Rosenbühl and Schwarzerde.

EASTERN ZONE

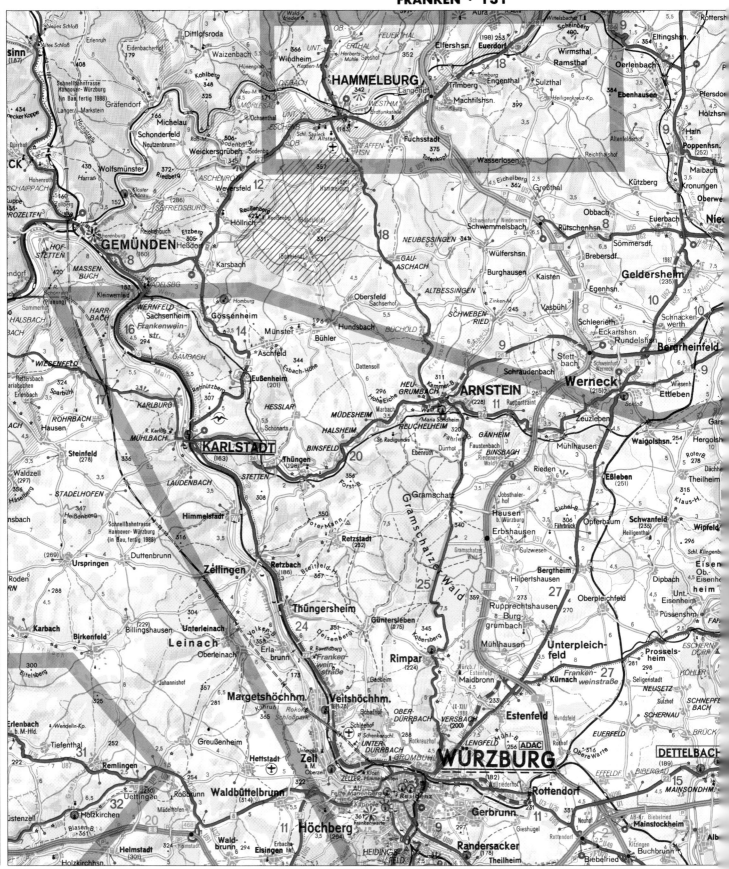

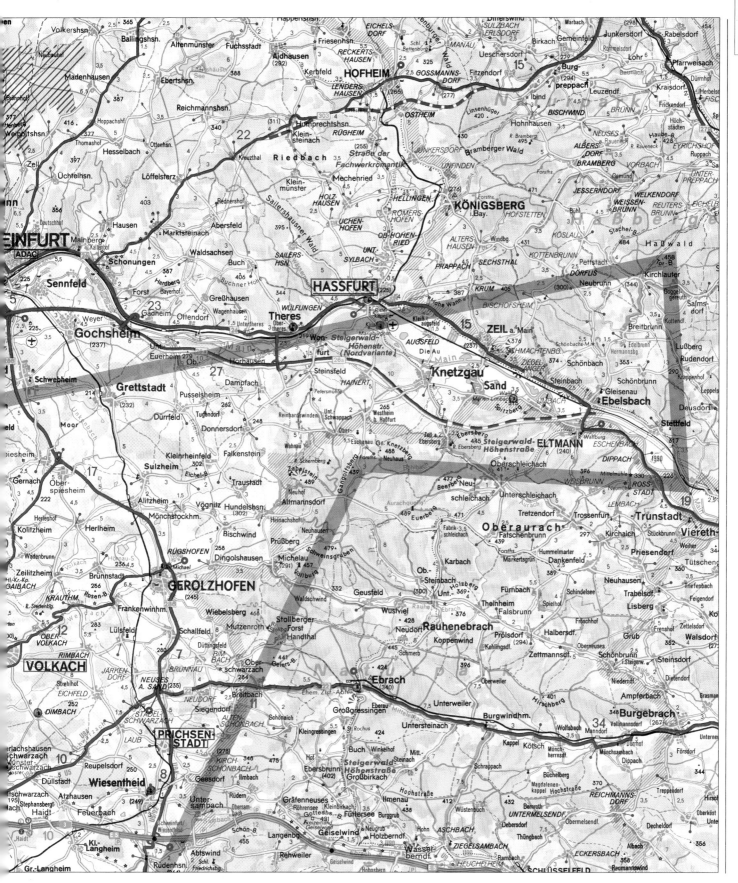

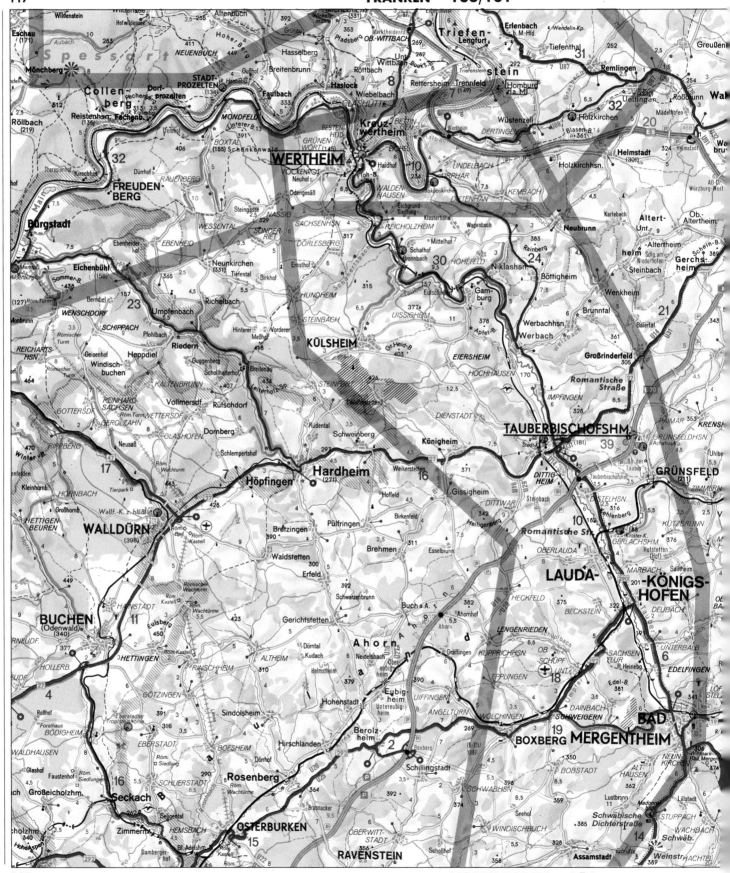

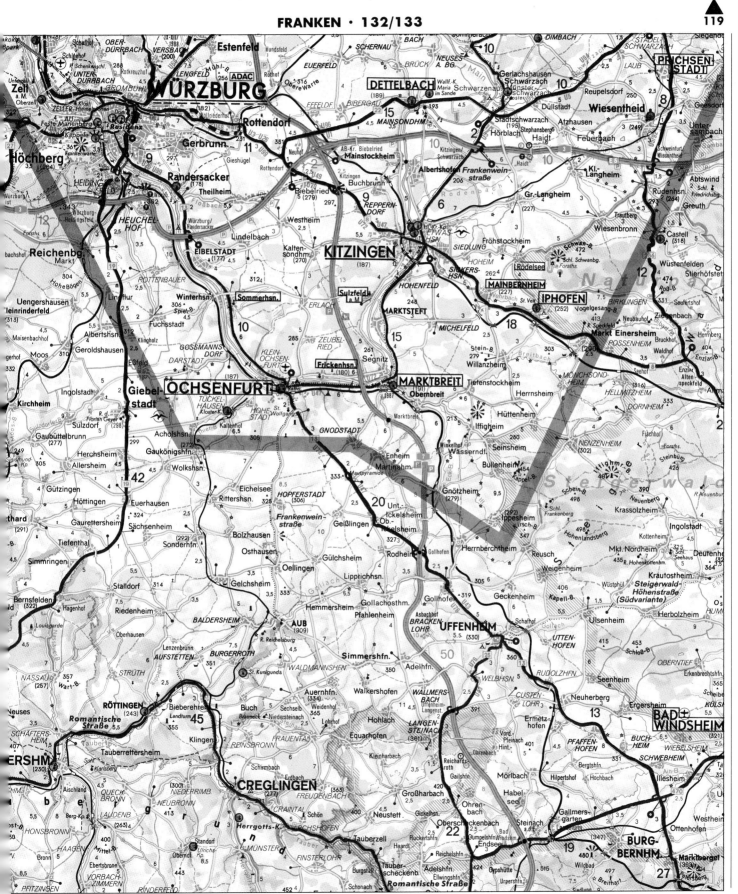

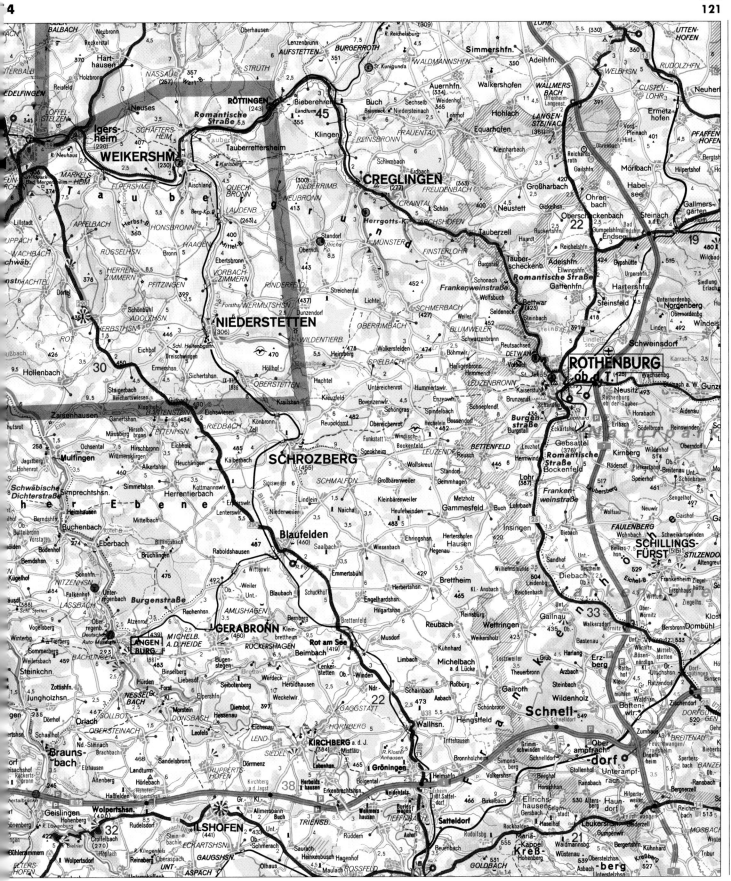

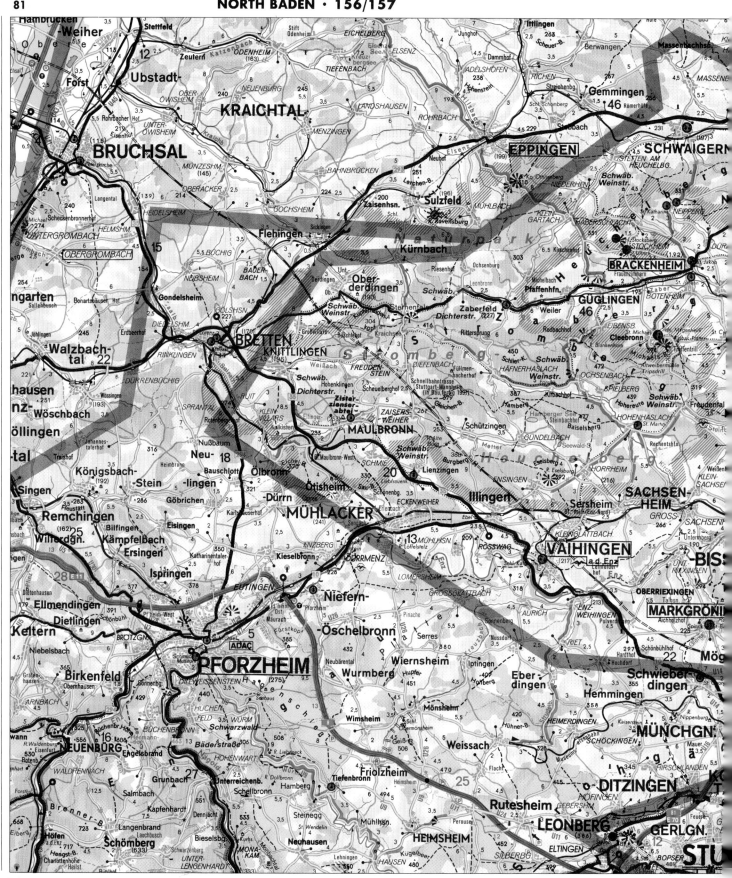

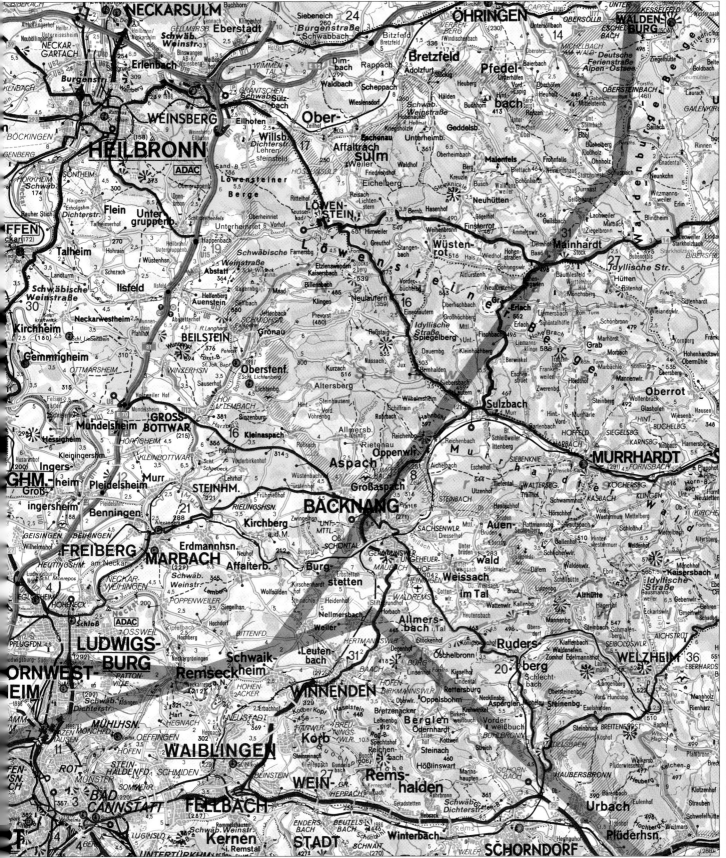

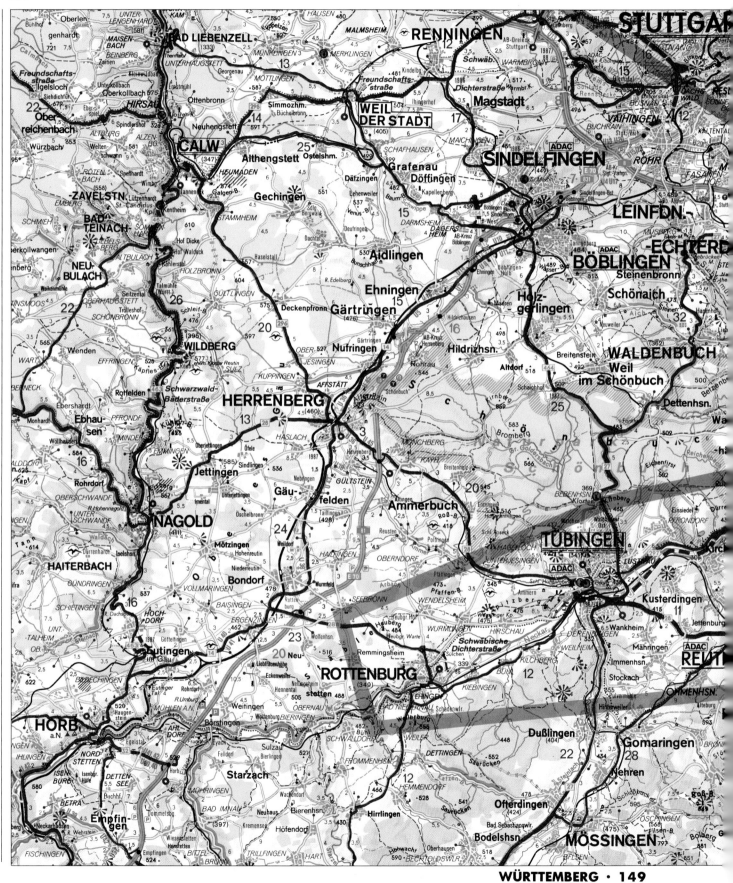

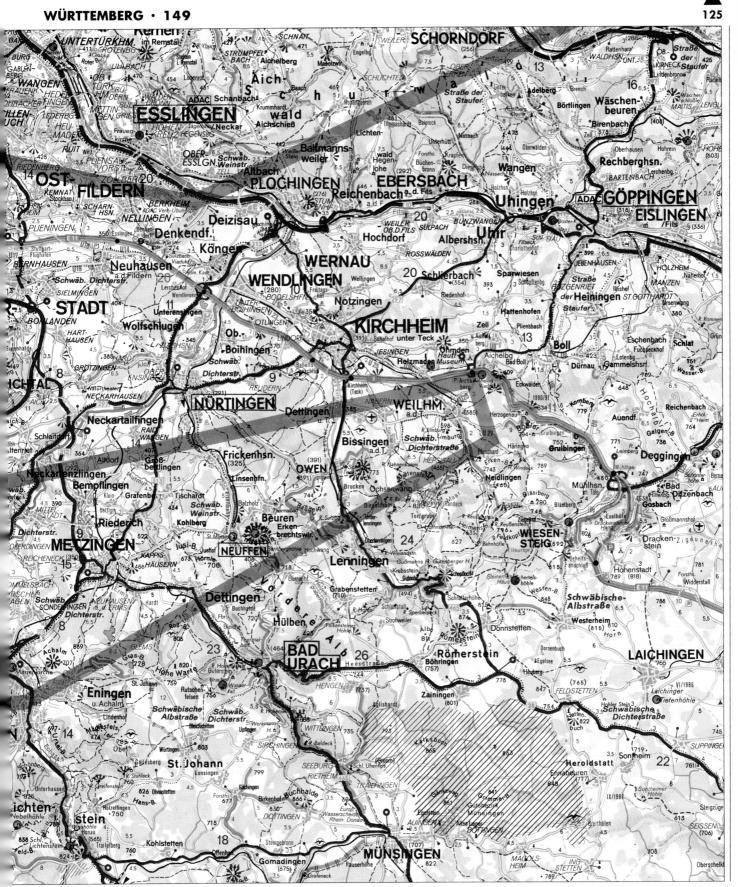

FRANKEN

Eighty kilometres (50 miles) east of the Rheingau, beyond the city of Frankfurt, the river Main, flowing to join the Rhine at Mainz, scribbles a huge drunken W through the irregular limestone and red marl hills of Franken (Franconia), the northern extremity of Bavaria.

The centre of the region is the baroque city of Würzburg. Its most famous vineyard, sloping down to the Main within the city itself, is Würzburger Stein. The name Stein has been traditionally borrowed by foreigners to describe Franconian wine generically (as the English shortened Hochheim to "hock" for all Rhine wines). "Steinwein" comes in fat flagons called Bocksbeutels, thus distinguishing itself from almost all other German wines, which come in elegant flasks. The Bocksbeutel has been used for centuries here: now it is reserved by law exclusively for Qualitätswein from Franken and (by long tradition) for certain wines from northern Baden, including the Tauber valley.

This is probably the extent of popular knowledge. It is a specialized subject, not least because its rarity value and local popularity keep the price higher than we are accustomed to pay for more famous names from the Rhine and Mosel. Most "Frankenwein" is drunk in Bavaria, particularly in Munich, or in the wealthy cities of northern Germany. Besides, the area is exceptionally diffuse and hard to comprehend. Vineyards are only found on exceptional south slopes. The climate is harsh and serious frosts are common; the season is too short for regular success with Riesling.

Traditionally, Franken has made its best wine with the Silvaner, only here (and in certain exceptional sites elsewhere, such as the Nierstein Rheinterrasse and parts of the Kaiserstuhl) a better-than-moderate variety. Silvaner here can produce full-bodied dry wines (and occasionally sweet ones) with a noble breadth and substance; dense, even sticky in their intensity. They are regularly compared with white burgundy, not for their flavour but for their vinosity and ability to match rich food at table.

Unfortunately the Müller-Thurgau has now gained the upper hand. It works well, but rarely if ever produces the remarkable low-key stylishness of Silvaner. Scheurebe and the new Perle can do better. Bacchus tends to be aggressively aromatic; out of keeping for the region. Kerner is also too aromatic, although many people find it acceptable. In a ripe year Rieslaner is a good compromise, making excellent Auslesen with the breadth of a Silvaner and the depth of a Riesling. 1976 in the Steigerwald produced some extraordinary wines with a bouquet like salty honey.

Auslesen, however, are rarer in Franken than elsewhere in Germany, and Beeren- and Trockenbeerenauslesen very rare indeed. Although one of the most famous wines of all time, a Würzburger Stein of the (almost literally) immortal vintage of 1546, was certainly as sweet as a Beerenauslese when it started on its long career (it was drunk, with awe, at the age of 420), the Franken style generally finds its best expression in Kabinett and Spätlesen – and sometimes indeed in QbA wines, when the addition of sugar has been nicely judged.

Franken has a wildly fluctuating production. There are years when very large yields can make the wine over-light, others where the poor farmer has his crop reduced to almost nil. For example, the yield in 1983 was 148 hl/ha, but in 1985 it was only 13 hl/ha. Vintages that are generally successful along the Rhine can sometimes be disappointing in Franken, partly for this reason.

There is a wider range of climate here than in other German wine regions. This unreliability can result in overproduction – as in '82 and '83 – of a harvest that is usually small and concentrated. It is worth investigating the Silvaner of the lesser vintages – not too young: it takes at least two years for the elusive flavours to knit and the singular soft texture to emerge.

This rambling region is divided into three Bereiche: Mainviereck for its lower reaches towards Frankfurt; Maindreieck for its heart, the district of Würzburg; and Steigerwald for its eastern extremities, with the sternest climate of all. The river Main is the unifying factor of the two western Bereiche, with the vineyards sited either on the river banks or in side-valleys. Further east the pattern becomes less clear. Bereich Steigerwald consists of a collection of scattered vineyards in a hundred warm corners, with no helpful river valley to string them together. The Bereich names are frequently used, partly because a great number of the far-flung vineyards are included in no Großlage. The majority of the wine, as in Rheinhessen and Baden, is made by cooperatives (some of which are described in the Producers section on page 138). Würzburg itself, however, boasts three of the oldest, biggest and best wine estates in Germany – the Bürgerspital, the Juliusspital and the Staatlicher Hofkeller.

TRAVEL INFORMATION

The sprawling wine region of Franken follows the river Main as it meanders through the forests of central Germany. The Rhine, with its lighthearted atmosphere, is left behind as the traveller enters the heart of Central Europe, a land of forests, ancient cities and baroque masterpieces.

Places to visit

Würzburg: one of the great historic cities of Germany, with too many treasures to list. Winelovers can imbibe culture as well as Franken wine at various ancient cellars such as that beneath the Bürgerspital (Theaterstraße, tel: 0931-13861) and the Juliusspital (Juliuspromenade, tel: 0931-54080). The baroque Residenz and the 12th century Marienberg, the fortress of the prince-bishops, are highlights in a city of marvels. Dettelbach: a small town on the main east of Würzburg, noted for its 36 towers. Iphofen: an old town deep in the countryside east of the Main, on the edge of the Steigerwald.

Wine festivals

Würzburg has a festival in late September, Gambach in late October. Others include: Röttingen (late May), Dettelbach & Stammheim (early June), Rimbach (3rd w/e in June), Obereisenheim (early July), Aschaffenburg (2nd w/e in July), Castell (3rd w/e in July), Homburg (end July), Volkach (mid Aug), Escherndorf (2nd w/e in Sept and also in Oct), Fahr (mid-Oct).

Food and drink

Franken is known for beer as well as wine: many towns and villages have their own breweries. Plum and other fruit brandies are also made here. Nowhere else in Germany has quite Franken's profusion of inns, serving food such as pig's knuckle and Sauerkraut, grilled sausages and *Meerfischli* — small fish from the rivers. Among hotels, the Schloß Steinburg has perhaps the perfect location for winelovers: it sits above the famous Stein vineyard just outside the city of Würzburg (tel: 0931-93061). The Schafhof near Amorbach, a little town south of the Main, is the former inn of a Benedictine abbey. The Zehntkeller inn at Iphofen offers a glimpse of old Franken (tel: 09323-3318); in Volkach the Hotel Zur Schwane serves regional specialities.

▲ The river Main describes a series of wobbly Ws through the scattered Franken wine-districts. Miltenberg, where the river right-angles north-westward, is typical in having only one vineyard site; the south-facing lower slopes of the Burgstadt, the forest-crowned hill that looms over the old tile roofs of the town.
▶ The village of Volkach, upstream from Würzburg, includes in its Großlage name of Kirchberg the great vineyards of Escherndorf, some of Franken's finest. Its famous Gothic church is known as Maria im Weingarten — "Mary in the vineyard".

VINEYARDS

ROAD MAP

116   117

OFFENBACH

ASCHAFFENBURG

Main

DARMSTADT

GROSS-
UMSTADT

BAD MERGENTHEIM

79   ROAD MAP   120

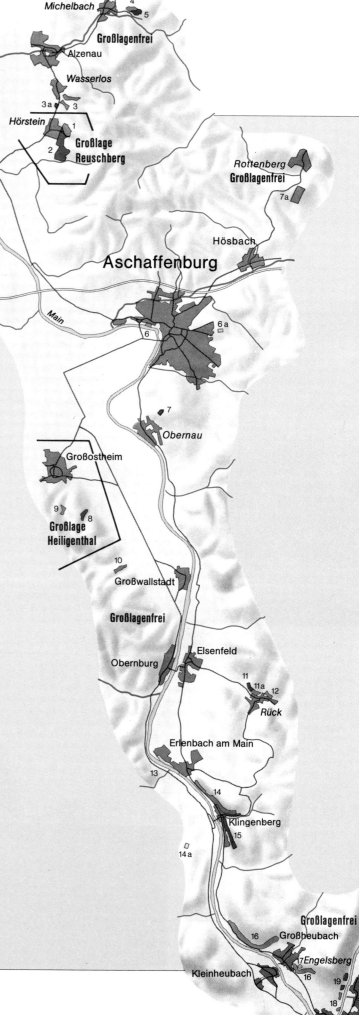

**BEREICH
MAINVIERECK**

**GROSSLAGE
REUSCHBERG**

Hörstein
(Ortsteil of Alzenau)
Abtsberg 1
Other vineyards 2

GROSSLAGENFREI

Wasserlos
(Ortsteil of Alzenau)
Schloßberg 3
Luhmannchen 3 a

Michelbach
(Ortsteil of Alzenau)
Steinberg 4
Apostelgarten 5

Aschaffenburg
Pompejaner 6
Godelsberg 6 a

Obernau
(Ortsteil of
Aschaffenburg)
Sanderberg 7

Rottenberg
(Ortsteil of Hösbach)
Gräfenstein 7 a

**GROSSLAGE
HEILIGENTHAL**

Großostheim
Reischklingeberg 8
Harstell 9
Also vineyards in the
parish of
Wenigumstadt

GROSSLAGENFREI

Großwaltstadt
Lützeltalerberg 10

Rück
(Ortsteil of Elsenfeld)
Johannisberg 11
Schalk 11 a
Jesuitenberg 12

Erlenbach am Main
Hochberg 13

**Klingenberg am
Main**
Hochberg 14
Einsiedel 14 a
Schloßberg 15

Großheubach
Bischofsberg 16

Engelsberg
(Ortsteil of
Großheubach)
Klostergarten 17

Miltenberg
Steingrübler 18

Bürgstadt
Mainhölle 19
Centgrafenberg 20

Dorfprozelten
Predigtstuhl 21

Kreuzwertheim
Kaffelstein 22

**BEREICH
MAINDREIECK**

GROSSLAGENFREI

Homburg am Main
(Ortsteil of
Triefenstein)
Kallmuth 23
Edelfrau 24

Lengfurt
(Ortsteil of
Triefenstein)
Alter Berg 25
Oberrot 26

**Erlenbach (bei
Marktheidenfeld)**
incl. Ortsteil
Tiefenthal
Krähenschnabel 27 P

Marktheidenfeld
Kreuzberg 27 a

Remlingen
Krähenschnabel 27 P
Sonnenhain 27 b

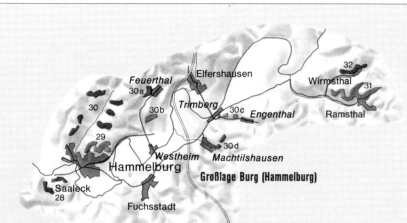

| 118 | **ROAD MAP** | 119 |

GROSSLAGE BURG (HAMMELBURG)

Saaleck
(Ortsteil of Hammelburg)
Schloßberg 28

Hammelburg
Heroldsberg 29
Trautlestal 30

Feuerthal
(Ortsteil of Hammelburg)
Kreuz 30 a

Westheim
(Ortsteil of Hammelburg)
Längberg 30 b

Trimberg
(Ortsteil of Elfershausen)
Schloßberg 30 c P

Engenthal
(Ortsteil of Elfershausen)
Schloßberg 30 c P

Machtilshausen
(Ortsteil of Elfershausen)
Sommerleite 30 d

Ramsthal
St. Klausen 31

Wirmsthal
(Ortsteil of Euerdorf)
Scheinberg 32

GROSSLAGE EWIG LEBEN

Randersacker
Teufelskeller 60
Sonnenstuhl 61
Pfülben 62
Marsberg 63

GROSSLAGE ÖLSPIEL

Sommerhausen
Steinbach 64 P
Reifenstein 65

Eibelstadt
Steinbach 64 P

GROSSLAGE TEUFELSTOR

Eibelstadt
Kapellenberg 66
Mönchsleite 67

Randersacker
Dabug 68 P

Lindelbach
(Ortsteil of
Randersacker)
Dabug 68 P

GROSSLAGENFREI

Adelsberg
(Ortsteil of
Gemünden)
Wernleite 68 a*

Margetshöchheim
Bärental 68 b

Tauberrettersheim
Königin 68 d*

Röttingen
Feuerstein 68 e*

Bergtheim
Harfenspiel 69

Kleinochsenfurt
(Ortsteil of
Ochsenfurt)
Herrenberg 69 a

Winterhausen
Kaiser Wilhelm 69 b

GROSSLAGE MARKGRAF BABENBERG

Frickenhausen
Fischer 70
Kapellenberg 71

GROSSLAGE HOFRAT (KITZINGEN)

Segnitz
Zobelsberg 73
Pfaffensteig 74

Marktbreit
Sonnenberg 75 P

Marksteft
Sonnenberg 75 P

Sulzfeld
Maustal 76
Cyriakusberg 77

Kitzingen
Wilhelmsberg 78
Eselsberg 78 a

– Ortsteil Eherieder
Mühle
Kaiser Karl 79 P

Repperndorf
(Ortsteil of Kitzingen)
Kaiser Karl 79 P

Buchbrunn
Heißer Stein 80

Mainstockheim
Hofstück 81

Albertshofen
Herrgottsweg 81 a

GROSSLAGE HONIGBERG

Dettelbach
Berg-Rondell 82
Sonnenleite 83 P

– Ortsteile Brück
and Schnepfenbach
Sonnenleite 83 P

– Ortsteil Bibergau
Vineyards not
registered as
Einz. 84

GROSSLAGE KIRCHBERG (VOLKACH)

Neuses am Berg
(Ortsteil of
Dettelbach)
Glatzen 85

Escherndorf
(Ortsteil of Volkach)
Fürstenberg 86 P
Berg 87 P
Lump 88

Köhler
(Ortsteil of Volkach)
Fürstenberg 86 P

Neusetz
(Ortsteil of
Dettelbach)
Fürstenberg 86 P

Untereisenheim
(Ortsteil of Markt
Eisenheim)
Berg 87 P
Sonnenberg 99
Small parts of the
above vineyard
belong to No. 100

Sommerach
Katzenkopf 89
Rosenberg 90 P

Hallburg
(Ortsteil of Volkach)
Rosenberg 90 P
Kreuzberg 92 P

Nordheim
Vögelein 91
Kreuzberg 92 P

Astheim
(Ortsteil of Volkach)
Karthäuser 93

Krautheim
(Ortsteil of Volkach)
Sonnenleite 94

Obervolkach
(Ortsteil of Volkach)
Landsknecht 95 P

Rimbach
(Ortsteil of Volkach)
Landsknecht 95 P

Gaibach
(Ortsteil of Volkach)
Kapellenberg 97

Volkach
(incl. Ortsteil Fahr)
Ratsherr 98

Obereisenheim
(Ortsteil of Markt
Eisenheim)
Höll 100

Stammheim
(Ortsteil of
Kolitzheim)
Eselsberg 101

Theilheim
(Ortsteil of
Waigolshausen)
Mainleite 101 a P

Hergolshausen
(Ortsteil of
Waigolshausen)
Mainleite 101 a P

Wipfeld
Zehntgraf 102

Frankenwinheim
Rosenberg 102 a

Zeilitzheim
(Ortsteil of
Kolitzheim)
Heiligenberg 102 b

Lindach
(Ortsteil of
Kolitzheim)
Kreuzpfad 102 c

Also vineyards in the
parishes of Neusetz,
Köhler (Ortsteil of
Volkach), Fahr and
Schwarzenau
(Ortsteil of
Schwarzenach)

GROSSLAGENFREI

Hallburg
(Ortsteil of Volkach)
Schloßberg 103

Gaibach
(Ortsteil of Volkach)
Schloßpark 103 a

Vogelsburg
(Ortsteil of Volkach)
Pforte 103 b

Schweinfurt
Peterstirn 103 c*
Mainleite 103 d*

Mainberg
(Ortsteil of
Schonungen)
Schloß 103 e*

Mönchsteckheim
(Ortsteil of Sulzheim)
Mönchberg 103 f

Kitzingen
Ortsteil Eherieder
Mühle
Eherieder Berg 104

Obernbreit
Kanzel 104 a

Tauberzell
(Ortsteil of
Adelshofen)
Hasennestle 104 b*

BEREICH STEIGERWALD

GROSSLAGE SCHILD (ABTSWIND)

Abtswind
Altenberg 105

Greuth
(Ortsteil of Castell)
Bastel 105 a

Prichsenstadt
Ortsteil
Kirchschönbach
Mariengarten 105 b

GROSSLAGE HERRENBERG

The sites 106 and
108 also belong to
Großlage Schild

Castell
Bausch 106
Hohnart 107
Kirchberg 108
Feuerbach 109
Kugelspiel 110
Reitsteig 111
Schloßberg 112
Trautberg 113

GROSSLAGE SCHLOSSBERG (RÖDELSEE)

Parts of Einz. 120
also belong to this
Großlage

Kleinlangheim
Wutschenberg 114

Wiesenbronn
Wachhügel 115
Geißberg 115 a

Großlangheim
Kiliansberg 116

Rödelsee
Schwanleite 117
Küchenmeister 118

Sickershausen
(Ortsteil of Kitzingen)
Storchenbrünnle 119

Also vineyards in
the parishes of
Mainbernheim and
Hoheim (Ortsteil of
Kitzingen)

GROSSLAGE BURGWEG (IPHOFEN)

Iphofen
Julius-Echter-Berg
120
Kalb 121
Kronsberg 121 a

Possenheim
(Ortsteil of Iphofen)
Vogelsang 122 P

Markt Einersheim
Vogelsang 122 P

Willanzheim
Vineyards not
registered as Einz.

GROSSLAGE SCHLOSSSTÜCK (FRANKENBERG)

Hüttenheim
(Ortsteil of
Willanzheim)
Tannenberg 123

Seinsheim
Hohenbühl 124

Bullenheim
(Ortsteil of
Ippesheim)
Paradies 125

Ippesheim
Herrschaftsberg 126

Ergersheim
Altenberg 127*

Weimersheim
(Ortsteil of Ipsheim)
Roter Berg 127 a

Ingolstadt
(Ortsteil of
Sugenheim)
Rotenberg 127 a*

Weigenheim
Hohenlandsberg
127 b P*

Reusch
(Ortsteil of
Weigenheim)
Hohenlandsberg
127 b T*

Ipsheim
Burg Hoheneck 127 c P*

Kaubenheim
(Ortsteil of Ipsheim)
Burg Hoheneck 127 c P*

VILLAGES

Walddachsbach
(Ortsteil of
Dietersheim)
Burg Hoheneck 127 c T*

Also vineyards in
Krassolzheim (Ortsteil
of Sugenheim),
Hump-
rechtsau, Rüdisbronn,
Külsheim, Ickelheim
(Orts. of Windsheim),
Walddachsbach and
Dottenheim (Orts. of
Dietersheim)

GROSSLAGENFREI

Martinsheim
Langenstein 128

Tiefenstockheim
(Ortsteil of
Seinsheim)
Stiefel 128 a

Iphofen
Domherr 128 b

Neundorf
(Ortsteil of
Sugenheim)
Hüßberg 128 c*
Mönchsbuck 128 d*
Sonneberg 128 e*
Wonne 128 f*

Bad Windsheim
Ortsteil Oberntief
Rosenberg 128 g*

GROSSLAGE KAPELLENBERG

Schmachtenberg
(Ortsteil of Zeil am
Main)
Eulengrund 129

Ziegelanger
(Ortsteil of Zeil am
Main)
Ölschnabel 130

Steinbach
(Ortsteil of
Ebelsbach)
Nonnenberg 131

Sand am Main
Kronberg 132

Oberschwappach
(Ortsteil of Knetzgau)
Sommertal 133

GROSSLAGENFREI

Zell am Ebersberg
(Ortsteil of Knetzgau)
Schloßberg 133 a

Sand am Main
Himmelsbühl 133 b

Zeil am Main
Mönchshang 134

– Ortsteil Krum
Himmelreich 134 a

**Königsberg in
Bayern
Ortsteil Unfinden**
Kinnleitenberg 134 b

Eltmann
Schloßleite 135

Weiher
(Ortsteil of Viereth)
Weinberge 135 a*

Bamberg
Alter Graben 135 b*

Altmannsdorf
(Ortsteil of Michelau)
Sonnenwinkel 136

Donnersdorf
Falkenberg 136 a

Mönchstockheim
(Ortsteil of Sulzheim)
Köhler 136 b P

Dingolshausen
Köhler 136 b P

– Ortsteil Bischwind
Köhler 136 b P

Gerolzhofen
Köhler 136 b P
Arlesgarten 136 c

Michelau
Vollburg 137

Oberschwarzach
(incl. Ortsteile
Mutzenroth and
Düttingsfeld)
Herrenberg 138

**– Ortsteil
Wiebelsberg**
Dachs 138 a

Handthal
(Ortsteil of
Oberschwarzach)
Stollberg 139

Kammerforst
(Ortsteil of
Oberschwarzach)
Teufel 140

Prichsenstadt
Krone 141

BEREICH MAINVIERECK
Bereich Mainviereck extends across the famous Spessart forest from Aschaffenburg in the northwest down to Kreuzwertheim in the first trough of the W described by the Main. The very limited vineyard area is all close to the river with the exception of Rück, in a little eastern side valley. The soils are largely sandstone based and loamy. Two Großlagen: Reuschberg (Hörstein) and Heiligenthal (Großostheim) and 15 villages where no Großlage applies.

GROSSLAGE REUSCHBERG
This Großlage consists of two vineyards close to the town of Hörstein.
Vineyards
Einzellagen: Abtsberg and other nearby sites, 17.8ha, W, steep.

GROSSLAGE HEILIGENTHAL
Two sites south of Großostheim.
Vineyards
Einzellagen: Reichsklingenberg, 5ha, SE, steep; Harstell, 7ha, SE, steep.

Villages with no Großlage but with *Einzellagen:* Rück: Jesuitenberg, 6.7ha, S, sloping/steep; Johannisberg, 10ha, SW, sloping/steep; Schalk, 10ha, S,SW, sloping/steep. Großheubach: Bischofsberg, 15ha, S,W, sloping/steep. Bürgstadt: Mainhölle, 8ha, SE, steep. Kreuzwertheim: Kaffelstein, 10ha, S,SW, steep.

BEREICH MAINDREIECK
Bereich Maindreieck includes Homburg and Lengfurt, next door to Kreuzwertheim, but then leaps over the central ridge of the W to an isolated area of vines on the tributary river Saale round Hammelburg. Here the soil is limestone (Muschelkalk), the soil of all the best Franconian vineyards. Nine Großlagen: Burg (Hammelburg), Roßtal (Karlstadt), Ravensburg (Thüngersheim), Ewig Leben (Randersacker), Ölspiel (Sommerhausen), Teufelstor (Eibelstadt), Hofrat (Kitzingen), Honigberg (Dettelbach) and Kirchberg (Volkach).

Villages with no Großlage but with *Einzellagen:* Homburg am Main: Kallmuth, 29.9ha, SW, steep. Lengfurt: Oberrot, 1ha, S,SE, steep; Alter Berg, 4.8ha, SW, steep.
Vineyards
Großlage Burg with *Einzellagen:* Feuerthal: Kreuz, 4.8ha, E, steep. Hammelburg: Heroldsberg, 14.9ha, E,W,S, steep; Trautlestal, 14.9ha, S,SW, sloping/steep. Saaleck: Schloßberg, 14.9ha, SW, steep.

The western trough of the W is the centre of Franconian wine production, with Würzburg at its heart. The main concentrations of vines are in the villages north and south of Würzburg along the river, all on limestone, down to Frickenhausen, the foot of the eastern trough of the W, and in bends in the river higher up around Escherndorf and Nordheim, still on limestone but here with an overlay of marly clay. The famous hill of Escherndorfer Lump makes great Silvaners from this soil structure.

The wines of all the principal vineyards can be tasted and compared at the big, bustling Weinstuben of the three great Würzburg estates. The Juliusspital, the Bürgerspital and the Staatliche Hofkeller all maintain wonderfully comfortable and convivial cafés for the appreciation of their wines in a city which is infiltrated with vineyards to its very heart. You can look up from its famous baroque statue-lined bridge (on feast days one long café from end to end) to see the steep vine-ramp of the Innere Leiste supporting the Marienberg Castle. The celebrated Stein vineyard covers the best parts of the south-facing hill overlooking the city – a skyline now sadly marred by ugly and intrusive new buildings. Steinwein begins to have real meaning when you have sipped a stiff Silvaner Spätlese at the Bürgerspital and gone on to marvel at Tiepolo's ceilings in the Residenz.

GROSSLAGE ROSSTAL
The vineyards of the Main around Karlstadt and of the tributary river Kahl.
Vineyards
Einzellagen: Gößenheim: Homburg (formerly Arnberg), 8ha, S, steep. Karlstadt: Im Stein, 8ha, SW, steep. Himmelstadt: Kelter, 20ha, SW,W, steep.

GROSSLAGE RAVENSBURG
The next stretch of the Main valley going south, just downstream from Würzburg.
Vineyards
Einzellagen: Retzbach: Benediktinusberg, 54.4ha, S,SW, steep. Thüngersheim: Johannisberg, 110ha, W,SW,S, steep; Scharlachberg, 129.7ha, W,S, sloping/steep. Erlabrunn: Weinsteig, 11.9ha, S,SE,E, steep. Veitshöchheim: Sonnenschein, 25ha, S,SW,W, steep.

Villages with no Großlage but with *Einzellagen:* Würzburg: Pfaffenberg, 49.9ha, S,SE, steep. Stein, 84.8ha, S, steep. Innere Leiste, 10.1ha, S, steep. Schloßberg, 5.4ha, E, steep. Abtsleite, 44.8ha, SE,S, steep. Kirchberg, 10.1ha, NE, steep.

GROSSLAGE EWIG LEBEN
A group of vineyards just south of the city of Würzburg, around Randersacker.
Vineyards
Einzellagen: Randersacker: Teufelskeller, 40ha, S,SW, steep. Pfülben, 14.9ha, SE,S, steep. Marsberg, 49.9ha, S,SW, steep. Sonnenstuhl, 49.9ha, S,SW, steep.

GROSSLAGE TEUFELSTOR
Four sites on the river banks around Eibelstadt and the splendidly-named Sommerhausen (on the south-facing bank) and Winterhausen across the river, facing northeast.
Vineyards
Einzellage: Eibelstadt: Kapellenberg, 69.9ha, SW, sloping/steep; Dabug, 10ha, SE, steep.

GROSSLAGE ÖLSPIEL

Two vineyards with advantageous exposure on the east bank of the Main.

Vineyards

Sommerhausen: Steinbach, 34.9ha, SW, steep. Reifenstein, 49.9ha, SSW,W, steep.

GROSSLAGE MARKGRAF BABENBERG

The Main makes one of its great bends here, giving the two vineyards of the Großlage a fine southerly exposure.

Vineyards

Einzellage: Frickenhausen: Fischer, 46.9ha, S, steep; Kapellenberg, 63ha, S, steep.

GROSSLAGE HOFRAT

Once again the Main flows from north to south, giving this collection of vineyards around Kitzingen less good sites.

Vineyard

Einzellagen: Marktbreit: Sonnenberg, 15.9ha, S-SW, steep.

GROSSLAGE KIRCHBERG

Sweeping bends around Volkach form some good sites as the vineyards thin out towards the north.

Vineyards

Einzellagen: Escherndorf: Lump, 34.9ha, S-SE, steep. Astheim: Karthäuser, 45ha, S, steep. Nordheim: Kreuzberg, 149.9ha, SW, sloping/steep. Vögelein, 249.5ha, SW,NW, sloping/steep. Sommerach: Rosenberg, 49.9ha, E-SW, sloping/steep; Katzenkopf, 199.5ha, SSE-SW, sloping/steep. Volkach: Ratsherr, 149.7ha, S, sloping/steep.

BEREICH STEIGERWALD

Wine communities to the east of the Main form this much smaller Bereich. The best known are Iphofen, Rödelsee and Castell, all on heavier marly clay soil which demands a fine summer but can deliver both full-bodied and nicely nuanced wines. Six Großlagen: Schild (Abtswind), Herrenberg (Castell), Schloßberg (Rödelsee), Burgweg (Iphofen), Schloßstück (Frankenberg) and Kapellenberg (Zeil).

GROSSLAGE SCHILD

Vineyard

Einzellage: Abtswind: Altenberg, 29.9ha, SW,NW, sloping/steep.

GROSSLAGE HERRENBERG

Vineyards

Einzellagen: Castell: Bausch, 13.9ha, NW,N, sloping/steep. Feuerbach, 3ha, NW,N, sloping/steep. Hohnart, 5.4ha, S, steep. Kirchberg, 1.6ha, E,NW,W, steep. Kugelspiel, 14.9ha, NW,N, sloping/steep. Reitsteig, 2ha, S, sloping/steep. Schloßberg, 6.9ha, S,SW, steep. Trautberg, 2ha, S, sloping/steep.

GROSSLAGE SCHLOSSBERG

Vineyard

Einzellage: Rödelsee: Küchenmeister, 59.8ha, NW, sloping/steep.

GROSSLAGE BURGWEG

Vineyards

Einzellagen: Iphof: Julius-Echter-Berg, 69.9ha, S,SW, steep. Kronsberg, 129.7ha, S,SW,SE, steep. Kalb, 64.8ha, S,W, steep.

Village with no Großlage but with *Einzellage:* Michelau: Vollburg, 10.1ha, S,SW, sloping/steep.

VISITING WÜRZBURG

The capital of Franken is an architectural masterpiece, the epicentre of the German Baroque. It is also the home of the greatest Franken wine estates (see facing page). These manage to combine art and wine in happy sympathy. The Bavarian State Cellars, for instance, houses its casks in the vaults beneath the great Residenz of the former prince-bishops of this most Catholic of cities. The cellars are grand enough, but the Residenz itself, with its Tiepolo ceilings and other decorations, is magnificent.

The Residenz was built in the mid-eighteenth century to the designs of Balthasar Neumann, the court architect. Tiepolo, the Venetian master of the fresco, was commissioned to depict two incidents in Barbarossa's life in the Kaisersaal or Imperial hall.

Earlier in the city's history the ruling prince-bishops built the Marienberg fortress, which now houses the Mainfränkisches Museum. The greatest treasures here are the works of the late Gothic sculptor Riemenschneider, the Master of Würzburg. He

specialized in superbly-detailed limewood altar-pieces and free-standing figures. The Romanesque St. Kilian Cathedral also houses works by Riemenschneider.

The State Cellars apart, the other two great wine estates of the city are the Juliusspital, which belongs to a church charity, and the Bürgerspital, a municipal one. The Juliusspital's cellar dates from 1699, the buildings of the Bürgerspital date from the Middle Ages. The charity, which is dedicated to the Holy Ghost, was founded in 1413 for the relief of

Würzburg's aged citizens.

The Residenz is more than a showplace: its galleries host exhibitions and the Kaisersaal is the venue for a *Mozartfest* during the second half of June.

PRODUCERS

Fürstlich Castell'sches Domänenamt

Schloßplatz 5, 8711 Castell, tel: 09325-60170.
Owner: Prince Albrecht zu Castell-Castell. 58.2
hectares. *Einzellagen:* Castell: Schloßberg (15ha),
Kugelspiel (30), Bausch (40), Hohnart, Kirchberg,
Trautberg, Reitsteig and Feuerbach (the last 2 for
red wine); Neundorf: Hüßberg (6.8), Sonneberg
(2.4), Wonne (0.6) and Mönchsbuck (2.6).
A gem of an operatic princely estate with classic
palace in a village on a hill, the vineyards sloping
up to perfectly kept oakwoods – the prince's
other pride. The Castells grow no Riesling but
make fine, admirably balanced wines of Müller-
Thurgau (33%), Silvaner (26%) and a catholic
range of newer varieties; also admirable Sekt
("Casteller Herrenberg"). The new varieties
tend to taste more or less "*schmalzig*" and trite
beside the dignified soft earthiness of the classic
Silvaner. Scheurebe is successfully spicy;
Rieslaner excellent for Silvaner-style Auslesen.
Visitors to this remote spot can taste the wines in
a beautiful tasting room decorated with *trompe
l'œil*, or in the "Weinstall", a stable-turned-
restaurant.

The estate also makes the wine from 70
hectares belonging to 75 growers in the local
producers' association (Erzeugergemeinschaft
Steigerwald). The association's wines bear a
label almost identical to those of the estate.

Weingut Weingroßkellerei Ernst Gebhardt

Hauptstraße 21–23, 8701 Sommerhausen, tel:
09333-287. *Owners:* The Hügelschäffer family. 15
hectares. *Einzellagen:* Sommerhausen: Reifenstein
and Steinbach (21ha); Eibelstadt: Kapellenberg;
Frickenhausen: Fischer and Markgraf Babenberg
(the latter now absorbed into the Frickenhausen
Einzellage Kapellenberg, under the new Großlage
Markgraf Babenberg), Winterhausen: Kaiser
Wilhelm; Randersacker: Teufelskeller, Sonnenstuhl;
Marktbreit: Sonnenberg.
An 18th-century family estate bought in 1888 by
the Hügelschäffer family, who are also wine
merchants. They make somewhat fruitier and
sweeter wines than the old Franconian style with
great skill, especially from their best sites:
Steinbach and the famous Teufelskeller. 26%
is Silvaner, 26% Müller-Thurgau, 20%
Scheurebe (a favourite, distinctly black-
curranty), 6% Bacchus, 6% Riesling (to be
increased). Their Weinstube in the Flemish
baroque style is a well-known attraction.

Bürgerspital zum Heiligen Geist

Theaterstraße 19, 8700 Würzburg, tel: 0931-50363.
Director: Heinz Zeller. 140 hectares. *Einzellagen:*
Würzburg: Stein (22.7ha), Pfaffenberg (42.8),
Abtsleite (18.8) and Innere Leiste (2.6);
Randersacker: Teufelskeller (6.4), Marsberg (1.5)
and Pfülben (2.1); Veitshöchheim: Sonnenschein
(4.8); Thüngersheim: Scharlachberg (2.2);
Michlelau: Vollburg (9.7); Gössenheim: Homburg-
Arnberg (7.5); Leinach: Himmelspfad (7.4). (No
Großlage names are used.)
A splendid charity founded in 1319 for the old
people of Würzburg by Johannes von Steren,
and although now somewhat overshadowed by
the even richer ecclesiastical upstart, the
Juliusspital (q.v.), still the fourth-biggest wine
estate in Germany, with the biggest share of
Würzburg's famous Stein and other good south
slopes. The vineyards are 25% Riesling, 20%
each Silvaner and Müller-Thurgau, the rest
include several new varieties.

Hearty, full-flavoured and dry Rieslings are
the pride of the house, though a tasting at the
huge 500-seater Weinstube in the venerable
hospital buildings leaves an impression of powerful and flavoury wines from almost any
variety. Dry Silvaner and Weißburgunder, particularly Spätlesen, are a speciality.

Weinbau-Weinkellerei Christoph Hans Herpfer

Paul-Eberstraße 5–7, 8710 Kitzingen, tel: 09321-
4305. *Director:* Peter Herpfer.
A democratically run producers' association
(not a cooperative) with members in
Escherndorf, Volkach, Nordheim, Sommerach,
Kitzingen, Rödelsee, Würzburg, Randersacker
and elsewhere. The object is individual wines
made by modern methods, entirely protected
from oxygen, dry in the regional style but with
very distinct fruitiness. Silvaners from the
limestone of Würzburg, Randersacker and
Escherndorf are probably their finest wines,
with Scheurebes for the richest wines in ripe
vintages.

Juliusspital-Weingut

Klinikstraße 5, 8700 Würzburg 1, tel: 0931-3084-
147. *Director:* H. Kolesch. 160 hectares.
Einzellagen: Würzburg: Stein (21), Pfaffenberg,
Innere Leiste and Abtsleite; Randersacker:
Teufelskeller and Pfülben (5); Escherndorf: Lump
(2); Iphofen: Julius-Echter-Berg (9) and
Kronsberg; Rödelsee: Küchenmeister (6); Volkach:
Karthäuser; Thüngersheim: Johannisberg;
Bürgstadt: Mainhölle. (No Großlage names are
used.)
A charitable foundation on a scale even grander
than the Hospices de Beaune, founded in 1576
by the Prince-Bishop Julius Echter von
Mespelbrunn and now the third-largest wine
estate in Germany, supporting a magnificent
hospital for the people of Würzburg. Its low-
vaulted cellar, 250 metres long, was built in 1699
under the great classical "Fürstenbau" wing by
Antonio Petrini. The vineyards are 35%
Silvaner, 24% Müller-Thurgau, 11% Riesling.
The remaining 30% includes Gewürztraminer,
Ruländer, Weißburgunder, Muskateller,
Scheurebe, Spätburgunder (in Bürgstadt) and
several new varieties. All are matured in oak
(some of the casks are over 100 years old). Aside
from the classic Silvaners, the Riesling and
Rieslaner are particularly fruity, extrovert and
powerful. All QmP white wines have black
labels (lesser white wines have green, and reds,
red). The wines can be tasted in the hospital's
own Weinstube.

Weinbau-Weinkellerei Knoll & Reinhart

Alte Poststraße 6, 8710 Kitzingen 2, tel: 09321-
4548. *Owner:* Erich Knoll. 3 hectares in the villages
of Sommerach, Rödelsee and Iphofen.
The second-generation firm claims to have
Germany's oldest cellars (dug in AD 745). They
supplement supplies with bought grapes: 33%
Silvaner, 30% Kanzler, plus Faber, Müller-
Thurgau and Optima. An unusual emphasis on
the Müller-Thurgau × Silvaner cross Kanzler,
apparently very reliable here for full-flavoured
wines even in mean years.

Weingut Müller

Nordheim. 6 hectares in Iphofen, Nordheim,
Sommerach, Frankenwinheim.
A typical 300-year-old family property making
fresh and charming Silvaner, pleasant Müller-
Thurgau, slightly earthy Riesling and excellent
crisp and spicy Scheurebe.

Weingut Ernst Popp KG

Rödelseerstraße 14–15, 8715 Iphofen, tel: 09323-
3371. *Owners:* Michael and Josef Popp. 14 hectares
plus 20 hectares on contract in Iphofen and
Rödelsee. *Einzellagen:* Iphofen: Julius-Echter-Berg
(3), Kalb (2) and Kronsberg (16); Rödelsee:
Schwanleite (2) and Küchenmeister (2).
A respected family firm since 1878 making dry,
"nutty" wines of character, typical of the region.
25% Silvaner, 50% Müller-Thurgau.

Schloß Saaleck-Städt. Weingut

Postfach 1220, 8783 Hammelburg, tel: 09732-
80226. *Owner:* the municipality of Hammelburg.
Director: Josef Kastner. 30 hectares. *Einzellagen:*
Saaleck: Schloßberg, Hammelburg: Heroldsberg
and Trautlestal; Feuerthal: Kreuz; Westheim:
Längberg.
The ancient Schloß Saaleck and its estate are the
property of the town of Hammelburg, down the
Main west of Würzburg. The vineyards are 50%
Müller-Thurgau, 20% Silvaner, 10% Bacchus
(which the director particularly favours) and
other new varieties. The wines are for the most
part dry with powerful fruit flavours.

Staatlicher Hofkeller

Residenzplatz 3, 8700 Würzburg, tel: 0931-50701.
Owner: The State of Bavaria. *Director:* Dr.
Eichelsbacher. 173 hectares. *Einzellagen:*
Würzburg: Stein (28ha) and Innere Leiste (6);
Randersacker: Pfülben (3) and Marsberg (5);
Hörstein: Abtsberg (12); Großheubach:
Bischofsberg (3, red wine); Handthal: Stollberg (6);
Abtswind: Altenberg (6) and Thüngersheim:
Scharlachberg (11)
The superlative vineyards of the lordly Prince-
Bishops of Würzburg, originating in the 12th
century, are now (since 1803) the Bavarian State
Domain, run by the Bayerische Landesanstalt
für Weinbau and Gartenbau. The great cellar
under the baroque Residency at Würzburg is
one of the most stirring sights in the world of
wine. The vines, all on steep or sloping sites, and
on many different soils, are 34% Müller-

Thurgau, 21% Riesling, 16% Silvaner, 11% Rieslaner (a Silvaner × Riesling cross), 8% Kerner and many others in small quantities, including Spätburgunder in the 3-hectare Bischofsberg vineyard. The object is wines of true Franconian style, balancing high acidity with powerful flavours, all either trocken or halbtrocken (except for Auslesen, etc.). The '76 Spätlesen of Riesling and Rieslaner were the estate's ideal: highly concentrated and aromatic dry wines. There are now plans to reduce the number of new crossings used but to continue their tradition of maturing in oak casks. The estate has a college at Veitshöchheim and restaurants in Würzburg, Schloß Aschaffenburg (another cellar) and Stollberg in the Steigerwald. 80% of its average annual production of 80,000 cases are consumed in Bavaria.

Weingut Hans Wirsching

Ludwigstraße 16, 8715 Iphofen, tel: 09323-3033. *Owners:* Hans and Dr. Heinrich Wirsching. 45 hectares. *Einzellagen:* Iphofen: Julius-Echter-Berg, Kronsberg and Kalb; Rödelsee: Küchenmeister. Großlagen: Burgweg and Schloßberg.

A family firm since 1630 with its original Gutshaus and cellars, as well as modern ones outside the village. Silvaner, Müller-Thurgau and Riesling are predominant; Kerner, Scheurebe and Bacchus are also grown, with a little Traminer and Rieslaner (Silvaner × Riesling crossing). Half the wines are fully dry; the rest not greatly sweetened. The Wirschings take great pride in the fact that their wines (Iphöfer Silvaner and Scheurebe) were served to the Pope during his visit to Germany in 1980. Most of their business is direct to consumers but a little is also exported to the UK, USA, Netherlands and other countries.

Gebietswinzergenossenschaft Franken eG

8710 Kitzingen-Repperndorf, tel: 09321-5163/4. 2904 members.

The massive union (in 1959) of 7 cooperatives, drawing mainly on the Steigerwald. 57% of the one-million case production is Müller-Thurgau, 24% Silvaner; small quantities of several other varieties are grown, red as well as white. 10 Großlagen and 70 Einzellagen are involved.

Winzergenossenschaft Hammelburg

Marktplatz 11, 8783 Hammelburg. *Director:* Herr Baier.

25 hectares in Hammelburg, in Einzellagen Trautlestal and Heroldsberg, both part of Großlage Burg. A tiny local cooperative offering principally Silvaner.

Winzergenossenschaft Nordheim eG

8711 Nordheim/Main, tel: 09381-2345. 251 members; 300 hectares, 220 of them in Nordheim. *Einzellagen:* Escherndorf: Lump and Fürstenberg; Nordheim: Vögelein and Kreuzberg; Sommerach: Katzenkopf and Rosenberg.

The principal cooperative for the upper Main wine villages: 55% Müller-Thurgau, 22% Silvaner plus various others – mainly new varieties – and 3% red-wine grapes. Most of the members live in Nordheim and go out to tend their scattered hectares. Most of the wine is happily drunk up in Bavaria.

Winzergenossenschaft Randersacker eG

Maingasse 33, 8701 Randersacker, tel: 0931-709001. 258 members; 122 hectares, mainly in Randersacker (85ha), Sommerhausen (20) and Würzburg (6). *Einzellagen:* Randersacker: Sonnenstuhl, Marsberg, Pfülben, Dabug and Teufelskeller; Sommerhausen: Steinbach and Reifenstein; Würzburg: Abtsleite and Kirchberg; Gerbrunn: Alter Berg and Neuberg; Rimpar: Kobersberg; Theilheim: Altenberg; Leinach: Himmelberg.

The cooperative of one of the best areas in Franken with high standards. Müller-Thurgau and Silvaner are the two main grapes with only moderate interest in more exotic kinds and only 2% Riesling. Good as the wines are, 80% is consumed locally.

Winzergenossenschaft Sommerach eG

Nordheimerstraße 12, 8711 Sommerach/Main, tel: 09381-3636.

The oldest cooperative cellar in Franken, established in 1901 in the "Kingdom of Bavaria", as it was then called. 245 members supply grapes from 153.8 hectares in villages from a wide area surrounding the town of Volkach. Amongst the best known of the 16 Einzellagen are the Iphöfer Kalb, Escherndorfer Lump, and Volkacher Ratsherr, but the largest holdings are at Sommerach (Rosenberg and Katzenkopf) covering 102 hectares. 45% of the vineyards are planted with Müller-Thurgau, 25% with

---

VISITING ESTATES AND WINE CELLARS

Tasting wine

There are plenty of opportunities to taste the local wines in every German wine district. Indeed, some estates rely on visitors, either tasters or those who come to eat in restaurants and bars, for much of their sales. Tastings are usually arranged on a more organized – though convivial – basis than in other wine countries. Visiting wine cellars is not quite as simple as it is in France, and the equivalent sign to "*Visitez nos caves*" is absent. Nevertheless, most estate and cooperative cellars are happy to welcome interested visitors during business hours – usually between 9 a.m. and 5 p.m. on week days – although they do expect advance warning, either by letter or by telephone. Some cellars set a firm maximum and minimum to the number of persons they will receive in any one party. If a tasting is provided free of charge, it is courteous to buy a few bottles when leaving. Most tastings, especially the organized ones, are charged for. Rates vary, as do the number of wines provided. Do not expect to taste great wines from venerable vintages: the grower will want to interest you in bottles on his current list. The Germans are, by nature, very hospitable, but the visitor to a small estate should remember that although tasting in a producer's cellar is one of the most enjoyable aspects of visiting a wine region, it may be occupying a large part of the estate owner's working day and the welcome should not be overstayed. The local wine promotion bodies in the regions have lists of the estates where visitors are welcome to taste the wines. Alternatively, travel along one of the wine roads or *Weinstraßen* – not many kilometres will go by before a tasting cellar is spotted. In some of the main wine towns there are central cellars where the wines of several growers can be sampled. This is a good way to get the flavour of a region. Many restaurants in wine districts will have a long list of local wines which can be bought by the glass.

Buying wine

Many estates sell almost all their wines directly to the consumer and have a wine bar or tasting room set aside for this purpose. While customers sit around tables the wines are served to them. Facilities for spitting at "sitting" tastings are not normally offered. General comment on the wines is made, after each has been introduced by the cellar master (Kellermeister) or by the estate owner (Weingutsbesitzer). Such tastings quickly become a social occasion, although the wines still receive proper attention. Their relatively low alcohol content makes it possible to taste many wines in this way and remain clear headed. (In the course of his duties the professional taster will willingly tackle 70 or more German white wines in one session. For wines with a higher alcohol content this would hardly be possible.)

Silvaner and 13% with Bacchus, Riesling accounts for only 2% and Kerner, Perle and Scheurebe for another 14%. Sales are exclusively in West Germany.

Winzergenossenschaft Thüngersheim eG

Untere Hauptstraße 272a, 8702 Thüngersheim, tel: 09364-1052/3. 364 members. 217 hectares. *Einzellagen:* Thüngersheim: Johannisberg and Scharlachberg; Retzbach: Benediktusberg; Veitshöchheim: Sonnenschein; Erlabrunn: Weinsteig; Himmelstadt: Kelter; Rück: Jesuitenberg and Schalk; Karlstadt: Roßtal (Großlage); Leinach: Himmelberg.
The major cooperative of the scattered wine villages of the lower Main, set up in 1930. More than half of its vines are Müller-Thurgau. Silvaner, Scheurebe, Kerner and Bacchus are also important, depending on the highly varied soil, from which red wine is also produced. Production is up to 250,000 cases of Bocksbeutel (the Franconian flagon-shaped bottle) and many of the wines win gold and silver medals. Only 6% is exported (to the UK, USA and Canada); a large part of the domestic share in the market is consumed in the Alps.

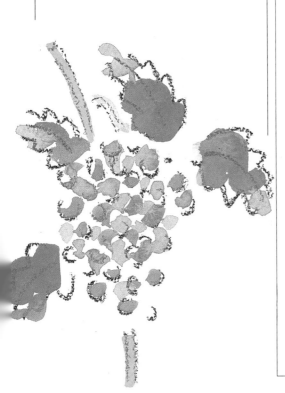

Sekt is the uncharacteristically short German word for what the EEC defined in 1979 as quality sparkling wine. Amongst other technical requirements, the bubbles in the wine must result from a secondary fermentation – either in bottle or in vat. Figures suggest that under 10% of German sparkling wine is made by the labour-intensive bottle fermentation method. The most important Sekt producers prefer fermentation in vat on technical as well as economic grounds, for it allows a complete and continuous control of the delicate process by which the sparkle is created in the base wine.

Bottle fermentation in Germany is reserved mainly for the small parcels of sparkling wine produced by contractors for private estates. These are possibly of more interest to the winelover than to the regular Sekt drinker. Many bear a vintage and the names of a region, village vineyard and vine variety. There are nearly 600 of these growers' sparkling wines ("Winzersekte") on the market, particularly from the Mosel-Saar-Ruwer and Rheinhessen. The impact they make on the total annual production of Sekt of over 23 million cases is as yet very small, but it is increasing. 86% of German Sekt is sold without any indication of the origin of the base wine, and this is how the German consumer likes it. The great variety and individuality of German still wine is not relevant when it comes to a choice of Sekt. What is wanted is a sparkling wine of consistent quality, which can be bought under a recognized and familiar brand name. So, the world of German Sekt is led, in terms of sales, by names such as Deinhard, Faber, Henkell, Herres, Rüttgers and Söhnlein. German Sekt production, like the Champagne trade, is big business and is starting to attract the attention of large international concerns looking for a stake in the German market.

Although the Sekt business seems a far cry from the almost cottage-industry level of some sections of German still wine production, Sekt manufacturers, with an eye for quality, also depend on the Riesling grape for the reputation of their best products. A Brut or Extra Dry Riesling Sekt embodies many of the characteristics of a good quality Riesling Kabinett wine from the Rheingau or Mosel-Saar-Ruwer: clean and uncloying, with refreshing acidity. As from September 1986 German Sekt labelled "Produce of Germany" must be made from German base wine.

SEKT

Some of the best Sekt producers are:

Burgeff & Co GmbH
Tank- and bottle-fermented Sekt makers since 1836. Now owned by Seagram.

Sektkellerei Carstens KG
Gas-stored from first fermentation gives Carstens its sparkle. Henkell-owned.

Deinhard & Co KGaA
Top Sekt makers since 1843, internationally known for Lila Riesling Sekt.

Deutz & Geldermann Sektkellerei GmbH
Sekt house with Champagne origins and connections. Mainly bottle-fermented.

Faber Sektkellerei Faber KG
Founded 1952, annual sales now reach 47 million bottles of cheap Sekt.

Fürst von Metternich Sektkellerei GmbH
Established by the Oetker-Gruppe in 1971 to sell up-market Sekt.

Georg Geiling & Co KG
Small family business making bottle-fermented top quality Sekt.

Sektkellereien Henkell & Co
Large producers, founded 1836, claiming over 50% of the Sekt export market.

Gräflich von Kageneck'sche Erzeuger-Weinvertrieb GmbH
The sparkling arm of the Baden cooperative movement. Established 1974.

G. C. Kessler & Co
Oldest Sekt house in Germany, founded 1826 by a former Veuve Clicquot employee.

Christian Adalbert Kupferberg & Cie KGaA
Founded 1850. Pioneers of bottle fermentation followed by filtration.

Matheus Müller KGaA
Seagram-owned, Sekt makers since 1838. Best known brand "MM Extra". Tank-fermented.

Sektkellerei Nikolaus Rüttgers GmbH
Henkell's huge cheap Sekt subsidiary.

Sektkellerei Schloß Wachenheim AG
Founded 1888; after much experimentation settled for bottle fermentation.

Söhnlein Rheingold KG Kellereien
Söhnlein "Rheingold" was christened personally by Wagner. Current owner: Oetker.

Erzeugergemeinschaft Winzersekt
An association of 350 winegrowers producing various Winzersekte.

WÜRTTEMBERG

The old principalities of Baden and Württemberg are united as a state, but remain separate as wine regions. Baden is much the bigger producer of the two, but a true Württemberger will argue that his wine is much the better – and, acting accordingly, consume his share and more.

The hard-working, productive Württembergers are some of Germany's great wine drinkers, and they prefer their own wine. As a result it is scarcely ever exported and the best bottles (which are expensive) almost never.

Growers therefore have the best of all possible motives to concentrate on quality: they, and their friends and acquaintances, are going to drink what they make themselves.

The landlocked regions of Germany only take on comprehensible shapes as they are encompassed and traversed by rivers. The river Neckar is almost a Mosel in Württemberg, ambling through the hills and fed by tributaries that provide the essential south slopes for vineyards. The climate here is harsher than that of Baden, with cold continental winters but correspondingly more sunshine in summer: a well-chosen site will ripen Riesling well, and even give more body and colour to a red wine than any other German vineyard. These considerations make the wine-map of Württemberg the most complicated in Germany; the vineyards preposterously disjointed and scattered, so that even in the area between Heilbronn and Ludwigsburg, the Württembergisch Unterland, where three-quarters of the vineyards are concentrated, only half a dozen valley-sides muster much more than a few hectares of vines. Württemberg, like the Mosel in this, too, concentrates on Riesling for its fine white wines. But its real speciality is red and rosé made of its own indigenous grape the Trollinger, and to a lesser extent the Schwarzriesling (the Pinot Meunier in French, with the German alias of Müllerrebe), the Portugieser, the Pinot Noir (Spätburgunder) and the Limberger, which may be a form of Burgundy's Gamay. Red plantings make up half the total; if the red is not fully red it is Weißherbst, rosé, as in Baden, or mixed with white grapes to make Schillerwein – a true local speciality.

As in Baden, the great majority of the production is by the cooperatives, with only a handful of relatively modest private estates. But even the cooperatives cannot simplify the complexity of a region with three Bereiche and 16 Großlagen. The best way to understand it is to follow the northwards flow of the Neckar. On the analogy of the Mosel picture, the huge car-factory city of Stuttgart is its Trier. Here and along the tributary Rems, flowing in from the east like the Ruwer to the Mosel, are the first and some of the best Württemberg vineyards, the Bereich Remstal-Stuttgart. Unlike the Mosel, however, the Neckar does not have the vines to itself. The side-valleys carry the vineyards west into the foothills of the Black Forest, east into Swabia, the rural heartland of southern Germany. The Großlagen roughly correspond to the side-valleys – roughly but not wholly. Exceptions abound, and careful use of the maps is needed to tie down the birthplace of a Württemberg wine.

▲ The tributary valleys of the Neckar conceal such gems as Strumpfelbach, in the Remstal only a few kilometres from Stuttgart, with its splendid Riesling and Trollinger vineyard, the Altenberg.
▶ In many of the wine regions, radical reshaping of old vineyards has taken place. Flurbereinigung is the term for this totally revised landscape, with old terraces removed and easy access by road to every part.

DLG (DEUTSCHE LANDWIRTSCHAFTS-GESELLSCHAFT)

The Württemberg wine-capital of Heilbronn is also, in one sense, the wine-capital of Germany. It is here that the DLG, the German Agricultural Society, holds its annual national competitive tastings for bronze, silver and gold medals (the latter now called the Großer Preis). Each German wine region has its own "Gebiet" and "Länder" wine competitions, for which medals are issued. Only wines that have scored at least 3.5 points out of the maximum five in the regional competitions may be entered for the DLG's National Wine Award, or Bundesweinprämierung.

At the DLG tasting 3.5 points give a bronze medal, 4 points a silver medal, and 4.5 points a Großer Preis. Juries judge the wines by region, grape variety and quality category. Marks out of five are given separately for "smell", "taste" and "harmony", then divided by three to give the overall mark. Disputed decisions are sent upstairs to an appeal committee, which often has a difficult task judging totally different styles of wine all at one sitting.

The proportion of entrants that are judged winners may seem suprisingly high. But to be considered for the final, national, DLG competition, wines have to pass their regional contests. Of the 150,000 individual batches of German wine bottled each year, about 3,000 get DLG medals. To protect the reputation of the DLG prize, no other national competitions are allowed.

TRAVEL INFORMATION

The winelands of the Neckar and its tributaries link classically romantic South German scenery and the rich modern city of Stuttgart. The locals are, statistics show, the leading wine drinkers in Germany and there are plenty of places to join them for a glass – so many that very little Württemberg wine leaves its homeland.

Places to visit

Stuttgart: shopping and conventions, ballet and museums are among attractions in this modern, prosperous city.
Eßlingen: both the old and the new Rathaus, and indeed the entire core of this little town, are charming. Heilbronn: town on the Neckar with a wealth of old buildings. Ludwigsburg: the largest Baroque castle in Germany, with open-air theatre in summer. Other places of interest include: Weinstadt, Brackenheim, Bad Mergentheim.

Wine roads

The *Schwäbische Weinstraße* runs north from Metzingen along the river to Stuttgart, then loops through the wine country to end at Bad Mergentheim in the northeast. There are educational vineyard trails at Stuttgart, Gemmrigheim, Neckarsulm, Fellbach, Kernen, Remshalden, Vaihingen, Beilstein, Großbottwar, Bad Mergentheim and Ingelfingen.

Wine festivals

Stuttgart-Bad Cannstatt (end May), Bretzfeld-Schwabbach (mid-June), Heilbronn (3rd w/e in June), Beilstein (end July), Ingelfingen (mid-Aug), Remshalden (mid-Aug), Großbottwar (end Aug), Weinstadt (early Sept), Laudenbach (mid-Sept), Eßlingen (mid Sept), Metzingen (end Oct).

Wine museum

Stuttgart's wine museum is based in a cellar close to the Rotenberg vineyard. There is a library, and a wine education trail (with tasting facilities) starts from the museum.

Food and drink

Perhaps it is the riches of Stuttgart, perhaps culinary traditions. Whatever the cause, Württemberg has plenty of good hotels and restaurants to add to the ever-present inns and Weinstuben. Castle hotels include the von Raßler family's Schloß Weitenburg, on the Neckar south of Stuttgart (tel: 07457-8051). The Restaurant Zum Ochsen in Kernen, the Krone near Metzingen and the beautifully situated Ulrichshöhe near Nürtingen are among many known for their cuisine. Stuttgart has hotels and restaurants in profusion. Among the Weinstuben, the Bäcke-Metzger in Bad Cannstatt, the Ratskeller in the marketplace and the Börse in Heustraße are noted.

VILLAGES

BEREICH REMSTAL-STUTTGART

Sixteen hundred hectares of vines are divided into five Großlagen.

Hohenneuffen is the uppermost of the river, round Neuffen, Frickenhausen and Metzingen. There is no Riesling here but light Silvaner, Müller-Thurgau and (for red) largely Schwarzriesling.

Weinsteige is the Großlage of Stuttgart, a city where the appearance of vineyards in its midst (or at least in its suburbs Bad Cannstatt, Mühlhausen and Zuffenhausen) is particularly surprising. The vines here are mainly Trollinger and Riesling, the best-known Einzellagen (of 26) Berg, Steinhalde and Zuckerle, and in Fellbach, facing west over the Neckar towards Stuttgart, Wetzstein, Goldberg, Lämmler (entirely red wine) and Hinterer Berg.

Vineyards

Großlage Weinsteige with *Einzellagen:* Bad Cannstatt/Stuttgart Zuffenhausen: Berg, 89.7ha, SW-S-SE, sloping/steep. Mühlhausen: Steinhalde, 20ha, SW-S-E, mainly steep terraces; Zuckerle, 20ha, W-S-SE, steep terraces. Fellbach: Wetzstein, 11.9ha, W-SW-SE, moderately sloping; Goldberg, 114.7ha, NW-S-E, moderately steep; Lämmler, 31.9ha, SW-S, steep; Hinterer Berg, 10.1ha, W-S, steep.

The valley of the Rems (Remstal) has three Großlagen: Kopf (13 Einzellagen) centred round Schorndorf, with a good deal of Trollinger but also some fair sites for Riesling; Wartbühl (20 Einzellagen) round Weinstadt and Korb, with Riesling and other white grapes in the majority; and Sonnenbühl (with four Einzellagen) south of Weinstadt and the Rems, which specializes in robust Trollinger red.

BEREICH WÜRTTEMBERGISCH UNTERLAND

Much the biggest area, with 7,000 of the 9,600 hectares of Württemberg's vines. The Bereich, with nine Großlagen, spreads across the Neckar valley north of Stuttgart from Baden (where it brushes the Kraichgau) to the Bottwar valley in the east.

GROSSLAGE SCHALKSTEIN

The first Großlage, following the Neckar north. Its 14 Einzellagen stretch from Ludwigsburg to Hessigheim, the wine centre, with red grapes in the majority, their best wines well coloured and full-bodied.

Vineyards

Hessigheim: Wurmberg, 49.9ha, W-SW-S-SE, terraced. Felsengarten, 296.4ha, W-SW-S-SE, steep terraces.

GROSSLAGE STROMBERG

A widely dispersed collection of 19 Einzellagen along the tributary Enz valley to the west, with Mühlhausen and Vaihingen as centres, stretching down the Neckar valley to Kirchheim and Bönnigheim. Two thirds are red vines, with considerable Limberger.

GROSSLAGE HEUCHELBERG

A more intensive viniferous district with 24 Einzellagen, just north of Stromberg to the west of the Neckar. The centres are Cleebronn and Schwaigern, responsible for some of Württemberg's best Rieslings from the lime-rich soil.

Vineyards

Neipperg: Vogelsang, 199.6ha, SW-S-SE, moderate to steep. Schwaigern: Ruthe, 6.9ha, S, sloping. Cleebronn: Michaelsberg, 229ha, N-W-S-E, moderate to steep.

GROSSLAGE KIRCHENWEINBERG

This is the real kernel of Württemberg's wine region, its 12 Einzellagen including the huge 456-hectare Katzenbeißer at Lauffen. Talheim and Flein, on the outskirts of Heilbronn, are its other centres. Schwarzriesling is the most popular grape in a predominantly red-wine vineyard.

Vineyards

Flein: Sonnenberg, 49.9ha, SW-S-SE, moderate to steep; Altenberg, 69.9ha, S-SE, moderate to steep; Eselsberg, 64.8ha, SW-S, moderate to steep. Talheim: Schloßberg, 149.7ha, SW-S-SE, moderate to steep.

GROSSLAGE WUNNENSTEIN

A limited district east of the Neckar, including the town of Großbottwar, with nine Einzellagen, mainly dedicated to red grapes.

GROSSLAGE SALZBERG

An important area east of Heilbronn, noted for some of Württemberg's best Rieslings. The 14 Einzellagen are spread between Eberstadt, Lehrensteinsfeld, Willsbach, Affaltrach, Eichelberg, Obersulm and Löwenstein.

Vineyards

Eberstadt: Sommerhalde, 58.9ha, SW-S, moderate to steep; Eberfürst, 89.7ha, SW-S, moderate to steep. Lehrensteinsfeld: Althälde, 59.8ha, SW-S-SE, moderate to steep; Steinacker, 64.8ha, SW-S, moderate to steep; Frauenzimmer, 8ha, SW-S, moderately sloping. Willsbach and Affaltrach: Dieblesberg, 169.7ha, SW-S-SE, moderate to steep; Zeilberg, 149.7ha, SW-S-SE, moderate to steep. Eichelberg: Obersulm Hundsberg, 74.7ha, SW, moderate to steep.

GROSSLAGE SCHOZACHTAL

A small area just north of Wunnenstein, with only five Einzellagen around Abstatt and Untergruppenbach. White wines are in the majority. Some good Riesling is grown here.

GROSSLAGE LINDELBERG

A more scattered region of mainly white wine, northeast of Heilbronn round the Brettach valley. Eight Einzellagen lie between Siebeneich, Untersteinbach and Neuenstein.

GROSSLAGE STAUFENBERG

Heilbronn is an important wine centre with a first-class cooperative and the seat of the all-Germany D.L.G. annual wine championship. Its vineyards and those of the Neckar downstream are in the Großlage Staufenberg, which has 12 Einzellagen divided almost equally between white grapes and red. The main centres are Gundelsheim, Erlenbach, Weinsberg and Heilbronn itself.

Vineyards

Gundelsheim: Himmelreich, 40ha, SW-S, 40% steep. Erlenbach: Kayberg, 249.3ha, W-S-E, sloping. Weinsberg: Ranzenberg, 139.8ha, SW-S-SE, sloping; Schemelsberg, 33.9ha, SW-S, sloping. Heilbronn: Stiftsberg, 399ha, W-S-E, moderately sloping; Wartberg, 42ha, SW-S, sloping; Stahlbühl, 20ha, SW-S, sloping.

BEREICH KOCHER-JAGST-TAUBER

The northern Württemberg Bereich is much the smallest, with 400 hectares and the only one to specialize (90%) in white wine. It straddles the valleys of the Kocher and Jagst, Neckar tributaries from the east, and the Tauber (which flows north to the Main).

GROSSLAGE KOCHERBERG

The southern half of the Bereich, with 12 Einzellagen, includes Ingelfingen and Niedernhall on the Kocher.

Vineyards

Ingelfingen: Hoher Berg, 109.7ha, SW-S-E, steep. Niedernhall: Burgstall, 29.9ha, W-SW-S, steep. Weißbacher: Altenberg, 4.8ha, W-S-E, steep.

GROSSLAGE TAUBERBERG

The isolated Tauber valley vineyards (7 Einzellagen) are centred on Bad Mergentheim, Weikersheim and Niederstetten. Both the limy soil and the use of Silvaner and Müller-Thurgau recall the fact that Franken is not far away.

Vineyard

Niederstetten: Schafsteige, 59.8ha, W-S-E, steep.

PRODUCERS

Weingut Graf Adelmann, "Brüssele"

Burg Schaubeck, 7141 Steinheim-Kleinbottwar, tel: 07148-6665. *Owner:* Michael, Graf Adelmann. A 15-hectare estate: 12 hectares in Kleinbottwar (*Einzellagen:* Oberer Berg and Süßmund, solely owned); 3ha in Hoheneck.

One of the best-known estates in Württemberg, instantly recognized by its pale-blue "lacy" label with the name "Brüssele" (after a former owner). Burg Schaubeck is a small but towering and venerable stronghold, apparently with Roman origins, owned by the Adelmanns since 1914. The vines are 48% red: 22% Trollinger, also Samtrot (see below), Clevner, Limberger (or Lemberger), Muskat-Trollinger; 52% white: 27% Riesling, also Traminer, Ruländer, Müller-Thurgau, Kerner, Muskateller and Silvaner.

Kleinbottwar is red marl, Hoheneck limestone; both are sloping sites.

The wines are originals, with distinct characters and yet notable delicacy that makes them sometimes almost timid. Acidity tends to be low but flavours dry and complex (90% is trocken): the estate is now aiming for higher acidity in its white wines. Specialities include Weißherbst and red wine from Muskat-Trollinger – a table grape elsewhere, making slightly raisiny wine; Samtrot (a Pinot Meunier mutation; a mature Auslese reminded me of Valpolicella); Muskateller, delicate and long despite its obvious spicy character; and a soft, low-key, smoky but elegant Riesling. The quality is as high as the wines are unusual.

Schloßkellerei Affaltrach

Am Ordensschloß 15, 7104 Obersulm. *Owner:* Dr. Reinhold Baumann. 7.5 hectares. *Einzellagen:* Affaltrach: Dieblesberg, planted with a wide variety of red and white grapes.

Originally a 13th-century foundation, bought by the present owners in 1928 and now consisting of a small estate and an associated company buying fresh must from some 200 small growers to make wine and Sekt. The estate wines are mainly trocken or halbtrocken, intended for use at table and made to improve in bottle when possible. Eisweine and Trockenbeerenauslesen with some of the highest must weights in the country are produced here.

Graf Bentzel-Sturmfeder'sches Weingut

Sturmfederstraße 4, 7129 Ilsfeld-Schozach, tel: 07133-7829. *Owner:* Count Hanfried von Bentzel-Sturmfeder-Horneck. 17.6 hectares. *Einzellage:* Schozach: Roter Berg.

An estate with 14th-century origins and 18th-century cellars. The vineyards are 28% Riesling, 22% Spätburgunder, 18% Samtrot (a Pinot Meunier mutation), 10% Schwarzriesling (Pinot Meunier), etc., on clay slopes which give body to the wines. The wines last well, even when the acidity is relatively low, with barrel-ageing giving them stability. Noble rot is a rare occurrence; most of the wines are dry, much appreciated in local restaurants.

Fürstlich Hohenlohe Langenburg'sche Weingüter

im Schloß, 6992 Weikersheim. *Director:* Karl-Heinz Schäfer. 26 hectares. *Einzellagen:* Weikersheim: Karlsberg (17ha, solely owned) and Schmecker (23); Tauberrettersheim: Königin (which is over the Württemberg border in Franken, 3).

The ancient cellars of Schloß Weikersheim are used for very modern wine-making. The limestone vineyards give light, aromatic wines with a certain *Bodenton* or *goût de terroir*. This is the transition from Württemberg to Franken. Vines are 30% Müller-Thurgau, 17% Riesling, 15% Kerner, 10% Silvaner, etc.

Fürst zu Hohenlohe-Öhringen'sche Schloßkellerei

7110 Öhringen, Schloß, tel: 07941-7081. *Owner:* Prince Kraft zu Hohenlohe-Öhringen. 22 hectares. *Einzellagen:* Verrenberg: Verrenberg (solely owned).

A princely estate since the 14th-century, with 17th-century cellars (and even a cask dated 1702). The Verrenberg is unusual in being one sweep of vines, producing almost uniformly dry whites, which they claim contain less than 6 grams/litre of sugar. The vines are 60% Riesling, 10% Limberger, 10% Müller-Thurgau, 8% Spätburgunder, 7% Kerner.

Weingüter und Schloßkellerei Graf von Neipperg

7103 Schwaigern, tel: 07138-5081. *Owner:* Count Karl-Eugen zu Neipperg. 36.6 hectares. *Einzellagen:* Schwaigern: Ruthe (6.5); Neipperg: Schloßberg (2.4), Klingenberg: Schloßberg (1.1).

Documents prove the family to have been making wine here since 1248, shortly after the building of Burg Neipperg, the original castle. There is now a Weinstube in Schloß Schwaigern over the cellars. Vines are 59% red: 23% Limberger (or Lemberger), 17% Schwarzriesling (Pinot Meunier), 11% Spätburgunder, 8% Trollinger; the whites are 26% Riesling, 2% Traminer, 5% Muskateller and 8% Müller-Thurgau. The Neippergs introduced the Limberger (or Lemberger) to make red wine of colour and tannin; their other speciality is spicy Traminer, although their Riesling is highly thought of. 97% of the wines are trocken or halbtrocken. Count Neipperg is also the owner of properties in St-Emilion: Châteaux Canon-la-Gaffelière and La Mondotte.

Weinbau Sonnenhof, Bezner-Fischer

7143 Vaihingen-Gündelbach, tel: 07042-21038. *Owners:* Albrecht and Charlotte Fischer. 22.5 hectares. *Einzellagen:* Gündelbach: Wachtkopf; Hohenhaslach: Kirchberg; Roßwag: Halde.

Highly successful estate with many awards and prizes to his credit. Harvesting is left as late as possible, producing wines (90% are trocken/halbtrocken) that are typical of their grape variety. The list includes red Eiswein from Trollinger and from Limberger (or Lemberger) grapes, light in colour but intense in flavour. The vineyards are also planted with Riesling (20.9%), Spätburgunder (8.5%), Müller-Thurgau (9%), and others including Dornfelder and Muskat-Trollinger.

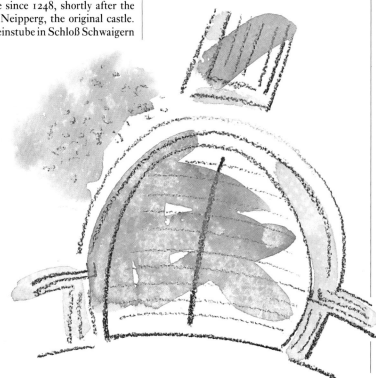

VINEYARDS

BEREICH KOCHER-JAGST-TAUBER

GROSSLAGE TAUBERBERG

Bad Mergentheim Ortsteil Markelsheim
Mönchsberg 1 P
Probstberg 2 P

Weikersheim
Hardt 3
Schmecker 4
Karlsberg 5

– Ortsteil Elpersheim
Mönchsberg 1 P
Probstberg 2 P

– Ortsteil Schäftersheim
Klosterberg 4 a

– Ortsteil Laudenbach
Schafsteige 6 P

– Ortsteil Haagen
Schafsteige 6 P

Niederstetten
Schafsteige 6 P

– Ortsteil Wermutshausen
Schafsteige 6 P

– Ortsteil Vorbachzimmern
Schafsteige 6 P

– Ortsteil Oberstetten
Schafsteige 6 P

GROSSLAGE KOCHERBERG

Dörzbach
Altenberg 7

Ingelfingen
Hoher Berg 8 P

– Ortsteil Criesbach
Hoher Berg 8 P
Burgstall 11 P

Künzelsau
Hoher Berg 8 P

– Ortsteil Belsenberg
Heiligkreuz 9

Niedernhall
Hoher Berg 8 P
Burgstall 11 P
Engweg 12 P
Altenberg 13 P

Weißbach
Engweg 12 P
Altenberg 13 P

Forchtenberg
Flatterberg 14 P

– Ortsteil Ernsbach
Flatterberg 14 P

Schöntal Ortsteil Bieringen
Schlüsselberg 15

Widdern
Hofberg 16 P

Neudenau Ortsteil Siglingen
Hofberg 16 P

Möckmühl
Hofberg 16 P
Ammerlanden 17

Hardthausen Ortsteil Kochersteinsfeld
Rosenberg 17 a

BEREICH WÜRTTEMBERGISCH UNTERLAND

(See map pages 146–147)

GROSSLAGE STAUFENBERG

Gundelsheim
Himmelreich 18

Bad Friedrichshall Ortsteil Duttenberg
Schön 19 P

– Ortsteil Offenau
Schön 19 P

Langenbrettach Ortsteil Brettach
Berg 20

Untereisesheim
Vogelsang 21

Oedheim
Kayberg 22 P

Erlenbach
Kayberg 22 P

Neckarsulm
Scheuerberg 23

Ellhofen
Ranzenberg 24 P

Weinsberg
Ranzenberg 24 P
Schemelsberg 25

– Ortsteil Gellmersbach
Dezberg 26 P

Eberstadt
Dezberg 26 P

Heilbronn
Stiftsberg 27 P
Wartberg 28
Stahlbühl 29

– Ortsteil Horkheim
Stiftsberg 27 P

Talheim
Stiftsberg 27 P

GROSSLAGE LINDELBERG

Neuenstein Ortsteil Kesselfeld
Schwobarjörgle 30 P

– Ortsteil Obersöllbach
Margarete 31 P

Öhringen Ortsteil Michelbach am Wald
Margarete 31 P
Dachsteiger 32 P

– Ortsteil Verrenberg
Goldberg 33 P
Verrenberg 35

Pfedelbach
Goldberg 33 P

– Ortsteil Untersteinbach
Dachsteiger 32 P

– Ortsteil Heuholz
Dachsteiger 32 P

– Ortsteil Harsberg
Dachsteiger 32 P

– Ortsteil Oberohrn
Dachsteiger 32 P

– Ortsteil Windischenbach
Goldberg 33 P

Wüstenrot Ortsteil Maienfels
Schneckenhof 36 P

Bretzfeld
Goldberg 33 P

– Ortsteil Geddelsbach
Schneckenhof 36 P

– Ortsteil Unterheimbach
Schneckenhof 36 P

– Ortsteil Adolzfurt
Schneckenhof 36 P

– Ortsteil Siebeneich
Himmelreich 37 P

– Ortsteil Schwabbach
Himmelreich 37 P

– Ortsteil Dimbach
Himmelreich 37 P

– Ortsteil Waldbach
Himmelreich 37 P

Langenbrettach Ortsteil Langenbeutingen
Himmelreich 37 P

GROSSLAGE SALZBERG

Eberstadt
Sommerhalde 39
Eberfürst 40

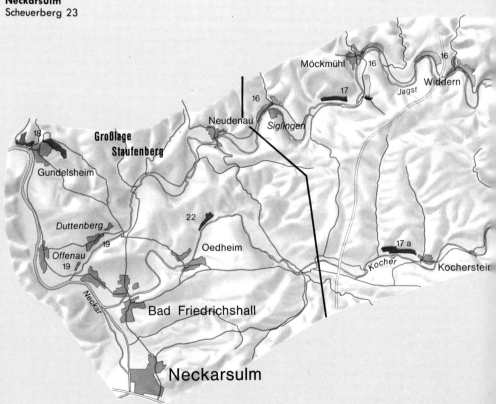

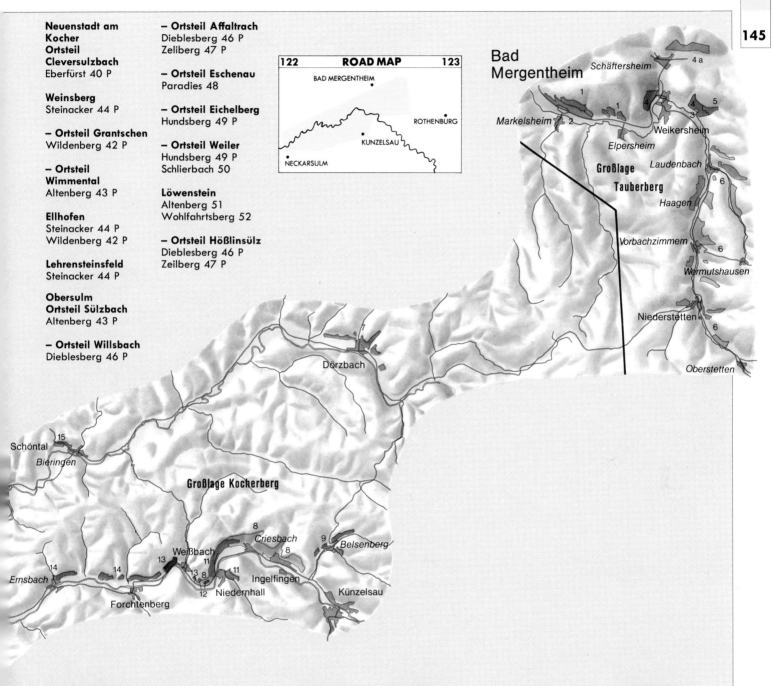

Neuenstadt am
Kocher
Ortsteil
Cleversulzbach
Eberfürst 40 P

Weinsberg
Steinacker 44 P

– Ortsteil Grantschen
Wildenberg 42 P

– Ortsteil
Wimmental
Altenberg 43 P

Ellhofen
Steinacker 44 P
Wildenberg 42 P

Lehrensteinsfeld
Steinacker 44 P

Obersulm
Ortsteil Sülzbach
Altenberg 43 P

– Ortsteil Willsbach
Dieblesberg 46 P

– Ortsteil Affaltrach
Dieblesberg 46 P
Zeliberg 47 P

– Ortsteil Eschenau
Paradies 48

– Ortsteil Eichelberg
Hundsberg 49 P

– Ortsteil Weiler
Hundsberg 49 P
Schlierbach 50

Löwenstein
Altenberg 51
Wohlfahrtsberg 52

– Ortsteil Hößlinsülz
Dieblesberg 46 P
Zeilberg 47 P

ROAD MAP
122 · 123
BAD MERGENTHEIM
ROTHENBURG
KUNZELSAU
NECKARSULM

Bad
Mergentheim
Schäftersheim
4 a
1
1
4
4
5
3
Markelsheim
2
Weikersheim
Elpersheim
Großlage
Tauberberg
Laudenbach
6
Haagen
Vorbachzimmern
6
Wermutshausen
Niederstetten
6
Oberstetten

Dörzbach

Schöntal 15
Bieringen

Großlage Kockerberg

8
Criesbach
9 Belsenberg
8
14   14
13 Weißbach
11
Ernsbach
13 8
11
12 Niedernhall Ingelfingen
Forchtenberg
Künzelsau

GROSSLAGE
SCHOZACHTAL

Löwenstein
Sommerberg 53 P

Untergruppenbach
Ortsteil Unterheinreit
Sommerberg 53 P

Abstatt
Sommerberg 53 P
Burgberg 54 P
Burg Wildeck 55

Ilsfeld
Rappen 56

– Ortsteil Auenstein
Burgberg 54 P
Schloßberg 57

GROSSLAGE
WUNNENSTEIN

Beilstein
Wartberg 58
Steinberg 59

– Ortsteil
Hohenbeilstein
Schloßwengert 60

Oberstenfeld
Forstberg 61 P
Lichtenberg 62 P
Harzberg 63 P

– Ortsteil Gronau
Forstberg 61 P

Ilsfeld
Lichtenberg 62 P

Großbottwar
Lichtenberg 62 P
Harzberg 63 P

– Ortsteil
Winzerhausen
Lichtenberg 62 P
Harzberg 63 P

– Ortsteile Hof and
Lembach
Lichtenberg 62 P
Harzberg 63 P

Steinheim
Lichtenberg 62 P

– Ortsteil
Kleinbottwar
Lichtenberg 62 P
Oberer Berg 64 P
Süßmund 65
Götzenberg 66

Ludwigsburg
Ortsteil Hoheneck
Oberer Berg 64 P

GROSSLAGE
KIRCHEN-
WEINBERG

Heilbronn
Sonnenberg 67 P
Altenberg 68 P

Flein
Sonnenberg 67 P
Altenberg 68 P
Eselsberg 69

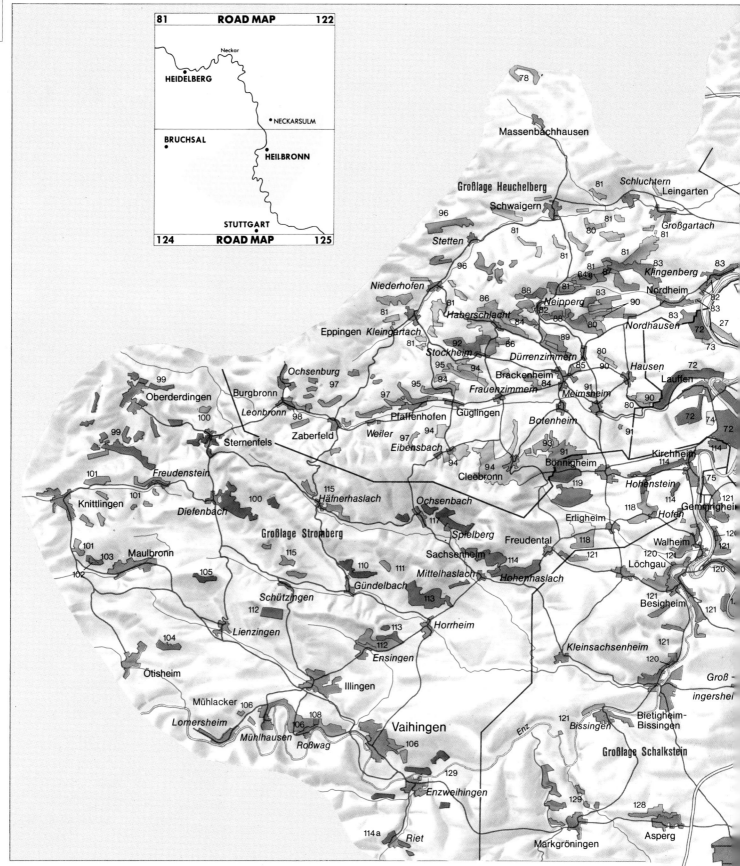

81 ROAD MAP 122

Neckar

HEIDELBERG

• NECKARSULM

BRUCHSAL

• HEILBRONN

STUTTGART

124 ROAD MAP 125

78

Massenbachhausen

Großlage Heuchelberg

Schluchtern

Leingarten

Schwaigern

81

81

Großgartach

96

80

81

Stetten

81

81

83

83

96

84 87 Klingenberg

Niederhofen

88

Neipperg

90

Nordheim

82

81

86

82

83

81

Haberschlacht

84

88

80

Nordhausen

72

27

Eppingen Kleingartach

81

86

89

73

92

Stockheim

Dürrenzimmern

80

Hausen

72

95

94

85 90

Ochsenburg

97

95

94

Brackenheim

91

Lauffen

Oberderdingen

99

Burgbronn

97

Frauenzimmern

84

Meimsheim

72

74

Leonbronn

98

Pfaffenhofen

Güglingen

Botenheim

80 90

99

Zaberfeld

Weiler

94

91

72

Sternenfels

97

Eibensbach

97

93

91

Kirchheim

114

101

Freudenstein

94

94

Bönnigheim

114

100

Häfnerhaslach

115

Cleebronn

Hohenstein

75

101

Knittlingen

119

101

Diefenbach

100

Ochsenbach

118

Hofen

Gemmrigheim

121

Maulbronn

103

Großlage Stromberg

117

Erligheim

114

121

102

115

Spielberg

Walheim

120

105

110

111

Freudental

118

121

120 121

Löchgau

Sachsenheim

114

Schützingen

Gündelbach

113

Hohenhaslach

121

Besigheim

121

112

Mittelhaslach

104

Lienzingen

113

Horrheim

Kleinsachsenheim

121

112

120

Ötisheim

Ensingen

Groß-

Illingen

121

ingershei

Mühlacker

106

Bissingen

Bietigheim-

Lomersheim

108

Bissingen

106

Vaihingen

Enz

Mühlhausen

Roßwag

106

Großlage Schalkstein

129

Enzweihingen

129

128

114a Riet

Markgröningen

Asperg

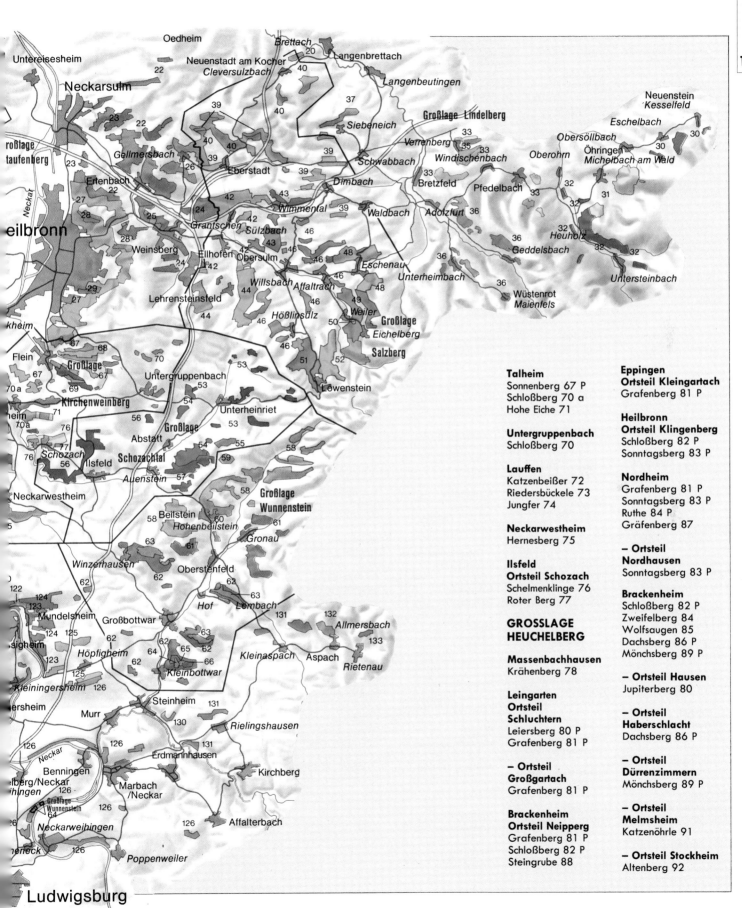

Talheim
Sonnenberg 67 P
Schloßberg 70 a
Hohe Eiche 71

Untergruppenbach
Schloßberg 70

Lauffen
Katzenbeißer 72
Riedersbückele 73
Jungfer 74

Neckarwestheim
Hernesberg 75

Ilsfeld
Ortsteil Schozach
Schelmenklinge 76
Roter Berg 77

GROSSLAGE
HEUCHELBERG

Massenbachhausen
Krähenberg 78

Leingarten
Ortsteil
Schluchtern
Leiersberg 80 P
Grafenberg 81 P

– Ortsteil
Großgartach
Grafenberg 81 P

Brackenheim
Ortsteil Neipperg
Grafenberg 81 P
Schloßberg 82 P
Steingrube 88

Eppingen
Ortsteil Kleingartach
Grafenberg 81 P

Heilbronn
Ortsteil Klingenberg
Schloßberg 82 P
Sonntagsberg 83 P

Nordheim
Grafenberg 81 P
Sonntagsberg 83 P
Ruthe 84 P
Gräfenberg 87

– Ortsteil
Nordhausen
Sonntagsberg 83 P

Brackenheim
Schloßberg 82 P
Zweifelberg 84
Wolfsaugen 85
Dachsberg 86 P
Mönchsberg 89 P

– Ortsteil Hausen
Jupiterberg 80

– Ortsteil
Haberschlacht
Dachsberg 86 P

– Ortsteil
Dürrenzimmern
Mönchsberg 89 P

– Ortsteil
Melmsheim
Katzenöhrle 91

– Ortsteil Stockheim
Altenberg 92

– Ortsteil
Mühlhausen
Steinhalde 139 P
Zuckerle 140 P

– Ortsteil Hofen
Zuckerle 140 P

– Ortsteil
Untertürkheim
Herzogenberg 142 P
Mönchberg 143 P
Altenberg 144
Gips 145 P
Wetzstein 146 P
Schloßberg 147 P

– Ortsteil Rotenberg
Schloßberg 147 P

– Ortsteil Uhlbach
Schloßberg 147 P
Steingrube 148
Götzenberg 149

– Ortsteil Galsburg
Abelsberg 150

– Ortsteil Wangen
Berg 137 p

– Ortsteil Hedelfingen
Lenzenberg 151 P

– Ortsteil Rohracker
Lenzenberg 151 P

– Ortsteil
Obertürkheim
Kirchberg 152 P
Ailenberg 153 P

Fellbach
Herzogenberg 142 P
Mönchberg 143 P
Gips 145 P
Wetzstein 146 P
Goldberg 154
Lämmler 155
Hinterer Berg 156

**Eßlingen
Ortsteil Mettingen**
Kirchberg 152 P
Ailenberg 153 P
Lerchenberg 157 P
Schenkenberg 159 P

Eßlingen
Lerchenberg 157 P
Schenkenberg 158 P
Burg 158 a

**GROSSLAGE
KOPF**

Korb
Sommerhalde 159
Berg 160 P
Hörnle 161 P

– Ortsteil
Kleinheppach
Greiner 162

Waiblingen
Hörnle 161 P

– Ortsteil Neustadt
Söhrenberg 163

– Ortsteil Beinstein
Großmulde 164

Winnenden
Berg 160 P
Holzenberg 165 P
Roßberg 166

– Ortsteil Hanweiler
Berg 160 P

– Ortsteil
Breuningsweiler
Holzenberg 165 P

– Ortsteil Bürg
Schloßberg 167

**Weinstadt,
Ortsteil Großheppach**
Wanne 168

**Remshalden
Ortsteil Grunbach**
Berghalde 169

Winterbach
Hungerberg 170

Schorndorf
Grafenberg 171

**GROSSLAGE
WARTBÜHL**

Winnenden
Haselstein 172 P

– Ortsteil
Hertmannsweiler
Himmelreich 173 P

– Ortsteil Baach
Himmelreich 173 P

– Ortsteil
Breuningsweiler
Haselstein 172 P

– Ortsteil Hanweiler
Maien 174

Waiblingen
Steingrüble 175 P

Korb
Steingrüble 175 P

– Ort. Kleinheppach
Steingrüble 175 P
Sonnenberg 176 a

**Weinstadt
Ortsteil
Großheppach**
Steingrüble 175 P
Zügernberg 177

– Ortsteil
Beutelsbach
Sonnenberg 176 P
Altenberg 178 P
Käppele 179

– Ortsteil Schnait
Sonnenberg 176 P
Altenberg 178 P

– Ortsteil
Endersbach
Wetzstein 180
Happenhalde 181

– Ortsteil
Strümpfelbach
Gastenklinge 182
Nonnenberg 183

**Remshalden
– Ortsteil Grunbach**
Klingle 184

– Ortsteil
Geradstetten
Sonnenberg 176 P
Lichtenberg 185 P

– Ortsteil Hebsack
Lichtenberg 185 P

**Aichwald
Ortsteil Aichelberg**
Luginsland 186

**Kernen
Ortsteil Stetten**
Pulvermächer 187
Lindhälder 188
Brotwasser 189
Häder 190 P

– Ortsteil
Rommelshausen
Häder 190 P

**GROSSLAGE
SONNENBÜHL**

**Weinstadt
Ortsteil
Beutelsbach**
Burghalde 192 P

– Ortsteil Schnait
Burghalde 192 P

– Ortsteil
Strümpfelbach
Altenberg 193

– Ortsteil Endersbach
Hintere Klinge 194

**Kernen
Ortsteil Stetten**
Mönchberg 195 P

– Ortsteil
Rommelshausen
Mönchberg 195 P

**GROSSLAGE
HOHENNEUFFEN**

Metzingen
Hofsteige 196 P
Schloßsteige 197 P

– Ortsteil Neuhausen
Hofsteige 196 P

Neuffen
Schloßsteige 197 P

– Ortsteil
Kappishäusern
Schloßsteige 197 P

Kohlberg
Schloßsteige 197 P

Frickenhausen
Schloßsteige 197 P

– Ortsteil Linsenhofen
Schloßsteige 197 P

Beuren
Schloßsteige 197 P

Weilheim
Schloßsteige 197 P

**BEREICH OBERER
NECKAR
Tübingen and
Ortsteile Hirschau
and Unterjesingen**
Sonnenhalden 198

**Ammerbuch
Ortsteil Breitenholz**
Hinterhalde 198 a

– Ortsteil Entringen
Pfaffenberg 198 b

**Rottenberg and
Ortsteile Wurmlingen
and Wendelsheim**
Kapellenberg 199

Reutlingen
Sommerhalde 199 a

GROSSLAGENFREI

Ravensburg
Rauenegg 200*

Staatliche Lehr- und Versuchsanstalt für Wein und Obstbau

Traubenplatz 5, 7102 Weinsberg, tel: 07134-5040. *Owner:* the State of Baden-Württemberg. *Director:* Dr. Gerhard Götz. 53 hectares. *Einzellagen:* Abstatt: Burg Wildeck (solely owned); Weinsberg: Ranzenberg and Schemelsberg (solely owned); Talheim: Schloßberg; Gundelsheim: Himmelreich; Lauda: Altenberg and Kirchberg; Lauffen: Katzenbeißer

The largest wine estate in Württemberg and the oldest wine school in Germany (founded in 1868); it has recently been rebuilt, and there are similar plans for the cellar. Experimentation and development form a major part of its work.

Of the circa 44 hectares in production, about 23% is Riesling, 17% Müller-Thurgau, 14% Kerner, 9% Spätburgunder, 8% Limberger (or Lemberger). A wide variety is in areas of less than 2 hectares. Methods are very modern and hygienic, aiming at maximum aroma by excluding air and avoiding sulphur. The wines are generally dry and full-bodied and the reds (especially Limberger) a good colour. Visits and tastings (by arrangement) are encouraged; both the vineyards and the wine are a great advertisement for Württemberg.

Württembergische Hofkammer-Kellerei

Hölderlinstraße 32, 7000 Stuttgart. *Owner:* Phillip Albrecht, Herzog von Württemberg. 23.5 hectares in 4 scattered areas, 1ha in Stuttgart (Untertürkheim: Mönchberg and Altenberg) and the others to the east, north and west at Stetten (Brotwasser), Mundelsheim (Käsberg), Hohenhaslach and Maulbronn (Eilfingerberg Klosterstück, solely owned).

More than half the vines are Riesling, with smaller parcels of Trollinger, Limberger (or Lemberger), etc. The grapes are pressed locally and the must brought to the medieval ducal cellars in Stuttgart for fermentation in oak casks. The wines are classically made and the estate is generally considered to be the flagship of Württemberg wines.

Weingärtnergenossenschaft Bad Cannstatt eG

Rommelstraße 20, 7000 Stuttgart-Bad Cannstatt, tel: 0711–542266.

The 55 hectares supplying this cooperative cellar push their way through the urban development of Württemberg's largest wine "village" – Stuttgart. The wines are much valued locally, particularly the Trollinger, and the Helfensteiner (Pinot Noir × Trollinger) does well in national (DLG) competitions. Most are sold within 50km (30 miles) of the city centre. As the burghers of Stuttgart consume more than twice the national average amount of wine per year, the cooperative's claim that there is only one thing wrong with its wine – there is not enough of it – seems justified. The holdings of the 90 members are planted mainly with Riesling (18%), Müller-Thurgau (10%), and, of course, Trollinger (60%).

Weingärtnergenossenschaft Flein-Talheim eG

Römerstraße 14, 7101 Flein, tel: 07131-52033.

A cooperative of 425 members serving two villages near Heilbronn. In Talheim, once a leading Jewish community with its own synagogue, there are 85 hectares supplying grapes, and in Flein, 185 hectares. The Flein Riesling wines are particularly successful in competitions, and rose to a Beerenauslese and an Eiswein in 1983. Riesling is, in fact, the most widely planted vine, covering 52% of sloping vineyards. Schwarzriesling accounts for 31%, and Kerner and Samtrot each 4%. All the wine is "estate bottled" and sold locally, mainly to the wine and grocery trades.

Genossenschaftskellerei Heilbronn-Erlenbach-Weinsberg eG

Binswangerstraße, 7100 Heilbronn, tel: 07131-10027.

An impressive cooperative of 600 members, lying in pleasant, undulating country, northeast of Heilbronn. As the title of the cellars suggests, grapes are supplied from 600 hectares in Heilbronn itself, Erlenbach, and the small town of Weinsberg, famous for its viticultural institute. There are 179 hectares of Riesling, 154 hectares of Trollinger, 63 hectares of Schwarzriesling, and 8 hectares of Kerner – one of the best known crossings from Weinsberg. The cooperative is certainly one of the best in the region, and wins many top awards for its wines.

Weingärtnergenossenschaft Lauffen eG

Im Brühl 48, 7128 Lauffen, tel: 07133-5088.

Lauffen, the birthplace of the poet Friedrich Hölderlin, can also boast of its excellent (510-hectare, 623-member) cooperative cellar. The holdings are in the Katzenbeißer and Jungfer (the first meaning "somebody who bites cats" and the second, more comprehensibly, a "virgin") Einzellagen. 98% of the production is consumed within Württemberg. The vineyards are planted 70% with Schwarzreisling (Pinot Meunier), 7% Trollinger, 6% Riesling and 4% Müller-Thurgau. There are also small amounts of Gewürztraminer, Kerner, Ruländer, Limberger and Samtrot (a mutation of Schwarzriesling).

Weingärtnergenossenschaft Nordheim eG

Südstraße 70, 7107 Nordheim, tel: 07133-5013/4.

The members of this cooperative own 180 hectares southeast of the substantial town of Heilbronn. The two Einzellagen Sonntagsberg and Gräfenberg are scattered around Nordheim, Nordhausen and Klingenberg. The steep, south-facing vineyards are planted with Riesling (29%), Schwarzriesling (18%), Trollinger (12%), Müller-Thurgau (10%), Kerner (9%) and Lemberger (7%). The concentration is a little in favour of white wine varieties, meeting the current demand. The

Trollinger and Lemberger wines are often made into blends, and as such, win awards at the national (DLG) competitions. 90% of the 145,000 cases, or their equivalent, sold each year, are consumed locally.

Weingärtnergenossenschaft Strombergkellerei eG

Cleebronnerstraße 70, 7124 Bönnigheim, tel: 07143-246.

A large cooperative of 620 members, as its name suggests, in the Großlage Stromberg, delivering 10% of its wine as a tithe to the Zentralkellerei at Möglingen, leaving some 241,500 cases to be distributed amongst the grocery trade (30%), the wine trade (30%), restaurants (10%) and directly to the consumer (23%). The 306 hectares are mainly at Bönningheim itself (130 hectares), Sachsenheim-Hohenhaslach (100 hectares), and Kirchheim (50 hectares). This is red-wine country: the holdings are Trollinger 21%, Schwarzriesling 20%, Lemberger 19%, Spätburgunder 8% and a small area of the new crossing, Dornfelder. White wine varieties are Kerner 11%, Riesling 10% and Müller-Thurgau 10%.

Weingärtnergenossenschaft Untertürkheim eG

Strümpfelbacherstraße 47, 7000 Stuttgart, tel: 0711-331092.

Founded in 1887, this is one of the oldest co-operative cellars in Württemberg. Here tradition counts. It is claimed that in the 19th century, when Württemberg was a kingdom, Untertürkheimer wine was widely known through the chain of connections linking the royal households of Europe, and eventually leading to the Czar. Today the Untertürkheimers buy the local wine, taking directly from the cooperative cellars 83% (59,000 cases) of the annual output in bottle. The 99 members own 70 hectares of sloping vineyard, planted 43% with Trollinger, 17% with Riesling, 15% with Müller-Thurgau and 6% with Kerner.

Württembergische Weingärtner-Zentral-Genossenschaft eG

Raiffeisenstraße 2, 7141 Möglingen, tel: 07141-48051.

In Württemberg 87% of vineyard owners have insufficient land to make a living from viticulture. As a result, they become members of cooperative cellars, which purchase the grapes from them. The WZG, the central cooperative cellars for the region, receives the total crop from 43 local cooperatives, and part of the crop from 49 others. The storage capacity amounts to the equivalent of 11.5 million cases, of which three-quarters are sold within Württemberg. This vast establishment, with a bottling capacity of nearly 4,000 cases per hour, is able to exert a stabilizing effect on the Württemberg wine market.

NORTH BADEN

Baden is the new force in German wine – at present only domestically, but soon no doubt on the world stage. Its vineyards have undergone no less than a revolution in recent years: they have been almost entirely rationalized and remodelled by Flurbereinigung, have doubled in size and quadrupled in output. They now lie third in yield in Germany, behind only Rheinpfalz and Rheinhessen.

Baden faces Alsace across the Rhine. It is Germany's warmest (although not necessarily its sunniest) wine region, with correspondingly ripe, high-alcohol and low-acid wines: the diametric opposite of Mosels in style and function. The best Mosel wines are for analytical sipping. Baden makes mealtime wines with a warm vinosity that approaches the French style. It is the choice of grape varieties and the taste for a trace of sweetness that distinguishes them from Alsace wines. The difference is reinforced by a slightly less favourable climate than the suntrap of the Vosges foothills.

Eighty per cent of Baden's vineyards lie in a 150-kilometre (80-mile) strip running from northeast to southwest, from Baden-Baden to Basel, in the foothills of the Black Forest where it meets the Rhine valley. The combination of dark forested-topped hills skirted by fresh green vineyards is not unique to Baden, but it reaches a picturesque poignancy along that ridge that makes it an unforgettable region to visit. Baden-Baden, the most stylish of spas, is an excellent natural centre for exploration for the main Baden vineyard areas. The balance is of purely local importance. The secondary areas lie southeast on the banks of the Bodensee (alias Lake Constance), north of Baden in the minor regions of the Kraichgau and Badische Bergstraße, respectively south and north of Heidelberg (but now united in one Bereich with both names – the Badische Bergstraße/Kraichgau), and far north on the border with Franken, a little region known logically enough as Bereich Badisches Frankenland. The main thrust of Baden viticulture is thus along the Rhine.

Baden is, even more than the southern Rheinpfalz, the land of the cooperative. More than 100 cooperatives process nearly 90 per cent of the crop, and half of all their output finds its way to the huge ZBW central cellars in Breisach on the Rhine. The ZBW bottles some 400–500 different types of wine. Baden has no powerful preference for one grape variety. Relics of local tradition in this most diverse and extended region are not so important today as well-judged selections for particular sites. The Müller-Thurgau is the workhorse grape, with about one-third of the vineyard area. Spätburgunder for red and light rosé comes second with about one-fifth. Then comes Ruländer, alias Pinot Gris or Tokay d'Alsace, which makes one of Baden's most striking wines: dense, almost thick, low in acid but high in extract and potentially the best wine of the region to accompany its often richly savoury food. In order of popularity Gutedel (or Chasselas) comes next, followed by Riesling (the prince of Baden's whites, as of all other regions), then Silvaner, Weißburgunder and Gewürztraminer. Baden's taste is clearly not for the highly aromatic new varieties; it conjures flavour and harmony out of relatively neutral grapes, regarding wine in the French manner as first and foremost an accompaniment to food. A relatively high alcohol content by German standards makes the analogy with France closer. In the jargon of the EEC Baden is the only German wine region to be classed as within Viticulture Zone B, with higher norms for natural grape sugar – hence strength. The rest of Germany is in

Zone A, a distinction shared only by the vineyards of Luxembourg. Baden shares Zone B with the French vineyards of Alsace, Champagne, Jura, Savoie and the Loire.

There are several regions of definite stylistic difference within the extended scope of Baden's vineyards. The climate of the Bodensee in the south is very different, for example, from that of the northerly borders of Franken – the northern extremity of Baden's vineyards.

The two Bereiche in the northern part of Baden have quite distinct characters. The remote little enclave known as Badisches Frankenland in viticultural logic is truly part of Franken. Only an awkwardly placed political boundary allies its Tauber valley wines to Baden at all. The Bereich Badische Bergstraße and Kraichgau, although clearly another political compromise, is truly Baden in feeling, its best wines deriving from Ruländer and Riesling, particularly south of Heidelberg round Wiesloch, where remarkably fine and harmonious wines are made. Müller-Thurgau outnumbers all other grapes, but Riesling still occupies one-fifth of the vineyards of the Bereich, and fully justifies its place. A certain amount of red wine is made, but the relative coolness of the region favours well-balanced whites.

▼ Hand-picking (here with a degree of clairvoyance) is still the rule in Germany. The quality vineyards are too steep for machines.

TRAVEL INFORMATION

The northern part of the Baden wine region includes one of Germany's major tourist centres, Heidelberg.

Places to visit
Heidelberg has Germany's oldest university, a superb castle and a perhaps over-selfconscious historic centre. In summer there is a drama festival and open-air concerts. The beauty of the Neckar valley, running east from Heidelberg, can perhaps best be seen from a boat.

Wine roads
The *Badische Weinstraße* starts north of Heidelberg and threads through the Bergstraße vineyards and on towards the Ortenau district (see South Baden).

Wine festivals
See South Baden

Food and drink
It is here that the climate becomes more benign and southern, with asparagus among the market-garden crops. Schwetzingen, near Heidelberg, is noted for asparagus; another local delicacy is *Hopfensprossen* – tiny hops dressed with butter or cream. Fruits such as wild raspberries (*Himbeeren*) and currants (*Johannisbeeren*) are also Baden specialities. Many towns have markets where local produce can be bought. In the Black Forest look out for *Bauernspeck*, country-smoked bacon, and anything involving kirsch, cream and cherries. Black Forest venison is famous: one noted dish is *Rehrücken* or saddle of venison with pears and cranberries.

The lower Neckar valley has a clutch of castle hotels such as Burg Guttenberg (tel: 06266-228), the Schloßhotel Hirschorn (tel: 06272-1373) and the Burghotel Hornberg (tel: 06261-4064). More domestic in scale is the Schloßhotel Heinsheim, 350 years in the same family (tel: 07264-1045) or the riverside Zum Ritter in the town of Neckargemünd (tel: 06223-7035).

The splendidly named village of

Heiligenkreuzsteinach-Eiterbach has the Goldener Pflug restaurant. Other noted restaurants are Pfeffer und Salz near Viernheim and Zum Ritter in Heidelberg.

▼ The contrast between the unreformed old narrow terraces and the broad new ones resulting from Flurbereinigung can still be seen in different parts of Baden's Kaiserstuhl.

VINEYARDS

ROAD MAP

78   79

DARMSTADT

GROSS-UMSTADT

Rhein

WORMS   BENSHEIM

FRANKENTHAL   WEINHEIM

MANNHEIM   Neckar

NEUSTADT   HEIDELBERG

LANDAU

BRUCHSAL

80   ROAD MAP   81

**BEREICH
BADISCHES
FRANKENLAND**

**GROSSLAGE
TAUBERKLINGE**

Dertingen
(Ortsteil of Wertheim)
Mandelberg 1
Sonnenberg 2 P

Kembach
(Ortsteil of Wertheim)
Sonnenberg 2 P

Lindelbach
(Ortsteil of Wertheim)
Ebenrain 4

Wertheim
Schloßberg 5

Reichholzheim
(Ortsteil of Wertheim)
Josefsberg 3 P
First 6
Satzenberg 7
Kemelrain 8 P

Bronnbach
(Ortsteil of Wertheim)
Josefsberg 3 P

Höhefeld
(Ortsteil of Wertheim)
Kemelrain 8 P

Uissigheim
(Ortsteil of Külsheim)
Stahlberg 9

Külsheim
Hoher Herrgott 10

Werbach
Hirschberg 11
Beilberg 12 P

Großrinderfeld
Beilberg 12 P

Impfingen
(Ortsteil of
Tauberbischofsheim)
Silberquell 13

Tauberbischofsheim
Edelberg 14

Distelhausen
(Ortsteil of
Tauberbischofsheim)
Kreuzberg 14 a

Dittigheim
(Ortsteil of
Tauberbischofsheim)
Steinschmetzer 14 b

Dittwar
(Ortsteil of
Tauberbischofsheim)
Ölkuchen 14 c

Königheim
Kirchberg 15

Gissigheim
(Ortsteil of Königheim)
Gützenberg 15 a

Gerlachsheim
(Ortsteil of Lauda-
Königshofen)
Herrenberg 16

Oberlauda
(Ortsteil of Lauda-
Königshofen)
Steinklinge 17
Altenberg 18 P

Lauda
(Ortsteil of Lauda-
Königshofen)
Altenberg 18 P
Frankenberg 19 P
Nonnenberg 20 P

Marbach
(Ortsteil of Lauda-
Königshofen)
Frankenberg 19 P

Beckstein
(Ortsteil of Lauda-
Königshofen)
Nonnenberg 20 P
Kirchberg 21 P

Königshofen
(Ortsteil of Lauda-
Königshofen)
Kirchberg 21 P
Walterstal 22 P
Turmberg 23

Unterbalbach
(Ortsteil of Lauda-
Königshofen)
Vogelsberg 23 a

Oberbalbach
(Ortsteil of Lauda-
Königshofen)
Mühlberg 23 b

Sachsenflur
(Ortsteil of Lauda-
Königshofen)
Walterstal 22 P
Kailberg 24

Unterschüpf
(Ortsteil of Boxberg)
Mühlberg 25

Oberschüpf
(Ortsteil of Boxberg)
Altenberg 26
Herrenberg 27

Krautheim
Heiligenberg 28 P

Klepsau
(Ortsteil of
Krautheim)
Heiligenberg 28 P

Dainbach
(Ortsteil of Bad
Mergentheim)
Alte Burg 28 a

Main

Wertheim

Dertingen

Lindelbach

Kembach

Reichholzheim

Bronnbach

Höhefeld

Uissigheim

Werbach

Groß-Rinderfeld

Külsheim

Tauber

Impfingen

Tauberbischofsheim

Großlage
Tauberklinge

Königheim

Dittigheim

Gissigheim

Dittwar

Distelhausen

Lauda

Gerlachsheim

Oberlauda

Marbach

Lauda-Königshofen

Beckstein

Königshofen

Oberschüpf

Sachsenflur

Unterbalbach

Oberbalbach

Unterschüpf

Boxberg

Dainbach

Bad Mergentheim

Krautheim

Klepsau

udenbach 29

Hemsbach

30

Sulzbach

31

Weinheim

32

Lützelsachsen

33

Hohensachsen

roßsachsen

34

35

tershausen

36

Großlage
Rittersber

38 39

40

chriesheim

38

41

Dossenheim

41

Handschuhsheim
42

43

Neckar

Heidelberg

120 ROAD MAP

Main

BAD
MERGENTHEIM ●

KUNZELSAU ●

● NECKARSULM

122 ROAD MAP

**BEREICH
BADISCHE
BERGSTRASSE/
KRAICHGAU**

**GROSSLAGE
RITTERSBERG**

Laudenbach
Sonnberg 29

Hemsbach
Herrnwingert 30 P

Sulzbach
(Ortsteil of Weinheim)
Herrnwingert 30 P

Weinheim
Hubberg 31
Wüstberg 32

Lützelsachsen
(Ortsteil of Weinheim)
Stephansberg 33 P

Hohensachsen
(Ortsteil of Weinheim)
Stephansberg 33 P

Großsachsen
(Ortsteil of Hirschberg)
Sandrocken 34

Leutershausen
(Ortsteil of Hirschberg)
Kahlberg 35
Staudenberg 36 P

Schriesheim
Staudenberg 36 P
Kuhberg 38
Madonnenberg 39
Schloßberg 40

Dossenheim
Ölberg 41

Heidelberg
Heiligenberg 42
Sonnenseife
  ob der Bruck 43

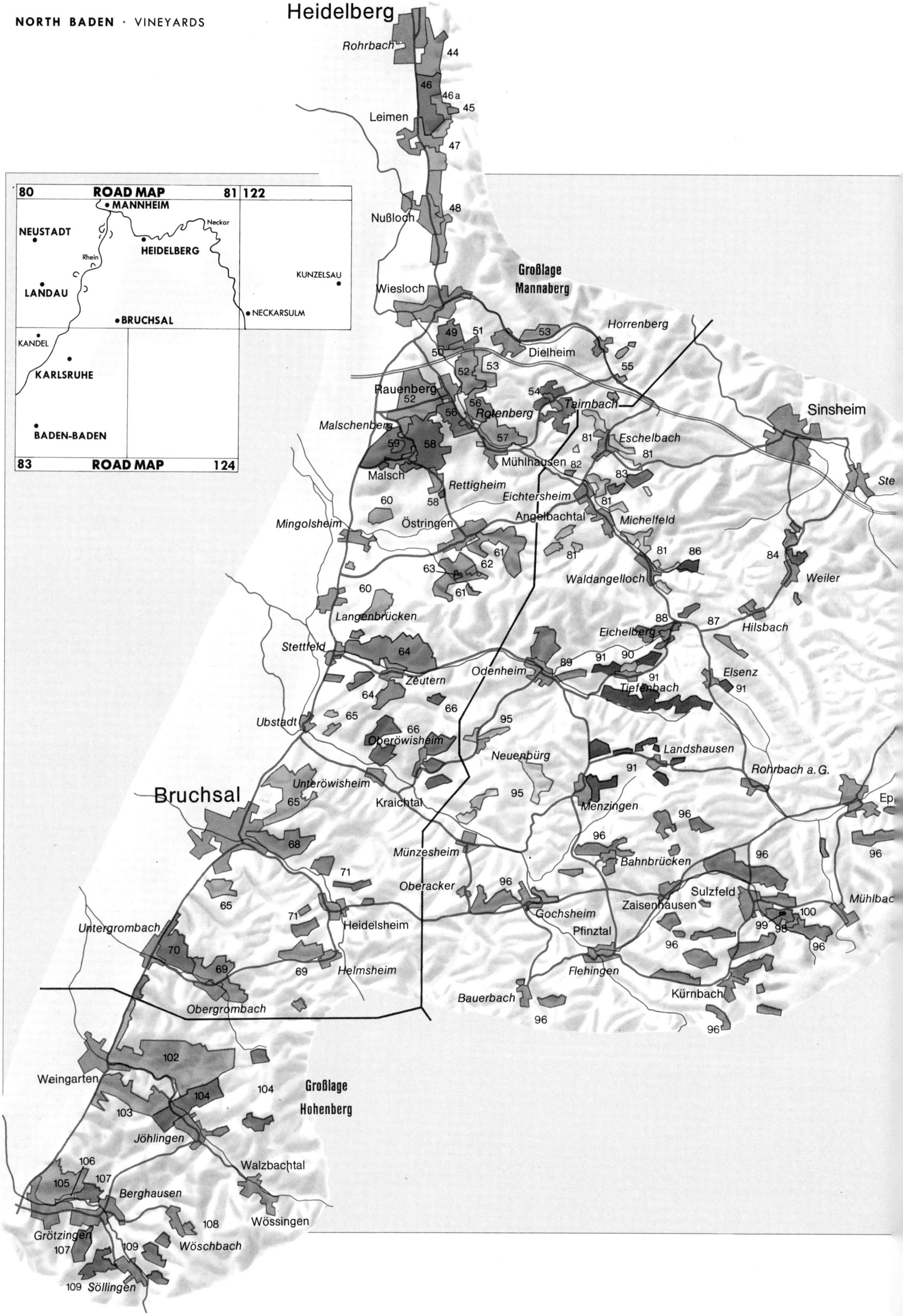

Heidelberg

Rohrbach

44

46

46a
45

Leimen

47

Nußloch

48

Großlage
Mannaberg

ROAD MAP

80 | 81 122

MANNHEIM

NEUSTADT

Neckar

HEIDELBERG

Rhein

KUNZELSAU

LANDAU

NECKARSULM

BRUCHSAL

KANDEL

KARLSRUHE

BADEN-BADEN

83 ROAD MAP 124

Wiesloch

49 51

50

53

Horrenberg

Dielheim

52 53

55

Sinsheim

Rauenberg

52

54

Tairnbach

56

Rotenberg

81

Eschelbach

81

Malschenberg

57

Mühlhausen

82

83

59 58

Rettigheim

Eichtersheim

81

Malsch

58

Angelbachtal

Michelfeld

60

Östringen

Mingolsheim

81

81

86

84

Weiler

61

62

Waldangelloch

63

65

60

61

Langenbrücken

88

87

Hilsbach

Stettfeld

64

Eichelberg

91

90

Elsenz

Zeutern

Odenheim

89

91

91

64

66

Tiefenbach

91

Ubstadt

65

66

95

Oberöwisheim

Neuenbürg

Landshausen

Bruchsal

Unteröwisheim

65

Kraichtal

95

91

Rohrbach a. G.

Ep

68

Münzesheim

96

Menzingen

96

71

Bahnbrücken

96

96

Sulzfeld

Mühlbac

65

Oberacker

96

Zaisenhausen

100

71

Heidelsheim

96

Gochsheim

99 98

96

Untergrombach

Pfinztal

96

70

69

69

Helmsheim

Flehingen

Kürnbach

Obergrombach

Bauerbach

96

96

102

Weingarten

104

Großlage
Hohenberg

104

103

104

Jöhlingen

106

Walzbachtal

105

107

Berghausen

108

Wössingen

Grötzingen

107

109

Wöschbach

109 Söllingen

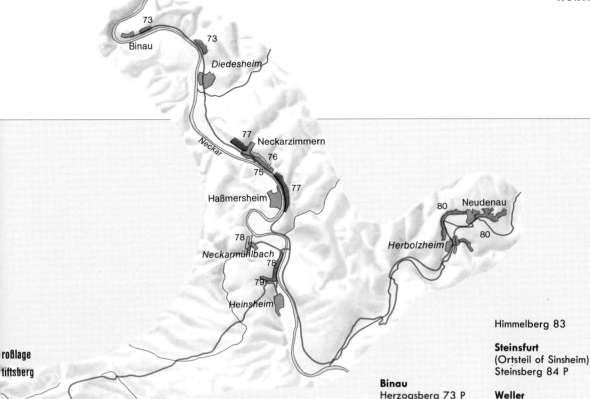

73 Binau
73 Diedesheim
Neckar
77 Neckarzimmern
76
75
77 Haßmersheim
78 Neckarmühlbach
78
79
Heinsheim
80 Neudenau
80
Herbolzheim

roßlage
tiftsberg
Kirchhardt
Berwangen
92
emmingen

GROSSLAGE MANNABERG

Heidelberg
Burg 44
Dachsbuckel 45
Herrenberg 46 P
Dormenacker 46 a

Leimen
Herrenberg 46 P
Kreuzweg 47

Nußloch
Wilhelmsberg 48

Weisloch
Bergwäldle 49
Spitzenberg 50
Hägenich 51

Rauenberg
Burggraf 52

Dielheim
Teufelskopf 53
Rosenberg 54 P

Tairnbach
(Ortsteil of
Mühlhausen)
Rosenberg 54 P

Horrenberg
(Ortsteil of Dielheim)
Osterberg 55

Rotenberg
(Ortsteil of
Rauenberg)
Scholßberg 56

Mühlhausen
Heiligenstein 57

Malschenberg
(Ortsteil of
Rauenberg)
Ölbaum 58 P

Rettigheim
(Ortsteil of
Mühlhausen)
Ölbaum 58 P

Malsch
Ölbaum 58 P
Rotsteig 59

**Mingolsheim and
Langenbrücken**
(Ortsteile of Bad
Schönborn)
Goldberg 60

Östringen
Ulrichsberg 61
Hummelberg 62
Rosenkranzweg 63

Zeutern
(Ortsteil of Ubstadt-
Weiher)
Himmelreich 64 P

Stettfeld
(Ortsteil of Ubstadt-
Weiher)
Himmelreich 64 P

Ubstadt
(Ortsteil of Ubstadt-
Weiher)
Weinhecke 65 P

Bruchsal
Weinhecke 65 P
Klosterberg 68

**Oberöwisheim,
Unteröwisheim**
(Ortsteil of Kraichtal)
Kirchberg 66

Obergrombach
(Ortsteil of Bruchsal)
Burgwingert 69 P

Helmsheim
(Ortsteil of Bruchsal)
Burgwingert 69 P

Untergrombach
(Ortsteil of Bruchsal)
Michaelsberg 70

Heidelsheim
(Ortsteil of Bruchsal)
Altenberg 71

GROSSLAGE STIFTSBERG

Eberbach
Schollerbuckel 74*

Binau
Herzogsberg 73 P

Diedesheim
(Ortsteil of Mosbach)
Herzogsberg 73 P

Neckarzimmern
Wallmauer 75
Götzhalde 76
Kirchweinberg 77 P

Haßmersheim
Kirchweinberg 77 P

Neckarmühlbach
(Ortsteil of
Haßmersheim)
Hohberg 78

Heinsheim
(Ortsteil of Bad
Rappenau)
Burg Ehrenberg 79

Herbolzheim
Berg 80 P

Neudenau
Berg 80 P

Eschelbach
(Ortsteil of Sinsheim)
Sonnenberg 81 P

Waldangelloch
(Ortsteil of Sinsheim)
Sonnenberg 81 P

Eichtersheim
(Ortsteil of
Angelbachtal)
Sonnenberg 81 P
Kletterberg 82

Michelfeld
(Ortsteil of
Angelbachtal)
Sonnenberg 81 P

Himmelberg 83

Steinsfurt
(Ortsteil of Sinsheim)
Steinsberg 84 P

Weller
(Ortsteil of
Sinsheim)
Steinsberg 84 P
Goldberg 86

Hilsbach
(Ortsteil of Sinsheim)
Eichelberg 87

Eichelberg
(Ortsteil of
Östringen)
Kapellenberg 88

Odenheim
(Ortsteil of
Östringen)
Königsbecher 89

Tiefenbach
(Ortsteil of
Östringen)
Schellenbrunnen 90
Spiegelberg 91 P

Elsenz
(Ortsteil of Eppingen)
Spiegelberg 91 P

**Landshausen and
Menzingen**
(Ortsteile of
Kraichtal)
Spiegelberg 91 P

Berwangen
(Ortsteil of Kirchardt)
Vogelsang 92 P

Gemmingen
Vogelsang 92 P

**Menzingen,
Münzesheim and
Neuenbürg**
(Ortsteile of Kraichtal)
Silberberg 95

**Bahnbrücken,
Gochsheim and
Oberacker**
(Ortsteile of
Kraichtal)
Lerchenberg 96 P

Eppingen
Lerchenberg 96 P

Rohrbach a. G.
(Ortsteil of Eppingen)
Lerchenberg 96 P

Mühlbach
(Ortsteil of Eppingen)
Lerchenberg 96 P

Zaisenhausen
Lerchenberg 96 P

Kürnbach
Lerchenberg 96 P

Flehingen
(Ortsteil of
Oberderdingen)
Lerchenberg 96 P

Sulzfeld
Lerchenberg 96 P
Burg Ravensburger
   Husarenkappe 98
Burg Ravensburger
   Löchle 99
Burg Ravensburger
   Dicker Franz 100

Bauerbach
(Ortsteil of Bretten)
Lerchenberg 96 P

**GROSSLAGE
HOHENBERG**

Weingarten
Katzenberg 102
Petersburg 103

Jöhlingen
(Ortsteil of
Walzbachtal)
Hasensprung 104

Grötzingen
(Ortsteil of Karlsruhe)
Lichtenberg 105
Turmberg 106 P

Berghausen
(Ortsteil of Pfinztal)
Sonnenberg 107

Wöschbach
(Ortsteil of Pfinztal)
Steinwengert 108

Söllingen
(Ortsteil of Pfinztal)
Rotenbusch 109

158

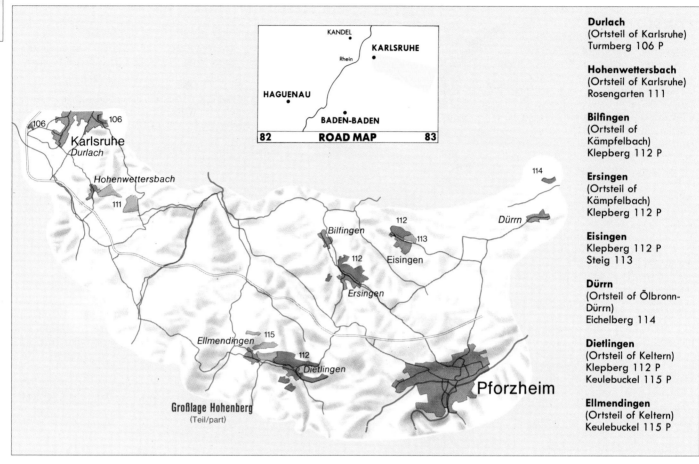

Durlach
(Ortsteil of Karlsruhe)
Turmberg 106 P

Hohenwettersbach
(Ortsteil of Karlsruhe)
Rosengarten 111

Bilfingen
(Ortsteil of
Kämpfelbach)
Klepberg 112 P

Ersingen
(Ortsteil of
Kämpfelbach)
Klepberg 112 P

Eisingen
Klepberg 112 P
Steig 113

Dürrn
(Ortsteil of Ölbronn-
Dürrn)
Eichelberg 114

Dietlingen
(Ortsteil of Keltern)
Klepberg 112 P
Keulebuckel 115 P

Ellmendingen
(Ortsteil of Keltern)
Keulebuckel 115 P

TRAVELLING THE VINEYARDS

Some German vineyards are easy to visit, as they follow closely the slopes of the river that holds the region together. Pick up the Mosel at Trier and you can discover all the well-known wine villages without any further help by simply travelling downstream to Koblenz. The vineyards of the Ahr and the Mittelrhein are similarly confined, and only now and again are vines allowed to establish themselves in attractive side valleys.

Other regions are more spread out and lack the reference point provided by a dissecting river. For them, a well signposted wine road is ideal. Probably the best known of these is the *Deutsche Weinstraße*, dating from 1935, that runs 80 kilometres (50 miles) from the north to the south of the Rheinpfalz, ending at the French border. Here at Schweigen, in the 1920s, the first Weinlehrpfad (instructional wine path) was

constructed in the vineyards. It set a trend that has since been enthusiastically followed, particularly in Baden and Württemberg.

Country walking in Germany is made easy by a comprehensive network of public footpaths, but the instructional wine path with its well-sited notice boards offers guidance in German on such matters as the vine varieties grown, the methods of training, the type of soil and the layout of the Einzellagen. It will always include in its tour one or more Weinstuben (wine bars), so that the effect on the wine of the

vineyard from which it comes can be judged on the spot.

Consumption of wine in Germany has remained at about 21 litres per head for the last ten years, and producers are faced with a difficult and competitive market. Efforts to build up a clear identity for the wine growing regions have been linked with the reconstruction (Flurbereinigung) of the vineyards, and the value of tourism has not been forgotten. The new Weinlehrpfade help to explain and therefore to sell German wine, and by the end of the 1970s practically all the eleven wine regions had their own Weinstraßen.

A natural adjunct to the wine roads are the Winzerfeste – the wine festivals – that fill the calendar from late April until October (details can be found in the Travel Information sections). These simple exercises in selling are natural tourist attractions, but

they offer a chance to enjoy wine, without being too serious about it. Details of when and where they take place can be obtained from:
Stabilisierungsfonds für Wein,
Gutenbergplatz 3–5,
6500 Mainz 1.
(Tel: 06131-28290)
Office hours are usually 9–12 a.m. and 2–4 p.m.

Visiting wine estates and cellars is described on p138.

VILLAGES

BEREICH BADISCHE BERGSTRASSE/KRAICHGAU

The northernmost section of the Baden vineyards of the Rhine is so diffuse that its union in one Bereich looks like a measure of desperation. The Kraichgau is the area south of Heidelberg between the Rhine and the converging River Neckar, flowing northwest from Heilbronn in Württemberg. The Badische Bergstraße is a southern extension of the Hessische Bergstraße, a narrow ridge of vineyards running north-south and straddling the university city of Heidelberg.

The Kraichgau boasts three Großlagen: Hohenberg in the south around Pforzheim, Stiftsberg to the east and Mannaberg in the northwest (and including the southern villages of the Bergstraße: the chief of these is Wiesloch). The northern Bergstraße has its own Großlage: Rittersberg. Its principal town is called, simply, Weinheim.

The whole Bereich has some 1,800 hectares of vineyard divided into 77 Einzellagen. Almost half its vines are Müller-Thurgau, only 10 per cent are red; the exceptional sites, such as they are, are planted with Riesling (20%) and Ruländer (13%). Neckarzimmern on the Neckar has the estate with the widest reputation.

GROSSLAGE MANNABERG

This Großlage covers the vineyards on the edge of the Rhine Valley, which here is a broad plain, and those in side-valleys running east into the Kraichgau hills. The area is a continuation southwards of the Großlage Rittersberg, which takes in the country north of Heidelberg, Müller-Thurgau is the most common grape, with Ruländer, Riesling, Silvaner, Spätburgunder and Weißburgunder also grown.

Vineyards

Einzellagen: Heidelberg: Burg, 10ha, SW-W, steep; Dachsbuckel, 7ha, SW-W, steep. Rauenberg: Burggraf, 157ha, S-NW, steep. Östringen: Ulrichsberg, 67ha, SE-W, steep; Hummelberg, 5ha, SW, steep; Rosenkranzweg, 3ha, S, steep. Stettfeld: Himmelreich, 124ha, SE-W, steep. Bruchsal: Klosterberg, 20ha, steep.

GROSSLAGE STIFTSBERG

The Stiftsberg vineyards are east of the Mannaberg, in a string of valleys amid the Kraichgau hills. The most far-flung are in the valley of the Neckar and its eastward tributary the Jagst.

Vineyards

Einzellagen: Neckarzimmern: Götzhalde, 1.2ha, 40% terraced; Wallmauer, 2ha, 40% terraced. Sulzfeld: Burg Ravensburger Dicker Franz, 6.5ha, 100% sloping; Burg Ravensburger Husarenkappe, 6.5ha, 45% steep; Burg Ravensburger Löchle, 8.5ha, 60% steep. Michelfeld: Himmelberg, 5.6ha, 50% steep; Sonnenberg, 65ha, 50% steep.

GROSSLAGE HOHENBERG

A group of sites around Weingarten continue the trend of the Mannaberg southwards, with a scattering of vineyards in the countryside to the south and east, towards Pforzheim.

BEREICH BADISCHES FRANKENLAND

But for political boundaries this remote outpost of Baden wine-growing would be attached to its natural ally, Franken. It produces wines in the Franken style, mainly from Müller-Thurgau, and bottles them in Franconian flagons. The whole area, with some 526 hectares of vines, is one Großlage, Tauberklinge, and its centres are the towns of Lauda, Tauberbischofsheim and Wertheim on the Main.

PRODUCERS

Weingut Burg Hornberg

6951 Neckarzimmern, tel: 06261-2348. *Owner:* Baron Hans-Wolf von Gemmingen Hornberg. 14.5 hectares. *Einzellagen:* Neckarzimmern: Götzhalde and Wallmauer; Michelfeld: Himmelberg.

An ancient steep vineyard site owned by this family since the 17th century, with 30% Riesling, 10% Müller-Thurgau, 6% Silvaner, 20% Spätburgunder, plus Muskateller, Traminer, Ruländer and Weißburgunder. The wines are made by traditional methods to extract the maximum from the warm site; the best are full-bodied and impressive. A restaurant provides a chance to taste a wide range.

Freiherr von Göler'sche Verwaltung

Haupstraße 44, 7519 Sulzfeld, tel: 07269-231. *Owner:* Freiherr von Göler. 14 hectares. *Einzellagen:* Sulzfeld: Burg Ravensburger Husarenkappe, Löchle, Dicker Franz.

A north Baden estate surrounding the castle of Ravensburg, owned by the von Göler family since the 13th century. Riesling predominates (50%), followed by Silvaner with 12%, plus Müller-Thurgau, Weißburgunder, Limberger (or Lemberger), Schwarzriesling (Pinot Meunier), Spätburgunder and Trollinger. At present 80% of the wines are medium sweet, which suits their slightly earthy full style. Even

so, the amount of dry wines made is likely to increase in the coming years.

Weingut Reichsgraf & Marquis zu Hoensbroech

6921 Angelbachtal-Michelfeld, tel: 07265-381. *Owner:* Rüdiger, Reichsgraf und Marquis zu Hoensbroech. 15 hectares. *Einzellagen:* Michelfeld: Himmelberg and Sonnenberg. The Großlage is Stiftsberg.

A small lordly estate of the Kraichgau, south of Heidelberg in north Baden. Powerful dry wines are made of Weißburgunder (30%), Silvaner (20%), Riesling and Spätburgunder (15%); also Schwarzriesling (Pinot Meunier), Rülander, Gewürztraminer and Müller-Thurgau. The latter is to be reduced, to the advantage of Silvaner. Dry Kabinett wines constitute the main produce.

Fürstlich Löwenstein-Wertheim-Rosenberg'sches Weingut

Rathausgasse 5, 6983 Kreuzwertheim, tel: 09342-6505. *Owner:* Prince Alois Konstantin zu Löwenstein-Wertheim-Rosenberg. 27 hectares. *Einzellagen:* Homburg: Kallmuth; Lengfurt: Alter Berg and Oberrot; Reichholzheim: Satzenberg and Kemelrain; Bronnbach: Josefsberg. (Reichholzheim and Bronnbach are in the Bereich Badisches Frankenland in Baden.)

An isolated estate on the north bank of the Main west of the main Franken vineyards. The old Cistercian vineyards dating from the 12th century were acquired by the princely family at their secularization.

The vines are 42% Silvaner, 19% Müller-Thurgau, 15% Spätburgunder, 8% Bacchus, 7% Kerner, only 5% Riesling, 3% Traminer and 1% Rieslaner. The soil is an odd mixture of sandstone and limestone, on good slopes which ripen well. The style is powerful, dry and altogether Franconian. No crop in 1985, due to late frosts.

Winzergenossenschaft Bad. Frankenland eG

St.-Georg-Straße 1–3, 6980 Wertheim-Reicholzheim, tel: 09342-1026.

A large cooperative cellar, handling half the crop of the Bereich Badisches Frankenland, a once large and concentrated area, cut down to a tenth of its size by vine diseases in the last century. 215,000 cases of wine in the Franconian flagon-shaped bottle ("Bocksbeutel") and 67,000 cases of litre bottles are sold each year, 98% of them in West Germany. 684 members have 336 hectares, distributed over a large number of villages, planted with 78% Müller-Thurgau, 8% Kerner and 6% Silvaner.

GERMAN WINE QUALITY CATEGORIES

QUALITY WINE (QbA, QmP)		TABLE WINE (DTW)		LANDWEIN
REGION	BEREICH	DISTRICT	SUB-DISTRICT	DISTRICT
Ahr	Walporzheim/Ahrtal			Ahrtaler Landwein
Hessische Bergstraße	Starkenburg, Umstadt	Rhein-Mosel	Rhein	Starkenburger Landwein
Mittelrhein	Bacharach, Rheinburgengau, Siebengebirge			Rheinburgen-Landwein
Nahe	Kreuznach, Schloß Böckelheim			Nahegauer Landwein
Rheingau	Johannisberg			Altrheingauer Landwein
Rheinhessen	Bingen, Nierstein, Wonnegau			Rheinischer Landwein
Rheinpfalz	Südliche Weinstraße, Mittelhaardt/Deutsche Weinstraße			Pfälzer Landwein
Mosel-Saar-Ruwer	Zell/Mosel, Bernkastel, Obermosel, Saar-Ruwer, Moseltor		Mosel	Landwein der Mosel
			Saar	Landwein der Saar
Franken	Steigerwald, Maindreieck, Mainviereck, Bayerischer Bodensee	Bayern	Main	Fränkischer Landwein (not used)
			Donau	Regensburger Landwein
			Lindau	Bayerischer Bodensee-Landwein
Württemberg	Remstal-Stuttgart, Württembergisch Unterland, Kocher-Jagst-Tauber, Württembergischer Bodensee	Neckar		Schwäbischer Landwein
Baden	Bodensee, Markgräflerland, Kaiserstuhl-Tuniberg, Breisgau, Ortenau	Oberrhein	Römertor	Südbadischer Landwein
	Badische Bergstraße/Kraichgau, Badisches Frankenland		Burgengau	Unterbadischer Landwein

Zentralkellerei Badischer Winzergenossenschaften (ZBW)

Zum Kaiserstuhl 6, 7814 Breisach, tel: 07667-820.
Director: Ludwig Strub.

The mammoth central cooperative of Baden, uniting no less than 100 local cooperatives at one of the largest, most modern plants in Europe at Breisach on the Rhine. The vineyards are scattered all over Baden's seven Bereiche – from Badisches Frankenland by the River Main to the banks of the Bodensee in the south – and they amount to 4,500 hectares. Altogether some 25,000 growers are involved. The vines are 45% Müller-Thurgau, 26% Spätburgunder, 7% Ruländer, 6% Riesling, 5% each of Weißburgunder and Gutedel, 3% Silvaner and 2% Gewürztraminer. Each vintage 400–500 different wines are produced, under 50 different Einzellage and Großlage names, with their grape varieties and qualities. Over 4 million cases are produced annually, and distribution is countrywide. Exports are mainly to the UK, USA, the Benelux countries and Scandinavia. It is impossible to generalize about the output of this great organization more than to say that its wines are well made and true to type and class across the whole spectrum.

▶ These are the official figures declared after the harvest. The varying proportions in the different quality levels are mainly a result of variation in weather conditions.
◀ German wine is divided into quality wine (Qualitätswein), table wine (Deutscher Tafelwein or DTW) and Landwein. This table relates the eleven German quality-wine regions to the table wine and Landwein districts.

SUMMARY OF RECENT VINTAGES IN THE FIVE MAIN EXPORTING REGIONS

		MOSEL-SAAR-RUWER	NAHE	RHEIN-GAU	RHEIN-HESSEN	RHEIN-PFALZ
TOTAL QUANTITY OF WINE DECLARED AT HARVEST, IN HECTOLITRES						
1985		1,195,000	263,000	180,000	1,082,000	1,388,000
1984		1,106,000	312,000	163,000	1,855,000	2,311,000
1983		1,829,000	612,000	298,825	3,400,000	3,252,000
1982		2,365,000	716,700	485,000	3,773,000	3,847,000
1981		1,113,500	249,900	171,500	1,724,500	2,166,700
1980		571,500	132,600	101,500	1,145,000	1,593,900
1979		1,090,000	265,000	280,000	1,480,000	2,550,000
1976		1,040,000	366,000	228,000	1,960,000	2,310,000
PERCENTAGE OF QUALITY WINE, BY CATEGORY						
1985	QbA	63	57	40	38	47
	Kabinett	27	27	53	28	32
	Spätlese	8	13	6	29	17
	Auslese	2	3	1	5	4
1984	QbA	79	82	73	78	75
	Kabinett	1	1	1	6	7
	Spätlese	—	—	—	1	2
	Auslese	—	—	—	—	—
1983	QbA	43	48	30	46	52
	Kabinett	12	15	50	19	23
	Spätlese	31	25	19	25	16
	Auslese	9	8	0	2	3
1982	QbA	61	67	74	73	72
	Kabinett	30	24	25	18	12
	Spätlese	4	5	0	7	4
	Auslese	2	1	0	0	0
1981	QbA	63	54	71	54	54
	Kabinett	28	35	25	35	33
	Spätlese	9	10	2	10	11
	Auslese	0	1	0	1	2
1980	QbA	75	60	83	57	62
	Kabinett	15	24	15	23	20
	Spätlese	2	9	0	17	12
	Auslese	0	1	0	3	2
1979	QbA	37	16	59	16	46
	Kabinett	14	25	32	21	28
	Spätlese	38	48	7	58	17
	Auslese	11	11	0	5	3
1976	QbA	8	11	11	6	20
	Kabinett	10	26	22	8	30
	Spätlese	34	38	46	64	33
	Auslese	46	25	20	22	15
	Beeren-auslese	2	1	1	2	2

SOUTHERN ZONE

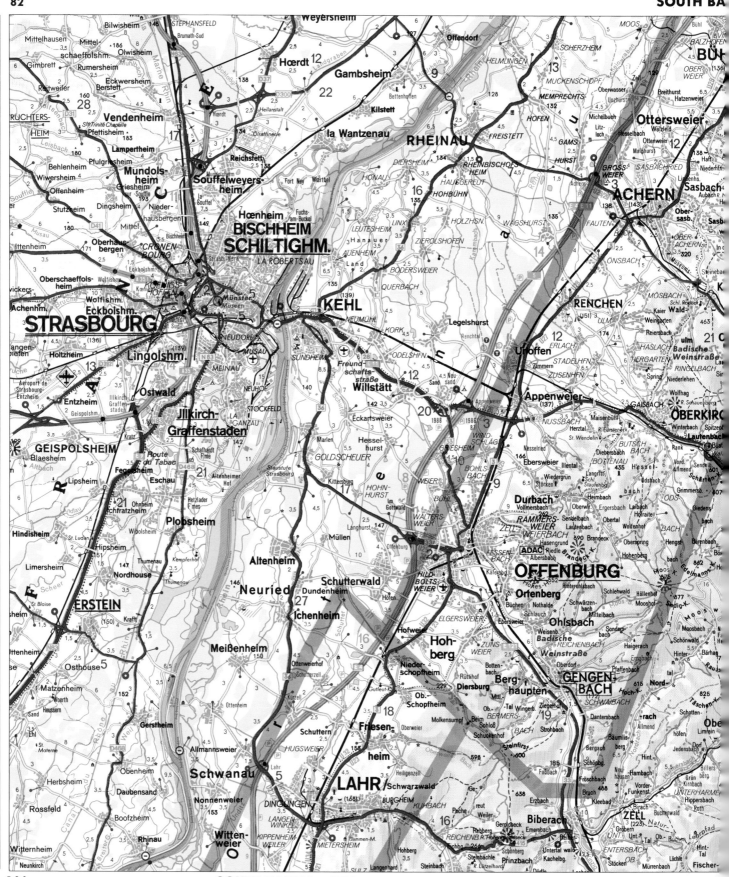

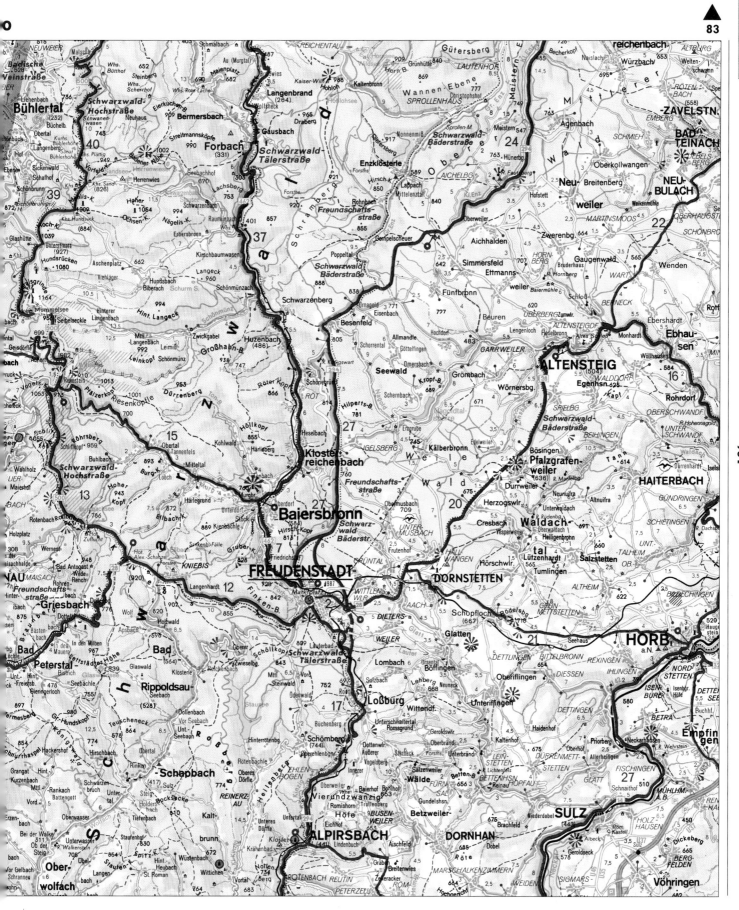

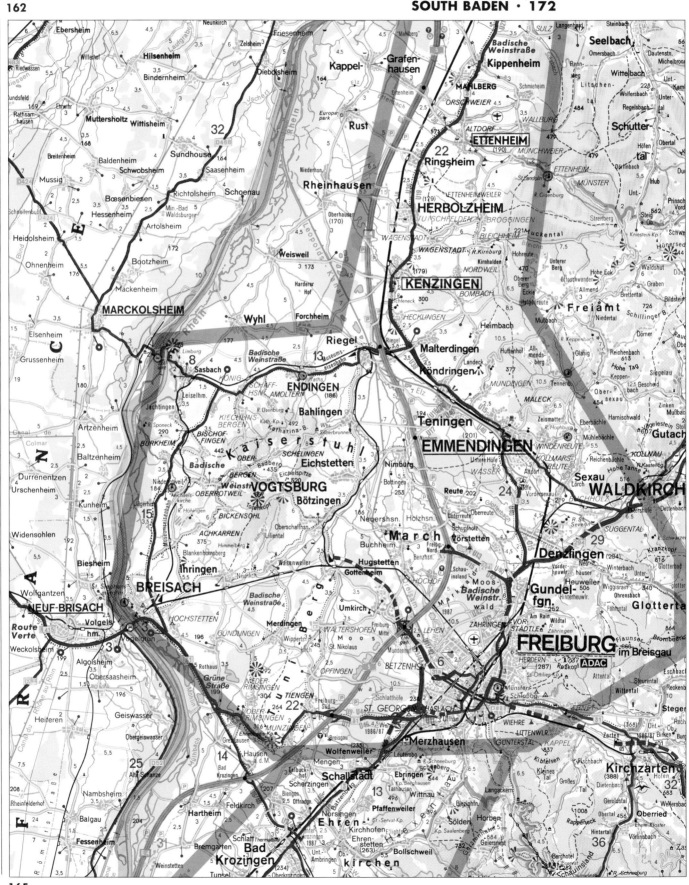

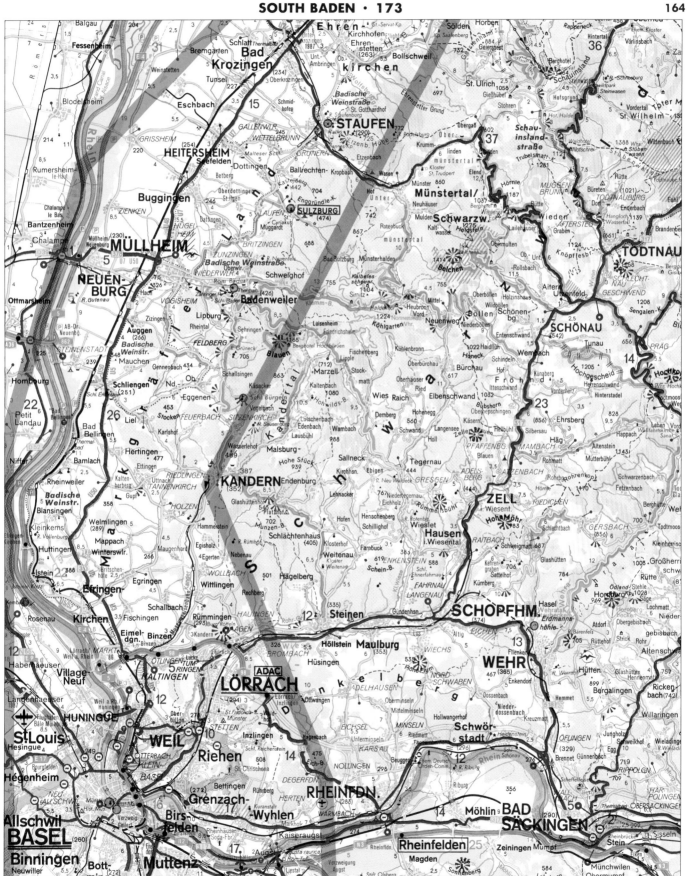

SOUTH BADEN

The Baden vineyards really begin in earnest south of Baden-Baden with the Bereich Ortenau, which in turn shades without a perceptible break into the Bereich Breisgau. Ortenau has a privileged climate that allows it to specialize in red and rosé wines: its red Spätburgunders have good colour and reasonable body and are very much to the local taste. Even more so are its pale pink Weißherbst and its curious and original Rotgold, made by fermenting the juices of Spätburgunder and Pinot Gris together. Rotgold has a smooth texture and slight sweetness which visitors can find disconcerting.

Undoubtedly the finest wines of the Ortenau are the Rieslings from steep hillsides at Ortenberg and Durbach (where they are called Klingelberger). Gewürztraminer (here known as Clevner) is the other Durbach speciality. These wines have the "breed", the length and the balance to put Baden on the international map – if any of them reach the frontier.

The Bereich Breisgau starts south of Offenburg, producing rather weighty dry white wines, largely of Müller-Thurgau and the superior Ruländer. Weißherbst is also popular here.

Considerably more important, and indeed the climax of Baden wine-growing, is the "island" Bereich of Kaiserstuhl-Tuniberg, an old volcano standing out in the Rhine valley, detached from the Black Forest, one of nature's pre-ordained vineyards whose climate and soil can give remarkable character to a wide range of wines. Inevitably the safe Müller-Thurgau is dominant, but a quarter of the vineyard is Spätburgunder, which here gives dark

wine with a curiously bitter finish, and almost another quarter Ruländer, which can give impressive (if not very refreshing) wine. Silvaner can be splendid in warm corners of the Kaiserstuhl.

Bereich Markgräflerland, stretching south to the Swiss border, offers no such fireworks as the old volcano, but specializes in gentle dry wines. Its Gutedel is often *spritzig* to lift its neutral character. Müller-Thurgau is useful as always. A more interesting wine is made of the Nobling, a cross between Gutedel and Silvaner with much more aroma than either.

To the visitor to the Bodensee the tiny Bereich on the north shores of the lovely lake is of consuming interest. To others it remains a legend.

TRAVEL INFORMATION

▲ Meersburg on the Bodensee (Lake Constance in English) is Germany's nearest approach to a southern port. The climate has attracted famous gardeners as well as winegrowers.
▶ Freiburg im Breisgau is noted for the charm of its ancient streets and the liveliness of its university.

This large region has everything from the sophisticated spa of Baden-Baden to cuckoo-clock-making villages deep in the Black Forest.

Places to visit
Baden-Baden: Germany is a country still much given to visiting – and using – spas, and Baden-Baden is the chief of them. It is both opulently nineteenth century and up-to-date: the waters are pronounced good for "diseases of modern civilization" as well as traditional over-indulgence. Gambling, culture and countryside are on offer as well as the waters. Freiburg: one of Europe's finest gothic spires towers over a medieval marketplace. Kaiserstuhl: range of volcanic hills with walking and fine views west to France and

east to the Black Forest. Schwarzwald (Black Forest): well-tended forest paths, farm holidays and folklore. Bodensee (Lake Constance): one of Europe's biggest lakes, with boating, swimming and historic towns such as Meersburg.

Wine roads
The *Badische Weinstraße* runs from north to south along the edge of the Black Forest, passing through Freiburg and ending at

▶ The beautiful Baroque edifice of Kloster Birnau at Oberuhldingen, just north of Meersburg on the Bodensee, overlooks the 32-hectare Einzellage Kirchhalde, planted with a typical regional selection of Müller-Thurgau and Spätburgunder, with an unusual proportion of the aromatic new Bacchus.

the Swiss frontier. A wine path – the *Breisgauer Weinwanderweg* – starts at Freiburg and threads the vineyards as far as Friesenheim, a walk of 97km which is split into 23 stages. The signpost is a goblet on a diamond shape.

Wine festivals
Bubbingen (mid-June), Freiburg (mid-June), Müllheim (end June), Reicholzheim (mid-July), Schloß Ortenberg & Durbach (early Aug), Affental (mid-Aug), Breisach (end Aug), Meersburg (mid-Sept), Heidelberg (end Sept); in October the festivals are too numerous to list.

Food and drink
Baden celebrates food as heartily as its neighbour across the Rhine, Alsace. Game, fruit and all manner of farm produce abound. The area is a popular one for holidaymakers, both German and foreign, and the *Fremdenzimmer* and *Zimmer Frei* signs hang thick in towns and villages. Such places, and the small guest houses and inns, offer good value. In the vineyard districts, they will often be run by winemaking families. Hotels include the comfortable Am Münster in Breisach (tel: 07667-7071). In Freiburg, the Panoramahotel am Jägerhäusle (tel: 0761-551011) has a splendid view of the city and the Kaiserstuhl. In the old town, the Rappen is right on the marketplace (tel: 0761-31353) and Zum Roten Bären (tel: 0761-36913) has been an inn since the year 1311. On the Bodensee, the Hotel Hecht in the historic city of Überlingen has a well-reputed restaurant. Deep in the Black Forest, the ancient Spielweg inn at Münstertal has a new wing with a swimming-pool.

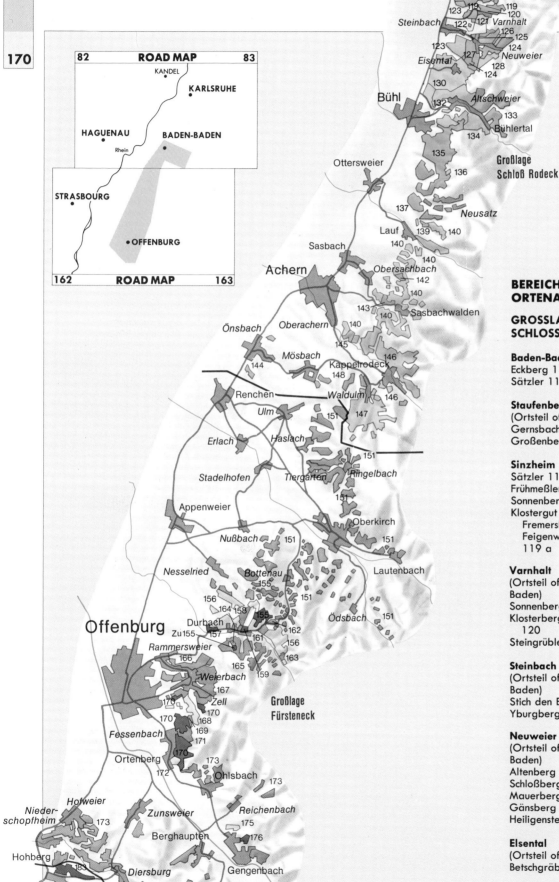

VINEYARDS

ROAD MAP 82 83
KANDEL
KARLSRUHE
HAGUENAU
BADEN-BADEN
Rhein
STRASBOURG
OFFENBURG
ROAD MAP 162 163

Baden-Baden

Altschweier
(Ortsteil of Bühl)
Sternenberg 132 P

Neusatz
(Ortsteil of Bühl)
Sternenberg 132 P
Wolfhag 135 P
Burg Windeck
 Kastanienhalde
 136

Bühlertal
Engelsfelsen 133
Klotzberg 134

Ottersweier
Wolfhag 135 P
Althof 137

Lauf
Gut Alsenhof 139
Alde Gott 140 P

Obersasbach
(Ortsteil of Sasbach)
Alde Gott 140 P
Eichwäldele 142

Sasbachwalden
Alde Gott 140 P
Klostergut
 Schelzberg 143

Önsbach
(Ortsteil of Achern)
Pulverberg 144

Oberachern
(Ortsteil of Achern)
Alde Gott 140 P
Bienenberg 145

Kappelrodeck
Hex vom Dasenstein
 146

Waldulm
(Ortsteil of
Kappelrodeck)
Pfarrberg 147
Kreuzberg 148 P

Renchen
Kreuzberg 148 P

Mösbach
(Ortsteil of Achern)
Kreuzberg 148 P

Obertsrot
(Ortsteil of
Gernsbach)
Grafensprung 149

Weisenbach
Kestellberg 150 P

BEREICH ORTENAU

GROSSLAGE SCHLOSS RODECK

Baden-Baden
Eckberg 116
Sätzler 117 P

Staufenberg
(Ortsteil of
Gernsbach)
Großenberg 116 a

Sinzheim
Sätzler 117 P
Frühmeßler 118
Sonnenberg 119 P
Klostergut
 Fremersberger
 Feigenwäldchen
 119 a

Varnhalt
(Ortsteil of Baden-
Baden)
Sonnenberg 119 P
Klosterbergfelsen
 120
Steingrübler 121

Steinbach
(Ortsteil of Baden-
Baden)
Stich den Buben 122
Yburgberg 123

Neuweier
(Ortsteil of Baden-
Baden)
Altenberg 124
Schloßberg 125
Mauerberg 126
Gänsberg 127
Heiligenstein 128

Elsental
(Ortsteil of Bühl)
Betschgräber 130

Hilpertsau
(Ortsteil of
Gernsbach)
Kestellberg 150 P

**GROSSLAGE
FÜRSTENECK**

Ulm
(Ortsteil of Renchen)
Renchtäler 151 P

Erlach
(Ortsteil of Renchen)
Renchtäler 151 P

Haslach
(Ortsteil of
Oberkirch)
Renchtäler 151 P

Stadelhofen
(Ortsteil of
Oberkirch)
Renchtäler 151 P

Tiergarten
(Ortsteil of
Oberkirch)
Renchtäler 151 P

Ringelbach
(Ortsteil of
Oberkirch)
Renchtäler 151 P

Ödsbach
(Ortsteil of
Oberkirch)
Renchtäler 151 P

Bottenau
(Ortsteil of
Oberkirch)
Renchtäler 151 P

Nußbach
(Ortsteil of
Oberkirch)
Renchtäler 151 P

Oberkirch
Renchtäler 151 P

Lautenbach
Renchtäler 151 P

Nesselried
(Ortsteil of
Appenweier)
Renchtäler 151 P
Schloßberg 155 P

Durbach
Schloßberg 155 P
Plauelrain 156
Ölberg 157
Josephsberg 158
Steinberg 159
Kapellenberg 161

Bienengarten 162
Kasselberg 163
Schloß Grohl 164
Kochberg 165

Rammersweier
(Ortsteil of
Offenburg)
Kreuzberg 166

Zell-Weierbach
(Ortsteil of
Offenburg)
Abtsberg 167

Fessenbach
(Ortsteil of
Offenburg)
Bergle 168
Franzensberger
169 P

Ortenberg
Franzensberger
169 P
Freudental 170
Andreasberg 171
Schloßberg 172

Ohlsbach
Kinzigtäler 173 P

Zunsweier
(Ortsteil of
Offenburg)
Kinzigtäler 173 P

Gengenbach
Kinzigtäler 173 P
Nollenköpfle 176

Reichenbach
(Ortsteil of
Gengenbach)
Kingzigtäler 173 P
Amselberg 175

Bermersbach
(Ortsteil of
Gengenbach)
Kinzigtäler 173 P

Berghaupten
Kinzigtäler 173 P

Diersburg
(Ortsteil of Hohberg)
Kinzigtäler 173 P
Schloßberg 181

Hofweier
(Ortsteil of Hohberg)
Kinzigtäler 173 P

Niederschopfheim
(Ortsteil of Hohberg)
Kinzigtäler 173 P

**BEREICH
BREISGAU**

**GROSSLAGE
SCHUTTER-
LINDENBERG**

Friesenheim
Kronenbühl 183 P

Oberschopfheim
(Ortsteil of
Friesenheim)
Kronenbühl 183 P

Oberweier
(Ortsteil of
Friesenheim)
Kronenbühl 183 P

Heiligenzell
(Ortsteil of
Friesenheim)
Kronenbühl 183 P

Lahr
Kronenbühl 183 P
Herrentisch 184

Hugsweier
(Ortsteil of Lahr)
Kronenbühl 183 P

Mietersheim
(Ortsteil of Lahr)
Kronenbühl 183 P

Sulz
(Ortsteil of Lahr)
Haselstaude 185 P

Mahlberg
Haselstaude 185 P

Kippenheim
Haselstaude 185 P

Schmieheim
(Ortsteil of
Kippenheim)
Kirchberg 186 P

Wallburg
(Ortsteil of Ettenheim)
Kirchberg 186 P

Münchweier
(Ortsteil of Ettenheim)
Kirchberg 186 P

**GROSSLAGE
BURG
LICHTENECK**

Ettenheim
Kaiserberg 189 P

Altdorf
(Ortsteil of Ettenheim)
Kaiserberg 189 P

Ringsheim
Kaiserberg 189 P

Herbolzheim
Kaiserberg 189 P

Tutschfelden
(Ortsteil of
Herbolzheim)
Kaiserberg 189 P

Broggingen
(Ortsteil of
Herbolzheim)
Kaiserberg 189 P

Bleichheim
(Ortsteil of
Herbolzheim)
Kaiserberg 189 P

Wagenstadt
(Ortsteil of
Herbolzheim)
Hummelberg 192 P

Kenzingen
Hummelberg 192 P
Roter Berg 193

Nordweil
(Ortsteil of
Kenzingen)
Herrenberg 194

Bombach
(Ortsteil of
Kenzingen)
Sommerhalde 195

Hecklingen
(Ortsteil of
Kenzingen)
Schloßberg 196

Malterdingen
Bienenberg 197 P

Heimsbach
(Ortsteil of Teningen)
Bienenberg 197 P

Köndringen
(Ortsteil of Teningen)
Alte Burg 198 P

Mundingen
(Ortsteil of
Emmendingen)
Alte Burg 198 P

**GROSSLAGE
BURG
ZÄHRINGEN**

Hochburg
(Ortsteil of
Emmendingen)
Halde 199

Sexau
Sonnhalde 200 P

Buchholz
(Ortsteil of
Waldkirch)
Sonnhalde 200 P

Denzlingen
Sonnhalde 200 P
Eichberg 203 P

Heuweiler
Eichberg 203 P

Glottertal
Eichberg 203 P
Roter Bur 205

Wildtal
(Ortsteil of
Gundelfingen)
Sonnenhof 207

Freiburg
Schloßberg 208

Lehen
(Ortsteil of Freiburg)
Bergle 209

**BEREICH
KAISERSTUHL-
TUNIBERG**

**GROSSLAGE
VULKANFELSEN**

Nimburg
(Ortsteil of Teningen)
Steingrube 210 P

Neuershausen
(Ortsteil of March)
Steingrube 210 P

Riegel
St. Michaelsberg 211

Bahlingen
Silberberg 212

Eichstetten
Herrenbuck 213
Lerchenberg 214
(The two sites 213
and 214 cannot be
shown separately, as
213 is situated
above 214 on a
steep slope)

Bötzingen
Lasenberg 215
Eckberg 216

Wasenweiler
(Ortsteil of Ihringen)
Lotberg 217

Kreuzhalde 218 P

Ihringen
Kreuzhalde 218 P
Fohrenberg 219
Winklerberg 220
Schloßberg 221 P
Castellberg 222 P
Steinfelsen 223 P

– Ortsteil Blanken-
hornsberg
Doktorgarten 224

Achkarren
(Ortsteil of
Vogtsburg im
Kaiserstuhl)
Schloßberg 221 P
Castellberg 222 P

Bickensohl
(Ortsteil of
Vogtsburg im
Kaiserstuhl)
Steinfelsen 223 P
Herrenstück 226

Oberrotweil
(Ortsteil of
Vogtsburg im
Kaiserstuhl)
Schloßberg 221 P
Käsleberg 227
Eichberg 228
Henkenberg 229
Kirchberg 230

Oberbergen
(Ortsteil of
Vogtsburg im
Kaiserstuhl)
Pulverbruck 231
Baßgeige 232

Schelingen
(Ortsteil of
Vogtsburg im
Kaiserstuhl)
Kirchberg 233

Bischoffingen
(Ortsteil of
Vogtsburg im
Kaiserstuhl)
Enselberg 234 P
Rosenkranz 235
Steinbuck 236

Burkheim
(Ortsteil of
Vogtsburg im
Kaiserstuhl)
Feuerberg 237
Schloßgarten 238

Jechtingen
(Ortsteil of Sasbach)
Enselberg 234 P
Steingrube 239
Hochberg 240
Eichert 241
Gestühl 242 P

Leiselheim
(Ortsteil of Sasbach)
Gestühl 242 P

Sasbach
Scheibenbuck 243
Lützelberg 244
Rote Halde 245
Limburg 246

Kiechlinsbergen
(Ortsteil of Endingen)
Teufelsburg 247
Ölberg 248

Königschaffhausen
(Ortsteil of Endingen)
Hasenberg 249
Steingrüble 250

Amoltern
(Ortsteil of Endingen)
Steinhalde 251

Endingen
Engelsberg 252
Steingrube 253
Tannacker 254

Breisach
Augustinerberg 255
Eckartsberg 256

**GROSSLAGE
ATTILAFELSEN**

Gottenheim
Kirchberg 257

Merdingen
Bühl 258

Waltershofen
(Ortsteil of Freiburg)
Steinmauer 259

Opfingen
(Ortsteil of Freiburg)
Sonnenberg 260

Niederrimsingen
(Ortsteil of Breisach)
Rotgrund 261

Tiengen
(Ortsteil of Freiburg)
Rebtal 262

Oberrimsingen
(Orteil of Breisach)
Franziskaner 263

Munzingen
(Ortsteil of Freiburg)
Kappellenberg 264

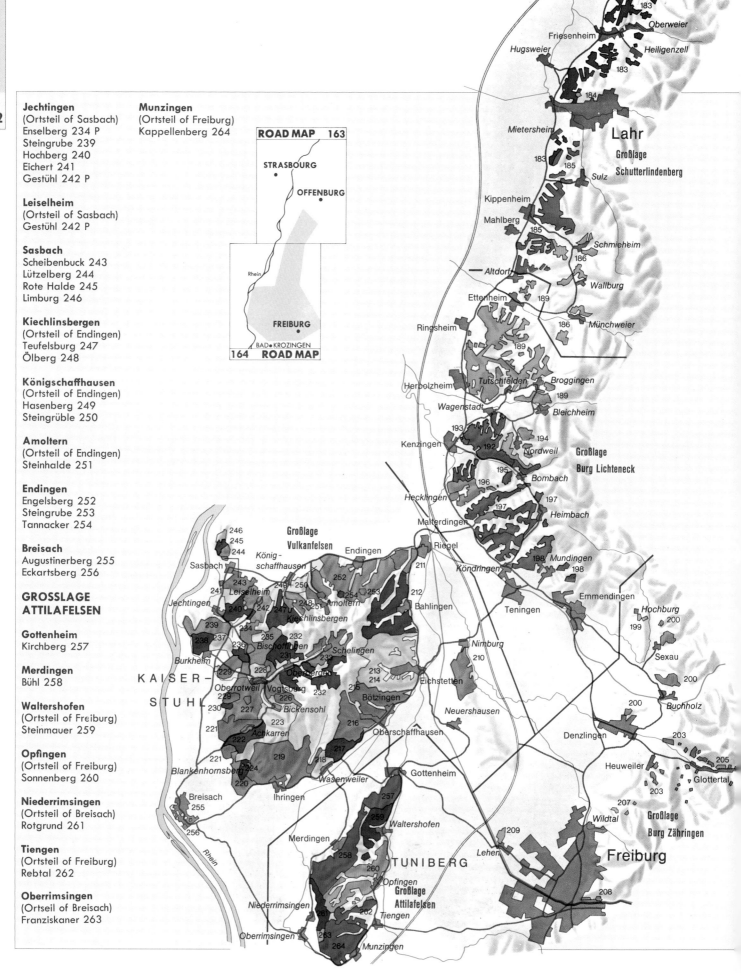

ROAD MAP 163

STRASBOURG

OFFENBURG

Rhein

FREIBURG

BAD · KROZINGEN

ROAD MAP 164

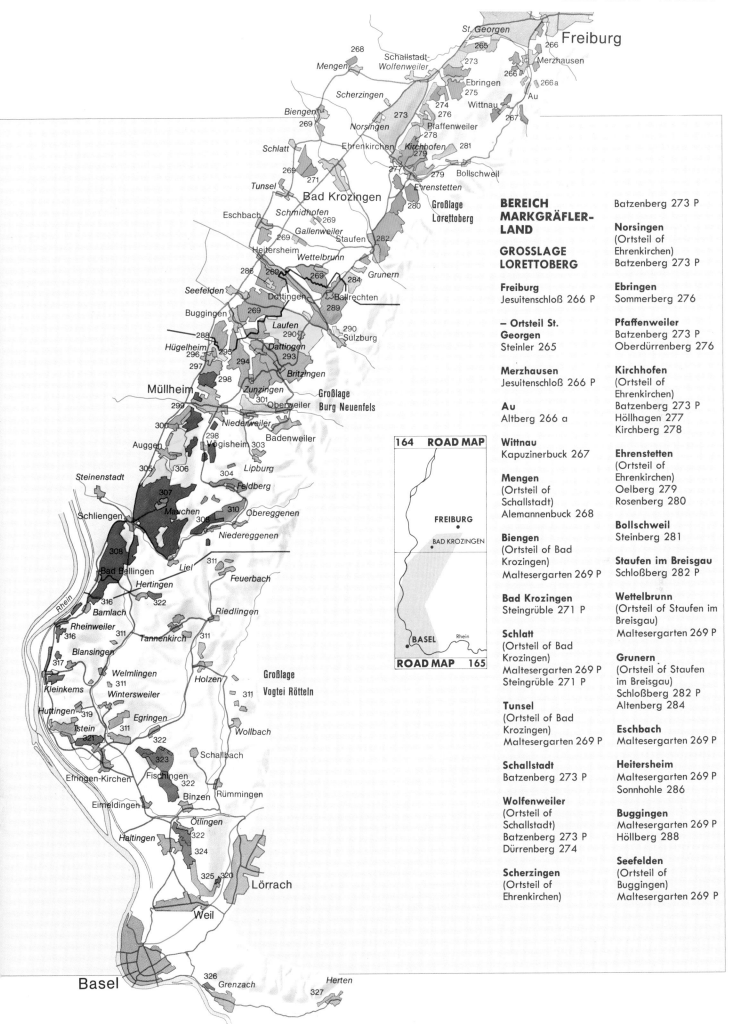

Freiburg

St. Georgen

265 266
268   273
Mengen   Schallstadt-
           Wolfenweiler   Merzhausen
                    266 266a
           Ebringen
           275   Au
Scherzingen   274 276
                    Wittnau
           273
Biengen   Pfaffenweiler 267
269   Norsingen   278
Schlatt   Ehrenkirchen Kirchhofen 281
                    279
269   277   279 Bollschweil
271
Tunsel Bad Krozingen   Ehrenstetten
Eschbach Schmidhofen   280 Großlage
269   269   Lorettoberg
269 Gallenweiler Staufen
Heitersheim   282
269   Wettelbrunn
286 269   269   284 Grunern
Seefelden   289
           Dattingen Ballrechten
Buggingen 269
288   Laufen 290
Hügelheim 290 Sulzburg
296 295 294 293
297   Britzingen
298
Müllheim Zunzingen   Großlage
299 301 Oberweiler   Burg Neuenfels
300   Niederweiler
       298 Badenweiler
Auggen Vögisheim 303
305 306   304   Lipburg
Steinenstadt   Feldberg
307
Schliengen Manchen 310
           308 Obereggenen
308   Niedereggenen
    Liel 311
Bad Bellingen Feuerbach
Hertingen
316 322   Riedlingen
Bamlach
Rheinweiler 311
316   Tannenkirch 311
Blansingen
317   Großlage
Kleinkems Welmlingen Vogtei Rötteln
       311
Huttingen Wintersweiler
319   Egringen 311
Istein 311
321   322
           Schallbach
       323
Efringen-Kirchen Fischingen
           322
       Binzen Rümmingen
Eimeldingen
       Ötlingen
Haltingen 322
       324
       325 320
       Lörrach

Weil

Rhein

164 ROAD MAP
FREIBURG
BAD KROZINGEN
BASEL Rhein
ROAD MAP 165

326 Grenzach Herten
327
Basel

BEREICH MARKGRÄFLER-LAND

GROSSLAGE LORETTOBERG

Freiburg
Jesuitenschloß 266 P

– Ortsteil St. Georgen
Steinler 265

Merzhausen
Jesuitenschloß 266 P

Au
Altberg 266 a

Wittnau
Kapuzinerbuck 267

Mengen
(Ortsteil of Schallstadt)
Alemannenbuck 268

Biengen
(Ortsteil of Bad Krozingen)
Maltesergarten 269 P

Bad Krozingen
Steingrüble 271 P

Schlatt
(Ortsteil of Bad Krozingen)
Maltesergarten 269 P
Steingrüble 271 P

Tunsel
(Ortsteil of Bad Krozingen)
Maltesergarten 269 P

Schallstadt
Batzenberg 273 P

Wolfenweiler
(Ortsteil of Schallstadt)
Batzenberg 273 P
Dürrenberg 274

Scherzingen
(Ortsteil of Ehrenkirchen)

Batzenberg 273 P

Norsingen
(Ortsteil of Ehrenkirchen)
Batzenberg 273 P

Ebringen
Sommerberg 276

Pfaffenweiler
Batzenberg 273 P
Oberdürrenberg 276

Kirchhofen
(Ortsteil of Ehrenkirchen)
Batzenberg 273 P
Höllhagen 277
Kirchberg 278

Ehrenstetten
(Ortsteil of Ehrenkirchen)
Oelberg 279
Rosenberg 280

Bollschweil
Steinberg 281

Staufen im Breisgau
Schloßberg 282 P

Wettelbrunn
(Ortsteil of Staufen im Breisgau)
Maltesergarten 269 P

Grunern
(Ortsteil of Staufen im Breisgau)
Schloßberg 282 P
Altenberg 284

Eschbach
Maltesergarten 269 P

Heitersheim
Maltesergarten 269 P
Sonnhohle 286

Buggingen
Maltesergarten 269 P
Höllberg 288

Seefelden
(Ortsteil of Buggingen)
Maltesergarten 269 P

GROSSLAGE BURG NEUENFELS

Ballrechten-Dottingen
Castellberg 289
Altenberg 290 P

Sulzburg
Altenberg 290 P

Laufen
(Ortsteil of Sulzburg)
Altenberg 290 P

Britzingen
(Ortsteil of Müllheim)
Altenberg 290 P
Sonnhole 293 P
Rosenberg 294 P

Dattingen
(Ortsteil of Müllheim)
Altenberg 290 P
Sonnhole 293 P
Rosenberg 294 P

Zunzingen
(Ortsteil of Müllheim)
Rosenberg 294 P

Hügelheim
(Ortsteil of Müllheim)
Höllberg 295
Gottesacker 296
Schloßgarten 297

Müllheim
Sonnhalde 298
Reggenhag 299
Pfaffenstück 300

Vöglsheim
(Ortsteil of Müllheim)
Sonnhalde 298 P

Niederweiler
(Ortsteil of Müllheim)
Römerberg 301 P

Badenweiler
Römerberg 301 P

Lipburg
(Ortsteil of Badenweiler)
Kirchberg 303

Feldberg
(Ortsteil of Mülheim)
Paradies 304

Auggen
Letten 305
Schäf 306 P

Mauchen
(Ortsteil of Schliengen)
Frauenberg 307

Sonnenstück 308 P

Schliengen
Sonnenstück 308 P

Steinenstadt
(Ortsteil of Neuenburg am Rhein)
Schäf 306 P
Sonnenstück 308 P

Niedereggenen
(Ortsteil of Schliengen)
Sonnenstück 308 P
Röthen 310 P

Lief
(Ortsteil of Schliengen)
Sonnenstück 308 P

Bad Bellingen
Sonnenstück 308 P

Obereggenen
(Ortsteil of Schliengen)
Röthen 310 P

GROSSLAGE VOGTEI RÖTTELN

Feuerbach
(Ortsteil of Kandern)
Steingässle 311 P

Tannenkirch
(Ortsteil of Kandern)
Steingässle 311 P

Riedlingen
(Ortsteil of Kandern)
Steingässle 311 P

Holzen
(Ortsteil of Kandern)
Steingässle 311 P

Wollbach
(Ortsteil of Kandern)
Steingässle 311 P

Welmlingen
(Ortsteil of Efringen-Kirchen)
Steingässle 311 P

Huttingen
(Ortsteil of Efringen-Kirchen)
Kirchberg 319 P

Istein
(Ortsteil of Efringen-Kirchen)
Kirchberg 319 P

Wintersweiler
(Ortsteil of Efringen-Kirchen)
Steingässle 311 P

Efringen-Kirchen
Steingässle 311 P
Kirchberg 319 P
Oelberg 321
Sonnhohle 322 P

Bamlach
(Ortsteil of Bad Bellingen)
Kapellenberg 316 P

Rheinweiler
(Ortsteil of Bad Bellingen)
Kapellenberg 316 P

Blansingen
(Ortsteil of Efringen-Kirchen)
Wolfer 317 P

Kleinkems
(Ortsteil of Efringen-Kirchen)
Wolfer 317 P

Lörrach
Sonnenbrunnen 320

Egringen
(Ortsteil of Efringen-Kirchen)
Sonnhohle 322 P

Hertingen
(Ortsteil of Bad Bellingen)
Sonnhohle 322 P

Schallbach
Sonnhohle 322 P

Fischingen
Weingarten 323

Rümmingen
Sonnhohle 322 P

Eimeldingen
Sonnhohle 322 P

Binzen
Sonnhohle 322 P

Ötlingen
(Ortsteil of Weil am Rhein)
Sonnhohle 322 P
Stiege 324 P

Haltingen
(Ortsteil of Weil am Rhein)
Stiege 324 P

Weil am Rhein
Stiege 324 P
Schlipf 325

Grenzach
(Ortsteil of Grenzach-Whylen)
Hornfelsen 326

Herten
(Ortsteil of Rheinfelden)
Steinacker 327

BEREICH BODENSEE

GROSSLAGENFREI

Rechberg
(Ortsteil of Klettgau)
Kapellenberg 347 P*

Erzingen
(Ortsteil of Klettgau)
Kapellenberg 347 P*

Nack
(Ortsteil of Lottstetten)
Steinler 348*

Gallingen
Ritterhalde 349*
Schloß Rheinburg 350*

Hohentengen
Ölberg 351*

GROSSLAGE SONNENUFER

Singen (Hohentwiel)
Elisabethenberg 345 P*
Olgaberg 346*

Hilzingen
Elisabethenberg 345 P*

Relchenau
Hochwart 328

Bodman
Königsweingarten 328 a*

Überlingen
Felsengarten 329

Oberuhldingen
(Ortsteil of Uhldingen-Mühlhof)
Kirchhalde 330

Meersburg
Chorherrenhalde 331
Fohrenberg 332 P
Rieschen 333
Jungfernstieg 334
Bengel 335
Haltnau 335 a
Lerchenberg 336 P
Sängerhalde 337 P

Stetten
Fohrenberg 332 P
Lerchenberg 336 P
Sängerhalde 337 P

Hagnau
Burgstall 340 P

Kirchberg
(Ortsteil of Salem)
Schloßberg 339

Kippenhausen
(Ortsteil of Immenstaad)
Burgstall 340 P

Immenstaad
Burgstall 340 P

Bermatingen
Leopoldsberg 341

Markdorf
Sängerhalde 337 P
Burgstall 340 P

Konstanz
Sonnhalde 344

The yellow area on this map represents the vineyards not registered as Einz.

BEREICH REMSTAL-STUTTGART

GROSSLAGENFREI

Kreßbronn/Bodensee
Berghalde 201

BEREICH BAYERISCHER BODENSEE

GROSSLAGE LINDAUER SEEGARTEN

Nonnenhorn
Seehalde 202
Sonnenbüchel 203

Lindau
Spitalhalde 204 P

Wasserburg
Spitalhalde 204 P

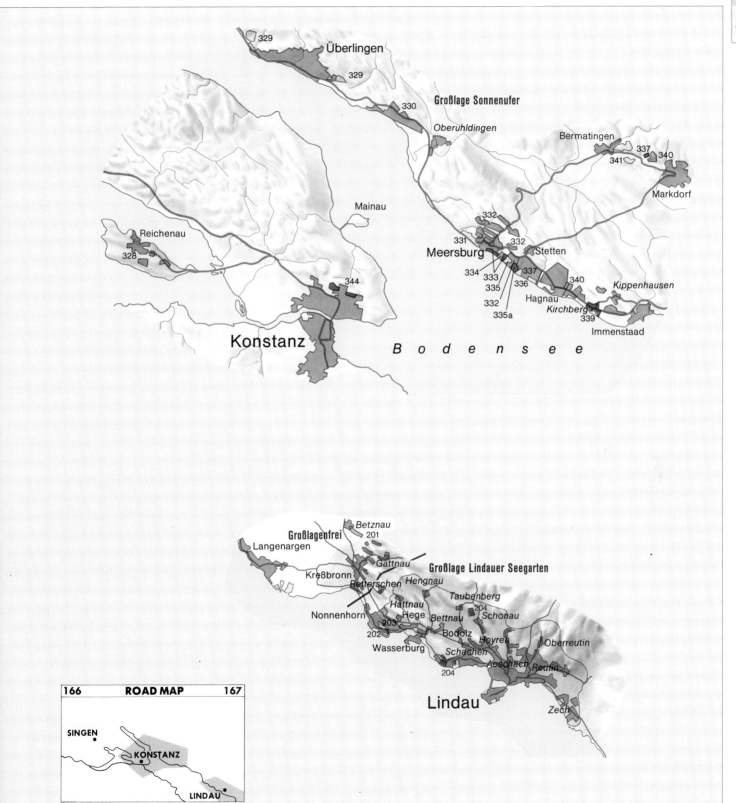

329
Überlingen
329
330
Großlage Sonnenufer
Oberuhldingen
Bermatingen
337 340
341
Markdorf
Mainau
332
331
332
Stetten
Meersburg
334 333 337
335 336 340
332 *Kippenhausen*
335a Hagnau
Kirchberg 339
Immenstaad
Reichenau
328
344
Konstanz
B o d e n s e e

Betznau
Großlagenfrei 201
Langenargen
Gattnau
Kreßbronn *Hengnau*
Retterschen **Großlage Lindauer Seegarten**
Taubenberg
Nonnenhorn *Hattnau* 204
Hege *Bettnau* *Schonau*
203
202 *Bodolz*
Hoyren *Oberreutin*
Wasserburg *Schachen*
Aeschach *Reutin*
204
Lindau
Zech

166 **ROAD MAP** 167

SINGEN
KONSTANZ
LINDAU

VILLAGES

BEREICH BODENSEE

The Bodensee and the Rhine which flows from its western end mark the German–Swiss border. The lake (Germany's biggest) counteracts the considerable altitude (about 450 metres [1,500 feet] above sea level) to produce a mild climate in which Spätburgunder and Müller-Thurgau both give refreshing, lightly fruity wines. The whites are often *spritzig*, the Spätburgunder either pale red or (its most attractive form) made into Weißherbst, the often very lively pale rosé which is the true local speciality.

The predominant grape varieties are Müller-Thurgau and Spätburgunder, with small amounts of Gewürztraminer and Ruländer. Slopes tend to be steep and exposure is almost always southerly, the vineyards benefiting from the lakeside microclimate.

The district makes up only about 3% of the total vineyard area in Baden and has only one Großlage: Sonnenufer. The main centres are on or near the lake shore: Bermatingen, Birnau, Kirchberg and Meersburg. Hagnau on the lake has a cooperative.

GROSSLAGE SONNENUFER
Vineyards
Einzellagen: Meersburg: Chorherrenhalde, 15.9ha, 100% steep. Bengel, 7ha, 100% steep. Fohrenberg, 25ha, 50% steep. Jungfernstieg, 4.8ha, 100% steep. Lerchenberg, 10.1ha, 80% sloping. Rieschen, 4ha, 100% steep. Bermatingen: Leopoldsberg, 18.2ha, 100% steep. Oberuhldingen: Kirchhalde, 32.3ha, 94% steep. Kirchberg: Schloßberg, 15ha, 85% sloping.

BEREICH MARKGRÄFLERLAND

Markgräflerland is the unexciting orchard corner of Germany between Basel and Freiburg, a district with its own taste in wine, marvellous cakes and very passable distillations of its abundant fruit. Its favourite grape is the Gutedel, the local name for what the Swiss call Fendant and the French Chasselas – in all cases a mild, not to say neutral wine maker, yet somehow very agreeable in its innocent freshness, dry and often *spritzig*. A cross between Gutedel and Silvaner called Nobling shows real promise, with surprising aroma and finesse. Otherwise the predominant grapes are Müller-Thurgau (here pleasantly aromatic) and Spätburgunder – often made as Weißherbst.

The Bereich is divided into three Großlagen, listed here from south to north (down the Rhine).

GROSSAGE VOGTEI RÖTTELN

Efringen-Kirchen is the seat of the considerable cooperative, which uses most of the 11 Einzellage names contained in the Großlage. Weil am Rhein is another centre.

Vineyards
Efringen-Kirchen: Steingässle, 120.8ha, 100% sloping. Wolfer, 29.9ha, 50% steep. Weil am Rhein Einzellagen: Schlipf, 14.9ha, 35% steep. Stiege, 28.8ha, 90% sloping.

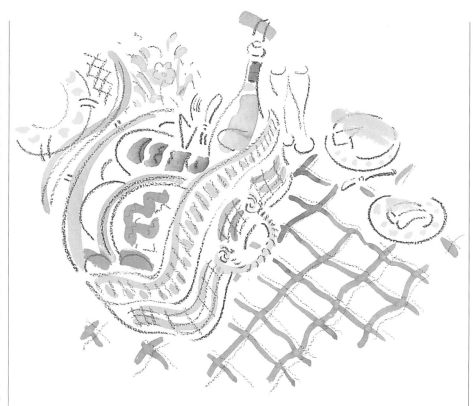

GROSSLAGE BURG NEUENFELS

Auggen, Bad Bellingen, Badenweiler, Müllheim, Laufen and Schliengen are centres of this hillier district with 18 Einzellagen.

Vineyards
Einzellagen: Auggen: Schäf, 170.5ha, 75% sloping. Bad Bellingen: Sonnenstück, 222ha, 50% steep. Badenweiler: Römerberg, 32.9ha, 100% sloping. Ballrechten-Dottingen: Altenberg, 25.8ha, 100% sloping. Müllheim: Reggenhag, 35.9ha, 80% sloping. Römerberg, 32.9ha, 40% steep. Ortsteil Laufen: Altenberg, 160.5ha, 100% sloping. Schliengen: Sonnenstück, 222.6ha, 100% sloping.

GROSSLAGE LORETTOBERG

This Großlage includes the southern outskirts of the lovely city of Freiburg. Its centres include Bad Krozingen, Ebringen, Pfaffenweiler and Ehrenkirchen, sharing 19 Einzellagen.

Vineyards
Einzellagen: Freiburg and Merzhausen: Jesuitenschloß, 32ha, 100% sloping.

BEREICH KAISERSTUHL-TUNIBERG

Northwest of Freiburg the Rhine is briefly diverted from its northward course by a volcanic outcrop from the plain, an advance guard for the Black Forest hills ranged along the eastern skyline. There are two lumps, the modest Tuniberg on the doorstep of Freiburg, then the dignified flat-topped hill of the Kaiserstuhl – "the Emperor's Seat". Breisach, home of the great central cooperative, is the Rhine port and bridge-town to France. This is the climax of the Baden wineland, with a third of all its vines and a good share of its best wine concentrated on its volcanic slopes.

The Kaiserstuhl slopes have been the subject of a spectacular re-landscaping to convert them into modern vineyards. The whole broad hill now has a distinctly man-made look. The Bereich is divided into only two Großlagen, whose Wagnerian names are therefore particularly well known. Vulkanfelsen covers the Kaiserstuhl and Atillafelsen the Tuniberg. Large parts of both hills are clothed in loess, the deep though light soil derived from the blown sand of past ice-ages. The loess warms up quickly, and is easy to reshape into the wide, efficient terraces of the new landscaping. One third of the whole region is planted with Müller-Thurgau, a quarter with Spätburgunder and another quarter with Ruländer, the Tokay d'Alsace, which performs exceptionally well on these iron-rich volcanic slopes. Low acid, always a characteristic of this grape, is compensated for by fiery concentrated flavours and density of texture, qualities that mature extremely well.

Much of the Spätburgunder is made into Weißherbst but the warmest vineyards, notably in Ihringen, Achkarren, Bickensohl and Oberrotweil on the south of the Kaiserstuhl, take pride in their red wines. Some of the best sites are also planted with Silvaner to good effect.

GROSSLAGE VULKANFELSEN
Vineyards

Einzellagen: Ihringen: Doktorgarten, 29ha, 60% steep. Oberrotweil: Eichberg, 84.8ha, 35% steep. Käsleberg, 261.3ha, 90% terraced. Henkenberg, 52.9ha, 100% sloping.

BEREICH BREISGAU

Breisgau is the name for the backdrop of Black Forest foothills running north behind the Kaiserstuhl-Tuniberg, from Freiburg almost to Offenburg. It has three Großlagen: Schutterlindenberg for its northern section centred on Lahr, with only four Einzellagen; Burg Lichteneck running south to Emmendingen, with eight Einzellagen including Hecklingen with its Schloßberg; and Burg Zähringen for the hills just north of Freiburg, with seven Einzellagen, the best known of which is the steep little 6-hectare Roter Bur in Glottertal, planted with 75 per cent Spätburgunder to produce a particularly lively Weißherbst.

GROSSLAGE SCHUTTERLINDENBERG
Vineyard

Lahr: Kronenbühl, 160.8ha, 75% terraced.

GROSSLAGE BURG LICHTENECK
Vineyard

Ortsteil Hecklingen, *Einzellage:* Schloßberg, 75.9ha, 60% terraced.

GROSSLAGE BURG ZÄHRINGEN
Vineyards

Einzellagen: Emmendingen: Hochburg, 4ha, steep. Glottertal: Roter Bur, 6ha, steep. Freiburg: Schloßberg, 4ha, steep; Bergle, 4ha, sloping.

BEREICH ORTENAU

The Black Forest foothills continue north from Offenburg to Baden Baden, the mixture of vineyard and forest with old villages and feudal castles producing unforgettable pictures. Once again there are two Großlagen: Fürsteneck for the southern half of the Ortenau; Schloß Rodeck for the northern. Durbach, near Offenburg, is the most distinguished of its villages by reason of its lordly ownership and the Riesling (here called Klingelberger) of its steep sand and granite slopes. Durbach has all or part of 10 of the 22 Einzellagen contained in the Großlage Fürsteneck, Ortenberg has four and Oberkirch most of the 309-hectare Einzellage Renchtäler.

Schloß Rodeck is divided into 33 Einzellagen, the better-known being Yburgberg and Stich den Buben at Steinbach near Baden-Baden, Mauerberg at Neuweier in the same hills, farther south the Alde Gott at Sasbachwalden, Hex vom Dasenstein at Kappelrodeck and Pfarrberg at Waldulm.

Ortenau is Spätburgunder country. From somewhere in its heart comes a large supply of a popular light red called Affentaler, distinguished only by the moulded figure of a monkey clutching the bottle. Much its best wines are its Klingelbergers and Ruländers, with some respectable Gewürztraminer and adequate Müller-Thurgau.

GROSSLAGE FÜRSTENECK
Vineyards

Einzellagen: Ortsteil Zell-Weierbach: Abtsberg, 88.8ha, 70% sloping. Fessenbach: Bergle, 34.9ha, 80% steep. Ortenberg: Andreasberg, 18.1ha, 95% steep; Schloßberg, 10.1ha, 100% steep. Durbach: Steinberg, 3ha; Kochberg, 104.6ha; Bienengarten, 4.8ha; Josephsberg, 10.1ha; Ölberg, 10.1ha. All 100% steep.

GROSSLAGE SCHLOSS RODECK
Vineyards

Einzellagen: Ortsteil Neuweier: Mauerberg, 38.8ha. 100% steep. Ortsteil Steinbach: Stich den Buben, 29.9ha, 90% steep; Yburgberg, 40ha, 100% sloping. Kappelrodeck: Hex vom Dasenstein, 105ha, 85% steep. Sasbach: Alde Gott, 147.9ha, 80% steep.

LANDWEIN

This category of German table wine was introduced in 1982 as a response to the success of French *vins de pays* – as standard drinking but of some local character, with more style and flavour than the totally anonymous Tafelwein. 15 areas with new names but roughly corresponding to the well-known basic regions of Germany have the right to christen a Landwein if the wine in question meets certain simple requirements. The alcohol content, for example, must be 0.5% higher than that of Tafelwein. An important regulation is that the sugar content must not be greater than 18 grams per litre – the upper limit for medium-dry\(halbtrocken) wines. Landwein is therefore intended as a relatively dry and briskly acidic wine suitable for mealtimes.

The 15 Landwein areas are as follows:

Ahrtaler Landwein Ahr

Starkenburger Landwein Hessische Bergstraße

Rheinburgen-Landwein Mittelrhein

Landwein der Mosel Mosel and Ruwer

Landwein der Saar Saar

Nahegauer Landwein Nahe

Altrheingauer Landwein Rheingau

Rheinischer Landwein Rheinhessen

Pfälzer Landwein Rheinpfalz

Fränkischer Landwein Franken (not used)

Regensburger Landwein a minuscule area on the Danube

Bayerischer Bodensee-Landwein a small area near Lindau on Lake Constance (Bodensee), which in QbA terms is part of Württemberg, although politically it belongs to Bavaria

Schwäbischer Landwein Württemberg
Unterbadischer Landwein northern part of Baden

Südbadischer Landwein southern part of Baden

(*See* also the table on German wine quality categories on p 160.)

PRODUCERS

Weingut Blankenhorn
Baslerstraße 2, 7846 Schliengen, tel: 07635-1092. *Owner:* Klaus Blankenhorn. 16.5 hectares. *Einzellagen:* Schliengen: Sonnenstück; Mauchen: Sonnenstück; Müllheim; Reggenhag; Badenweiler: Römerberg; Auggen: Schäf. *Großlage:* Burg Neuenfels.

A well-known producer of the light, juicy Gutedel and typical dry red of the region. Vines are 45% Gutedel, 25% Riesling, 12% Spätburgunder, 2% Müller-Thurgau, plus others, including Nobling (Silvaner × Gutedel crossing), Silvaner and Weißburgunder.

Weingut Hermann Dörflinger
Mühlenstraße 7, 7840 Müllheim, tel: 07631-2207. *Owner:* Hermann Dorflinger. 12 hectares. *Einzellagen:* Müllheim: Reggenhag, Pfaffenstück and Sonnhalde; Badenweiler: Römerberg.

An estate entirely devoted to the production of fresh, dry wines. The sloping vineyards are planted in Gutedel (50%), Müller-Thurgau (12%), Spätburgunder (14%), Ruländer, Silvaner, Weißburgunder and Gewürztraminer.

Stiftungskellerei Freiburg
Deutschordensstraße 2, 7800 Freiburg, tel: 0761-2108128. *Owner:* Heiliggeistspitalstiftung. 12.3 hectares. *Einzellagen:* Freiburg: Schloßberg (1.3ha) and Jesuitenschloß (11).

A religious institution claiming origins in 1298, currently producing attractive, dry Spätlesen from Riesling. Main vine varieties grown are Müller-Thurgau (50%), Spätburgunder (21%), Gutedel (13%) and Silvaner (6%).

Weingut Freiherr von Gleichenstein
Bahnhofstraße 12, 7818 Oberrotweil, tel: 07662-288. *Owner:* Hans-Joachim von Gleichenstein. *Einzellagen:* Oberrotweil: Eichberg, Henkenberg and Käsleberg. *Großlage:* Vulkanfelsen. The vines are 30% Müller-Thurgau, 40% Spätburgunder, 10% Ruländer, and 2% each of Muskateller, Silvaner, Nobling, Traminer, Riesling, Weißburgunder and Findling.

An estate founded in the 17th century, in even older buildings, making conservative wines, 80% dry, the reds fermented on the skins, tannic, dry and full of character. Dry Weißherbst Spätlese, pale but full of flavour, is the unusual speciality of the house.

Schloßgut Istein
7859 Efringen-Kirchen, tel: 07628-1284. *Owners:* the Rural District of Lörrach, and Albert Soder. 6 hectares. *Einzellage:* Istein: Kirchberg.

Small estate near the Swiss border, once the property of the Bishop of Basel, producing fully fermented wines, including a Gewürztraminer Auslese with 16.8 degrees of alcohol. Apart from this rarity of almost sherry strength, wine is also made from 1.8 hectares of Gutedel (a local speciality) and a range of other red and white vine varieties, (Riesling, Weißburgunder, Ruländer, Müller-Thurgau, Silvaner, etc.).

Weingut Andreas Männle
Heimbach 293, 7601 Durbach, tel: 0781-41486. *Director:* Heinrich Männle. About 17 hectares. *Einzellagen:* Durbach: Bienengarten (15ha) and Kochberg.

The vines are 20% each of Müller-Thurgau, Spätburgunder and Riesling, 12% each of Ruländer and Clevner (Traminer), 8% Scheurebe. On the face of it a simple guesthouse wine farmer, but a specialist in fine sweet wines with some remarkable successes including extraordinary Weißherbst Eiswein. The sweet reds are a very German taste.

Weingut Heinrich Männle
Sendelbach 86, 7601 Durbach, tel: 0781-41101. *Owners:* Heinrich and Willma Männle. 5 hectares. *Einzellagen:* Durbach: Kochberg (3.5ha), Plauelrain (1.5) and Ölberg.

An estate that regularly achieves top awards for its wines. Although 62% of the production is in white wine, Herr Männle is particularly well-known for his cask-matured Spätburgunder. The range of vine varieties includes Müller-Thurgau (15%), Scheurebe (13%), Ruländer (13%), Clevner (Traminer, 7%) and Klingelberger (Riesling, 7%).

Staatsweingut Meersburg
Seminarstraße 6, 7758 Meersburg, tel: 07532-6085. *Owner:* the State of Baden-Württemberg. *Director:* Helmut Häußermann. 59.1 hectares. *Einzellagen:* Meersburg: Lerchenberg, Bengel, Sängerhalde, Jungfernstieg, Rieschen, Chorherrenhalde and Fohrenberg; Hohentwiel bei Singen: Olgaberg; Gailingen am Hochrhein: Ritterhalde. *Großlage:* Sonnenufer.

Formerly the estate of the Prince-Bishops of Meersburg. In 1802 it became Germany's first state domain, largely in Meersburg on the banks of the Bodensee (Lake Constance). In 1956 frosts destroyed the vineyards and total reconstitution brought them up to date in varieties and methods. The vines are 39% Müller-Thurgau, 46% Spätburgunder, 3.5% Ruländer and 9.5% Weißburgunder, Traminer and Riesling. More red varieties are to be planted. The specialities are Müller-Thurgau of the gentler kind and pinky-gold *spritzig* Spätburgunder.

Gräflich Wolff-Metternich'sches Weingut
Grohl 117, 7601 Durbach, tel: 0781-42779. *Owner:* Count Paul Josef Wolff-Metternich. *Einzellagen:* Durbach: Schloß Grohl (5.5ha); Schloßberg (16, both solely owned); Lahr: Herrentisch (6).

A 36-hectare hillside estate in Durbach and Lahr, of ancient origin, particularly proud of its late-harvest and aromatic wines. 30% Riesling, 21% Spätburgunder (Pinot Noir), 20% Müller-Thurgau, 15% Traminer and Gewürztraminer, 10% Weißburgunder and Ruländer, 4% other varieties.

Weingut Freiherr von Neveu
7601 Durbach. *Owner:* Heinrich, Freiherr von Neveu. 12 hectares. *Einzellagen:* Durbach:

Josephsberg and Ölberg. *Großlage:* Fürsteneck.

A neighbour of Schloß Staufenberg with similarly stylish wines, perhaps more full-blooded with good acidity. 41% Riesling, 22% Müller-Thurgau, 14.5% Spätburgunder, 14% Clevner, 4% Gewürztraminer, 4% Scheurebe. Müller-Thurgau is being reduced in favour of Riesling and Spätburgunder. The wines are made and matured at the estate but bottled and distributed by the ZBW cooperative at Breisach.

St. Andreas Hospital Fonds, Weingut der Stadt Offenburg
Steingrube 7, 7601 Ortenberg. *Director:* Alfons Decker. 30.5 hectares. *Einzellagen:* Ortenberg: Andreasberg; Offenburg: Spitalhalde; Fessenbach: Bergle; Zell-Weierbach: Abtsberg.

The hospital was founded in 1300 by the citizens of Offenburg and acquired vineyards in the 19th century. A medieval almshouse taken over by the town of Offenburg in 1936 as an inn. 36% Müller-Thurgau, 17% Riesling, 17% Spätburgunder, 6.6% Kerner, 5% Gewürztraminer and Traminer, 4.3% Scheurebe, 2.1% Muskateller, 1.6% Ruländer, 1.5% Weißburgunder and about 5% others. Its standard drinking is principally Müller-Thurgau; Riesling Kabinetts are the speciality, as are the Beerenauslesen.

Weinbauversuchsgut Schloß Ortenberg des Ortenaukreises
Burgweg 19a, 7601 Ortenberg, tel: 0781-34848. *Director:* Herbert Dresel. 7.5 hectares. *Einzellage:* Ortenberg: Schloßberg.

Established in 1950 as a teaching institute on former castle land, with a modern cellar and exemplary standards. 23% Müller-Thurgau, 19% Riesling, 15% Burgunder, 11% Ruländer, 8% Traminer, 8% Gewürztraminer, 8% Scheurebe, 3% Silvaner, 3% Kerner, 5% Muskateller and others. The best wines are Klingelbergers (Riesling), whether "slim" and refreshing or splendidly ripe and sweet.

Schloß Salem
7777 Salem. *Owner:* Max, Markgraf von Baden. 77 hectares in three estates: Birnau, Schloß Kirchberg and Bermatingen.

All the estates specialize in Müller-Thurgau and Spätburgunder Weißherbst. Schloß Salem is the Bodensee residence of the Margrave of Baden and the very modern central cellar of the widespread estate. *See also* Schloß Staufenberg.

Weingut Hartmut Schlumberger
Weinstraße 19, Laufen, 7811 Sulzburg, tel: 07634-8992. *Owner:* Hartmut Schlumberger. 5 hectares. *Einzellage:* Laufen: Altenberg. *Großlage:* Burg Neuenfels.

An old family manor between Freiburg and Basel in the heart of the Markgräflerland, planted with 45% Gutedel, 20% Spätburgunder, 10% Müller-Thurgau, 5% Ruländer and Gewürztraminer. The wines, generally dry and refreshing, are "made with love and developed in wood".

Staatliches Weinbauinstitut

Merzhauserstraße 119, 7800 Freiburg, tel: 0761-40026. *Owner:* the State of Baden-Württemberg. *Director:* Dr. Günter Staudt. 42 hectares. *Einzellagen:* Freiburg: Schloßberg, Jesuitenschloß (9ha); Müllheim: Reggenhag (1.5); Blankenshornberg: Doktorgarten (25); Hecklingen: Schloßberg (3); Durbach: Steinberg (2.5, solely owned).

The teaching institute of the State of Baden-Württemberg, founded in 1920 and including the 19th-century estate of the Blankenhorn brothers at Ihringen, known as Versuchs- und Lehrgut Blankenhornsberg (q.v.), the most considerable on the Kaiserstuhl. The vineyards are planted with a variety of vines, including Traminer (often known as Clevner in Baden's Bereich Ortenau, and labelled as such at the institute). The wines are made with exemplary care.

Staatliches Weinbauinstitut Freiburg Versuchs- und Lehrgut Blankenhornsberg

7817 Ihringen, tel: 07668-217. *Owner:* the State of Baden-Württemberg. *Director:* Erich Meinke. 35 hectares. *Einzellage:* Blankenhornsberg: Doktorgarten (solely owned).

The outstanding Kaiserstuhl estate, on steep volcanic slopes, planted with 18% Müller-Thurgau, 18% Spätburgunder, 13% Riesling, 11% Ruländer, 10% Weißburgunder, 30% other varieties and new crossings. Up to 70% of the wines are normally made dry, but with powerful acidity and flavours. 1976 was an exception, an *annus mirabilis* for sweet wines. *See* Staatliches Weinbauinstitut.

Markgräflich Badisches Weingut, Schloß Staufenberg

7601 Durbach, tel: 07811-42778. *Owner:* H.M. Max, Markgraf von Baden. 27 hectares. *Einzellage:* Durbach: Schloß Staufenberg (which belongs exclusively to the Weingut).

A homely old manor on a hill with very steep skirting vineyards at a height of about 350 metres. 40% Riesling (alias Klingelberger), 28% Müller-Thurgau, 8.3% Traminer (alias Clevner), some Ruländer, Spätburgunder and new varieties. A place of great charm, with delicate and distinguished Rieslings. Two thirds of the wines are dry; one third medium-sweet. The Margrave also owns Schloß Salem (q.v.), and Schloß Eberstein-Murgtal (11 hectares), whose Spätburgunder is made at Schloß Staufenberg.

Affentaler Winzergenossenschaft Bühl eG

7580 Bühl-Eisental, tel: 07223-24376.
Each of the 980 members of this cooperative cellar in the Bereich Ortenau owns on average a little over a quarter of a hectare of vineyard. From this almost kitchen-garden viticulture come more medals for Spätburgunder (in the monkey-embossed bottle) than anywhere else in Germany. The Affental, literally translated as "monkey's valley" (but probably a corruption of "Ave Maria Tal"), with its Spätburgunder, is a speciality much appreciated in all its Germanic variety – dry, medium-dry, medium-sweet, sweet, from Kabinett to Auslese and beyond. In fact, 60% of the 280 hectares of sloping vineyards are planted with Riesling, for which the town of Bühl is also well known. Spätburgunder occupies a further 25% and Müller-Thurgau 12%.

Winzergenossenschaft eG Ballrechten-Dottingen

Franz-Hesstraße 2, 7801 Ballrechten-Dottingen, tel: 07634-8233.
A cooperative cellar of 139 members with 120 hectares in the 165-hectare Ballrechten-Dottingen Castellberg Einzellage. 99% of the wines are sold in bottle to the wholesale trade, restaurants and the consumer. In a region where cooperative cellars handle most of the crop, Ballrechten-Dottingen is well placed to influence the local market, with a storage capacity over 3 times the size of the average harvest. A small plantation of Gewürztraminer helps the quality image of the cooperative by winning many awards, but the main vine varieties grown are Gutedel (Chasselas) 34%, Müller-Thurgau 38% and Spätburgunder 10%.

Winzergenossenschaft Bickensohl eG

Neulindenstraße 25, 7818 Vogtsburg-Bickensohl, tel: 07622-213.
A 220-member cooperative established in 1924 in the warm, rustic, southwest corner of the Bereich Kaiserstuhl-Tuniberg. The wines from the two Einzellagen in Bickensohl, Herrenstück and Steinfelsen, are 98% "estate bottled". 30% of the holdings in the volcanic soil are planted with Müller-Thurgau, 25% with Ruländer, 20% with Spätburgunder and 15% with Weißburgunder.

Winzergenossenschaft Bischoffingen am Kaiserstuhl eG

Bacchusstraße 14, 7818 Vogtsburg-Bischoffingen, tel: 07662-756.
One of several excellent, award-winning cooperative cellars in the middle of the warmest part of the German vineyards, the Bereich Kaiserstuhl-Tuniberg. Most of the wine from the 305 members is sold in litre bottles, but some 49,000 cases of QmP in 0.75 litre bottles are also produced annually, depending on the vintage. Müller-Thurgau occupies 31% of the vineyard holdings, Ruländer 29%, Spätburgunder 24% and Silvaner 9%.

Winzergenossenschaft Britzingen eG

Markgräflerstraße 25/27, 7840 Müllheim-Britzingen, tel: 07631-4011.
A cooperative supplied by 232 members with holdings of 180 hectares on the outskirts of the main wine-producing town of the Bereich Markgräflerland, Müllheim. Founded in 1950, most of the wine (the equivalent of about 143,000 cases per annum) is "estate bottled", and all is sold in West Germany. The holdings on the sand and clay slopes of the Einzellagen Sonnhole and Rosenberg are planted mainly with Gutedel (43%), Müller-Thurgau (27%), Weißburgunder (7%) and Spätburgunder (7%).

Winzergenossenschaft Durbach eG

Nachtweide 1, 7601 Durbach, tel: 0781-31061.
A cooperative cellar whose 320 members supply grapes from 305 hectares in the steep slopes around Durbach. The wines win many of the top awards at the national (DLG) tasting competitions, and were particularly successful in the 1983 vintage. Spätburgunder covers 33% of the vineyards, Müller-Thurgau 27%, Riesling 16%, Traminer (known locally as Clevner) 11% and Ruländer also 11%.

Erste Markgräfler Winzergenossenschaft

Am Sonnenstück 1, 7846 Schliengen, tel: 07635-1094.
This, as its name implies, the first cooperative cellar in the Bereich Markgräflerland, lies about 20 kilometres (12 miles) north of the Swiss border. 240 members, with 157 hectares between them, produce the equivalent of about 179,000 cases per year. Two-thirds of this quantity are sold in litre bottles, particularly suited to the restaurant trade which forms a strong local market. The holdings on the slopes of the 223-hectare Sonnenstück Einzellage, divided between Schliengen and neighbouring communities, are 41% Gutedel, 23% Müller-Thurgau and 19% Spätburgunder, with 17% of a variety of others, from Riesling to Auxerrois.

Winzergenossenschaft eG, Hügelheim

Baslerstraße 12, 7840 Müllheim.
This relatively small cooperative cellar, founded in 1952, receives grapes from 106 members, exclusively in the commune of Hügelheim. The wines are sold under the Einzellage names of Schloßgarten and Höllberg, and part of the crop from the steep 1-hectare Gottesacker site is also delivered to the cellars. In the vineyards are grown Gutedel (38%), Müller-Thurgau (30%), Spätburgunder (14%) and Nobling, a Silvaner × Gutedel cross (8%), with 10% other varieties, including Muskateller.

Kaiserstühler Winzergenossenschaft, Ihringen eG

Winzerstraße 6, 7817 Ihringen, tel: 07668-622.
One of the largest local cooperative cellars in West Germany, with 950 members owning 400 hectares of vineyard. The positively flavoured wines from the volcanic soil are sold 98% on the home market with a small amount (about 6,000 cases) exported annually. Ihringen is an enclave for Silvaner: here it ignores the trend elsewhere and maintains its stake in the vineyards. It

180

covers 39% of the area supplying the cooperative. Other vines grown are Müller-Thurgau
(27%), Spätburgunder (21%) and Ruländer
(8%).

Winzergenossenschaft Kirchhofen eG
Herrenstraße 11, 7801 Ehrenkirchen, tel: 07633-
7027.
Cooperative cellar founded in 1951 that sells all
its annual production of approximately 143,000
cases in bottle. The 240 members deliver the
grapes from 110 hectares of vineyards on heavy
clay soil a little south of Freiburg. The wines are
sold under the Kirchhofener Einzellage names
Batzenberg, Kirchberg and Höllhagen. The
sloping vineyards are planted with 50% Gutedel
– the Markgräflerland favourite, 30% Müller-
Thurgau, 8% Spätburgunder and 8%
Ruländer.

Winzergenossenschaft Königschaffhausen am Kaiserstuhl eG
7833 Endingen-Königschaffhausen, tel: 07642-1003.
Established in 1933 on the northern edge of the
Bereich Kaiserstuhl-Tuniberg, this cooperative
receives the grapes of its 340 members from 140
hectares in the neighbourhood of
Königschaffhausen. The wines are sold under
the local Einzellage names of Hasenberg or
Steingrüble, as Endinger Engelsberg, or less
often under the Großlage name, Vulkanfelsen.
All (approximately 166,700 cases per annum)
are "estate bottled". The vineyards are planted
with 40% Müller-Thurgau, 30% Spätburgunder, 20% Ruländer and 3% Gewürztraminer. As happens elsewhere, the small
amount of Gewürztraminer produced wins
many awards. Half the Spätburgunder is made
into red wine and the rest into Weißherbst.

Markgräfler Winzergenossenschaft Müllheim eG
Werderstraße 51, 7840 Müllheim, tel: 07631-4074.
A cooperative of 151 members with 100 hectares
in the Bereich Markgräflerland, selling 90% of
its wines locally. Whilst annual production
varies between 500,000 and 1,500,000 litres, the
storage capacity amounts to a luxurious
3,500,000 litres. Good reserves of wine can be
held and even the largest harvests can be
accommodated with ease. The Markgräflerland
speciality Gutedel (Chasselas) covers 35% of the
vineyard holdings, Müller-Thurgau 30%,
Spätburgunder 12%, Ruländer 8% and
Nobling (Silvaner × Gutedel) 7%.

Bezirkskellerei "Markgräflerland" eG
Winzerstraße 2, 7859 Efringen-Kirchen, tel: 07628-
778. 708 members in 27 villages. *Einzellagen:*
Hornfelsen, Schlipf, Sonnhole, Weingarten,
Kapellenberg, Wolfer, Kirchberg, Ölberg,
Steingässle. Großlage: Vogtei Rötteln.
Vines are 52% Gutedel, 26% Müller-Thurgau,
12% Spätburgunder. The major cooperative of
the region, producing typical light dry wine.
Exports to Switzerland.

Renchtäler Winzergenossenschaft eG
Renchenerstraße 42, 7602 Oberkirch, tel: 07802-
3044.
A large cooperative cellar with a storage capacity
of 8,500,000 litres, whose 615 members own 452
hectares of mainly sloping or steep vineyards.
Like so many in the region, it does remarkably
well in the national (DLG) competitions, winning 15 of the highest awards (the Großer DLG-
Preis) in 1985. The wines are sold exclusively
under the name of the large Oberkircher
Renchtäler Einzellage. 32% of the vineyards are
Spätburgunder, 29% Müller-Thurgau, 23%
Riesling, 9% Ruländer and 7% Traminer. No
export.

Winzergenossenschaft Sasbach eG
Jechtingerstraße 26, 7831 Sasbach, tel: 07642-7282.
A cooperative of 276 members, receiving grapes
from 100 hectares, all at Sasbach on the northern
edge of the Bereich Kaiserstuhl-Tuniberg. The
annual production amounts to the equivalent of
97,600 cases, of which about 80% are sold in litre
bottles. The cooperative's wines of the Pinot
family (Weißburgunder, Ruländer and
Spätburgunder) achieve many top awards. In
1985 these included a 1983 Sasbacher Limburg
Weißburgunder Trockenbeerenauslese, as well
as a self-confessed speciality, red wine from
Spätburgunder (Pinot Noir). Most are sold
locally. The vineyard holdings are planted with
40% Spätburgunder, 33% Müller-Thurgau,
16% Ruländer and 5% Weißburgunder.

Winzergenossenschaft Sasbachwalden eG
Talstraße 2, 7595 Sasbachwalden, tel: 07841-4033.
220 hectares, of which 120 are at Sasbachwalden
itself, supply the grapes for this cooperative
cellar. Other holdings are at Oberachern,
Obersasbach, Lauf and Neusatz, a few
kilometres south of Baden-Baden. Annual production amounts to the equivalent of about
178,000 cases, averaging 68 hl/ha. Eleven top
awards (Großer DLG-Preis) were won by the
Spätburgunder wines from the steep slopes of
the Sasbachwalden Alde Gott Einzellage in
1985. The Spätburgunder, in fact, covers 50%
of the vineyard holdings, followed by Riesling
(20%) and Müller-Thurgau (also 20%).

Zentralkellerei Badischer Winzergenossenschaften (ZBW)
See p161 (this cooperative has vineyards all
over the extensive Baden wine region).

AGEING GERMAN WINES

Good-quality German wines have a much
longer lifespan, and benefit much more by
being kept in bottle, than fashion suggests
or most people suppose. The wine industry
and trade have little to gain from older
bottles, and have tacitly agreed that
German wines are ready to drink within
months of being bottled. With the
enormous crops (and hence the high water
content) of standard-quality modern QbA
wines there is indeed no gain from
keeping bottles more than six months or a
year. But almost all the superior-grade
(QmP) wines, delectable as they may
taste in their flower-and-fruity youth,
have the potential to put on another
dimension of flavour with maturity. When
they are first offered for sale they are at
their most brisk and lively, with acidity
and fruitiness often tending to cancel each
other out in a generally tingling and
exciting effect. Some fine wines
(particularly Rieslings) at this stage have
remarkably little aroma.

Sometimes after a year or two in
bottle the first rapture goes without
maturer flavours taking its place; the wine
you bought with enthusiasm seems to be
letting you down. Be patient. The subtle
alchemy takes longer. It may be four or
five years before the mingled savours of
citrus and spice and oil emerge.

Each vintage has its own timespan, but
as a generalization Kabinett wines from a
first-rate grower need at least three
years in bottle and may improve for
seven or eight, Spätlesen will improve for
anything from four to ten years, and
Auslesen and upwards will benefit from
five or six years up to 20 or even more.

There are signs of a trend back
towards ageing German wines after a
period in which freshness and youth have
been the most desirable qualities. Some
estates are promoting their wines as
worthy of keeping. One, the von
Kesselstatt estate in Trier, guarantees that
its Rieslings will last for ten years. If they
don't the customers can have their money
back.

(On p160 is a key to the quality
categories of German wine. On p161 is
a table summarizing the quantities of
wine produced in recent vintages in the
five main exporting regions; a second
table gives a breakdown into quality
categories.)

EXPORTING HOUSES

Deinhard & Co KGaA
Deinhardplatz 3, 5400 Koblenz, tel: 0261-1040. *Owners:* Hanns-Christof and Rolf Wegeler.
Internationally known wine merchants, established by the forefathers of the present owners in 1794. Apart from important vineyard holdings of over 100 hectares, based in Bernkastel, Oestrich and Deidesheim, Deinhard is one of the oldest producers of sparkling wine in Germany and exports to 84 countries. They also import leading branded drinks of various sorts.

Louis Guntrum Weinkellerei GmbH
Rheinallee 62, 6505 Nierstein/Rhein, tel: 06133-5101. *Principals:* Lorenz and Hanns Joachim Guntrum.
Merchants with their own estates in Rheinhessen producing mostly Riesling. They sell over 250,000 cases a year of non-estate-bottled wines in Germany and abroad, including Canada, the UK, Japan and Sweden.

Adolph Huesgen GmbH
Am Bahnhof 21–24, 5580 Traben-Trarbach, tel: 06541-9281.
A 250-year-old family firm of merchants dealing in their own bottlings of wines from all over West Germany, as well as estate bottlings, sold 90% on the export market to a wide variety of countries, including those in the Far East.

Hermann Kendermann OHG
Mainzerstraße 57, 6530 Bingen. *Owners:* Herr Hans-Walter Kendermann and Jürgen Kendermann.
Specialities are Black Tower Liebfraumilch, Green Gold Moselle, German generic and estate-bottled wines.

Langenbach & Co. GmbH
Alzeyerstraße 31, 6520 Worms, tel: 06241-591053. *Owner:* Whitbread & Co. PLC, Great Britain.
A respected exporting house, founded in 1852, possibly best known for its quality Liebfraumilch, "Crown of Crowns". Owners of part of the Liebfrauenstift-Kirchenstück vineyard, the original source of Liebfraumilch.

Sigmund Loeb GmbH
Engelstraße 18, 5500 Trier, tel: 0651-42614. *Owners:* Christopher M. Jevell, London and Josef Steinlein, Trier.
Export house established in Trier in 1874, with a London (UK) office opened in 1937. No brand wines are offered, and Loebs are best known and respected for their impeccable list of fine estate bottlings. Wines of Mosel-Saar-Ruwer, Rheingau, Rheinpfalz, Rheinhessen, Nahe and Württemberg. Exports to both northern Europe and the USA.

Peter Meyer Wineries GmbH
Cusanusstraße 14, 5550 Bernkastel-Kues, tel: 06531-3071. *Owner:* Peter J. F. Meyer.
A firm of wine merchants based in Bernkastel-Kues. The annual turnover is equivalent to 1.25 million cases of inexpensive QbA, QmP and wine from its own Hermann Freiherr von Schorlemer estate (q.v.). The cellars are amongst the most modern on the Mosel, and the wines (some of which are "bag-in-a-box") are much exported.

Rudolf Müller GmbH & Co.
5586 Reil an der Mosel, tel: 06532-3004. *Principals:* Walter Müller, Dr. Richard Müller, Margrit Müller-Burggraef.
The company owns estates in the Mosel (14.5 hectares) and sells wines from other estates in Nierstein (Rheinhessen; about 50 hectares).

Franz Reh & Sohn GmbH & Co. KG
Römerstraße 27, 5559 Leiwen, tel: 06507-3031. *President:* Herbert Reh. Two estates with about 13 hectares. *Einzellagen:* Leiwen: Laurentiuslay and Klostergarten; Trittenheim: Apotheke and Altärchen; Piesport: Goldtröpfchen, Gärtchen (solely owned), Günterslay and Treppchen; Dhron: Hofberg.
A highly successful merchant house with the brands Kellerprinz, Klosterprinz and Hockprinz. Also the owners of two estates, Josefinengrund at Leiwen and Marienhof at Piesport.

Rheinberg Kellerei GmbH
Mainzerstraße 162–170, 6530 Bingen, tel: 06721-1890.
In business as wine merchants since 1939, the company is owned by the well-known grocery chain Edeka. Grape juice or wines are purchased to produce modern, efficiently-made wines. Annual turnover over 4m. cases.

St. Augustus Weinkellerei GmbH
Bernhardstraße 1, 5500 Trier, tel: 0651-31041. *Owners:* Roberto Anz and KMU Geschäftsvermittlungs GmbH.
A firm of wine exporters established in recent years, supplying its own bottlings under well-known Großlage names. Annual turnover is a little short of 900,000 cases.

St. Ursula Weingut und Weinkellerei GmbH
Mainzerstraße 184, 6530 Bingen, tel: 06721-70225. *Owner:* the Nestlé Gruppe Deutschland.
Vast capacity sometimes equals inferior quality. This is not the case with this cellar. St. Ursula, with 2.5 million cases per year (not all German wine), buys quality grape juice and wine, much of which supplies their Goldener Oktober range. Given the style of wine required, the cellars are equipped and maintained to the highest standard. St. Ursula owns the Weingut Villa Sachsen.

Scholl & Hillebrand GmbH
Geisenheimerstraße 9, 6220 Rüdesheim, tel: 06722-1028. *Owner:* Bernhard Breuer and Partner. (Herr Breuer is also a partner in Weingut G. Breuer.)
A family firm of wine merchants established in 1880, selling wine from its own holding in the Rüdesheimer Berg Roseneck Einzellage, as well as estate-bottled wines from elsewhere in the Rheingau, and wines that it buys in bulk. There is a strong emphasis on elegant Rieslings and the well-balanced brand wine, Riesling Dry QbA.

Weingut/Weinkellerei Carl Sittmann
Wormserstraße 61, 6504 Oppenheim, tel: 06133-2021. *Owner:* Walter Sittmann-Haury.
Established in 1879, this estate produces wines of a wide variety from about 80 hectares (in Nierstein, Oppenheim, Dienheim and Alsheim), including the Alsheimer Rheinblick Weißherbst QbA. As wine merchants and exporters they have sales in the region of 104,000 cases worldwide. Exports to seven countries, particularly the UK, USA, Japan and Canada.

H. Sichel Söhne GmbH
Werner-von-Siemensstraße 14–18, 6508 Alzey, tel: 06731-4060. *Managing Directors:* Riquet Hess, Friedrich Weidmann, Peter and Ronald Sichel.
One of the best known shipping houses established in 1857, whose major brand, Blue Nun Liebfraumilch, is sold throughout the world. Besides this famous wine, Sichels deal in a full range of Großlage names, and also have long-established connections with a number of fine estates. The Sichel family has played an important part in the German wine trade, Walter (in London) and Peter (in New York) being internationally recognized as experts and spokesmen. Their USA and UK exports total 2.2m. cases.

Steiner'scher Keller
6740 Landau, tel: 06341-4001. *Owners:* The Heinz Steiner family.
A wine merchants' business established in 1752 in Landau in the south of the Rheinpfalz. The owners, the Steiner family, also have a small holding in the Altes Löhl and Königsgarten vineyards. The annual turnover is the equivalent of about 330,000 cases. Grapes, "must" and wine are bought in. Most of the wines are dry with wines suitable for diabetics a speciality.

A. Weigand
Mainzerstraße 54–56, 6530 Bingen am Rhein, tel: 06721-13311. *Owners:* Ludwig Ebling and Heinrich Schwarz.
These wine merchants manage the estates and sales of Weingut Nonnenberg in the Rheingau and Weingut Sonnenhof in Rheinhessen. They also produce Sekt at their Bingen address. Exports are to the UK and USA.

Zimmermann-Graef & Co KG
Marientaler Au, 5583 Zell an der Mosel, tel: 06542-419-0. *Owners:* Paula and Johannes Hübinger.
A wine merchants' business set up in 1886, which has expanded to handle the equivalent of 1.33 million cases per annum. "Must" or wine is purchased. The company also has its own holdings in the Zeller Burglay-Felsen and Petersborn-Kabertchen Einzellagen. Sales are worldwide.

GLOSSARY

Abfüllung (or Abzug)
Bottling (e.g., Erzeuger-Abfüllung, bottled by the grower or producer).

Amtliche Prüfung
Certification of standard quality by chemical analysis and tasting. Compulsory since 1971 for all QbA and QmP wines (qq.v.). Each wine is given an AP number which must be displayed on the label.

Anbaugebiet
Official EEC term for a specified wine region, of which there are 11 in West Germany (e.g., Mosel-Saar-Ruwer, Baden).

Anreichern
To "enrich": adding sugar to must or wine to increase the alcohol; the equivalent of the French chaptalization. In Germany no sugar may be added to QmP wines but all Tafelwein and QbA wine may be assumed to have been "enriched".

Auslese
Literally "selected": the third category of QmP wines, made only in ripe vintages and usually naturally sweet. Auslesen often have a slight degree of "noble rot" which adds subtlety to their fruity sweetness. Good Auslesen deserve ageing in bottle for several years to allow their primary sweetness to mellow to more adult flavours.

Beerenauslese
Literally "selected grapes": the category of QmP wine beyond Auslese in sweetness and price, and theoretically in quality. Only very overripe and "nobly rotten" grapes are used to make intensely sweet, often deep-coloured wines which age admirably.

Blau
"Blue"; when used of grapes, means "red" or "black".

Bereich
One of over 30 districts or subregions (e.g., Bereich Bernkastel) within 11 Anbaugebiete. Bereich names are commonly used for quality wines (QbA and QmP) and in some circumstances for table wine (DTW) blended from the less-distinguished vineyards of the district.

Bundesweinprämierung
A national wine competition organized by the DLG (q.v.) for wines selected from regional prize winners. The tastings are held at Heilbronn in Württemberg. 3.5 points out of 5 wins a bronze medal, 4 a silver medal and 4.5 a "Großer Preis". Wines normally display their achievement by a strip label between the neck and body

labels or by a small circular label.

Charta
A new association of Rheingau Riesling producers dedicated to high-quality dry Rieslings with standards considerably above the legal minimum.

Deutsche(r)
"German"; distinguishes Tafelwein from German grapes from inferior mixtures of the wines of "various EEC countries", often sold with pseudo-German labels.

Deutsches Weinsiegel
A seal of quality given by the DLG (q.v.) to quality wines that achieve a laid-down level of points higher than that required to obtain an Amtliche Prüfungs (q.v.) number. The standard seal is red, but green seals are awarded to medium-dry wines and yellow seals to dry wines. About 10–12% of all quality wines produced in West Germany are granted a seal.

Diabetikerwein
Must contain less than 4 g/l of residual sugar, and no more than 25 mg/l of free sulphur dioxide and 12% alcohol, before it can be recommended, after medical advice, for consumption by a diabetic.

DLG
The German Agricultural Society (Deutsche Landwirtschafts-gesellschaft), the body that judges and presents the national wine awards. *See* Bundesweinprämierung.

Domäne
"Domain" – in Germany a term used mainly to describe the six estates owned by federal German States, the biggest in the Rheingau and Franken and the best on the Nahe.

Edelfäule
Noble rot. A fungus that in the right conditions greatly enhances the quality of the grapes and is essential in the making of fine Riesling Beerenauslese wines.

Eigenem
"Own." "Aus eigenem Lesegut" means "from his own harvest".

Einzellage
An individual vineyard site recognized by the law. There are some 2,600 Einzellagen in Germany. Before 1971 there were 10 times as many. Officially the minimum size for an Einzellage is 5 hectares although there are a number much smaller than this. Not all Einzellagen are in contiguous parcels, particularly in Baden and Württemberg. A Großlage (q.v.) is a unit of several Einzellagen supposedly of the same quality and

character. The Einzellage or Großlage name follows the village (Gemeinde) name on the label.

Eiswein
Wine made by pressing grapes that have been left hanging on the vine into mid-winter (sometimes February) and are gathered and pressed in early morning, while frozen solid. Since it is the water content of the grape that freezes, the juice, separated from the ice, is concentrated sugar, acidity and flavour. The result is extraordinarily sweet and piquant wines with almost limitless ageing capacity, less rich but more penetrating than Beeren- or Trockenbeerenauslese, often fetching spectacular prices.

Erzeugerabfüllung
"Own bottling", the equivalent of the French *mis au domaine* or *mis au château*.

Erzeugergemeinschaft
A producers' association, usually for sales purposes, as distinct from a cooperative for making wine.

Faß
A cask, traditionally on the Rhine a Halbstück (610 litres), and on the Mosel a Halbfuder (500 litres).

Flasche
Bottle – the same word as the English "flask".

Flurbereinigung
The term for the Government-sponsored "consolidation" and re-allocation of vineyard holdings by remodelling the landscape, a process that has revolutionized the old system of terracing in most parts of Germany, making the land workable by tractors and rationalizing scattered holdings.

Fuder
The Mosel barrel, an oak oval holding 1,000 litres or about 111 cases.

Gemeinde
Village, parish or commune. The village name always comes before the vineyard on German labels.

Großlage
A "collective vineyard", consisting of a number of Einzellagen (q.v.) of similar character and quality. The Bereiche contain 150 Großlagen and 2,600 Einzellagen. Unfortunately the wine law does not permit the label to distinguish between a Großlage and an Einzellage name. Großlage names are normally used for wines below the top quality, but also sometimes for such wines as Trockenbeeren-auslesen when a single Einzellage cannot produce enough grapes to fill even a small barrel.

Jahrgang
Vintage (year).

Halbtrocken
"Half-dry" – wine with no more than 18 grams of unfermented sugar a litre, therefore drier than most modern German wines but sweeter than a trocken wine (q.v.).

Kabinett
The first category of natural, unsugared, Qualitätswein mit Prädikat. Fine Kabinett wines have qualities of lightness and delicacy which make them ideal refreshment, not inferior in the right context to heavier (and more expensive) Spätlese or Auslese wines.

Kellerei
Wine cellar; by inference a merchant's rather than a grower's establishment (which would be called a Weingut).

Landespreismünze
Regional wine prizes, which act as the "heats" for the National Bundesweinprämierung (q.v.).

Landwein
A category for Tafelwein from one of 14 designated areas, of not more than 18 grams a litre residual sugar and therefore trocken or halbtrocken.

Lesegut
Crop.

Liebfraumilch
A much-abused name for a mild "wine of pleasant character" officially originating in Rheinpfalz, Rheinhessen, Rheingau or Nahe. It must be in the QbA category and should be predominantly of Riesling, Silvaner, Müller-Thurgau or Kerner grapes. Since neither its character nor quality is remotely consistent, varying widely from shipper to shipper, its popularity can only be ascribed to its simple and memorable name.

Mostgewicht
"Must weight". The sugar content of the must is ascertained by measuring its specific gravity on the Oechsle (q.v.) scale.

Neuzüchtung
New (grape) variety. German breeders have produced a score of new varieties which are slowly being accepted or rejected by growers.

Oechsle
The specific gravity, therefore sweetness, of German must is measured by the method invented by Ferdinand Oechsle (1774–1852). Each gram by which a litre of grape juice is heavier than a litre of water is one degree Oechsle.

Ortsteil
A place-name (a suburb or part of a

GLOSSARY

village) with a standing independent from its Gemeinde or village. Certain famous estates, such as Schloß Vollrads are allowed to omit the village names from their labels.

Perlwein
Slightly fizzy Tafelwein, often artificially carbonated under pressure.

Pokalwein
Wine served "open" in a large glass (Pokal) in a café or Weinstube.

Prädikat
See QmP.

Prüfungsnummer
The individual AP number given to each "quality" wine after testing. *See* Amtliche Prüfung.

QbA
Qualitätswein bestimmter Anbaugebiete: "quality wine of a designated region". The category of wine above Tafelwein and Landwein but below QmP (q.v.). QbA wine has had its alcohol enhanced with added sugar. It must be from one of 11 Anbaugebiete (unblended), from approved grapes, reach a certain level of ripeness before sugaring and pass an analytical and tasting test to gain an AP number. In certain underripe vintages a high proportion of German wine comes into this category and can be very satisfactory, although never reaching the delicacy and distinction of QmP wine.

QmP
Qualitätswein mit Prädikat. "Quality wine with special attributes" is the awkward official description of all the finest German wines, beginning with the Kabinett category and rising in sweetness, body and value to Trockenbeerenauslese. QmP wines must originate in a single Bereich (q.v.) and are certificated at each stage of their career from the vineyard on.

Rebe
Vine (Rebsorte: vine variety).

Restsüße
"Residual sugar": the sugar remaining unfermented in a wine at bottling, whether fermentation has stopped or maximum Süßreserve has been added. The minimum, in a wine for diabetics, is about 4 grams a litre. In a Trockenbeerenauslese it may reach astonishing figures of more than 180 grams a litre, with very little of the sugar converted to alcohol.

Roseewein, Roséwein
Pale pink wine from red grapes.

Rotling
Pale red wine from mixed red and white grapes.

Rotwein
Red wine.

Säure
Acidity (measured in units per 1,000 of tartaric acid). The essential balancing agent to the sweetness in German (or any) wine. As a rule of thumb a well-balanced wine has approximately one unit per 1,000 (ml.) of acid for each 10 degrees Oechsle (q.v.). Thus an 80° Oechsle wine needs an acidity of approximately 0.8.

Schaumwein
Sparkling wine – a general term for low-priced fizz. Quality sparkling wines are called Sekt.

Schillerwein
A pale red (Rotling) of QbA or QmP status, produced only in Württemberg.

Schloß
Castle.

Schoppenwein
Another term for Pokalwein – wine served "open" in a large glass.

Sekt
Quality sparkling wine, subject to similar controls to QbA wines.

Spätlese
Literally "late-gathered". The QmP category above Kabinett and below Auslese, with wines of a higher alcoholic degree and greater body and vinosity than Kabinetts. Also often considerably sweeter but not necessarily so. A grower must notify the authorities of his intention to pick a Spätlese crop, and tasting panels establish a consensus of what constitutes proper Spätlese style in each vintage and region. Spätlesen, particularly dry ones, are often the best German wines to drink with a meal and have greater potential for long bottle-ageing than most Kabinetts.

Spitzen
"Top", a favourite German term, whether applied to a vineyard, a grower or a vintage.

Stück
The standard traditional oak cask of the Rhine, holding 1,200 litres or about 133 cases. There are also Doppelstücke, Halbstücke and Viertel- (quarter) stücke, holding the logical quantities.

Süßreserve
Unfermented grape juice with all its natural sweetness, held in reserve for "back-blending" with dry, fully fermented wines to arrive at the wine maker's ideal of a balanced wine. This sweetening (which also lowers the alcoholic content) is often overdone, but a judicious hint of

extra sweetness can enhance fruity flavours and make an average wine considerably more attractive.

Tafelwein
"Table wine", the humblest category of German wine. (Without the prefix Deutsche it is not German, however Gothic the label.) The origin, alcohol content and grape varieties are all controlled but Tafelwein is never more than a light wine for quenching thirst, and frequently fails even in this.

TBA
See Trockenbeerenauslese.

Trocken
"Dry" – the official category for wines with less than 9 grams of unfermented sugar a litre. Trocken wines have recently been much in fashion for use with meals, but frequently taste arid, hollow and unbalanced compared with halbtrocken (q.v.) versions of the same wines, adjusted with Süßreserve (q.v.).

Trockenbeerenauslese
"Selected dried grapes" (frequently shortened to TBA). Ironically the precise opposite of the last entry, the "dry" here referring to the state of the overripe grapes when picked in a shrivelled state from "noble rot" and desiccation on the vine. Such is the concentration of sugar, acid and flavours that Oechsle readings of Trockenbeerenauslese must (never in more than minute quantities) can reach more than 300°. Trockenbeerenauslese wines are reluctant to ferment and rarely exceed 6% alcohol, the remaining intense sweetness acting as a natural preservative and slowing down maturation for many years. Only Eisweine (q.v.) mature more slowly.

Weinberg
Vineyard, even when it is not a "berg" (hill) but flat.

Weingut
Wine estate. The term may only be used by growers who grow all their own grapes.

Weinprobe
Wine tasting.

Weinstein
The thick deposit of potassium tartrate crystals forming a glittering rock-like lining to old barrels.

Weißherbst
A rosé wine of QbA status made from red grapes of a single variety, the speciality of Baden and Württemberg, but also the fate of some sweet reds of other regions which fail to achieve a full red colour.

("Noble rot" attacks the pigments and often makes red Auslesen excessively pale.)

Winzer
Wine grower.

Winzergenossenschaft, Winzerverein
Growers' cooperative.

Zuckerrest
The same as Restsüße (q.v.).

VINEYARD REGISTER

The alphabetical index of vineyards that follows lists every vineyard site, be it Einzellage or Großlage, registered in West Germany. (A few small, unregistered "einzellagenfreie" vineyards mentioned in the vineyard lists in the main body of this Atlas, but not shown on the vineyard maps, are not listed here.)

The first column lists the Einzellagen (individual vineyard sites) and Großlagen (collective vineyards) in alphabetical order. Großlage names are shown in bold type.

The second column shows the Gemeinde (village or town) with which each Einzellage is linked. The Ortsteil (parish or town suburb) occasionally listed in the third column is an even smaller geographical unit linked with the Einzellage. (A few wine estates are themselves registered as Ortsteile: these are shown by the abbreviation "Ortst." followed by a letter rather than a number.)

The last column shows each Einzellage's official number, preceded by the name of the wine region in which it is situated. These numbers correspond to those used in the vineyard maps and their accompanying lists. (See below for a key to the abbreviations and for page-number references to each wine region.)

A "T" following the number indicates an Einzellage that extends over more than one Gemeinde or Ortsteil (the latter are listed in the second and third columns).

To find a vineyard, look it up in the first column, note the number and abbreviation in the last column, then turn to the relevant page for the region in question.

A	=	Ahr p38
MSR	=	Mosel-Saar-Ruwer p43–51
Mrh	=	Mittelrhein p60
Rhg	=	Rheingau p66
N	=	Nahe p89
Rhh	=	Rheinhessen p96
Rhpf	=	Rheinpfalz p104–106
HB	=	Hessische Bergstraße p114
F	=	Franken p130–132
W	=	Württemberg p144–149
B	=	Baden p154–175

Site	Town	Ortsteil	Region & Site No.
Abelsberg	Stuttgart	Gaisburg	W 150
Abtei	Bernkastel-Kues	Wehlen	MSR 235
Abtei	Sponheim	–	N 169
Abteiberg	Mesenich	–	MSR 96
Abtei Kloster Stuben	Bremm	–	MSR 103
Abtei Ruppertsberg	Bingen	Bingerbrück	N 3 T
Abtey	**Appenheim**	–	**Rhh 37–61**
	Gau-Algesheim	–	
	Nieder-Hilbersheim	–	
	Ober-Hilbersheim	–	
	Partenheim	–	
	Sankt Johann	–	
	Sprendlingen	–	
	Wolfsheim	–	
Abtsberg	Alzenau	Hörstein	F 1
Abtsberg	Graach	–	MSR 241
Abtsberg	Impflingen	–	Rhpf 302
Abtsberg	Mertesdorf	Maximin Grünhaus	MSR 414
Abtsberg	Offenberg	Zell-Weierbach	B 167
Abtsfronhof	Bad Dürkheim	–	Rhpf 124
Abtsleite	Würzburg	–	F 58
Adelberg	**Armsheim**	–	**Rhh 93–118**
	Bermersheim v.d.H.	–	
	Bornheim	–	
	Ensheim	–	
	Erbes-Büdesheim	–	
	Flonheim	–	
	Lonsheim	–	
	Nack	–	
	Nieder-Wiesen	–	
	Sülzheim	–	
	Wendelsheim	–	
	Wörrstadt	–	
Adelpfad	Engelstadt	–	Rhh 134
Adelsberg	Bayerfeld-Steck-weiler	–	N 255
Adler	Zell	Merl	MSR 140
Äffchen	Wöllstein	–	Rhh 88
Affenberg	Worms	Heppenheim	Rhh 433
Agritiusberg	Konz	Oberemmel	MSR 442
Ahrenberg	Nack	–	Rhh 94
Ailenberg	Eßlingen	Mettingen	W 153 T
	Stuttgart	Obertürkheim	
Albachtaler	Wasserliesch	–	MSR 501
Alde Gott	Achern	Oberachern	B 140 T
	Lauf	–	
	Sasbach	Obersasbach	
	Sasbachwalden	–	
Alemannenbuck	Schallstadt	Mengen	B 268
Allenberg	Raumbach/Glan	–	N 222
Alsterweiler Kapellenberg	Maikammer	–	Rhpf 218
Altärchen	Trittenheim	–	MSR 314
Altarberg	Ellenz-Poltersdorf	–	MSR 70
Altberg	Au	–	B 266 a
Altdörr	Dalheim	–	Rhh 225
Altdörr	Friesenheim	–	Rhh 225 a
Alte Burg	Bad Mergentheim	Dainbach	B 28 a
Alte Burg	Emmendingen	Mundingen	B 198 T
	Tenningen	Köndringen	
Alte Burg	Zwingenberg	–	HB 9
Alte Lay	Bad Neuenahr-Ahrweiler	Walporzheim	A 20
Altenberg	Abtswind	–	F 105
Altenberg	Bad Bergzabern	–	Rhpf 321
Altenberg	Baden-Baden	Neuweier	B 124
Altenberg	Ballrechten-Dottingen	–	B 290 T
	Müllheim	Britzingen	
	Müllheim	Dattingen	
	Sulzburg	–	
	Sulzburg	Laufen	
Altenberg	Brackenheim	Stockheim	W 92
Altenberg	Boxberg	Oberschüpf	B 26
Altenberg	Bruchsal	Heidelsheim	B 71
Altenberg	Dörzbach	–	W 7
Altenberg	Ergersheim	–	F 127
Altenberg	Flein	–	W 68 T
	Heilbronn	–	
Altenberg	Hillesheim	–	Rhh 292
Altenberg	Kanzem	–	MSR 430 T
	Konz	Filzen	
	Konz	Hamm	
Altenberg	Konz	Krettnach	MSR 437
Altenberg	Konz	Oberemmel	MSR 439
Altenberg	Lauda-Königshofen	Lauda	B 18 T
	Lauda-Königshofen	Oberlauda	
Altenberg	Löwenstein	–	W 51
Altenberg	Meddersheim	–	N 201
Altenberg	Niedernhall	–	
	Weißbach	–	
Altenberg	Obersulm	Sülzbach	W 43 T
	Weinsberg	Wimmental	
Altenberg	Staufen im Breisgau	Grunern	B 284
Altenberg	Stuttgart	Untertürkheim	W 144
Altenberg	Theilheim	–	F 59 a
Altenberg	Trier	Kürenz	MSR 364
Altenberg	Weinstadt	Beutelsbach	W 178 T
	Weinstadt	Schnait	
Altenberg	Weinstadt	Strümpfelbach	W 193
Altenberg	Weisenheim am Sand	–	Rhpf 79
Altenberg	Wellen	–	MSR 507
Altenburg	Wachenheim	–	Rhpf 143
Altenburg	Waldlaubersheim	–	N 20
Altenforst	Burrweiler	–	Rhpf 265
Alter Berg	Aspach	Allmersbach	W 132
Alter Berg	Triefenstein	Lengfurt	F 25
Alter Berg	Römerberg (bei Speyer)	Mechtersheim	Rhpf 264 c T
	Römerberg (bei Speyer)	Heiligenstein	
Alter Graben	Bamberg	–	F 135 b
Alte Römerstraße	Freilaubersheim	–	Rhh 64 T
	Volxheim	–	
Alte Römerstraße	Mandel	–	N 151
Altes Löhl	Landau in der Pfalz mit Queichheim und Mörlheim		Rhpf 283
Althof	Ottersweier	–	B 137
Ameisenberg	St. Goar	–	Mrh 52 T
	St. Goar	Werlau	
Am Gaisberg	Herxheimweier	–	Rhpf 305
Am heiligen Häuschen	Worms	Pfeddersheim	Rhh 427
Am hohen Stein	Rittersheim	–	Rhpf 4
Ammerlanden	Möckmühl	–	W 17
Amselberg	Gengenbach	Reichenbach	B 175
Amtgarten	Mülheim	–	MSR 262
Andreasberg	Ortenberg	–	B 171

Site	Town	Ortsteil	Region & Site No.
Andreasberg	Trier	Tarforst	MSR 369
Annaberg	Kallstadt	–	Rhpf 105
Annaberg	Schweich	–	MSR 351
Antoniusberg	Serrig	–	MSR 485
Antoniusbrunnen	Saarburg	–	MSR 478
Apostelberg	Guldental	Heddesheim und Waldhilbersheim	N 38
Apostelgarten	Alzenau	Michelbach	F 5
Apotheke	Trittenheim	–	MSR 315
Arlesgarten	Gerolzhofen	–	F 136 c
Arrasburg Schloßberg	Alf	–	MSR 132
Arzley	Cochem	Cond	MSR 77
Aspenberg	Bayerfeld-Steckweiler	–	N 257
Aspenberg	Oberndorf	–	N 250
Attilafelsen	**Breisach** **Breisach** **Freiburg** **Freiburg** **Freiburg** **Freiburg** **Gottenheim** **Merdingen**	**Niederrimsingen** **Oberrimsingen** **Munzingen** **Opfingen** **Tiengen** **Waltershofen** **–** **–**	**B 257– 264**
Auf dem Zimmerberg	Oberstreit	–	N 209
Auf der Heide	Traben-Trarbach	Wolf	MSR 198
Auf der Wiltingerkupp	Konz	Kommlingen	MSR 421
Auflangen	**Nierstein** **Nierstein**	**–** **Schwabsburg**	**Rhh 260– 267**
Augenscheiner	Trier	Biewer	MSR 384
Augustinerberg	Breisach	–	B 255
Aulenberg	Uelversheim	–	Rhh 300
Aulerde	Westhofen	–	Rhh 371
Ausoniusstein	Lehmen	–	MSR 25
Authental	Guntersblum	–	Rhh 306

Site	Town	Ortsteil	Region & Site No.
Backöfchen	Wallhausen	–	N 86
Backofen	Kaub	–	Mrh 81
Badstube	**Bernkastel-Kues Lieser**	**Bernkastel** **–**	**MSR 243– 250, 252**
Bärental	Margetshöchheim	–	F 68 b
Baiken	Eltville	Rauenthal	Rhg 77
Baron	St. Martin	–	Rhpf 226
Baßgeige	Vogtsburg im Kaiserstuhl	Oberbergen	B 232
Bastei	Traisen	–	N 278
Bastel	Castell	Greuth	F 105a
Batterieberg	Enkirch	–	MSR 180
Batzenberg	Ehrenkirchen Ehrenkirchen Ehrenkirchen Pfaffenweiler Schallstadt Schallstadt	Kirchhofen Norsingen Scherzingen – – Wolfenweiler	B 273 T
Bausch	Castell	–	F 106
Becherbrunnen	Mandel	–	N 155
Beilberg	Großrinderfeld Werbach	– –	B 12 T
Belz	Wachenheim	–	Rhpf 139
Benediktinerberg	Trier	Oleweg	MSR 382
Benediktinusberg	Zellingen	Retzbach	F 44
Bengel	Meersburg	–	B 335
Benn	Obrigheim	Mühlheim	Rhpf 28
Benn	Westhofen	–	Rhh 367
Berg	Asperg Markgröningen	– –	W 128 T
Berg	Bad Kreuznach	Winzenheim	N 127
Berg	Bad Neuenahr-Ahrweiler	Heppingen	A 4
Berg	Felsberg (Schwalm-Eder-Kreis)	Böddiger	Rhg 116
Berg	Hochheim Mainz	– Kostheim	Rhg 101 T
Berg	Korb Winnenden Winnenden	– – Hanweiler	W 160 T
Berg	Langenbrettach	Brettach	W 20
Berg	Markt Eisenheim Volkach	Untereisenheim Escherndorf	F 87 T
Berg	Neudenau Neudenau	– Herbolzheim	B 80 T
Berg	Neustadt an der Weinstraße	Diedesfeld	Rhpf 209
Berg	Roxheim	–	N 156
Berg	Stuttgart Stuttgart Stuttgart Stuttgart Stuttgart	Bad Cannstatt Feuerbach Münster Wangen Zuffenhausen	W 137 T
Berg	Unkel	–	Mrh 9
Berg-Bildstock	Walluf	Niederwalluf	Rhg 86
Bergborn	Langenlonsheim	–	N 63
Bergel	Edenkoben	–	Rhpf 228
Bergel	Grünstadt	–	Rhpf 37
Berghalde	Remshalden	Grunbach	W 169
Berghalde	Kreßbronn/Bodensee	–	W 201
Berg Kaisersteinfels	Rüdesheim	Aulhausen	Rhg 11
Bergkirche	Nierstein	–	Rhh 262

Site	Town	Ortsteil	Region & Site No.
Bergkloster	**Bermersheim**	–	**Rhh 354–371**
	Eppelsheim	–	
	Esselborn	–	
	Flomborn	–	
	Gundersheim	–	
	Gundheim	–	
	Hangen-Weisheim	–	
	Westhofen	–	
Bergle	Freiburg	Lehen	B 209
Bergle	Offenburg	Fessenbach	B 168
Bergpfad	Friesenheim	–	Rhh 228
Berg-Rondell	Dettelbach	–	F 82
Berg Roseneck	Rüdesheim	–	Rhg 12
Berg Rottland	Rüdesheim	–	Rhg 13
Bergschlößchen	Saarburg	–	MSR 479
Berg Schloßberg	Rüdesheim	–	Rhg 14
Bergwäldle	Wiesloch	–	B 49
Bernstein	Oberwesel	Engehöll	Mrh 63
Betschgräber	Bühl	Eisental	B 130
Bettelhaus	Bad Dürkheim	Ungstein	Rhpf 96
Beulsberg	Oberwesel	Urbar	Mrh 63
Beutelstein	Oberndorf	–	N 251
Bienenberg	Achern	Oberachern	B 145
Bienenberg	Malterdingen	–	B 197 T
	Teningen	Heimbach	
Bienenberg	Niederburg	–	Mrh 65
Bienenberg	Oberwesel	–	Mrh 65 a
Bienengarten	Durbach	–	B 162
Bienengarten	Koblenz	Güls	MSR 2
Bienengarten	Senheim	–	MSR 100
Bienenlay	Ediger-Eller	Eller	MSR 114
Biengarten	Frankweiler	–	Rhpf 287
Biengarten	Neustadt an der Weinstraße	Gimmeldingen an der Weinstraße	Rhpf 185
Bildberg	Freimersheim	–	Rhpf 254
Bildstock	Nierstein	–	Rhpf 252
Bildstock	Worms	Abenheim	Rhh 418
Bingerberg	Flonheim	–	Rhh 98 T
	Flonheim	Uffhofen	
	Erbes-Büdesheim	–	
Birkenberg	Roxheim	–	N 161
Birkenberg	Sommerloch	–	N 89
Bischofstein	Burgen	–	MSR 40
Bischofsberg	Arnstein	–	F 40 T
	Arnstein	Halsheim	
	Arnstein	Heugrumbach	
	Arnstein	Müdesheim	
	Arnstein	Reuchelheim	
Bischofsberg	Großheubach	–	F 16
Bischofsberg	Rüdesheim	–	Rhg 15
Bischofsgarten	Forst an der Weinstraße	–	Rhpf 133 T
	Friedelsheim	–	
	Wachenheim	–	
Bischofshub	Oberdiebach	–	Mrh 100
Bischofskreuz	**Böchingen**	–	**Rhpf 265–282**
	Burrweiler	–	
	Flemlingen	–	
	Gleisweiler	–	
	Knöringen	–	
	Landau in der Pfalz	**Dammheim**	
	Landau in der Pfalz	**Nußdorf**	
	Roschbach	–	
	Walsheim	–	
Bischofstuhl	Cochem	Sehl (Ebernach)	MSR 65
Bischofsweg	Neustadt an der Weinstraße	Mußbach an der Weinstraße	Rhpf 193

Site	Town	Ortsteil	Region & Site No.
Blattenberg	Mehring	–	MSR 342
Bleidenberg	Alken	–	MSR 31
Blücherhöhe	Edenkoben	–	Rhpf 233
Blücherpfad	Ober-Flörsheim	–	Rhh 395
Blüchertal	Kaub	–	Mrh 83
Blümchen	Nittel	–	MSR 510
Blume	Rech	–	A 34
Blume	Stadecken-Elsheim	Elsheim	Rhh 198
Bocksberg	Feilbingert	–	N 239
Bockshaut	Gau-Bickelheim	–	Rhh 120 T
	Wöllstein	–	
Bockstein	Ingelheim	Groß-Winternheim	Rhh 142
Bockstein	Ockfen	–	MSR 465
Bockstein	Stadecken-Elsheim	Elsheim	Rhh 196
Bodental-Steinberg	Lorch	–	Rhg 7
Böhlig	Wachenheim	–	Rhpf 138
Börnchen	Harxheim	–	Rhh 185
Bopser	Gerlingen	–	W 134
Bornpfad	Guntersblum	–	Rhh 305
Bottchen	Wittlich	–	MSR 214
Bräunersberg	Ottersheim/Zellertal	–	Rhpf 15
Bratenhöfchen	Bernkastel-Kues	Bernkastel	MSR 245
Brauneberg	Bekond	–	MSR 329
Brauneberg	Hetzerath Rivenich	–	MSR 321 T
Brauneberg	Klotten	–	MSR 58
Brauneberg	Oberfell	–	MSR 27
Braune Kupp	Wiltingen	–	MSR 449
Braunfels	Wiltingen	–	MSR 452
Brautrock	Bullay	–	MSR 135
Breinsberg	Rüssingen	–	Rhpf 16
Brotwasser	Kernen	Stetten	W 189
Bruderberg	Mertesdorf	Maximin Grünhaus	MSR 413
Brudersberg	Nierstein	–	Rhh 257
Bruderschaft	Klüsserath	–	MSR 326
Brückchen	Nierstein	–	Rhh 253
Brückes	Bad Kreuznach	–	N 117
Brückstück	Winningen	–	MSR 8
Brüderberg	Langsur	–	MSR 498
Bründelsberg	Schwegenheim	–	Rhpf 264 a
Brünnchen	Nochern	–	Mrh 56
Brunnenhäuschen	Westhofen	–	Rhh 369
Bubeneck	Ellerstadt	–	Rhpf 112
Bubenstück	Bingen	Gaulsheim	Rhh 5
Bühl	Merdingen	–	B 258
Bürgel	Flörsheim-Dalsheim	Dalsheim	Rhh 401
Bürgergarten	Neustadt an der Weinstraße	Haardt an der Weinstraße	Rhpf 198
Burg	Esslingen	–	W 158 a
Burg	Heidelberg	–	B 44
Burg	**Elfershausen**	**Engenthal**	**F 28–32**
	Elfershausen	**Machtilshausen**	
	Elfershausen	**Trimberg**	
	Euerdorf	**Wirmsthal**	
	Hammelburg	–	
	Hammelburg	**Feuerthal**	
	Hammelburg	**Saaleck**	
	Hammelburg	**Westheim**	
	Ramsthal	–	
Burgberg	Abstatt	–	W 54 T
	Ilsfeld	Auenstein	

Site	Town	Ortsteil	Region & Site No.
Burgberg	Alken	—	MSR 32
Burgberg	Dorsheim	—	N 46
Burgberg	Ingelheim	Groß-Winternheim	Rhh 148
Burgberg	Lösnich	—	MSR 202
Burgberg	Mayschoß	—	A 38
Burgberg	Steinheim	—	W 130
Burgberg	Traben-Trarbach	Trarbach	MSR 185
Burgberg	Trier	Olewig	MSR 373
Burg Bischof-steiner	Löf	Hatzenport	MSR 39
Burg Coreidel-steiner	Klotten	—	MSR 56
Burg Ehrenberg	Bad Rappenau	Heinsheim	B 79
Burggarten	Bad Neuenahr-Ahrweiler	Heimersheim	A 3 T
Burggarten	Bad Neuenahr-Ahrweiler	Heppingen	
Burggarten	Bockenheim an der Weinstraße	—	Rhpf 21
Burggarten	Dernau	—	A 31
Burggraf	Alf	—	MSR 130
Burggraf	Rauenberg	—	B 52
Burg Gutenfels	Kaub	—	Mrh 84
Burghalde	Weinstadt	Beutelsbach	W 192 T
	Weinstadt	Schnait	
Burg Hammerstein	**Bad Hönningen**	—	**Mrh 9—**
	Dattenberg	—	**23**
	Hammerstein	—	
	Ohlenberg	**Kasbach**	
	Leubsdorf	—	
	Leutesdorf	—	
	Linz	—	
	Rheinbrohl	—	
	Unkel	—	
Burg Hoheneck	Dietersheim	Walddachsbach	F 127 c T
	Ipsheim	—	
	Ipsheim	Kaubenheim	
Burg Katz	St. Goarshausen	—	Mrh 60
Burglay	Kröv	Kövenig	MSR 223
Burglay	Minheim	—	MSR 293
Burgley-Felsen	Zell	—	MSR 146
Burg Lichteneck	**Emmendingen**	**Mundingen**	**B 189—**
	Ettenheim	—	**198**
	Ettenheim	**Altdorf**	
	Herbolzheim	—	
	Herbolzheim	**Bleichheim**	
	Herbolzheim	**Broggingen**	
	Herbolzheim	**Tutschfelden**	
	Herbolzheim	**Wagenstadt**	
	Kenzingen	—	
	Kenzingen	**Bombach**	
	Kenzingen	**Hecklingen**	
	Kenzingen	**Nordweil**	
	Malterdingen	—	
	Ringsheim	—	
	Teningen	**Heimbach**	
	Teningen	**Köndringen**	
Burgmauer	Schweich	—	MSR 352
Burg Maus	St. Goarshausen	Wellmich und Ehrental	Mrh 58

Site	Town	Ortsteil	Region & Site No.
Burg Neuenfels	**Auggen**	—	**B 289—**
	Bad Bellingen	—	**310**
	Badenweiler	—	
	Badenweiler	**Lipburg**	
	Ballrechten-Dottingen	—	
	Müllheim	—	
	Müllheim	**Britzingen**	
	Müllheim	**Dattingen**	
	Müllheim	**Feldberg**	
	Müllheim	**Hügelheim**	
	Müllheim	**Niederweiler**	
	Müllheim	**Vögisheim**	
	Müllheim	**Zunzingen**	
	Neuenburg am Rhein	**Steinenstadt**	
	Schliengen	—	
	Schliengen	**Liel**	
	Schliengen	**Mauchen**	
	Schliengen	**Niedereggenen**	
	Schliengen	**Obereggenen**	
	Sulzburg	—	
	Sulzburg	**Laufen**	
Burg Ravensburger Dicker Franz	Sulzfeld	—	B 100
Burg Ravensburger Husarenkappe	Sulzfeld	—	B 98
Burg Ravensburger Löchle	Sulzfeld	—	B 99
Burg Rheinfels	**St. Goar**	—	**Mrh 50—**
	St. Goar	**Werlau**	**53**
Burg Rodenstein	**Bermersheim**	—	**Rhh 395—**
	Flörsheim-Dalsheim	**Dalsheim**	**405**
	Flörsheim-Dalsheim	**Niederflörsheim**	
	Mörstadt	—	
	Ober-Flörsheim	—	
Burgstall	Hagnau	—	B 340 T
	Immenstaad	—	
	Immenstaad	Kippenhausen	
	Markdorf	—	
Burgstall	Ingelfingen	Criesbach	W 11 T
	Niedernhall	—	
Burg Warsberg	Wincheringen	—	MSR 513
Burgweg	Bodenheim	—	Rhh 171
Burgweg	Großkarlbach	—	Rhpf 65
Burgweg	Kindenheim	—	Rhpf 27
Burgweg	Lambsheim	—	Rhpf 75 T
	Weisenheim am Sand	—	
Burgweg	Worms	Weinsheim	Rhh 431
Burgweg	**Geisenheim**	—	**Rhg 1—7**
	Lorch	—	**11—22, 24,**
	Lorch	**Lorchhausen**	**26, 27**
	Rüdesheim	—	
Burgweg	**Altenbamberg**	—	**N 261—**
	Bad Münster am Stein Ebernburg	**Ebernburg**	**323**
	Bad Münster am Stein Ebernburg	**Münster**	
	Duchroth	—	
	Niederhausen an der Nahe	—	
	Norheim	—	
	Oberhausen an der Nahe	—	
	Schloßböckelheim	—	
	Traisen	—	
	Waldböckelheim	—	
Burgweg	**Iphofen**	—	**F 110—**
	Iphofen	**Possenheim**	**122 a**
	Markt Einersheim	—	
	Willanzheim	—	
Burg Wildeck	Abstatt	—	W 55
Burg Windeck Kastanienhalde	Bühl	Neusatz	B 136
Burgwingert	Bruchsal	Helmsheim	B 69 T
	Bruchsal	Obergrombach	

Site	Town	Ortsteil	Region & Site No.
Calmont	Bremm	–	MSR 118 a
Calmont	Ediger-Eller	Eller	MSR 118
Carlsberg	Veldenz	–	MSR 266
Carlsfelsen	Palzem	–	MSR 517
Castellberg	Ballrechten-Dottingen	–	B 289
Castellberg	Vogtsburg im Kaiserstuhl	Achkarren	B 222 T
	Ihringen	–	
Centgericht	Heppenheim	–	HB 19
Centgrafenberg	Bürgstadt	–	F 20
Chorherrenhalde	Meersburg	–	B 331
Cyriakusberg	Sulzfeld	–	F 77

Site	Town	Ortsteil	Region & Site No.
Burg Zähringen	**Denzlingen**	**–**	**B 199–**
	Emmendingen	**Hochburg**	**209**
	Freiburg	**–**	
	Freiburg	**Lehen**	
	Glottertal	**–**	
	Gundelfingen Wiedtal	**–**	
	Heuweiler	**–**	
	Sexau	**–**	
	Waldkirch	**Buchholz**	
Busslay	Erden	–	MSR 203

Site	Town	Ortsteil	Region & Site No.
Dabug	Randersacker	–	F 68 T
	Randersacker	Lindelbach	
Dachgewann	Zornheim	–	Rhh 240
Dachs	Oberschwarzach	Wiebelsberg	F 138 a
Dachsberg	Brackenheim	–	W 86 T
	Brackenheim	Haberschlacht	
Dachsberg	Oestrich-Winkel	Winkel	Rhg 37
Dachsberg	Wiesbaden	Schierstein	Rhg 92
Dachsbuckel	Heidelberg	–	B 45
Dachsteiger	Öhringen	Michelbach am Wald	W 32 T
	Pfedelbach	Harsberg	
	Pfedelbach	Heuholz	
	Pfedelbach	Oberohrn	
	Pfedelbach	Untersteinbach	
Daubhaus	Appenheim	–	Rhh 42
Daubhaus	Bad Neuenahr-Ahrweiler	Ahrweiler	A 11
Daubhaus	Oppenheim	–	Rhh 268
Daubhaus	**Mainz**	**Kostheim**	**Rhg 98–114 a**
	Hochheim	**–**	
	Hochheim	**Massenheim**	
	Flörsheim	**–**	
	Flörsheim	**Wicker**	
Dautenpflänzer	Münster-Sarmsheim	–	N 7
Dechantsberg	Treis-Karden	Karden	MSR 49
Dellchen	Mandel	–	N 153
Dellchen	Norheim	–	N 287
Deuslay	Mesenich	–	MSR 98
Deutelsberg	**Eltville**	**Erbach**	**Rhg 48–55a, 58-67D**
	Eltville	**Hattenheim**	
Deutschherrenberg	Ober-Flörsheim	–	Rhh 396
Deutschherrenberg	Trier	–	MSR 376 T
	Trier	Olewig	
Deutschherrenberg	Zeltingen-Rachtig	–	MSR 229
Deutschherrenköpfchen	Trier	Olewig	MSR 375
Dezberg	Eberstadt	–	W 26 T
	Weinsberg	Gellmersbach	
Dickkopp	Ellerstadt	–	Rhpf 111
Dieblesberg	Löwenstein	Hößlinsülz	W 46 T
	Obersulm	Affaltrach	
	Obersulm	Willsbach	
Doctor	Bernkastel-Kues	Bernkastel	MSR 247
Doktor	Dexheim	–	Rhh 222
Doktor	Venningen	–	Rhpf 252
Doktorberg	Waldrach	–	MSR 398
Doktorgarten	Ihringen	Blankenhornsberg	B 224
Domberg	Sobernheim	–	N 205
Domblick	**Hohen-Sülzen**	**–**	**Rhh 406–414**
	Mölsheim	**–**	
	Monsheim	**–**	
	Monsheim	**Kriegsheim**	
	Offstein	**–**	
	Wachenheim	**–**	
Domdechaney	Hochheim	–	Rhg 107
Domgarten	Winningen	–	MSR 9
Domherr	Iphofen	–	F 128 b
Domherr	Piesport	–	MSR 300
Domherr	**Essenheim**	**–**	**Rhh 190–215**
	Gabsheim	**–**	
	Klein Winternheim	**–**	
	Ober-Olm	**–**	
	Saulheim	**–**	
	Schornsheim	**–**	
	Stadecken-Elsheim	**Elsheim**	
	Stadecken-Elsheim	**Stadecken**	
	Udenheim	**–**	

Site	Town	Ortsteil	Region & Site No.
Domherrenberg	Trier	Kürenz	MSR 363 T
	Trier	Ruwer	
Domherrenberg	Zell	–	MSR 150
Dominikanerberg	Kasel	–	MSR 404
Dominikanerberg	Morscheid	–	MSR 390
Domlay	Bad Neuenahr-Ahrweiler	Walporzheim	A 22
Domprobst	Graach	–	MSR 239
Doosberg	Oestrich-Winkel	Oestrich	Rhg 47
Dormenacker	Heidelberg	–	B 46 a
Dornpfad	Gabsheim	–	Rhh 213
Drachenbrunnen	Waldböckelheim	–	N 314
Drachenfels	Bad Honnef	Rhöndorf	Mrh 7 T
	Königswinter	–	
Drachenstein	Rüdesheim	–	Rhg 16
Drosselborn	Appenheim	–	Rhh 45
Dürrenberg	Schallstadt	Wolfenweiler	B 274
Dullgärten	Igel	–	MSR 496

Site	Town	Ortsteil	Region & Site No.
Ebenrain	Wertheim	Lindelbach	B 4
Eberfürst	Eberstadt	–	W 40 T
	Neustadt am Kocher	Cleversulzbach	
Ebersberg	Bodenheim	–	Rhh 172
Ebersberg	Nierstein	–	Rhh 251 T
	Nierstein	Schwabsburg	
Eck	Altenahr	–	A 42 T
	Altenahr	Reimerzhoven	
Eckartsberg	Breisach	–	B 256
Eckberg	Baden-Baden	–	B 116
Eckberg	Bötzingen	–	B 216
Eckweg	Heppenheim	–	HB 23
Edelberg	Enkirch	–	MSR 174
Edelberg	Lauschied	–	N 203
Edelberg	Meddersheim	–	N 202
Edelberg	Tauberbischofsheim	–	B 14
Edelfrau	Triefenstein	Homburg am Main	F 24
Edelmann	Mainz	Laubenheim	Rhh 165
Edelmann	Oestrich-Winkel	Mittelheim	Rhg 43
Edle Weingärten	Dittelsheim-Heßloch	Heßloch	Rhh 379
Eherieder Berg	Kitzingen	Eherieder Mühle	F 104
Ehrenberg	Gerlingen	–	W 134 a
Ehrenberg	Waldrach	–	MSR 397
Eichberg	Denzlingen	–	B 203 T
	Glottertal	–	
	Heuweiler	–	
Eichberg	Vogtsburg im Kaiserstuhl	Oberrotweil	B 228
Eichelberg	Fürfeld	–	Rhh 76
Eichelberg	Mühlacker	Lienzingen	W 105
Eichelberg	Neu-Bamberg	–	Rhh 76 a
Eichelberg	Ölbronn-Dürrn	Dürrn	B 114
Eichelberg	Sinsheim	Hilsbach	B 87
Eichert	Sasbach	Jechtingen	B 241
Eichwäldle	Sasbach	Obersasbach	B 142
Eilfingerberg	Maulbronn	–	W 102
Eilfingerberg Klosterstück	Maulbronn	–	W 103
Einsiedel	Klingenberg am Main	–	F 14 a
Eiserne Hand	Guntersblum	–	Rhh 287
Elfenley	Boppard	–	Mrh 48
Elisabethenberg	Hilzingen	–	B 345 T
	Singen (Hohentwiel)	–	
Elisenberg	Mülheim	–	MSR 259 T
	Veldenz	–	
Elkersberg	Alsenz	–	N 244
Ellergrub	Enkirch	–	MSR 181
Elster	Forst an der Weinstraße	–	Rhpf 150
Elzhofberg	Ediger-Eller	Ediger	MSR 109
Engelgrube	Neumagen-Dhron	Neumagen	MSR 310
Engelmannsberg	Eltville	Hattenheim	Rhg 54
Engelsberg	Endingen	–	B 252
Engelsberg	Herxheim bei Landau in der Pfalz	–	Rhpf 304
Engelsberg	Nackenheim	–	Rhh 244
Engelsberg	Offstein	–	Rhh 413
Engelsfelsen	Bühlertal	–	B 133
Engelstein	Boppard	Bopparder Hamm	Mrh 42 T
	Spay	–	
Engelströpfchen	Ediger-Eller	Eller	MSR 116

Site	Town	Ortsteil	Region & Site No.
Enggaß	Thörnich	–	MSR 330
Engweg	Niedernhall	–	W 12 T
	Weißbach	–	
Enselberg	Sasbach	Jechtingen	B 234 T
	Vogtsburg im Kaiserstuhl	Bischoffingen	
Erkenbrecht	Neustadt an der Weinstraße	–	Rhpf 201
Erkenbrecht	Geisenheim	–	
Erntebringer	**Geisenheim**	–	**Rhg 23, 25, 28–35, 37, 42–44, A**
	Geisenheim	**Johannisberg**	
	Oestrich-Winkel	**Mittelheim**	
	Oestrich-Winkel	**Winkel**	
Erzgrube	Bad Münster am Stein-Ebernburg	Ebernburg	N 267
Eselsberg	Flein	–	W 69
Eselsberg	Kitzingen	–	F 78 a
Eselsberg	Kolitzheim	Stammheim	F 101
Eselsbuckel	Niederotterbach	–	Rhpf 328
Eselshaut	Neustadt an der Weinstraße	Mußbach an der Weinstraße	Rhpf 189
Eselspfad	Appenheim	–	Rhh 44
Eselstreiber	Eckelsheim	–	Rhh 91
Esper	Kerzenheim	–	Rhpf 17
Euchariusberg	Konz	–	MSR 420
Euchariusberg	Konz	Krettnach	MSR 436 T
	Konz	Niedermennig	
	Konz	Obermennig	
Eulengrund	Zeil am Main	Schmachtenberg	F 129
Ewig Leben	**Randersacker**	–	**F 60–63**

Site	Town	Ortsteil	Region & Site No.
Fächern	Niederfell	–	MSR 19
Fässerlay	Boppard	Bopparder Hamm	Mrh 47
Fahrberg	Kobern-Gondorf	Kobern	MSR 12
Fahrberg	Lehmen	Moselsürsch	MSR 29 T
	Löf	Kattenes	
Falkenberg	Alsenz	–	N 246
Falkenberg	Dienheim	–	Rhh 275
Falkenberg	Donnersdorf	–	F 136 a
Falkenberg	Piesport	–	MSR 297
Falklay	Burg	–	MSR 172
Falklay	Reil	–	MSR 166
Fels	Freilaubersheim	–	Rhh 71
Fels	Konz	Könen	MSR 422
Fels	St. Katharinen	–	N 148
Felsen	Eppelsheim	–	Rhh 357
Felsenberg	Durchroth	–	N 316 a
Felsenberg	Eckenroth	–	N 25
Felsenberg	Oberhausen an der Nahe	–	N 316
Felsenberg	Schloßböckelheim	–	N 303
Felseneck	Bad Münster am Stein-Ebernburg	Münster am Stein	N 277
Felseneck	Gutenberg	–	N 98
Felseneck	Wallhausen	–	N 78
Felsengarten	Besigheim	–	W 121 T
	Bietigheim-Bissingen	Bissingen	
	Gemmrigheim	–	
	Hessigheim	–	
	Löchgau	–	
	Walheim	–	
Felsengarten	Überlingen	–	B 329
Felsenköpfchen	Bretzenheim	–	N 137
Felsenkopf	Trittenheim	–	MSR 316
Felsensteyer	Niederhausen an der Nahe	–	N 291
Felsentreppchen	Wittlich	–	MSR 215
Felslay	Mertesdorf	Orenzhof	MSR 411
Fettgarten	Zell	Merl	MSR 143
Feuer	Neustadt an der Weinstraße	Hambach an der Weinstraße	Rhpf 204
Feuerbach	Castell	–	F 109
Feuerberg	Bad Münster am Stein-Ebernburg	Ebernburg	N 270
Feuerberg	Duchroth	–	N 323
Feuerberg	Ediger-Eller	Ediger	MSR 111
Feuerberg	Ernst	–	MSR 66
Feuerberg	Feilbingert	–	N 237
Feuerberg	Flomborn	–	Rhh 355
Feuerberg	Vogtsburg im Kaiserstuhl	Burkheim	B 237
Feuerberg	**Bad Dürkheim**	**–**	**Rhpf 102–113**
	Bobenberg am Berg	**–**	
	Ellerstadt	**–**	
	Gönnheim	**–**	
	Kallstadt	**–**	
	Weisenheim am Berg	**–**	
Feuerley	Boppard	Bopparder Hamm	Mrh 44
Feuermännchen	Neuleiningen	–	Rhpf 42
Feuerstein	Röttingen	–	F 68 c
Feuersteinrossel	Oberndorf	–	N 249
Findling	Nierstein	–	Rhh 248
First	Eußenheim	–	F 38
First	Wertheim	Reichholzheim	B 6

Site	Town	Ortsteil	Region & Site No.
Fischer	Frickenhausen	–	F 70
Fischerpfad	Alsheim	–	Rhh 327
Flatterberg	Forchtenberg	–	W 14 T
	Forchtenberg	Ernsbach	
Försterlay	Lösnich	–	MSR 201
Fohrenberg	Ihringen	–	B 219
Fohrenberg	Meersburg	–	B 332 T
	Stetten	–	
Forst	Bad Kreuznach	–	N 112
Forst	Edesheim	–	Rhpf 245
Forstberg	Bad Neuenahr-Ahrweiler	Ahrweiler	A 12
Forstberg	Leutesdorf	–	Mrh 21
Forstberg	Oberstenfeld	–	W 61 T
	Oberstenfeld	Gronau	
Forstgrube	Illingen	–	W 108 T
	Vaihingen	Roßwag	
Forstweg	Walsheim	–	Rhpf 277
Frankenberg	Lauda-Königshofen	Lauda	B 19 T
	Lauda-Königshofen	Marbach	
Frankenhell	Damscheid	–	Mrh 66
Frankenstein	Freimersheim	–	Rhh 353
Frankenthal	Rüdesheim	Assmannshausen und Aulhausen	Rhg 8
Franzensberger	Offenburg	Fessenbach	B 169 T
	Ortenburg	–	
Franziskaner	Breisach	Oberrimsingen	B 263
Frauenberg	Bremm	–	MSR 121 T
	Neef	–	
Frauenberg	Flörsheim-Dalsheim	Niederflörsheim	Rhh 403
Frauenberg	Schliengen	Mauchen	B 307
Frauengarten	Wintersheim	–	Rhh 294
Frauenländchen	Kleinkarlbach	–	Rhpf 48
Freudental	Ortenberg	–	B 170
Freundstück	Forst an der Weinstraße	–	Rhpf 148
Fröhlich	Bechenheim	–	Rhh 337
Froher Weingarten	Niederheimbach	–	Mrh 108
Frohnwingert	Oberhausen	–	Rhpf 316
Frohwingert	St. Goar	–	Mrh 51 T
	St. Goar	Werlau	
Fronhof	Bad Dürkheim	–	Rhpf 125
Frühlingsplätzchen	Monzingen	–	N 190
Frühmess	Gleiszellen-Gleishorbach	–	Rhpf 319
Frühmesse	Alsheim	–	Rhh 328
Frühmeßler	Sinzheim	–	B 118
Fuchs	Saarburg	–	MSR 473
Fuchsberg	Geisenheim	–	Rhg 24
Fuchsen	Laubenheim	–	N 58
Fuchshöhle	Kobern-Gondorf	Gondorf	MSR 16
Fuchsloch	Gau-Odernheim	–	Rhh 314
Fuchsloch	Hochdorf-Assenheim	–	Rhpf 166 T
	Rödersheim-Gronau	–	
Fuchsloch	Wincheringen	–	MSR 514
Fuchsmantel	Bad Dürkheim	–	Rhpf 126 T
	Wachenheim	–	
Funkenberg	Müden	–	MSR 44
Fürstenberg	Dettelbach	Neusetz	F 86 T
	Volkach	Escherndorf	
	Volkach	Köhler	
Fürstenberg	Oberdiebach	–	Mrh 101 T
	Oberdiebach	Rheindiebach	

Site	Town	Ortsteil	Region & Site No.
Fürsteneck	**Appenweier**	**Nesselried**	**B 151—**
	Berghaupten	**—**	**181**
	Durbach	**—**	
	Gengenbach	**—**	
	Gengenbach	**Bermersbach**	
	Gengenbach	**Reichenbach**	
	Hohberg	**Diersburg**	
	Hohberg	**Hofweier**	
	Hohberg	**Niederschopfheim**	
	Lautenbach	**—**	
	Oberkirch	**—**	
	Oberkirch	**Bottenau**	
	Oberkirch	**Haslach**	
	Oberkirch	**Nußbach**	
	Oberkirch	**Ödsbach**	
	Oberkirch	**Ringelbach**	
	Oberkirch	**Stadelhofen**	
	Oberkirch	**Tiergarten**	
	Offenburg	**Fessenbach**	
	Offenburg	**Rammersweier**	
	Offenburg	**Zell-Weierbach**	
	Offenburg	**Zunsweier**	
	Ohlsbach	**—**	
	Ortenberg	**—**	
	Renchen	**Erlach**	
	Renchen	**Ulm**	
Fürstenlager	Bensheim	Auerbach	HB 11

Site	Town	Ortsteil	Region & Site No.
Gäns	Kobern-Gondorf	Gondorf	MSR 15
Gänsberg	Baden-Baden	Neuweier	B 127
Gärkammer	Bad Neuenahr-Ahrweiler	Walporzheim	A 19
Gärtchen	Piesport	Niederemmel	MSR 301
Gässel	Neustadt an der Weinstraße	Geinsheim	Rhpf 217
Gaisböhl	Ruppertsberg	—	Rhpf 174
Gaispfad	Traben-Trarbach	Traben	MSR 183
Galgenberg	Bad Kreuznach	Bosenheim	N 100
Galgenberg	Badenheim	—	Rhh 23
Galgenberg	Hackenheim	—	Rhh 68
Galgenberg	Kandel	—	Rhpf 332
Gartenlay	Leutesdorf	—	Mrh 22
Gastenklinge	Weinstadt	Strümpfelbach	W 182
Gedeonseck	**Brey**	**—**	**Mrh 39—48**
	Boppard	**Bopparder Hamm**	
	Rhens	**—**	
	Spay	**—**	
Gehrn	Eltville	Rauenthal	Rhg 78
Geiersberg	Armsheim	—	Rhh 112
Geiersberg	Dittelsheim-Heßloch	Dittelsheim	Rhh 377
Geierslay	Wintrich	—	MSR 292
Geiershöll	Klein-Winternheim	—	Rhh 190
Geisberg	Bockenau	—	N 175
Geisberg	Ockfen	—	MSR 468
Geisberg	Rivenich	—	MSR 319
Geisberg	Schoden	—	MSR 461
Geisberg	Zell	—	MSR 151
Geißberg	Heidesheim	—	Rhh 160
Geißberg	Wiesenbronn	—	F 115 a
Geißenkopf	Niedermoschel	—	N 233 T
	Obermoschel	—	
Geißkopf	Kirchheim an der Weinstraße	—	Rhpf 74
Geisterberg	Erbes-Büdesheim	—	Rhh 102 T
	Flonheim	—	
	Flonheim	Uffenhofen	
Gertrudenberg	Dattenberg	—	Mrh 13
Gerümpel	Friedelsheim	—	Rhpf 165
Gerümpel	Wachenheim	—	Rhpf 142
Gestühl	Sasbach	Jechtingen	B 242 T
	Sasbach	Leiselheim	
Gewürzgärtchen	Horrweiler	—	Rhh 14
Gewürzgarten	Hackenheim	—	Rhh 69
Geyersberg	Bechtheim	—	Rhh 390
Geyersberg	Gau-Weinheim	—	Rhh 127
Geyersberg	Sankt Johann	—	Rhh 56
Giebelhöll	Weinähr	—	Mrh 27
Gipfel	**Fellerich**	**—**	**MSR 500—**
	Nittel	**—**	**519**
	Nittel	**Köllig**	
	Nittel	**Rehlingen**	
	Oberbillig	**—**	
	Onsdorf	**—**	
	Palzem	**—**	
	Palzem	**Helfant und Esingen**	
	Palzem	**Kreuzweiler**	
	Palzem	**Wehr**	
	Temmels	**—**	
	Wasserliesch	**—**	
	Wellen	**—**	
	Wincheringen	**—**	

Site	Town	Ortsteil	Region & Site No.
Gips	Fellbach	–	W 145 T
	Stuttgart	Untertürkheim	
Glatzen	Dettelbach	Neuses am Berg	F 85
Glockenberg	Gau-Bischofsheim	–	Rhh 181
Glockenzehnt	Neustadt an der Weinstraße	Mußbach an der Weinstraße	Rhpf 190
Glöck	Nierstein	–	Rhh 263
Godelsberg	Aschaffenburg	–	F 6 a
Goetheberg	Obernhof	–	Mrh 28
Götterlay	Bruttig-Frankel	Bruttig	MSR 68
Götzenberg	Steinheim	Kleinbottwar	W 66
Götzenberg	Stuttgart	Uhlbach	W 149
Götzenborn	Wolfsheim	–	Rhh 57
Götzenfels	Bad Münster am Stein-Ebernburg	Ebernburg	N 272
Götzenfels	Norheim	–	N 282
Götzhalde	Neckarzimmern	–	B 76
Goldapfel	Worms	Abenheim	Rhh 415
Goldatzel	Geisenheim	Johannisberg	Rhg 34
Goldbächel	Wachenheim	–	Rhpf 141
Goldbäumchen	**Briedern**	**–**	**MSR 41–73**
	Bruttig-Fankel	**Bruttig**	
	Cochem	**–**	
	Cochem	**Sehl**	
	Ellenz-Poltersdorf	**–**	
	Ernst	**–**	
	Klotten	**–**	
	Moselkern	**–**	
	Müden	**–**	
	Pommern	**–**	
	Senheim	**Senhals**	
	Treis-Karden	**Karden**	
Goldberg	Alsheim	–	Rhh 291 T
	Eich	–	
	Mettenheim	–	
Goldberg	Bad Schönborn	Mingolsheim und Langenbrücken	B 60
Goldberg	Bissersheim	–	Rhpf 70
Goldberg	Bretzfeld	–	W 33 T
	Öhringen	Verrenberg	
	Pfedelbach	–	
	Pfedelbach	Windischenbach	
Goldberg	Esselborn	–	Rhh 354
Goldberg	Erpolzheim	–	Rhpf 80 T
	Freinsheim	–	
	Weisenheim am Sand	–	
Goldberg	Fellbach	–	W 154
Goldberg	Flörsheim-Dalsheim	Niederflörsheim	Rhh 402
Goldberg	Flomborn	–	Rhh 356
Goldberg	Gau-Algesheim	–	Rhh 39
Goldberg	Gensingen	–	Rhh 13
Goldberg	Grünstadt	Asselheim	Rhpf 34
Goldberg	Horrweiler	–	Rhh 13 a
Goldberg	Jugenheim	–	Rhh 131
Goldberg	Monzernheim	–	Rhh 381
Goldberg	Nieder-Olm	–	Rhh 218
Goldberg	Oestrich-Winkel	Mittelheim	Rhg 44
Goldberg	Osthofen	–	Rhh 394
Goldberg	Pommern	–	MSR 53
Goldberg	Sinsheim	Weiler	B 86
Goldberg	Udenheim	–	Rhh 207
Goldberg	Undenheim	–	Rhh 230
Goldberg	Vendersheim	–	Rhh 129
Goldberg	Wawern	–	MSR 458
Goldberg	Worms	Horchheim	Rhh 430

Site	Town	Ortsteil	Region & Site No.
Goldblume	Löf	–	MSR 35
Goldemund	Damscheid	–	Mrh 68
Goldemund	Oberwesel	–	Mrh 68 a
Goldene Luft	Nierstein	–	Rhh 259
Goldenes Horn	Siefersheim	–	Rhh 83
Goldfüßchen	Königswinter	Niederdollendorf	Mrh 4
Goldgrube	Bockenheim an der Weinstraße	–	Rhpf 24
Goldgrube	Köngernheim	–	Rhh 231
Goldgrube	Rüdesheim	–	N 163
Goldgrube	Staudernheim	–	N 211
Goldgrube	Traben-Trarbach	Wolf	MSR 197
Goldgrübchen	Mesenich	–	MSR 97
Goldkaul	Dernau	–	A 32
Goldkupp	Mehring	–	MSR 343
Goldlay	Niederfell	–	MSR 21
Goldlay	Oberfell	–	MSR 26
Goldlay	Pünderich	–	MSR 161
Goldlay	Reil	–	MSR 165
Goldloch	Dorsheim	–	N 48
Goldloch	Gauersheim	–	Rhpf 5
Goldstückchen	Armsheim	–	Rhh 111
Goldtröpfchen	Neumagen-Dhron	Dhron	MSR 298 T
	Piesport	–	
	Piesport	Niederemmel	
Goldwingert	Ürzig	–	MSR 208
Gollenberg	Bellheim	–	Rhpf 259 T
	Knittelsheim	–	
Gottesacker	Altdorf	–	Rhpf 250
Gottesacker	Müllheim	Hügelheim	B 296
Gottesacker	Walluf	Niederwalluf	Rhg 88 a
Gottesfuß	Wiltingen	–	MSR 450
Gottesgarten	Selzen	–	Rhh 233
Gotteshilfe	**Bechtheim**	**–**	**Rhh 389–394**
	Osthofen	**–**	
Gottesthal	**Oestrich-Winkel**	**Oestrich**	**Rhg 45–47, C**
Graben	Bernkastel-Kues	Bernkastel	MSR 246
Gräfenberg	Freckenfeld	–	Rhpf 331
	Kiedrich	–	Rhg 69
	Nordheim	–	W 87
Gräfenstein	Rottenberg	–	F 7 a
Graf Beyßel-Herrenberg	Bullay	–	MSR 134
Grafenberg	Brackenheim	Neipperg	W 81 T
	Eppingen	Kleingartach	
	Leingarten	Großgartach	
	Leingarten	Schluchtern	
	Nordheim	–	
	Schwaigern	–	
	Schwaigern	Niederhofen	
Grafenberg	Neumagen-Dhron	Dhron	MSR 304 T
	Piesport	–	
Grafenberg	Schorndorf	–	W 171
Grafenberg	Sponheim	–	N 170
Grafensprung	Gernsbach	Obertsrot	B 149
Grafenstück	**Bockenheim an der Weinstraße**	**–**	**Rhpf 18–32**
	Kindenheim	**–**	
	Obrigheim	**–**	
	Obrigheim	**Mühlheim**	

Site	Town	Ortsteil	Region & Site No.
Grafschaft	Alf	—	MSR 106–
	Beuren	—	138
	Bremm	—	
	Bullay	—	
	Ediger-Eller	Ediger	
	Neef	—	
	Nehren	—	
	St. Aldegrund	—	
	Zell	Merl	
Grafschafter Sonnenberg	Veldenz	—	MSR 265
Grain	Neustadt an der Weinstraße	—	Rhpf 200
Grainhübel	Deidesheim	—	Rhpf 155
Graukatz	Gaugrehweiler	—	N 259
Graukatz	Kalkofen	—	N 243
Graukatz	Münsterappel	—	N 259 b
Graukatz	Niederhausen an der Appel	—	N 259 c
Graukatz	Oberhausen an der Appel	—	N 259 a
Graukatz	Tiefenthal	—	Rhh 74
Graukatz	Winterborn	—	N 260
Greifenberg	Sulzheim	—	Rhh 116
Greiner	Korb	Kleinheppach	W 162
Greth	Treis-Karden	Treis	MSR 75
Großenberg	Gernsbach	Staufenberg	B 116 a
Großer Hengelberg	Neumagen-Dhron	Drohn	MSR 307
Großer Herrgott	Wintrich	—	MSR 289
Großlay	Müden	—	MSR 48
Großmulde	Waiblingen	Beinstein	W 164
Güldenkern	Aspach	Rietenau	W 133
Güldenmorgen	Dienheim	—	Rhh 268–
	Oppenheim	—	278
	Uelversheim	—	
Günterslay	Piesport	—	MSR 299 T
	Minheim	—	
Gützenberg	Königheim	Gissigheim	B 15 a
Guldenmorgen	Zornheim	—	Rhh 238
Guldenzoll	Heppenheim	—	HB 22
Gut Alsenhof	Lauf	—	B 139
Gutenberg	Oestrich-Winkel	Mittelheim	Rhg 36 T
	Oestrich-Winkel	Winkel	
Gutenhölle	Hüffelsheim	—	N 181
Gutental	Bad Kreuznach	—	N 120
Gutes Domtal	Dalheim	—	Rhh 216–
	Dexheim	—	243
	Friesenheim	—	
	Hahnheim	—	
	Köngernheim	—	
	Mommenheim	—	
	Nackenheim	—	
	Nieder-Olm	—	
	Nierstein	Schwabsburg	
	Selzen	—	
	Sörgenloch	—	
	Undenheim	—	
	Weinolsheim	—	
	Zornheim	—	
Gutleuthaus	Oppenheim	—	Rhh 274

Site	Town	Ortsteil	Region & Site No.
Guttenberg	Bad Bergzabern	—	Rhpf 323–
	Dierbach	—	333
	Dörrenbach	—	
	Freckenfeld	—	
	Kandel	—	
	Kapsweyer	—	
	Minfeld	—	
	Niederotterbach	—	
	Oberotterbach	—	
	Schweigen-Rechtenbach	—	
	Schweighofen	—	
	Steinfeld	—	
	Vollmersweiler	—	

Site	Town	Ortsteil	Region & Site No.
Haarberg-Katzensteg	Wöllstein	–	Rhh 86
Häder	Kernen Kernen	Rommelshausen Stetten	W 190 T
Hägenich	Wiesloch	–	B 51
Hähnchen	Bornheim	–	Rhh 104
Hämmchen	Brey	–	Mrh 41
Häs'chen	Neumagen-Dhron	Dhron	MSR 308
Hahn	Bacharach	–	Mrh 90
Hahn	Rehborn	–	N 219
Hahnen	Weisenheim am Sand	–	Rhpf 76
Hahnenberg	Zaberfeld Zaberfeld	Leonbrunn Ochsenburg	W 98 T
Hahnenkamm	Bubenheim	–	Rhpf 13
Hahnenschrittchen	Burg	–	MSR 170
Hahnhölle	Niedermoschel	–	N 235
Halde	Emmendingen	Hochburg	B 199
Halde	Illingen Mühlacker Mühlacker Vaihingen Vaihingen	– Mühlhausen Lomersheim – Roßwag	W 106 T
Halde	Stuttgart	Bad Cannstadt	W 141
Halde	Weisenheim am Sand	–	Rhpf 78
Halenberg	Monzingen	–	N 192
Haltnau	Meersburg	–	B 335 a
Hambusch	Bacharach	Steeg	Mrh 89
Hamm	Koblenz Koblenz	Lay Moselweiß	MSR 5 T
Hamm	Waldböckelheim	–	N 312
Hamm	Winningen	–	MSR 10
Hammerstein	Trier	Kürenz	MSR 367
Hansenberg	Geisenheim	Johannisberg	Rhg 33
Happenhalde	Weinstadt	Endersbach	W 181
Hardt	Weikersheim	–	W 3
Hardtberg	Dernau	–	A 28
Hardtberg	Rech	–	A 33
Harfenspiel	Bergtheim	–	F 69
Harstell	Großostheim	–	F 9
Harzberg	Großbottwar Großbottwar Großbottwar Oberstenfeld Oberstenfeld	– Hof und Lembach Winzerhausen – Gronau	W 63 T
Haselstaude	Kippenheim Lahr Mahlberg	– Sulz –	B 185 T
Haselstein	Winnenden Winnenden	– Breuningsweiler	W 172 T
Hasen	Eschbach	–	Rhpf 297
Hasenberg	Bad Ems Dausenau	– –	Mrh 25 T
Hasenberg	Endingen	Königschaffhausen	B 249
Hasenberg	Perl	–	MSR 525
Hasenbiß	Osthofen	–	Rhh 392
Hasenlauf	Bermersheim	–	Rhh 364
Hasenläufer	Burgen	–	MSR 274
Hasennestle	Adelshofen	Tauberzell	F 104 b
Hasensprung	Bechtheim	–	Rhh 383
Hasensprung	Dorn-Dürkheim	–	Rhh 331
Hasensprung	Ediger-Eller	Ediger	MSR 108
Hasensprung	Jugenheim	–	Rhh 132

Site	Town	Ortsteil	Region & Site No.
Hasensprung	Oestrich-Winkel	Winkel	Rhg 40
Hasensprung	Wallhausen	–	N 84
Hasensprung	Walzbachtal	Jöhlingen	B 104
Hasenzeile	Weisenheim am Sand	–	Rhpf 77
Hassel	Eltville	Hattenheim	Rhg 51
Haßmannsberg	Bockenheim an der Weinstraße	–	Rhpf 20
Haubenberg	Saulheim	–	Rhh 204
Heerkretz	Neu-Bamberg	–	Rhh 82
Heerkretz	Siefersheim	–	Rhh 82 a
Heide	Weyher in der Pfalz	–	Rhpf 241
Heidegarten	Edenkoben	–	Rhpf 231
Heilgraben	Dieblich	–	MSR 18
Heil	Frettenheim	–	Rhh 372
Heil	Wallertheim	–	Rhh 124
Heilgarten	Manubach	–	Mrh 99
Heiligborn	Albisheim	–	Rhpf 7
Heiligenbaum	Nierstein	–	Rhh 265
Heiligenberg	Eltville	Hattenheim	Rhg 52
Heiligenberg	Heidelberg	–	B 42
Heiligenberg	Illingen Sachsenheim	Schützingen Häfnerhaslach	W 115 T
Heiligenberg	Kolitzheim	Zeilitzheim	F 102 b
Heiligenberg	Krautheim Krautheim	– Klepsau	B 28 T
Heiligenberg	Maikammer	–	Rhpf 221
Heiligenberg	Weiler bei Monzingen	–	N 186
Heiligenborn	Albisheim	–	Rhpf 7
Heiligenborn	Serrig	–	MSR 490
Heiligenhäuschen	Jugenheim	–	Rhh 133
Heiligenhäuschen	Morscheid Riveris Waldrach	– – –	MSR 389 T
Heiligenhäuschen	Stetten	–	Rhpf 6
Heiligenhaus	Saulheim	–	Rhh 206
Heiligenkirche	Bockenheim an der Weinstraße	–	Rhpf 25
Heiligenpfad	Wendelsheim	–	Rhh 95
Heiligenstein	Baden-Baden	Neuweier	B 128
Heiligenstein	Mühlhausen	–	B 57
Heiligenstock	**Kiedrich**	**–**	**Rhg 66, 68–71**
Heiligenthal	**Großostheim**	**–**	**F 8–9**
Heiliger Blutberg	Alzey	Weinheim	Rhh 344
Heilige Tanne	Brensbach	–	HB 5 a
Heilighäuschen	Ingelheim	Groß-Winterheim	Rhh 143
Heiligkreuz	Bechtheim	–	Rhh 384
Heilig Kreuz	Edenkoben	–	Rhpf 229
Heilig Kreuz	Künzelsau	Belsenberg	W 9
Heimberg	Schloßböckelheim	–	N 306
Heißer Stein	Buchbrunn	–	F 80
Heisterberg	Königswinter	Niederdollendorf	Mrh 6
Heitersbrünnchen	Bodenheim	–	Rhh 173
Held	Bissersheim	–	Rhpf 67
Held	Kenn	–	MSR 353
Held	Köwerich	–	MSR 325
Held	Langsur	Mesenich	MSR 499
Held	Pölich	–	MSR 340
Helenenkloster	Mülheim	–	MSR 261
Hellenpfad	Braunweiler	–	N 146

Site	Town	Ortsteil	Region & Site No.
Hemsberg	Bensheim Bensheim Bensheim	– Zell Gronau	HB 16 T
Hendelberg	Eltville Oestrich-Winkel	Hattenheim Hallgarten	Rhg 59 T
Hengstberg	Desloch	–	N 224
Henkenberg	Vogtsburg im Kaiserstuhl	Oberrotweil	B 229
Heppenstein	Ockfen	–	MSR 464
Herbstthal	Karlstadt	Wiesenfeld	F 43 a
Hermannsberg	Niederhausen an der Nahe	–	N 300
Hermannshöhle	Niederhausen an der Nahe	–	N 299
Heroldsberg	Hammelburg	–	F 29
Herrenberg	Alf	–	MSR 129
Herrenberg	Bad Dürkheim	Ungstein	Rhpf 118
Herrenberg	Boos Staudernheim	– –	N 210 T
Herrenberg	Boxberg	Oberschüpf	B 27
Herrenberg	Briedern	–	MSR 92
Herrenberg	Cochen	–	MSR 59
Herrenberg	Dienheim Oppenheim	– –	Rhh 270 T
Herrenberg	Enkirch	–	MSR 178
Herrenberg	Erden	–	MSR 204
Herrenberg	Flörsheim Hochheim	– –	Rhg 110 T
Herrenberg	Heidelberg Leimen	– –	B 46 T
Herrenberg	Kasel	–	MSR 403
Herrenberg	Kenzingen	Nordweil	B 194
Herrenberg	Kesten	–	MSR 286
Herrenberg	Kleinkarlbach	–	Rhpf 46
Herrenberg	Konz Konz	Falkenstein Niedermennig	MSR 434 T
Herrenberg	Konz	Filzen	MSR 428
Herrenberg	Kröv	Kövenig	MSR 224
Herrenberg	Landau in der Pfalz	Nußdorf	Rhpf 274
Herrenberg	Lauda-Königshofen	Gerlachsheim	B 16
Herrenberg	Longuich Schweich	– –	MSR 350 T
Herrenberg	Mertesdorf Mertesdorf	– Maximin Grünhaus	MSR 415 T
Herrenberg	Minfeld	–	Rhpf 333
Herrenberg	Oberschwarzach Oberschwarzach Oberschwarzach	– Düttingsfeld Mutzenroth	F 138 T
Herrenberg	Ochsenfurt	Kleinochsenfurt	F 69 a
Herrenberg	Ockfen	–	MSR 463
Herrenberg	Rech	–	A 35
Herrenberg	Rehborn	–	N 217
Herrenberg	Schoden	–	MSR 460
Herrenberg	Serrig	–	MSR 493
Herrenberg	Trier	Kürenz	MSR 365
Herrenberg	Valwig	–	MSR 82
Herrenberg	**Dörscheid** **Kaub**	**–** **–**	**Mrh 78–85**
Herrenberg	**Castell**	**–**	**F 106–113**
Herrenberger	Ayl mit Ortsteil Biebelhausen		MSR 470
Herrenberger	Wawern	–	MSR 457

Site	Town	Ortsteil	Region & Site No.
Herrenbuck	Eichstetten	–	B 213
Herrenbuckel	Flemlingen	–	Rhpf 270
Herrengarten	Dienheim Oppenheim	– –	Rhh 282 T
Herrenletten	Neustadt an der Weinstraße	Haardt an der Weinstraße	Rhpf 197
Herrenmorgen	Bad Dürkheim	Leistadt	Rhpf 107
Herrenpfad	Heuchelheim-Klingen Göcklingen	– –	Rhpf 307 T
Herrenstück	Vogtsburg im Kaiserstuhl	Bickensohl	B 226
Herrentisch	Lahr	–	B 184
Herrenwingert	Steinfeld	–	Rhpf 327
Herrenzehntel	Weiler bei Monzingen	–	N 185
Herrgottsacker	Deidesheim	–	Rhpf 151
Herrgottsacker	Dirmstein	–	Rhpf 55
Herrgottsacker	Kleinkarlbach	–	Rhpf 45
Herrgottsblick	Zellertal	Harxheim	Rhpf 12
Herrgottshaus	Klein-Winternheim	–	Rhh 192
Herrgottsrock	Pellingen	–	MSR 445
Herrgottspfad	Gau-Odernheim	–	Rhh 312
Herrgottsweg	Albertshofen	–	F 81 a
Herrlesberg	Neckarwestheim	–	W 75
Herrlich	**Eschbach** **Göcklingen** **Herxheim bei Landau in der Pfalz** **Herxheimweyher** **Ilbesheim** **Impflingen** **Insheim** **Landau in der Pfalz** **Landau in der Pfalz** **Leinsweiler** **Rohrbach**	**–** **–** **–** **–** **–** **–** **–** **Mörzheim** **Wollmersheim** **–** **–**	**Rhpf 296–305**
Herrnberg	Gau-Bischofsheim	–	Rhh 184
Herrnberg	Flörsheim Hochheim	– –	Rhg 110 T
Herrnberg	Groß-Umstadt	–	HB 5
Herrnberg	Wiesbaden Wiesbaden	Frauenstein Schierstein	Rhg 96 T
Herrnwingert	Hemsbach Weinheim	– Sulzbach	B 30 T
Herrnwingert	Bensheim	Schönberg	HB 12
Herrschaftsberg	Ippesheim	–	F 126
Herrschaftsgarten	Hergenfeld	–	N 77
Herzchen	Briedel	–	MSR 158
Herzfeld	Bad Dürkheim	Leistadt	Rhpf 101
Herzlay	Bausendorf	Olkenbach	MSR 209
Herzog	Neustadt an der Weinstraße	Haardt an der Weinstraße	Rhpf 196
Herzogenberg	Fellbach Stuttgart Stuttgart	– Bad Cannstatt Untertürkheim	W 142 T
Herzogsberg	Binau Mosbach	– Diedesheim	B 73 T
Hessern	St. Goarshausen	–	Mrh 59
Heßweg	Odernheim am Glan	–	N 213

Site	Town	Ortsteil	Region & Site No.
Heuchelberg	**Brackenheim**	**—**	**W 78—98**
	Brackenheim	**Botenheim**	
	Brackenheim	**Dürrenzimmern**	
	Brackenheim	**Haberschlacht**	
	Brackenheim	**Hausen**	
	Brackenheim	**Meimsheim**	
	Brackenheim	**Neipperg**	
	Brackenheim	**Stockheim**	
	Cleebronn	**—**	
	Eppingen	**Kleingartach**	
	Güglingen	**—**	
	Güglingen	**Eibensbach**	
	Güglingen	**Frauenzimmern**	
	Heilbronn	**Klingenberg**	
	Leingarten	**Großgartach**	
	Leingarten	**Schluchtern**	
	Massenbachhausen	**—**	
	Nordheim	**—**	
	Nordheim	**Nordhausen**	
	Pfaffenhofen	**—**	
	Pfaffenhofen	**Weiler**	
	Schwaigern	**—**	
	Schwaigern	**Niederhofen**	
	Schwaigern	**Stetten**	
	Zaberfeld	**—**	
	Zaberfeld	**Leonbronn**	
	Zaberfeld	**Michelbach**	
	Zaberfeld	**Ochsenburg**	
Hexelberg	Eimsheim	—	Rhh 297
Hex vom Dasenstein	Kappelrodeck	—	B 146
Hildegardisberg	Bermersheim v. d. H.	—	Rhh 110
Hildegardis-brünnchen	Bingen	Bingerbrück	N 1
Himmelacker	Alzey	Dautenheim	Rhh 351
Himmelberg	Angelbachtal	Michelfeld	B 83
Himmelberg	Leinach	Oberleinach	F 49 T
	Leinach	Unterleinach	
Himmelchen	Bad Neuenahr-Ahrweiler	Walporzheim	A 17
Himmelgarten	Bad Kreuznach	Ippesheim	N 129
Himmelreich	Bretzfeld	Dimbach	W 37 T
	Bretzfeld	Siebeneich	
	Bretzfeld	Schwabbach	
	Bretzfeld	Waldbach	
	Langenbrettach	Langenbeutingen	
Himmelreich	Graach	—	MSR 240
Himmelreich	Gundelsheim	—	W 18
Himmelreich	Herxheim am Berg	—	Rhpf 89
Himmelreich	Sand am Main	Krum	F 134 a
Himmelreich	St. Aldegund	—	MSR 124
Himmelreich	Ubstadt-Weiher	Stettfeld	B 64 T
	Ubstadt-Weiher	Zeutern	
Himmelreich	Winnenden	Baach	W 173 T
	Winnenden	Hertmannsweiler	
Himmelreich	Zeltingen-Rachtig	—	MSR 230
Himmelsbühl	Sand am Main	—	F 133 b
Himmelthal	Guntersblum	—	Rhh 307
Hinkelstein	Bad Kreuznach	—	N 111
Hintere Klinge	Weinstadt	Endersbach	W 194
Hinterer Berg	Fellbach	—	W 156
Hinterhalde	Ammerbuch	Breitenholz	W 198 a
Hinterkirch	Rüdesheim	Assmannshausen und Aulhausen	Rhg 10
Hipperich	Guldental	Heddesheim und Waldhilbersheim	N 44
Hipping	Nierstein	—	Rhh 258
Hirschberg	Werbach	—	B 11
Hirschlay	Longuich	—	MSR 348
Hirtengarten	Oberbillig	—	MSR 502
Hirtenhain	Bad Kreuznach	Bosenheim	N 133

Site	Town	Ortsteil	Region & Site No.
Hitzlay	Kasel	—	MSR 406
Hoch	Bodenheim	—	Rhh 176
Hochbenn	Bad Dürkheim	—	Rhpf 123
Hochberg	Erlenbach am Main	—	F 13
Hochberg	Sasbach	Jechtingen	B 240
Hochberg	Klingenberg am Main	—	F 14
Hochberg	Worms	Herrnsheim	Rh 425 T
	Worms	Pfeddersheim	
Hochgericht	Altdorf	—	Rhpf 251
Hochgericht	Obrigheim	Mühlheim	Rhpf 29
Hochlay	Cochem	Sehl	MSR 62
Hochmess	**Bad Dürkheim**	**—**	**Rhpf 120—123**
	Ungstein	**—**	
Hockenmühle	Ockenheim	—	Rhh 32
Hochwart	Reichenau	—	B 328
Höchstes Kreuz	Feilbingert	—	N 241
Höhe	Landau in der Pfalz	Dammheim	Rhpf 282
Höhlchen	Dienheim	—	Rhh 277
Höhlchen	Bad Münster am Stein-Ebernburg	Münster	N 275
Höhlchen	Spabrücken	—	N 71
Höll	Ediger-Eller	Eller	MSR 115
Höll	Markt Eisenheim	Obereisenheim	F 100
Höllberg	Bensheim	Auerbach	HB 10
Höllberg	Buggingen	—	B 288
Höllberg	Müllheim	Hügelheim	B 295
Höllberg	Siefersheim	—	Rhh 84
Hölle	Alf	—	MSR 133
Hölle	Alsenz	—	N 247
Hölle	Alzey	Weinheim	Rhh 341
Hölle	Eckenroth	—	N 26
Hölle	Geisenheim	Johannisberg	Rhg 32
Hölle	Gleisweiler	—	Rhpf 269
Hölle	Guldental	Heddesheim und Waldhilbersheim	N 43
Hölle	Hammerstein	—	Mrh 19
Hölle	Hochheim	—	Rhg 106
Hölle	Nierstein	—	Rhh 255
Hölle	Pfaffen-Schwabenheim	—	Rhh 18
Hölle	Rümmelsheim	—	N 15
Hölle	Saulheim	—	Rhh 203
Hölle	Sprendlingen	—	Rhh 51
Hölle	Wiesbaden	Schierstein	Rhg 93
Hölle	Wiltingen	—	MSR 447
Hölle	Wöllstein	—	Rhh 89
Hölle	Wonsheim	—	Rhh 79
Höllenberg	Heidesheim	—	Rhh 162
Höllenberg	Nußbaum	—	N 194
Höllenberg	Rüdesheim	Assmannshausen	Rhg 9 T
	Rüdesheim	Aulhausen	
Höllenbrand	Bad Kreuznach	Bosenheim	N 99
	Bad Kreuznach	Planig	
Höllenbrand	Gundersheim	—	Rhh 359
Höllenpfad	Burgsponheim	—	N 173
Höllenpfad	Roxheim	—	N 159
Höllenpfad	Wallhausen	—	N 83

Site	Town	Ortsteil	Region & Site No.
Höllenpfad	**Battenberg**	–	**Rhpf 33–50**
	Grünstadt	–	
	Grünstadt	**Asselheim**	
	Grünstadt	**Sausenheim**	
	Kleinkarlbach	–	
	Mertesheim	–	
	Neuleiningen	–	
Höllenweg	Ingelheim	Groß-Winternheim	Rhh 154
Höllhagen	Ehrenkirchen	Kirchhofen	B 277
Hoeppslei	Serrig	–	MSR 491
Hörecker	Kanzem	–	MSR 431
Hörnchen	Laubenheim	–	N 60
Hörnchen	Wallhausen	–	N 79
Hörnle	Korb	–	W 161 T
	Waiblingen	–	
Hofberg	Bernkastel-Kues	Wehlen	MSR 234
Hofberg	Konz	Falkenstein	MSR 419
Hofberg	Möckmühl	–	W 16 T
	Neudenau	Siglingen	
	Widdern	–	
Hofberger	Neumagen-Dhron	Dhron	MSR 305 T
	Piesport	Niederemmel	
Hofgarten	Bad Kreuznach	–	N 107
Hofgut	Bretzenheim	–	N 139
Hofmeister	Hochheim	–	Rhg 103
Hofrat	**Albertshofen**	–	**F 73–81 a**
	Buchbrunn	–	
	Kitzingen	–	
	Kitzingen	**Eherieder Mühle**	
	Mainstockheim	–	
	Marktbreit	–	
	Marktsteft	–	
	Segnitz	–	
	Sulzfeld	–	
Hofsteige	Metzingen	–	W 196 T
	Metzingen	Neuhausen	
Hofstück	Mainstockheim	–	F 81
Hofstück	**Deidesheim**	–	**Rhpf 160–180**
	Ellerstadt	–	
	Friedelsheim	–	
	Gönnheim	–	
	Hochdorf-Assenheim	–	
	Meckenheim	–	
	Niederkirchen	–	
	Rödersheim-Gronau	–	
	Ruppertsberg	–	
Hohberg	Haßmersheim	Neckarmühlbach	B 78
Hohberg	Lörzweiler	–	Rhh 189
Hohberg	Weinolsheim	–	Rhh 226
Hoheburg	Ruppertsberg	–	Rhpf 173
Hohenberg	Pfaffenhofen	–	W 97 T
	Pfaffenhofen	Weiler	
	Zaberfeld	–	
	Zaberfeld	Michelbach	
Hohenberg	**Eisingen**	–	**B 102–115**
	Kämpfelbach	**Bilfingen**	
	Kämpfelbach	**Ersingen**	
	Karlsruhe	**Durlach**	
	Karlsruhe	**Grötzingen**	
	Karlsruhe	**Hohenwettersbach**	
	Keltern	**Dietlingen**	
	Keltern	**Ellmendingen**	
	Ölbronn-Dürrn	**Dürrn**	
	Pfinztal	**Berghausen**	
	Pfinztal	**Söllingen**	
	Pfinztal	**Wöschbach**	
	Walzbachtal	**Jöhlingen**	
	Weingarten	–	
Hohenbühl	Seinsheim	–	F 124
Hohenlandsberg	Weigenheim	–	F 127 b T
	Weigenheim	Reusch	

Site	Town	Ortsteil	Region & Site No.
Hohenmorgen	Deidesheim	–	Rhpf 156
Hohenneuffen	**Beuren**	–	**W 196–197**
	Frickenhausen	–	
	Frickenhausen	**Linsenhofen**	
	Kohlberg	–	
	Metzingen	–	
	Metzingen	**Neuhausen**	
	Neuffen	–	
	Neuffen	**Kappishäusern**	
	Weilheim	–	
Hohenrain	Eltville	Erbach	Rhg 65
Hohenrain	Knöringen	–	Rhpf 281
Hoher Berg	Ingelfingen	–	W 8 T
	Ingelfingen	Criesbach	
	Künzelsau	–	
	Niedernhall	–	
Hoher Hergott	Külsheim	–	B 10
Hohnart	Castell	–	F 107
Holzenberg	Winnenden	–	W 165 T
	Winnenden	Breuningsweiler	
Homberg	Albig	–	Rhh 323
Homberg	Bechtolsheim	–	Rhh 310
Homberg	Wiesbaden	Frauenstein	Rhg 95
Homburg	Gössenheim	–	F 33
Honigberg	Bad Kreuznach	Winzenheim	N 126
Honigberg	Biebelsheim	–	Rhh 16
Honigberg	Bingen	Dromersheim	Rhh 27
Honigberg	Bubenheim	–	Rhh 137
Honigberg	Dorsheim	–	N 47
Honigberg	Eltville	Erbach	Rhg 63
Honigberg	Guldental	Heddesheim und Waldhilbersheim	N 39
Honigberg	Ludwigshöhe	–	Rhh 283
Honigberg	Maring-Noviand	–	MSR 267
Honigberg	Nieder-Hilbersheim	–	Rhh 46
Honigberg	Sprendlingen	–	Rhh 50
Honigberg	Sulzheim	–	Rhh 117
Honigberg	**Geisenheim**	**Johannisberg**	**Rhg 29, 36 38–40, 42, 43, A, B**
	Oestrich-Winkel	**Mittelheim**	
	Oestrich-Winkel	**Winkel**	
Honigberg	**Dettelbach**	–	**F 82–84**
	Dettelbach	**Bibergau**	
	Dettelbach	**Brück**	
	Dettelbach	**Schnepfenbach**	
Honigsack	Grünstadt	Sausenheim	Rhpf 40
Honigsack	Herxheim am Berg	–	Rhpf 90
Honigsäckel	**Bad Dürkheim**	**Ungstein**	**Rhpf 117–119**
Horn	Ingelheim	Groß-Winternheim	Rhh 151
Horn	Kallstadt	–	Rhpf 116
Horn	Wachenheim	–	Rhh 409
Hornberg	Framersheim	–	Rhh 318
Hornfelsen	Grenzach-Whylen	Grenzach	B 326
Hubacker	Flörsheim-Dalsheim	Dalsheim	Rhh 398
Hubberg	Weinheim	–	B 31
Hubertusberg	Nittel	–	MSR 508 T
	Onsdorf	–	
Hubertusberg	Waldrach	–	MSR 392
Hubertusborn	Koblenz	Lay	MSR 6
Hubertuslay	Bausendorf	Olkenbach	MSR 210
Hubertuslay	Kinheim	–	MSR 200
Hühnerberg	Traben-Trarbach	Trarbach	MSR 188
Hüßberg	Sugenheim	Neundorf	F 128 c
Hütt	Grünstadt	Sausenheim	Rhpf 39

Site	Town	Ortsteil	Region & Site No.
Hüttberg	Mainz	Ebersheim	Rhh 168
Hütte	Konz	Oberemmel	MSR 440
Hüttenberg	Roxheim	–	N 157
Hütte-Terrassen	Bornheim	–	Rhh 105
Hummelberg	Herbolzheim Kenzingen	Wagenstadt –	B 192 T
Hummelberg	Östringen	–	B 62
Hundert	Oberwesel	Langscheid	Mrh 76
Hundertgulden	Appenheim	–	Rhh 43
Hundsberg	Obersulm Obersulm	Eichelberg Weiler	W 49 T
Hundskopf	Albis	–	Rhh 322
Hungerberg	Winterbach	–	W 170
Hungerbiene	Gundheim	–	Rhh 363
Hungriger Wolf	Bad Kreuznach	–	N 124
Hunnenstein	Alken	–	MSR 33
Hunolsteiner	Merxheim	–	N 189

Site	Town	Ortsteil	Region & Site No.
Idig	Neustadt an der Weinstraße	Königsbach an der Weinstraße	Rhpf 182
Im Felseneck	Bockenau	–	N 178
Im Heubusch	Morschheim	–	Rhpf 1
Immengarten	Maikammer	–	Rhpf 22O
Im Neuberg	Bockenau	–	N 177
Im Röttgen	Koblenz Winningen	Güls –	MSR 4 T
Im Sonnenschein	Siebeldingen	–	Rhpf 291
Im Stein	Karlstadt	–	F 41
In den Felsen	Schloßböckelheim	–	N 305
In den Layfelsen	Hammerstein	–	Mrh 18
In den siebzehn Morgen	Bad Kreuznach	Winzenheim	N 125
Inkelhöll	Lettweiler	–	N 227
Innere Leiste	Würzburg	–	F 57
Insel Heylesen Werth	Bacharach	–	Mrh 91

Site	Town	Ortsteil	Region & Site No.
Jesuitenberg	Elsenfeld	Rück	F 12
Jesuitenberg	Wawern	—	MSR 456
Jesuitengarten	Bad Neuenahr-Ahrweiler	Marienthal	A 24
Jesuitengarten	Forst an der Weinstraße	—	Rhpf 146
Jesuitengarten	Neustadt an der Weinstraße	Königsbach an der Weinstraße	Rhpf 183
Jesuitengarten	Oestrich-Winkel	Winkel	Rhg 39
Jesuitengarten	Pellingen	—	MSR 444
Jesuitengarten	Waldrach	—	MSR 401
Jesuitenhofgarten	Dirmstein	—	Rhpf 56
Jesuitenschloß	Freiburg Merzhausen	— —	B 266 T
Jesuitenwingert	Trier	Olewig	MSR 374
Johannesberg	Sobernheim Waldböckelheim	Steinhard —	N 207 T
Johannisberg	Aspisheim	—	Rhh 25
Johannisberg	Dreis	—	MSR 22O
Johannisberg	Elsenfeld	Rück	F 11
Johannisberg	Franzenheim	—	MSR 385
Johannisberg	Gau-Algesheim	—	Rhh 38
Johannisberg	Mainz	Laubenheim	Rhh 164
Johannisberg	Mertesdorf	—	MSR 412
Johannisberg	Rümmelsheim mit Ortsteil Burg Layen	—	N 17
Johannisberg	Thüngersheim	—	F 45
Johannisberg	Wallhausen	—	N 81
Johannisberg	Zotzenheim	—	Rhh 21
Johannisbrünnchen	Bernkastel-Kues	Bernkastel	MSR 251
Johanniskirchel	Neustadt an der Weinstraße	Diedesfeld an der Weinstraße	Rhpf 207
Johannisweg	Wallhausen	—	N 81 a
Johannitergarten	Neustadt an der Weinstraße	Mußbach an der Weinstraße	Rhpf 194
Josefsberg	Wertheim Wertheim	Bronnbach Reicholzheim	B 3 T
Josephsberg	Durbach	—	B 158
Josephshöfer	Graach	—	MSR 242
Judenkirch	Wiesbaden	Dotzheim	Rhg 97
Juffer	Brauneberg	—	MSR 277
Juffermauer	Treis-Karden	Karden	MSR 51
Juffer Sonnenuhr	Brauneberg	—	MSR 278
Julius-Echter-Berg	Iphofen	—	F 120
Jungbrunnen	Dorsheim	—	N 52
Jungfer	Eltville Oestrich-Winkel	Hattenheim Hallgarten	Rhg 58 T
Jungfer	Lauffen	—	W 74
Jungfernberg	Waldrach	—	MSR 394
Jungfernstieg	Meersburg	—	B 334
Junker	Bad Kreuznach	Ippesheim	N 130
Junker	Laubenheim	—	N 59
Jupiterberg	Brackenheim	Hausen	W 90

Site	Town	Ortsteil	Region & Site No.
Kachelberg	Ensheim	—	Rhh 114 a
Kachelberg	Wörrstadt	Rommersheim	Rhh 114
Käppele	Weinstadt	Beutelsbach	W 179
Käsberg	Hessigheim Mundelsheim	— —	W 122 T
Käsleberg	Vogtsburg im Kaiserstuhl	Oberrotweil	B 227
Kätzchen	Osann-Monzel	Monzel	MSR 282
Kafels	Norheim	—	N 289
Kaffelstein	Kreuzwertheim	—	F 22
Kahlberg	Hirschberg	Leutershausen	B 35
Kahlenberg	Bad Kreuznach	—	N 108
Kahlenberg	Feilbingert	—	N 240
Kahlenberg	Ottersheim	—	Rhpf 258
Kahllay	Niederfell	—	MSR 20
Kailberg	Lauda-Königshofen	Sachsenflur	B 24
Kaiserberg	Duchroth	—	N 321
Kaiserberg	Ettenheim Ettenheim Herbolzheim Herbolzheim Herbolzheim Ringsheim	— Altdorf — Bleichheim Broggingen Tutschfelden —	B 189 T
Kaiserberg	Göcklingen	—	Rhpf 298
Kaiserberg	Güglingen Güglingen	— Frauenzimmern	W 95 T
Kaiserberg	Landau in der Pfalz	Nußdorf	Rhpf 275
Kaisergarten	Gau-Weinheim	—	Rhh 126
Kaiser Karl	Kitzingen Kitzingen	Eherieder Mühle Repperndorf	F 79 T
Kaiserpfalz	**Bubenheim Engelstadt Heidesheim Ingelheim Ingelheim Jugenheim Schwabenheim Wackernheim**	**— — — — Groß-Winternheim — — —**	**Rhh 130–162**
Kaiserstuhl	Neustadt an der Weinstraße	Hambach an der Weinstraße	Rhpf 202
Kaiser Wilhelm	Winterhausen	—	F 69 b
Kalb	Iphofen	—	F 121
Kalbenstein	Karlstadt	Gambach	F 35
Kalbspflicht	Eltville	—	Rhg 76
Kallenberg	Bubenheim	—	Rhh 136
Kallmuth	Triefenstein	Homburg am Main	F 23
Kalkberg	Neustadt an der Weinstraße	Duttweiler	Rhpf 216
Kalkgasse	Bensheim	—	HB 13
Kalkgrube	Frankenweiler	—	Rhpf 286
Kalkofen	Bad Dürkheim	Leistadt	Rhpf 99
Kalkofen	Deidesheim	—	Rhpf 154
Kammer	Brauneberg	—	MSR 279
Kanzel	Obernbreit	—	F 104 a
Kapellberg	Laumersheim	—	Rhpf 62
Kapellchen	Minheim	—	MSR 294
Kapelle	Bodenheim	—	Rhh 177
Kapelle	Gau-Bickelheim	—	Rhh 122
Kapelle	Hainfeld	—	Rhpf 243
Kapellenberg	Alf	—	MSR 127
Kapellenberg	Alzey Alzey	— Weinheim	Rhh 343 T
Kapellenberg	Bad Bellingen Bad Bellingen	Bamlach Rheinweiler	B 316 T

Site	Town	Ortsteil	Region & Site No.
Kapellenberg	Bad Neuenahr-Ahrweiler	Ehlingen	A 1
Kapellenberg	Bingen	Kempten	Rhh 3
Kapellenberg	Briedern	–	MSR 93
Kapellenberg	Bruttig-Fankel Bruttig-Fankel	Bruttig Fankel	MSR 85 T
Kapellenberg	Durbach	–	B 161
Kapellenberg	Eibelstadt	–	F 66
Kapellenberg	Freiburg	Munzingen	B 264
Kapellenberg	Frickenhausen	–	F 71
Kapellenberg	Fürfeld	–	Rhh 75
Kapellenberg	Klettgau Klettgau	Erzingen Rechberg	B 347 T
Kapellenberg	Lorch	–	Rhg 4
Kapellenberg	Münster-Sarmsheim	–	N 6
Kapellenberg	Neustadt an der Weinstraße	Gimmeldingen an der Weinstraße	Rhpf 186
Kapellenberg	Nittel	Rehlingen	MSR 512
Kapellenberg	Ober-Olm	–	Rhh 193
Kapellenberg	Odernheim am Glan	–	N 216
Kapellenberg	Östringen	Eichelberg	B 88
Kapellenberg	Palzem	Helfant und Esingen	MSR 516
Kapellenberg	Rottenburg	Wurmlingen und Wendelsheim	W 199
Kapellenberg	Treis-Karden	Treis	MSR 74
Kapellenberg	Volkach	Gaibach	F 97
Kapellenberg	**Ebelsbach Knetzgau Sand am Main Zeil am Main Zeil am Main**	**Steinbach Oberschwappach – Schmachtenberg Ziegelanger**	**F 129–133**
Kapellengarten	Dackenheim	–	Rhpf 84
Kapellenpfad	Bad Kreuznach	–	N 115
Kapellenstück	Worms	Abenheim	Rhh 417
Kapplay	Ediger-Eller	Eller	MSR 113
Kapuzinerbuck	Wittnau	–	B 267
Kardinalsberg	Bernkastel-Kues	Kues	MSR 255
Karlsberg	Konz	Oberemmel	MSR 438
Karlsberg	Weikersheim	–	W 5
Karlskopf	Bad Neuenahr-Ahrweiler	Bachem	A 8
Karthäuser	Laubenheim	–	N 56
Karthäuser	Volkach	Astheim	F 93
Karthäuserhofberg	Trier	Eitelsbach	MSR 357
Karthäuser Klosterberg	Konz	–	MSR 416
Kasselberg	Durbach	–	B 163
Kastanienbusch	Birkweiler	–	Rhpf 293
Kastaniengarten	Edenkoben	–	Rhpf 236
Kastell	Boos Waldböckelheim	– –	N 208 T
Katergrube	Weinsheim	–	N 165
Katzebuckel	Mörstadt	–	Rhh 405
Katzenbeißer	Lauffen	–	W 72
Katzenberg	Weingarten	–	B 102
Katzenhölle	Bad Kreuznach	Planig	N 132
Katzenkopf	Alf	–	MSR 128
Katzenkopf	Sommerach	–	F 89
Katzenöhrle	Brackenheim	Meimsheim	W 91
Katzenstein	Kindenheim	–	Rhpf 26
Kaulenberg	Auen	–	N 182

Site	Town	Ortsteil	Region & Site No.
Kauzenberg in den Mauern	Bad Kreuznach	–	N 105
Kauzenberg-Oranienberg	Bad Kreuznach	–	N 103
Kauzenberg-Rosenhügel	Bad Kreuznach	–	N 104
Kayberg	Erlenbach-Binswangen Erlenbach-Binswangen Oedheim	Binswangen Erlenbach –	W 22 T
Kehr	Weinolsheim	–	Rhh 227
Kehrberg	Kobern-Gondorf	Gondorf	MSR 17
Kehrenberg	Altenbamberg	–	N 263
Kehrnagel	Kasel	–	MSR 405
Kellerberg	Weinsheim	–	N 166
Kellersberg	Gau-Bischofsheim	–	Rhh 183
Kelter	Himmelstadt	–	F 42
Kelterberg	Aspach Kirchberg Marbach/Neckar	Kleinaspach – Rielingshausen	W 131 T
Kemelrain	Wertheim Wertheim	Höhefeld Reichholzheim	B 8 T
Kertz	Niederhausen an der Nahe	–	N 297
Kestellberg	Gernsbach Weisenbach	Hilpertsau –	B 150 T
Keulebuckel	Keltern Keltern	Dietlingen Ellmendingen	B 115 T
Kickelskopf	Traisen	–	N 279
Kieselberg	Biebelsheim	–	Rhh 17
Kieselberg	Bobenheim am Berg	–	Rhpf 103
Kieselberg	Deidesheim	–	Rhpf 153
Kieselberg	Erpolzheim	–	Rhpf 81
Kieselberg	Kleinkarlbach	–	Rhpf 49
Kieselberg	Oberhausen an der Nahe	–	N 317
Kiliansberg	Großlangheim	–	F 116
Kilzberg	Geisenheim Geisenheim	– Johannisberg	Rhg 25 T
Kinnleitenberg	Königsberg in Bayern	Unfinden	F 134 b
Kinzigtäler	Berghaupten Gengenbach Gengenbach Gengenbach Hohberg Hohberg Hohberg Offenburg Ohlsbach	– – Bermersbach Reichenbach Diersburg Hofweiler Niederschopfheim Zunsweier –	B 173 T
Kirchberg	Albersweiler	–	Rhpf 289
Kirchberg	Badenweiler	Lipburg	B 303
Kirchberg	Barbelroth	–	Rhpf 315
Kirchberg	Bensheim	–	HB 14
Kirchberg	Bingen	Kempten	Rhh 2
Kirchberg	Bönnigheim Bönnigheim Freudental Kirchheim Sachsenheim Sachsenheim	– Hohenstein – – Hohenhaslach Kleinsachsenheim	W 114 T
Kirchberg	Burgen	–	MSR 273
Kirchberg	Castell	–	F 108
Kirchberg	Eckelsheim	–	Rhh 90
Kirchberg	Edenkoben	–	Rhpf 232

Site	Town	Ortsteil	Region & Site No.
Kirchberg	Efringen-Kirchen	–	B 319 T
	Efringen-Kirchen	Huttingen	
	Efringen-Kirchen	Istein	
Kirchberg	Ehrenkirchen	Kirchhofen	B 278
Kirchberg	Eßlingen	–	W 152 T
	Stuttgart	Obertürkheim	
Kirchberg	Ettenheim	Münchweier	B 186 T
	Ettenheim	Wallburg	
	Kippenheim	Schmieheim	
Kirchberg	Freilaubersheim	–	Rhh 70 a
Kirchberg	Gabsheim	–	Rhh 214
Kirchberg	Gleiszellen-Gleishorbach	–	Rhpf 318
Kirchberg	Gottenheim	–	B 257
Kirchberg	Groß- und Kleinfischlingen	–	Rhpf 253
Kirchberg	Hackenheim	–	Rhh 70
Kirchberg	Konz	Könen	MSR 423
Kirchberg	Königheim	–	B 15
Kirchberg	Kraichtal	Oberöwisheim, Unteröwisheim	B 66
Kirchberg	Lauda-Königshofen	Beckstein	B 21 T
	Lauda-Königshofen	Königshofen	
Kirchberg	Löf	Hatzenport	MSR 38
Kirchberg	Moselkern	–	MSR 42
Kirchberg	Neustadt an der Weinstraße	Hambach an der Weinstraße	Rhpf 203
Kirchberg	Osthofen	–	Rhh 388
Kirchberg	St. Martin	–	Rhpf 225
Kirchberg	Udenheim	–	Rhh 209
Kirchberg	Uettingen	–	F 52 b
Kirchberg	Vaihingen	Riet	W 114 a
Kirchberg	Vogtsburg im Kaiserstuhl	Schelingen	B 233
Kirchberg	Vogtsburg im Kaiserstuhl	Oberrotweil	B 230
Kirchberg	Veldenz	–	MSR 263
Kirchberg	Waldböckelheim	–	N 310
Kirchberg	Würzburg	Heidingsfeld	F 59
Kirchberg	**Dettelbach**	**Neuses am Berg**	**F 85–102, 104, 104 a**
	Dettelbach	**Neusetz**	
	Fahr	**–**	
	Frankenwinheim	**–**	
	Kolitzheim	**Lindach**	
	Kolitzheim	**Stammheim**	
	Kolitzheim	**Zeilitzheim**	
	Markt Eisenheim	**Obereisenheim**	
	Markt Eisenheim	**Untereisenheim**	
	Neusetz	**–**	
	Nordheim	**–**	
	Schwarzach	**Schwarzenau**	
	Sommerach	**–**	
	Volkach	**–**	
	Volkach	**Astheim**	
	Volkach	**Escherndorf**	
	Volkach	**Fahr**	
	Volkach	**Gaibach**	
	Volkach	**Hallburg**	
	Volkach	**Köhler**	
	Volkach	**Krautheim**	
	Volkach	**Obervolkach**	
	Volkach	**Rimbach**	
	Volkach	**Vogelsburg**	
	Waigolshausen	**Hergolshausen**	
	Waigolshausen	**Theilheim**	
	Wipfeld	**–**	
Kirchenpfad	Rüdesheim	–	Rhg 17
Kirchenstück	Alzey	Weinheim	Rhh 342
Kirchenstück	Bad Dürkheim	Leistadt	Rhpf 100
Kirchenstück	Bornheim	–	Rhh 106
Kirchenstück	Ellerstadt	–	Rhpf 160
Kirchenstück	Forst an der Weinstraße	–	Rhpf 147
Kirchenstück	Herxheim am Berg	–	Rhpf 88
Kirchenstück	Hainfeld	–	Rhpf 244
Kirchenstück	Hochheim	–	Rhg 108
Kirchenstück	Ingelheim	Groß-Winternheim	Rhh 149
Kirchenstück	Kallstadt	–	Rhpf 115
Kirchenstück	Landau in der Pfalz	Nußdorf	Rhpf 276
Kirchenstück	Maikammer	–	Rhpf 219
Kirchenstück	Mainz	Hechtsheim	Rhh 163
Kirchenweinberg	**Flein**	**–**	**W 67–77**
	Heilbronn	**–**	
	Ilsfeld	**Schozach**	
	Lauffen	**–**	
	Neckarwestheim	**–**	
	Talheim	**–**	
	Untergruppenbach	**–**	
Kirchgärtchen	Welgesheim	–	Rhh 15
Kirchhalde	Uhldingen-Mühlhof	Oberuhldingen	B 330
Kirchhöh	Dierbach	–	Rhpf 329
Kirchlay	Ernst	–	MSR 67
Kirchlay	Kröv	–	MSR 227
Kirchlay	Osann-Monzel	Osann	MSR 283
Kirchplatte	Nierstein	–	Rhh 249
Kirchspiel	Westhofen	–	Rhh 370
Kirchstück	Hohen-Sülzen	–	Rhh 412
Kirchtürmchen	Bad Neuenahr-Ahrweiler	Neuenahr	A 7
Kirchweinberg	Haßmersheim	–	B 77 T
	Neckarzimmern	–	
Kirchweingarten	Bullay	–	MSR 137
Kirschgarten	Erpolzheim	–	Rhpf 94
Kirschgarten	Laumersheim	–	Rhpf 64
Kirschheck	Norheim	–	N 286
Kirschheck	Wallhausen	–	N 82
Kirschwingert	Neu-Bamberg	–	Rhh 81
Kläuserweg	Geisenheim	–	Rhg 23 T
	Geisenheim	Johannisberg	
Klamm	Niederhausen an der Nahe	–	N 298
Klaus	Geisenheim	–	Rhg 29 T
	Geisenheim	Johannisberg	
	Oestrich-Winkel	Winkel	
Klausenberg	Worms	Abenheim	Rhh 416
Klepberg	Eisingen	–	B 112 T
	Kämpfelbach	Bilfingen	
	Kämpfelbach	Ersingen	
	Keltern	Dietlingen	
Kletterberg	Angelbachtal	Eichtersheim	B 82
Kletterberg	Neu-Bamberg	–	Rhh 80
Klingle	Remshalden	Grunbach	W 184
Kloppberg	Dittelsheim-Heßloch	Dittelsheim	Rhh 376
Kloppenberg	Mommenheim	–	Rhh 243
Klosterberg	Bechtolsheim	–	Rhh 311
Klosterberg	Bengel	Springiersbach	MSR 208 a
Klosterberg	Bernkastel-Kues	Wehlen	MSR 237
Klosterberg	Bruchsal	–	B 68
Klosterberg	Kiedrich	–	Rhg 68
Klosterberg	Lehmen	–	MSR 23
Klosterberg	Mainz	Laubenheim	Rhh 166
Klosterberg	Maring-Noviand	–	MSR 268
Klosterberg	Nieder-Olm	–	Rhh 216

Site	Town	Ortsteil	Region & Site No.
Klosterberg	Norheim	–	N 288
Klosterberg	Oberheimbach	–	Mrh 105
Klosterberg	Oestrich-Winkel	Oestrich	Rhg 45
Klosterberg	Osthofen	–	Rhh 386
Klosterberg	Perl	Sehndorf	MSR 522
Klosterberg	Platten	–	MSR 221
Klosterberg	Rüdesheim	–	Rhg 18
Klosterberg	Saarburg	–	MSR 472
Klosterberg	Sachsenheim Vaihingen	Hohenhaslach Horrheim	W 113 T
Klosterberg	Schleich	–	MSR 339
Klosterberg	Traben-Trarbach	Wolf	MSR 196
Klosterberg	Weikersheim	Schäftersheim	W 4 a
Klosterberg	Wiltingen	–	MSR 451
Klosterberg	Zell	Merl	MSR 144
Klosterberg	**Ahrbrück**	**Pützfeld**	**A 1—43**
	Altenahr	**–**	
	Altenahr	**Kreuzberg**	
	Altenahr	**Reimerzhoven**	
	Bad Neuenahr-Ahrweiler	**Ahrweiler**	
	Bad Neuenahr-Ahrweiler	**Bachem**	
	Bad Neuenahr-Ahrweiler	**Ehlingen**	
	Bad Neuenahr-Ahrweiler	**Heimersheim**	
	Bad Neuenahr-Ahrweiler	**Heppingen**	
	Bad Neuenahr-Ahrweiler	**Lohrsdorf**	
	Bad Neuenahr-Ahrweiler	**Marienthal**	
	Bad Neuenahr-Ahrweiler	**Neuenahr**	
	Bad Neuenahr Ahrweiler	**Walporzheim**	
	Dernau	**–**	
	Mayschoß	**–**	
	Rech	**–**	
Klosterberg-felsen	Baden-Baden	Varnhalt	B 120
Klosterbruder	Ingelheim	Groß-Winternheim	Rhh 141
Kloster Disibodenberg	Odernheim am Glan	–	N 212
Kloster Fürstental	Bacharach	Medenscheid und Neurath	Mrh 95
Klostergarten	Bad Neuenahr-Ahrweiler	Marienthal	A 26
Klostergarten	Bermersheim v. d. H.	–	Rhh 109
Klostergarten	Bingen Weiler	Bingerbrück –	N 2 T
Klostergarten	Brauneberg	Filzen	MSR 276
Klostergarten	Cochem	Sehl (Ebernach)	MSR 63
Klostergarten	Edenkoben	–	Rhpf 230
Klostergarten	Flonheim	–	Rhh 101
Klostergarten	Gönnheim	–	Rhpf 163
Klostergarten	Großheubach	Engelsberg	F 17
Klostergarten	Grünstadt	Sausenheim	Rhpf 41
Klostergarten	Hackenheim	–	Rhh 66
Klostergarten	Landau in der Pfalz	Godramstein	Rhpf 284
Klostergarten	Leiwen	–	MSR 323
Klostergarten	Lustadt Zeiskam	– –	Rhpf 263 T
Klostergarten	Niederkirchen	–	Rhpf 169
Klostergarten	Nierstein	–	Rhh 247
Klostergarten	Sankt Johann	–	Rhh 54
Klostergarten	St. Katharinen	–	N 149
Klostergarten	Schwabenheim	–	Rhh 140
Klostergarten	Sponheim	–	N 171
Klostergarten	Sprendlingen	–	Rhh 49
Klostergarten	Zotzenheim	–	Rhh 22
Klostergut Fremersberger Feigenwäldchen	Sinzheim	–	B 119 a
Klostergut Schelzberg	Sasbachwalden	–	B 143
Klosterhofgut	Bernkastel-Kues	Wehlen	MSR 236
Klosterkammer	St. Aldegund	–	MSR 126
Klosterlay	Rüdesheim	–	Rhg 19
Kloster Liebfrauenberg	**Bad Bergzabern**	**–**	**Rhpf 306—322**
	Barbelroth	**–**	
	Billigheim-Ingenheim	**Appenhofen, Billigheim, Ingenheim, Mühlhofen**	
	Gleiszellen-Gleishorbach	**–**	
	Göcklingen	**–**	
	Hergersweiler	**–**	
	Heuchelheim-Klingen	**–**	
	Kapellen-Drusweiler	**–**	
	Klingenmünster	**–**	
	Niederhorbach	**–**	
	Oberhausen	**–**	
	Pleisweiler-Oberhofen	**–**	
	Rohrbach	**–**	
	Steinweiler	**–**	
	Winden	**–**	
Klosterpfad	Dorsheim	–	N 50
Klosterpfad	Rhodt unter Rietburg	–	Rhpf 237
Kloster-schaffnerei	Bockenheim an der Weinstraße	–	Rhpf 22
Klosterstück	Einselthum Zellertal	– Zell	Rhpf 8 T
Klosterweg	Bingen	Dromersheim	Rhh 29
Klosterweg	Gerolsheim	–	Rhpf 61
Klosterweg	Hupperath Wittlich	– –	MSR 219 T
Klosterweg	Ockenheim	–	Rhh 34
Klosterweg	Wittlich	–	MSR 218
Klotzberg	Bühlertal	–	B 134
Knopf	Friesenheim	–	Rhh 229
Knopf	Hahnheim	–	Rhh 235
Kobersberg	Rimpar	–	F 52
Kobnert	**Bad Dürkheim**	**Leistadt**	**Rhpf 83—101**
	Bad Dürkheim	**Ungstein**	
	Dackenheim	**–**	
	Erpolzheim	**–**	
	Freinsheim	**–**	
	Herxheim am Berg	**–**	
	Kallstadt	**–**	
	Ungstein	**–**	
	Weisenheim am Berg	**–**	
Kochberg	Durbach	–	B 165
Kocherberg	**Dörzbach**	**–**	**W 7—17 a**
	Forchtenberg	**–**	
	Forchtenberg	**Ernsbach**	
	Hardthausen	**Kochersteinsfeld**	
	Ingelfingen	**–**	
	Ingelfingen	**Criesbach**	
	Künzelsau	**–**	
	Künzelsau	**Belsenberg**	
	Möckmühl	**–**	
	Möckmühl	**Siglingen**	
	Neudenau	**Siglingen**	
	Niedernhall	**–**	
	Schöntal	**Bieringen**	
	Weißbach	**–**	
	Widdern	**–**	

Site	Town	Ortsteil	Region & Site No.
Köhler	Dingolshausen	–	F 136 b T
	Dingolshausen	Bischwind	
	Gerolzhofen	–	
	Sulzheim	Mönchstockheim	
Köhler-Köpfchen	Bad Münster am Stein-Ebernburg	Ebernburg	N 268
König	Sternenfels	–	W 100 T
	Sternenfels	Diefenbach	
Königin	Tauberrettersheim	–	F 68 a
Königin Viktoriaberg	Hochheim	–	Rhg 102
König Johann Berg	Kastel-Staadt	–	MSR 494
König Johann Berg	Serrig	–	MSR 484
Königsbecher	Östringen	Odenheim	B 89
Königsberg	Klüsserath	–	MSR 327
Königsberg	Steinheim	Höpfigheim	W 125
Königsberg	Traben-Trarbach	Traben	MSR 191
Königsberg	**Igel**	**–**	**MSR 496–**
	Igel	**Liersberg**	**499**
	Langsur	**–**	
	Langsur	**Grewenich**	
	Langsur	**Mesenich**	
	Langsur	**Metzdorf**	
	Ralingen	**Edingen**	
	Ralingen	**Godendorf**	
	Ralingen	**Wintersdorf**	
Königsfels	Duchroth	–	N 320 T
Königsfels	Koblenz	Güls	MSR 3
Königsfels	Schloßböckelheim	–	N 307 T
	Waldböckelheim	–	
Königsgarten	Bad Münster am Stein-Ebernburg	Ebernburg	N 273
Königsgarten	Feilbingert	–	N 238
Königsgarten	**Albersweiler**	**–**	**Rhpf 283–**
	Albersweiler	**St.Johann**	**295**
	Birkweiler	**–**	
	Frankweiler	**–**	
	Landau in der Pfalz mit Queichheim und Mörlheim		
	Landau in der Pfalz	**Arzheim**	
	Landau in der Pfalz	**Godramstein**	
	Ranschbach	**–**	
	Siebeldingen	**–**	
Königslay-Terrassen	Zell	Merl	MSR 141
Königsschild	Langenlonsheim	–	N 65
Königsschloß	Münster-Sarmsheim	–	N 12
Königstuhl	Gundersheim	–	Rhh 360
Königstuhl	Lörzweiler	–	Rhh 219
Königsweg	Zellertal	Niefernheim	Rhpf 10 T
	Zellertal	Zell	
Königsweingarten	Bodman	–	B 328 a
Königswingert	Wachenheim	–	Rhpf 127
König Wenzel	Rhens	–	Mrh 39
König-Wilhelms-Berg	Flörsheim	Wicker	Rhg 113
Kopf	**Korb**	**–**	**W 159–**
	Korb	**Kleinheppach**	**171**
	Remshalden	**Grunbach**	
	Schorndorf	**–**	
	Waiblingen	**–**	
	Waiblingen	**Beinstein**	
	Waiblingen	**Neustadt**	
	Weinstadt	**Großheppach**	
	Winnenden	**–**	
	Winnenden	**Breuningsweiler**	
	Winnenden	**Bürg**	
	Winnenden	**Hanweiler**	
	Winterbach	**–**	
Koppelstein	Braubach	–	Mrh 33 T
	Lahnstein	–	

Site	Town	Ortsteil	Region & Site No.
Krähenberg	Massenbachhausen	–	W 78
Krähenschnabel	Erlenbach (bei Marktheidenfeld) mit Ortsteil Triefenthal		F 27 T
	Remlingen	–	
Kräuterberg	Bad Neuenahr-Ahrweiler	Walporzheim	A 18
Kräuterberg	Oberdiebach	–	Mrh 102
Kräuterhaus	Traben-Trarbach	Traben	MSR 192
Kranzberg	Dalheim	–	Rhh 224
Kranzberg	Nierstein	–	Rhh 260
Krapfenberg	Vollmersweiler	–	Rhpf 330
Kreidkeller	Kallstadt	–	Rhpf 106
Kreuz	Dienheim	–	Rhh 273 T
	Oppenheim	–	
Kreuz	Friedelsheim	–	Rhpf 131
Kreuz	Hammelburg	Feuerthal	F 30 a
Kreuz	Kirchheim an der Weinstraße	–	Rhpf 71
Kreuz	Ockenheim	–	Rhh 35
Kreuzberg	Achern	Mösbach	B 148 T
	Kappelrodeck	Waldulm	
	Renchen	–	
Kreuzberg	Bodenheim	–	Rhh 180
Kreuzberg	Dolgesheim	–	Rhh 295
Kreuzberg	Koblenz	Ehrenbreitstein	Mrh 31
Kreuzberg	Einselthum	–	Rhpf 9 T
	Zellertal	Niefernheim	
	Zellertal	Zell	
Kreuzberg	Marktheidenfeld	–	F 27 a
Kreuzberg	Neustadt an der Weinstraße	Duttweiler	Rhpf 214
Kreuzberg	Nordheim	–	F 92 T
	Volkach	Hallburg	
Kreuzberg	Offenburg	Rammersweier	B 166
Kreuzberg	Tauberbischofsheim	Distelhausen	B 14 a
Kreuzberg	Traben-Trarbach	Trarbach	MSR 189
Kreuzblick	Worms	Wies-Oppenheim	Rhh 432
Kreuzhalde	Ihringen	–	B 218 T
	Ihringen	Wasenweiler	
Kreuzkapelle	Guntersblum	–	Rhh 303
Kreuzlay	Zell	–	MSR 149
Kreuzpfad	Kolitzheim	Lindach	F 102 c
Kreuzweg	Framersheim	–	Rhh 317
Kreuzweg	Leimen	–	B 47
Kreuzwingert	Piesport	Niederemmel	MSR 302
Kriegsberg	Stuttgart	–	W 136
Kroatenpfad	Neustadt an der Weinstraße	Lachen/ Speyerdorf	Rhpf 213
Krötenbrunnen	**Alsheim**	**–**	**Rhh 279–**
	Dienheim	**–**	**301**
	Dolgesheim	**–**	
	Eich	**–**	
	Eimsheim	**–**	
	Gimbsheim	**–**	
	Guntersblum	**–**	
	Hillesheim	**–**	
	Ludwigshöhe	**–**	
	Mettenheim	**–**	
	Oppenheim	**–**	
	Uelversheim	**–**	
	Wintersheim	**–**	
Krötenpfuhl	Bad Kreuznach	–	N 116
Kronberg	Sand am Main	–	F 132
Krone	Laubenheim	–	N 61
Krone	Lorch	–	Rhg 5
Krone	Prichsenstadt	–	F 141

Site	Town	Ortsteil	Region & Site No.
Krone	Waldrach	–	MSR 395
Kroneberg	Bullay	–	MSR 136
Kronenberg	Alf	–	MSR 131
Kronenberg	Kallstadt	–	Rhpf 97
Kronenberg	**Bad Kreuznach**	**–**	**N 99–**
	Bad Kreuznach	**Bosenheim**	**143**
	Bad Kreuznach	**Ippesheim**	
	Bad Kreuznach	**Planig**	
	Bad Kreuznach	**Winzenheim**	
	Bretzenheim	**–**	
	Hargesheim	**–**	
Kronenbühl	Friesenheim	–	B 183 T
	Friesenheim	Heiligenzell	
	Friesenheim	Oberschopfheim	
	Friesenheim	Oberweier	
	Lahr	–	
	Lahr	Hugsweier	
	Lahr	Mietersheim	
Kronenfels	Waldböckelheim	–	N 313
Kronsberg	Iphofen	–	F 121 a
Küchenmeister	Rödelsee	–	F 118
Kugelspiel	Castell	–	F 110
Kuhberg	Schriesheim	–	B 38
Kuhnchen	Riveris	–	MSR 388
Kuhstall	St. Goar	–	Mrh 53
Kupferflöz	Dörscheid	–	Mrh 79
Kupfergrube	Schloßböckelheim	–	N 302
Kupferhalde	Oberderdingen mit Großvillars		W 99
Kupp	Ayl mit Ortsteil Biebelhausen		MSR 469
Kupp	Ockfen	–	MSR 462
Kupp	Saarburg	–	MSR 475
Kupp	Serrig	–	MSR 488
Kupp	Trier	Kürenz	MSR 366
Kupp	Wiltingen	–	MSR 448
Kupp	Wittlich	–	MSR 212
Kurfürst	Ellenz-Poltersdorf	–	MSR 69
Kurfürst	Neustadt an der Weinstraße	Mußbach an der Weinstraße	Rhpf 191
Kurfürstenberg	Waldrach	–	MSR 402
Kurfürsten- hofberg	Trier	Olewig	MSR 381
Kurfürstenstück	**Gau-Bickelheim**	**–**	**Rhh 119–**
	Gau-Weinheim	**–**	**129**
	Gumbsheim	**–**	
	Vendersheim	**–**	
	Wallertheim	**–**	
	Wöllstein	**–**	
Kurfürstlay	**Bernkastel-Kues**	**Andel**	**MSR 251–**
	Bernkastel-Kues	**Bernkastel**	**292**
	Bernkastel-Kues	**Kues**	
	Brauneberg	**–**	
	Brauneberg	**Filzen**	
	Burgen	**–**	
	Kesten	**–**	
	Maring-Noviand	**–**	
	Mülheim	**–**	
	Osann-Monzel	**Monzel**	
	Osann-Monzel	**Osann**	
	Veldenz	**–**	
	Wintrich	**–**	

Site	Town	Ortsteil	Region & Site No.
Laacherberg	Mayschoß	–	A 40
Laberstall	Ockenheim	–	Rhh 31
Lämmler	Fellbach	–	W 155
Längberg	Hammelburg	Westheim	F 30 b
Lahntal	**Bad Ems**	**–**	**Mrh 24–**
	Dausenau	**–**	**28**
	Fachbach		
	Nassau	**–**	
	Obernhof	**–**	
	Weinähr	**–**	
Landsknecht	Volkach	Obervolkach	F 95 T
	Volkach	Rimbach	
Landskrone	Bad Neuenahr- Ahrweiler	Heimersheim	A 2 T
	Bad Neuenahr- Ahrweiler	Lohrsdorf	
Lange Els	Heßheim	–	Rhpf 59
Langenberg	Eltville	Martinsthal	Rhg 84
Langenberg	Odernheim am Glan	–	N 216 a
Langenberg	Retzstadt	–	F 43
Langenmorgen	Deidesheim	–	Rhpf 158
Langenstein	Martinsheim	–	F 128
Langenstein	Neustadt an der Weinstraße	Lachen- Speyerdorf	Rhpf 211
Langenstück	Eltville	–	Rhg 73
Langenstück	Eltville	Rauenthal	Rhg 81
Langenstück	Walluf	Oberwalluf	Rhg 90
Langgarten	Manubach	–	Mrh 96
Langhölle	Obermoschel	–	N 232
La Roche	Flonheim	–	Rhh 99
Lasenberg	Bötzingen	–	B 215
Latt	Albersweiler	St. Johann	Rhpf 288
Laudamusberg	Neumagen-Dhron	Neumagen	MSR 311
Lauerweg	Langenlonsheim	–	N 64
Laurentiusberg	Altenbamberg	–	N 261
Laurentiusberg	Bremm	–	MSR 120
Laurentiusberg	Königswinter	Oberdollendorf	Mrh 2
Laurentiusberg	Saarburg mit Ortsteil Krutweiler		MSR 480
Laurentiusberg	Waldrach	–	MSR 396
Laurentiusberg	Wallhausen	–	N 88
Laurentiuslay	Köwerich	–	MSR 324
Laurentiuslay	Leiwen	–	MSR 324 a
Laurenziweg	Dorsheim	–	N 51
Lay	Bernkastel-Kues	Bernkastel	MSR 243
Lay	Lehmen	–	MSR 22
Lay	Palzem	–	MSR 518
Lay	Senheim	–	MSR 105
Lay	Wittlich	–	MSR 213
Layenberg	Bruttig-Fankel	Fankel	MSR 87
Layenberg	Niedermoschel	–	N 236
Laykaul	Korlingen	–	MSR 387
Leckerberg	Armsheim	Schimsheim	Rhh 113
Leckerberg	Dittelsheim-Heßloch	Dittelsheim	Rhh 373
Leckmauer	Müden	–	MSR 45
Leckzapfen	Osthofen	–	Rhh 393 a
Leidhecke	Bodenheim	–	Rhh 178
Leiersberg	Leingarten	–	W 80
Leikaul	Trier	Filsch	MSR 370
Leinhöhle	Deidesheim	–	Rhpf 157
Leistenberg	Oberhausen an der Nahe	–	N 318

Site	Town	Ortsteil	Region & Site No.
Leiterchen	Nittel	–	MSR 509
Leiterchen	Trittenheim	–	MSR 317
Lenchen	Oestrich-Winkel	Oestrich	Rhg 46
Lenchen	Stadecken-Elsheim	Stadecken	Rhh 199
Lennenborn	Bacharach	Steeg	Mrh 87
Lenzenberg	Stuttgart	Hedelfingen	W 151 T
	Stuttgart	Rohracker	
Leopoldsberg	Bermatingen	–	B 341
Lerchelsberg	Worms	Herrnsheim	Rhh 423
Lerchenberg	Bönnigheim	Hofen	W 118 T
	Erligheim	–	
Lerchenberg	Bretten	Bauerbach	B 96 T
	Eppingen	–	
	Eppingen	Mühlbach	
	Eppingen	Rohrbach a. G.	
	Kraichtal	Bahnbrücken, Gochsheim und Oberacker	
	Kürnbach	–	
	Oberderdingen	Flehingen	
	Sulzfeld	–	
	Zaisenhausen	–	
Lerchenberg	Eichstetten	–	B 214
Lerchenberg	Eßlingen	–	W 157 T
	Eßlingen	Mettingen	
Lerchenberg	Kapsweyer	–	Rhpf 326
Lerchenberg	Meersburg	–	B 336 T
	Stetten	–	
Lerchenböhl	Neustadt an der Weinstraße	Lachen-Speyerdorf	Rhpf 212
Lerchenspiel	Gerolsheim	–	Rhpf 60
Letten	Auggen	–	B 305
Letten	Deidesheim	–	Rhpf 137
Letten	Hainfeld	–	Rhpf 242
Letterlay	Kröv	–	MSR 226
Lichtenberg	Großbottwar	–	W 62 T
	Großbottwar	Hof und Lembach	
	Großbottwar	Winzerhausen	
	Ilsfeld	–	
	Oberstenfeld	–	
	Steinheim	–	
	Steinheim	Kleinbottwar	
Lichtenberg	Karlsruhe	Grötzingen	B 105
Lichtenberg	Remshalden	Geradstetten	W 185 T
	Remshalden	Hebsack	
Liebehöll	Münster-Sarmsheim	–	N 10
Liebenberg	Osthofen	–	Rhh 387
Liebenberg	Sachsenheim	Ochsenbach	W 117 T
	Sachsenheim	Spielberg	
Liebeneck-Sonnenlay	Osterspai	–	Mrh 37
Liebenstein-Sterrenberg	Kamp-Bornhofen	–	Mrh 55 T
	Kestert	–	
Liebesbrunnen	Dackenheim	–	Rhpf 85
Liebesbrunnen	Hochstätten	–	N 242
Liebfrau	Volxheim	–	Rhh 65
Liebfrauenberg	Dittelsheim-Heßloch	Heßloch	Rhh 378
Liebfrauenberg	Konz	Filzen	MSR 424
Liebfrauenberg	Meddersheim	–	N 198

Site	Town	Ortsteil	Region & Site No.
Liebfrauenmorgen	**Worms**	**–**	**Rhh 415–434**
	Worms	**Abenheim**	
	Worms	**Heppenheim**	
	Worms	**Herrnsheim**	
	Worms	**Hochheim**	
	Worms	**Horchheim**	
	Worms	**Leiselheim**	
	Worms	**Pfeddersheim**	
	Worms	**Pfiffligheim**	
	Worms	**Weinsheim**	
	Worms	**Wiesoppenheim**	
Liebfrauenstift-Kirchenstück	Worms	–	Rhh 421
Liebfrauenthal	Gimbsheim	–	Rhh 290
Lieseberg	Waldlaubersheim	–	N 22
Lieth	Harxheim	–	Rhh 187
Limburg	Sasbach	–	B 246
Lindauer Seegarten	**Bodolz**	**–**	**W 202–204**
	Lindau	**–**	
	Nonnenhorn	**–**	
	Wasserburg	**–**	
Lindelberg	**Bretzfeld**	**–**	**W 30–38**
	Bretzfeld	**Adolzfurt**	
	Bretzfeld	**Dimbach**	
	Bretzfeld	**Geddelsbach**	
	Bretzfeld	**Schwabbach**	
	Bretzfeld	**Siebeneich**	
	Bretzfeld	**Unterheimbach**	
	Bretzfeld	**Waldbach**	
	Langenbrettach	**Langenbeutingen**	
	Neuenstein	**Eschelbach**	
	Neuenstein	**Kesselfeld**	
	Neuenstein	**Obersöllbach**	
	Öhringen	**Michelbach am Wald**	
	Öhringen	**Verrenberg**	
	Pfedelbach	**–**	
	Pfedelbach	**Harsberg**	
	Pfedelbach	**Heuholz**	
	Pfedelbach	**Oberohrn**	
	Pfedelbach	**Untersteinbach**	
	Pfedelbach	**Windischenbach**	
	Wüstenrot	**Maienfels**	
Lindhälder	Kernen	Stetten	W 188
Linsenbusch	Ruppertsberg	–	Rhpf 172
Lochmühlerlay	Mayschoß	–	A 41
Löhrer Berg	Langenlonsheim	–	N 62
Lohrberger Hang	Frankfurt	–	Rhg 115
Longenburgerberg	Königswinter	Niederdollendorf	Mrh 5
Loreley Edel	St. Goarshausen	–	Mrh 61
Loreleyfelsen	**Bornich**	**–**	**Mrh 54–62**
	Kamp-Bornhofen	**–**	
	Kestert	**–**	
	Nochern	**–**	
	Patersberg	**–**	
	St. Goarshausen	**–**	

Site	Town	Ortsteil	Region & Site No.
Lorettoberg	**Au**	**—**	**B 265–**
	Bad Krozingen	**—**	**288**
	Bad Krozingen	**Biengen**	
	Bad Krozingen	**Schlatt**	
	Bad Krozingen	**Tunsel**	
	Bollschweil	**—**	
	Buggingen	**—**	
	Buggingen	**Seefelden**	
	Ebringen	**—**	
	Ehrenkirchen	**Ehrenstetten**	
	Ehrenkirchen	**Kirchhofen**	
	Ehrenkirchen	**Norsingen**	
	Ehrenkirchen	**Scherzingen**	
	Eschbach	**—**	
	Freiburg	**—**	
	Freiburg	**St. Georgen**	
	Heitersheim	**—**	
	Merzhausen	**—**	
	Pfaffenweiler	**—**	
	Schallstadt	**—**	
	Schallstadt	**Mengen**	
	Schallstadt	**Wolfenweiler**	
	Staufen im Breisgau	**—**	
	Staufen im Breisgau	**Grunern**	
	Staufen im Breisgau	**Wettelbrunn**	
	Wittnau	**—**	
Lotberg	Ihringen	Wasenweiler	B 217
Lottenstück	Ingelheim	Groß-Winternheim	Rhh 156
Lützelberg	Sasbach	—	B 244
Lützeltalerberg	Großwallstadt	—	F 10
Luginsland	Aichwald	Aichelberg	W 186
Luginsland	Wachenheim	—	Rhpf 134
Luhmännchen	Alzenau	Wasserlos	F 3 a
Luisengarten	Bad Münster am Stein-Ebernburg	Ebernburg	N 271
Lump	Kirschroth	—	N 197
Lump	Volkach	Escherndorf	F 88

Site	Town	Ortsteil	Region & Site No.
Madonnenberg	Schriesheim	—	B 39
Mäuerchen	Geisenheim	—	Rhg 26
Mäuerchen	Mertesdorf	Lorenzhof	MSR 410
Mäushöhle	Deidesheim	—	Rhpf 152
Magdalenenkreuz	Rüdesheim	—	Rhg 20
Maiberg	Heppenheim	—	HB 21 T
	Heppenheim	Hambach	
	Heppenheim	Erbach	
Maien	Winnenden	Hanweiler	W 174
Mainhölle	Bürgstadt	—	F 19
Mainleite	Schweinfurt	—	F 103 d
Mainleite	Waigolshausen	Hergolshausen	F 101 a T
	Waigolshausen	Theilheim	
Mainzerweg	Bingen	Dromersheim	Rhh 30
Maltesergarten	Bad Krozingen	Biengen	B 269 T
	Bad Krozingen	Schlatt	
	Bad Krozingen	Tunsel	
	Buggingen	—	
	Buggingen	Seefelden	
	Eschbach	—	
	Heitersheim	—	
	Staufen im Breisgau	Wettelbrunn	
Mandelbaum	Pfaffen-Schwabenheim	—	Rhh 19
Mandelberg	Alzey	Weinheim	Rhh 340
Mandelberg	Birkweiler	—	Rhpf 294
Mandelberg	Kirrweiler	—	Rhpf 223
Mandelberg	Laumersheim	—	Rhpf 63
Mandelberg	Lonsheim	—	Rhh 108
Mandelberg	Neustadt an der Weinstraße	Duttweiler	Rhpf 215
Mandelberg	Offenheim	—	Rhh 338
Mandelberg	Wertheim	Dertingen	B 1
Mandelbrunnen	Gundheim	—	Rhh 362
Mandelgarten	Gönnheim	—	Rhpf 162
Mandelgarten	Neustadt an der Weinstraße	Gimmeldingen an der Weinstraße	Rhpf 187
Mandelgarten	Obrigheim	Mühlheim	Rhpf 31
Mandelgarten	Wachenheim	—	Rhpf 128
Mandelgarten	Weisenheim am Berg	—	Rhpf 86
Mandelgraben	Brauneberg	—	MSR 275 T
	Brauneberg	Filzen	
Mandelhang	Edesheim	—	Rhpf 246
Mandelhöhe	**Kirrweiler**	**—**	**Rhpf 218–**
	Maikammer	**—**	**224**
	Maikammer		
	Asterweiler		
Mandelpfad	Billigheim-Ingenheim	Billigheim	Rhpf 308 T
	Rohrbach	—	
Mandelpfad	Dirmstein	—	Rhpf 57
Mandelpfad	Obrigheim	—	Rhpf 31
Mandelring	Neustadt an der Weinstraße	Haardt an der Weinstraße	Rhpf 195
Mandelröth	Dackenheim	—	Rhpf 83
Mandelstein	Boppard	Bopparder Hamm	Mrh 45

Site	Town	Ortsteil	Region & Site No.
Mannaberg	**Bad Schönborn**	**Langenbrücken und Mingolsheim**	**B 44–71**
	Bruchsal	–	
	Bruchsal	**Heidelsheim**	
	Bruchsal	**Helmsheim**	
	Bruchsal	**Obergrombach**	
	Bruchsal	**Untergrombach**	
	Dielheim	–	
	Dielheim	**Horrenberg**	
	Heidelberg	–	
	Kraichtal	**Oberöwisheim und Unteröwisheim**	
	Leimen	–	
	Malsch	–	
	Mühlhausen	–	
	Mühlhausen	**Rettigheim**	
	Mühlhausen	**Tairnbach**	
	Nußloch	–	
	Östringen	–	
	Rauenberg	–	
	Rauenberg	**Malschenberg**	
	Rauenberg	**Rotenberg**	
	Ubstadt-Weiher	**Stettfeld**	
	Ubstadt-Weiher	**Ubstadt**	
	Ubstadt-Weiher	**Zeutern**	
	Wiesloch	–	
Mannberg	Eltville	Hattenheim	Rhg 48
Marbach	Sobernheim	–	N 204
Marcobrunn	Eltville	Erbach	Rhg 60 T
	Eltville	Hattenheim	
Margarete	Neuenstein	Obersöllbach	W 31 T
	Öhringen	Michelbach am Wald	
Maria Magdalena	Klingenmünster	–	Rhpf 306
Marienberg	Koblenz	Güls	MSR 1 T
	Koblenz	Metternich	
Marienberg	Perl	Sehndorf	MSR 523
Marienburg	Pünderich	–	MSR 164
Marienburger	Zell	Kaimt	MSR 153
Mariengarten	**Deidesheim**	–	**Rhpf 138–159**
	Forst an der Weinstraße	–	
	Wachenheim	–	
Mariengarten	Prichsenstadt	Kirchschönbach	F 105 b
Marienholz	Trier	Eitelsbach	MSR 356 T
	Trier	Ruwer	
Marienpforter Klosterberg	Waldböckelheim	–	N 315
Markgraf Babenberg	**Frickenhausen**	–	**F 70–71**
Marksburg	**Braubach**	–	**Mrh 29–38**
	Filsen	–	
	Koblenz	–	
	Koblenz	**Ehrenbreitstein und Niederberg**	
	Lahnstein	–	
	Osterspai	–	
	Urbar	–	
	Vallendar	–	
Marmorberg	Braubach	–	Mrh 36
Marsberg	Randersacker	–	F 63
Marschall	Wiesbaden	Frauenstein	Rhg 94
Martinsberg	Sieversheim	–	Rhh 85 T
	Wonsheim	–	
Martinsborn	Bruttig-Fankel	Fankel	MSR 86
Martinshöhe	Gönnheim	–	Rhpf 113
Matheisbildchen	Bernkastel-Kues	Bernkastel	MSR 244
Mathias Weingarten	Bacharach	Medenscheid und Neurath	Mrh 94
Mauerberg	Baden-Baden	Neuweier	B 126
Maustal	Sulzfeld	–	F 76
Maximiner	Trier	Ruwer	MSR 362
Maximiner Burgberg	Fell (mit Ortsteil Fastrau)		MSR 347
Maximiner-Herrenberg	Longuich	–	MSR 349
Maximiner Hofgarten	Kenn	–	MSR 354
Maximiner Klosterlay	Detzem	–	MSR 337
Maximin Prälat	Kastel-Staadt	–	MSR 495
Meerspinne	**Neustadt an der Weinstraße**	–	**Rhpf 181–199**
	Neustadt an der Weinstraße	**Gimmeldingen an der Weinstraße**	
	Neustadt an der Weinstraße	**Haardt an der Weinstraße**	
	Neustadt an der Weinstraße	**Königsbach an der Weinstraße**	
	Neustadt an der Weinstraße	**Mußbach an der Weinstraße**	
Mehrhölzchen	**Eltville**	**Erbach**	**Rhg 45, 56–59**
	Oestrich-Winkel	**Hallgarten**	
	Oestrich-Winkel	**Oestrich**	
Meisenberg	Waldrach	–	MSR 400
Michaeliskapelle	Braunweiler	–	N 144
Michaelsberg	Cleebronn	–	W 94 T
	Güglingen		
	Güglingen	Eibensbach	
	Güglingen	Frauenzimmern	
Michaelsberg	Bruchsal	Untergrombach	B 70
Michelmark	Eltville	Erbach	Rhg 64
Michelsberg	Bad Dürkheim	–	Rhpf 120 T
	Bad Dürkheim	Ungstein	
Michelsberg	Mettenheim	–	Rhh 333
Michelsberg	Weyer in der Pfalz	–	Rhpf 240
Michelsberg	**Hetzerath**	–	**MSR 293–322 a**
	Klausen	**Krames**	
	Minheim	–	
	Neumagen-Dhron	**Dhron**	
	Neumagen-Dhron	**Neumagen**	
	Piesport	–	
	Piesport	**Niederemmel**	
	Rivenich	–	
	Sehlem	–	
	Trittenheim	–	
Mittelberg	Bayerfeld-Steckweiler		N 258
Mittelhölle	Geisenheim	Johannisberg	Rhg 35
Mönchbäumchen	Zornheim	–	Rhh 239
Mönchberg	Bad Kreuznach	–	N 121
Mönchberg	Fellbach	–	W 143 T
	Stuttgart	Bad Cannstatt	
	Stuttgart	Untertürkheim	
Mönchberg	Hergenfeld	–	N 75
Mönchberg	Hüffelsheim	–	N 179
Mönchberg	Kernen	Rommelshausen	W 195 T
	Kernen	Stetten	
Mönchberg	Mayschoß	–	A 36
Mönchberg	Sulzheim	Mönchsteckheim	F 103 f
Mönchberg	Volxheim	–	Rhh 63
Mönchgarten	Neustadt an der Weinstraße		Rhpf 199
Mönchhalde	Stuttgart	–	W 135 T
	Stuttgart	Bad Cannstatt	
	Stuttgart	Zuffenhausen	
Mönchhube	Dittelsheim-Heßloch	Dittelsheim	Rhh 375
Mönchpforte	Nieder-Hilbersheim	–	Rhh 48 T
	Ober-Hilbersheim	–	
Mönchsberg	Bad Mergentheim	Markelsheim	W 1 T
	Weikersheim	Elpersheim	

Site	Town	Ortsteil	Region & Site No.
Mönchsberg	Brackenheim	–	W 89 T
	Brackenheim	Dürrenzimmern	
Mönchsbuck	Sugenheim	Neundorf	F 128 d
Mönchsgewann	Flörsheim	Wicker	Rhg 112
Mönchshang	Zeil am Main	–	F 134
Mönchsleite	Eibelstadt	–	F 67
Mönchspfad	Bodenheim	–	Rhh 170
Mönchspfad	Geisenheim	–	Rhg 27
Mönchspfad	Schornsheim	–	Rhh 210
Mönchspfad	Siebeldingen	–	Rhpf 290
Mönchwingert	Manubach	–	Mrh 98
Mollenbrunnen	Bad Kreuznach	–	N 110
Mollenbrunnen	Hargesheim	–	N 143
Mondschein	Dittelsheim-Heßloch	Heßloch	Rhh 380
Monte Jup	Rheinbrohl	–	Mrh 16
Monteneubel	Enkirch	–	MSR 175
Montfort	Odernheim am Glan	–	N 214
Moosberg	Hahnheim	–	Rhh 236
Moosberg	Sörgenloch	–	Rhh 236 a
Morgenbachtaler	Trechtingshausen	–	Mrh 112
Morstein	Westhofen	–	Rhh 368
Moullay-Hofberg	Reil	–	MSR 167
Muckerhöhle	Waldböckelheim	–	N 309
Mühlbächer	Mundelsheim	–	W 123
Mühlberg	Boxberg	Unterschüpf	B 25
Mühlberg	Braubach	–	Mrh 35
Mühlberg	Edenkoben	–	Rhpf 234
Mühlberg	Lauda-Königshofen	Oberbalbach	B 23 b
Mühlberg	Schloßböckelheim	–	N 304
Mühlberg	Sponheim	–	N 168
Mühlberg	Veldenz	–	MSR 264
Mühlberg	Waldböckelheim	–	N 308
Mühlenberg	Ensch	–	MSR 333
Mühlenberg	Roxheim	–	N 160
Mühlenberg	Wallhausen	–	N 80
Münsterberg	Treis-Karden	Karden	MSR 50
Münsterstatt	Temmels	–	MSR 506
Münzberg	Landau in der Pfalz	Godramstein	Rhpf 285
Münzlay	**Bernkastel-Kues**	**Wehlen**	**MSR 229–242**
	Graach	**–**	
	Zeltingen-Rachtig	**–**	
	Zeltingen-Rachtig	**Zeltingen**	
Mütterle	Landau in der Pfalz	Wollmesheim	Rhpf 300
Mundklingen	Seeheim	–	HB 1 b
Musenhang	Forst an der Weinstraße	–	Rhpf 144
Musikantenbuckel	Freinsheim	–	Rhpf 91

Site	Town	Ortsteil	Region & Site No.
Nacktarsch	**Kröv**	**–**	**MSR 223–228**
	Kröv	**Kövenig**	
Narrenberg	Hergersweiler Winden	–	Rhpf 314 T
Narrenberg	Römerberg (bei Speyer)	Berghausen	Rhpf 264 d T
	Römerberg (bei Speyer)	Heiligenstein	
Narrenkappe	Bad Kreuznach	–	N 122
Neckarhälde	Affalterbach	–	W 126 T
	Benningen	–	
	Erdmannshausen	–	
	Freiberg/Neckar	Beihingen	
	Ludwigsburg	Hoheneck	
	Ludwigsburg	Neckarweihingen	
	Ludwigsburg	Poppenweiler	
	Marbach	–	
	Murr	–	
Neroberg	Wiesbaden	–	Rhg 91
Neuberg	Bornheim	–	Rhpf 261
Neuberg	Meckenheim	–	Rhpf 180
Neuberg	Osthofen	–	Rhh 393
Neuwies	Ockfen	–	MSR 467
Neuwingert	Brodenbach	–	MSR 34
Niederberg	Rivenich	–	MSR 318
Niederberg-Helden	Lieser	–	MSR 249
Nies'chen	Kasel	–	MSR 407
Nikolausberg	Cochem	Cond	MSR 79
Nill	Kallstadt	–	Rhpf 114
Nixenberg	Dorsheim	–	N 53
Nollenköpfle	Gengenbach	–	B 176
Nonnberg	Flörsheim	Wicker	Rhg 114
Nonnenberg	Bernkastel-Kues	–	MSR 238
Nonnenberg	Eltville	Rauenthal	Rhg 82
Nonnenberg	Ebelsbach	Steinbach	F 131
Nonnenberg	Lauda-Königshofen	Beckstein	B 20 T
	Lauda-Königshofen	Lauda	
Nonnenberg	Weinstadt	Strümpfelbach	W 183
Nonnengarten	Bad Dürkheim	–	Rhpf 109
Nonnengarten	Bad Kreuznach	Planig	N 134
Nonnengarten	Briedel	–	MSR 159
Nonnengarten	Mörstadt	–	Rhh 404
Nonnengarten	Pünderich	–	MSR 163
Nonnengarten	Traisen	–	N 281
Nonnenwingert	Worms	Hochheim	Rhh 429 T
	Worms	Leiselheim	
	Worms	Pfeddersheim	
	Worms	Pfiffligheim	
Nonnenstück	Deidesheim	–	Rhpf 171
Nußberg	Zell	–	MSR 145
Nußbien	Ruppertsberg	–	Rhpf 177
Nußbrunnen	Eltville	Hattenheim	Rhg 49
Nußriegel	Bad Dürkheim	Ungstein	Rhpf 119
Nußwingert	Neumagen-Dhron	Dhron	MSR 309

Site	Town	Ortsteil	Region & Site No.
Oberberg	Norheim	–	N 285
Oberberg	Walluf	Niederwalluf	Rhg 88
Oberdürrenberg	Pfaffenweiler	–	B 276
Obere Heimbach	Meisenheim	–	N 225
Oberer Berg	Ludwigsburg Steinheim	Hoheneck Kleinbottwar	W 64 T
Oberrot	Triefenstein	Lengfurt	F 26
Oberschloß	Kirrweiler	–	Rhpf 224
Ochsenberg	Brackenheim	Botenheim	W 93
Odinstal	Wachenheim	–	Rhpf 129
Ölbaum	Malsch Mühlhausen Rauenberg	– Rettigheim Malschenberg	B 58 T
Ölberg	Dossenheim	–	B 41
Ölberg	Durbach	–	B 157
Oelberg	Efringen-Kirchen	–	B 321
Oelberg	Ehrenkirchen	Ehrenstetten	B 279
Ölberg	Endingen	Kiechlinsbergen	B 248
Ölberg	Gau-Odernheim	–	Rhh 313
Ölberg	Grolsheim	–	Rhh 12
Ölberg	Hohentengen	–	B 351
Ölberg	Neustadt an der Weinstraße	Königsbach an der Weinstraße	Rhpf 181
Ölberg	Nierstein	–	Rhh 264
Ölberg	Wöllstein	–	Rhh 87
Ölgässel	Neustadt an der Weinstaße	Diedesfeld an der Weinstraße	Rhpf 206
Ölgild	Lörzweiler	–	Rhh 188
Ölkuchen	Tauberbischofsheim	Dittwar	B 14 c
Ölsberg	Oberwesel	–	Mrh 70
Ölschnabel	Zeil am Main	Ziegelanger	F 130
Ölspiel	**Eibelstadt Sommerhausen**	– –	**F 64–65**
Ohlenberg	Boppard	Bopparder Hamm	Mrh 43
Ohligsberg	Wintrich	–	MSR 291
Ohligpfad	Bobenheim am Berg	–	Rhpf 102
Olgaberg	Singen	–	B 346
Onkelchen	Norheim	–	N 284
Orbel	Nierstein	–	Rhh 266
Ordensgut	**Edesheim Hainfeld Rhodt unter Rietburg Weyher in der Pfalz**	– – – –	**Rhpf 237–248**
Orlenberg	Bissersheim	–	Rhpf 69
Ortelberg	Böbingen	–	Rhpf 249
Oschelskopf	Freinsheim	–	Rhpf 92
Osterberg	Bad Dürkheim	Ungstein	Rhpf 95
Osterberg	Bingen	Gaulsheim	Rhh 6
Osterberg	Dielheim	Horrenberg	B 55
Osterberg	Essingen	–	Rhpf 257
Osterberg	Großkarlbach	–	Rhpf 66
Osterberg	Mommenheim	–	Rhh 234 a
Osterberg	Selzen	–	Rhh 234
Osterberg	Spiesheim	–	Rhh 326
Osterberg	Wolfsheim	–	Rhh 58
Osterbrunnen	Niederkirchen	–	Rhpf 168
Osterhöll	Bad Kreuznach	–	N 106
Osterlämmchen	Ediger-Eller	Ediger	MSR 107
Otterberg	Waldlaubersheim	–	N 23
Palmberg	Valwig	–	MSR 81
Palmberg Terrassen	St. Aldegund	–	MSR 125
Palmengarten	Mandel	–	N 154
Palmenstein	Bingen	Sponsheim	Rhh 11
Paradies	Bad Kreuznach	Bosenheim	N 135
Paradies	Ippesheim	Bullenheim	F 125
Paradies	Kröv	–	MSR 228
Paradies	Müllheim	Feldberg	B 304
Paradies	Neustadt an der Weinstraße	Diedesfeld an der Weinstraße	Rhpf 208
Paradies	Obersulm	Eschenau	W 48
Paradiesgarten	Deidesheim	–	Rhpf 159
Paradiesgarten	**Alsenz Auen Bayerfeld-Steckweiler Boos Desloch Feilbingert Gaugrehweiler Hochstätten Kalkhofen Kirschroth Lauschied Lettweiler Mannweiler-Cölln Martinstein Meddersheim Meisenheim Merxheim Monzingen Münsterappel Nußbaum Niederhausen an der Appel Niedermoschel Oberhausen an der Appel Obermoschel Oberndorf Oberstreit Odernheim am Glan Raumbach/Glan Rehborn Sobernheim Sobernheim Staudernheim Unkenbach Waldböckelheim Weiler bei Monzingen Winterborn**	– Steinhard – – – –	**N 182–260**
Pares	Ingelheim	Groß Winternheim	Rhh 152
Pastorei	Bretzenheim	–	N 140
Pastorenberg	Wallhausen	–	N 85
Paterberg	Nierstein	–	Rhh 254
Paterhof	Dienheim Oppenheim	– –	Rhh 281 T
Paulinsberg	Kasel	–	MSR 408
Paulinsberg	Kesten	–	MSR 287
Paulinshofberger	Kesten	–	MSR 285
Paulinslay	Osann-Monzel	Monzel	MSR 281
Paulus	Bensheim	–	HB 17
Pechstein	Forst an der Weinstraße	–	Rhpf 145
Pelzerberger	Beuren	–	MSR 133 a
Petersberg	Neef	–	MSR 122
Petersberg	Weingarten	–	B 103

Site	Town	Ortsteil	Region & Site No.
Petersberg	**Bad Honnef**	**Rhöndorf**	**Mrh 1–7**
	Königswinter	**–**	
	Königswinter	**Niederdollendorf**	
	Königswinter	**Oberdollendorf**	
Petersberg	**Albig**	**–**	**Rhh 308–**
	Alzey	**–**	**326**
	Bechtolsheim	**–**	
	Biebelnheim	**–**	
	Framersheim	**–**	
	Gau-Heppenheim	**–**	
	Gau-Odernheim	**–**	
	Gau-Odernheim	**Gau-Köngernheim**	
	Spiesheim	**–**	
Petersborn-Kabertchen	Zell	–	MSR 147
Peterstirn	Schweinfurt	–	F 103 c
Pettenthal	Nierstein	–	Rhh 256
Pfaffenberg	Ammerbuch	Entringen	W 198 b
Pfaffenberg	Bad Neuenahr-Ahrweiler	Walporzheim	A 21
Pfaffenberg	Billigheim-Ingenheim	Ingenheim	Rhpf 312
Pfaffenberg	Burgsponheim	–	N 174
Pfaffenberg	Ediger-Eller	Ediger	MSR 110
Pfaffenberg	Eltville	Hattenheim	Rhg 55
Pfaffenberg	Flonheim	Uffenhofen	Rhh 97
Pfaffenberg	Landau in der Pfalz	Mörzheim	Rhpf 301
Pfaffenberg	Würzburg	–	F 53 T
	Würzburg	Unterdürrbach	
Pfaffengarten	Saulheim	–	Rhh 205
Pfaffengrund	**Neustadt an der Weinstraße**	**Diedesfeld an der Weinstraße**	**Rhpf 209–**
	Neustadt an der Weinstraße	**Duttweiler**	**217**
	Neustadt an der Weinstraße	**Geinsheim**	
	Neustadt an der Weinstraße	**Hambach an der Weinstraße**	
	Neustadt an der Weinstraße	**Lachen/Speyerdorf**	
Pfaffenhalde	Alzey	Schafhausen	Rhh 349
Pfaffenkappe	Nierstein	Schwabsburg	Rhh 221
Pfaffenmütze	Dittelsheim-Heßloch	Dittelsheim	Rhh 374
Pfaffenpfad	Alsenz	–	N 245
Pfaffensteig	Segnitz	–	F 74
Pfaffenstein	Niederhausen an der Nahe	–	N 294
Pfaffenstück	Müllheim	–	B 300
Pfaffenweg	Gau-Bischofsheim	–	Rhh 182
Pfaffenwies	Lorch	–	Rhg 6
Pfalzgrafenstein	Kaub	–	Mrh 85
Pfarrberg	Kappelrodeck	Waldulm	B 147
Pfarrgarten	Bingen	Gaulsheim	Rhh 4 T
	Bingen	Kempten	
Pfarrgarten	Bruttig-Fankel	Bruttig	MSR 83
Pfarrgarten	Filsen	–	Mrh 38
Pfarrgarten	Gau-Heppenheim	–	Rhh 320
Pfarrgarten	**Dalberg**	**–**	**N 69–**
	Gutenberg	**–**	**98**
	Hergenfeld	**–**	
	Schöneberg	**–**	
	Sommerloch	**–**	
	Spabrücken	**–**	
	Wallhausen	**–**	
Pfarrwingert	Dernau	–	A 29
Pfingstweide	Niederhausen an der Nahe	–	N 290
Pfirsichgarten	Ediger-Eller	Eller	MSR 112

Site	Town	Ortsteil	Region & Site No.
Pforte	Volkach	Vogelsburg	F 103 b
Pfülben	Randersacker	–	F 62
Pilgerberg	Igel	Liersberg	MSR 497
Pilgerpfad	Kamp-Bornhofen	–	Mrh 54
Pilgerpfad	**Bechtheim**	**–**	**Rhh 372–**
	Dittelsheim-Heßloch	**Dittelsheim**	**388**
	Dittelsheim-Heßloch	**Heßloch**	
	Frettenheim	**–**	
	Monzernheim	**–**	
	Osthofen	**–**	
Pilgerstein	Biebelnheim	–	Rhh 324
Pilgerweg	Zornheim	–	Rhh 241
Pinnerkreuzberg	Cochem	–	MSR 60
Pittermännchen	Dorsheim	–	N 49
Pittersberg	Münster-Sarmsheim	–	N 9
Plauelrain	Durbach	–	B 156
Pomerell	Zell	–	MSR 148
Pompejaner	Aschaffenburg	–	F 6
Portnersberg	Wittlich	–	MSR 217
Posten	Bacharach	–	Mrh 93
Prälat	Erden	–	MSR 206
Präsent	Medersheim	–	N 200
Predigtstuhl	Dorfprozelten	–	F 21
Probstberg	Bad Mergentheim	Markelsheim	W 2 T
	Weikersheim	Elpersheim	
Probstberg	**Fell (mit Ortsteil Fastrau)**		**MSR 345–**
	Kenn	**–**	**354**
	Longuich	**–**	
	Riol	**–**	
	Schweich	**–**	
Probsteiberg	Boppard	Hirzenach	
Probstey	Saulheim	–	Rhh 201
Pulchen	Konz	Filzen	MSR 426
Pulverberg	Ackern	Onsbach	B 144
Pulverbuck	Vogtsberg im Kaiserstuhl	Oberbergen	B 231
Pulvermächer	Kernen	Stetten	W 187

Site	Town	Ortsteil	Region & Site No.
Rabenkopf	Ingelheim	Groß-Winternheim	Rhh 157
Rabenkopf	Wackernheim	–	Rhh 157 a
Ranzenberg	Ellhofen	–	W 24 T
	Weinsberg	–	
Rappen	Ilsfeld	–	W 56
Rathausberg	Bruttig-Fankel	Bruttig	MSR 84
Ratsgrund	Sommerloch	–	N 92
Ratsherr	Volkach mit Ortsteil Fahr		F 98
Ravensburg	**Erlabrunn**	–	**F 44–50**
	Güntersleben	–	
	Leinach	**Oberleinach**	
	Thüngersheim	–	
	Veitshöchheim	–	
	Zellingen	–	
	Zellingen	**Retzbach**	
Rauenegg	Ravensburg	–	W 200
Raul	Konz	Oberemmel	MSR 441
Rausch	Saarburg	–	MSR 477
Rauschelay	Kaub	–	Mrh 82
Rebstöckel	**Neustadt an der Weinstraße**	–	**Rhpf 200–208**
	Neustadt an der Weinstraße	**Diedesfeld an der Weinstraße**	
	Neustadt an der Weinstraße	**Hambach an der Weinstraße**	
Rebtal	Freiburg	Tiengen	B 262
Rechbächel	Wachenheim	–	Rhpf 140
Reggenhag	Müllheim	–	B 299
Rehbach	**Nierstein**	–	**Rhh 256–259**
Reichesthal	Hochheim	–	Rhg 98 T
	Mainz	Kostheim	
Reichshalde	Knittlingen	–	W 101 T
	Knittlingen	Freudenstein	
	Maulbronn		
Reichskeller	Freilaubersheim	–	Rhh 73
Reichsritterstift	Bodenheim	–	Rhh 174
Reifenstein	Sommerhausen	–	F 65
Reifersley	Niederheimbach	–	Mrh 110
Reinig auf der Burg	Wasserliesch	–	MSR 500
Reischklingeberg	Großostheim	–	F 8
Reiterpfad	Neustadt an der Weinstraße	Königsbach an der Weinstraße	Rhpf 184
Reiterpfad	Ruppertsberg	–	Rhpf 175
Reitsteig	Castell	–	F 111
Remeyerhof	Worms	–	Rhh 422
Renchtäler	Appenweier	Nesselried	B 151 T
	Lautenbach	–	
	Oberkirch	–	
	Oberkirch	Bottenau	
	Oberkirch	Haslach	
	Oberkirch	Nussbach	
	Oberkirch	Ödsbach	
	Oberkirch	Ringelbach	
	Oberkirch	Stadelhofen	
	Oberkirch	Tiergarten	
	Renchen	Erlach	
	Renchen	Ulm	
Reuschberg	**Alzenau**	**Hörstein**	**F 1–2**
Rheinberg	Eltville	–	Rhg 75
Rheinberg	Oberdiebach	Rheindiebach	Mrh 103
Rheinblick	Münster-Sarmsheim	–	N 5
Rheinblick	Osthofen	–	Rhh 385
Rheinblick	Worms	Herrnsheim	Rhh 419
Rheinblick	**Alsheim**	–	**Rhh 327–334**
	Dorn-Dürkheim	–	
	Mettenheim	–	

Site	Town	Ortsteil	Region & Site No.
Rheingarten	Eltville	Erbach	Rhg 55 a T
	Eltville	Hattenheim	
Rheingasse	Lettweiler	–	N 226
Rheingoldberg	Niederburg	–	Mrh 64
Rheingrafenberg	Freilaubersheim	–	Rhh 72
Rheingrafenberg	Meddersheim	–	N 199
Rheingrafenberg	Wörrstadt	–	Rhh 115
Rheingrafenstein	**Eckelsheim**	–	**Rhh 62–92**
	Freilaubersheim	–	
	Fürfeld	–	
	Hackenheim	–	
	Neu-Bamberg	–	
	Pleitersheim	–	
	Siefersheim	–	
	Stein-Bockenheim	–	
	Tiefenthal	–	
	Volxheim	–	
	Wöllstein	–	
	Wonsheim	–	
Rheinhell	Eltville	Erbach	Rhg 67
Rheinhöhe	Ingelheim	Groß-Winternheim	Rhh 146
Rheinhöller	Linz	–	Mrh 12
Rheinnieder	Urbar	–	Mrh 29 T
	Vallendar	–	
Rheinpforte	Selzen	–	Rhh 232
Riedersbückele	Lauffen	–	W 73
Riegelfeld	Bad Neuenahr-Ahrweiler	Ahrweiler	A 15
Rieschen	Meersburg	–	B 333
Ritsch	Thörnich	–	MSR 331
Ritterberg	Schornsheim	–	Rhh 211
Rittergarten	Bad Dürkheim	–	Rhpf 122
Ritterhalde	Gailingen	–	B 349
Ritterhölle	Dalberg	–	N 73
Ritterpfad	Kanzem	–	MSR 455 T
	Wawern		
Rittersberg	Ilbesheim	–	Rhpf 299
Rittersberg	**Dossenheim**	–	**B 29–43**
	Heidelberg	–	
	Hemsbach	–	
	Hirschberg	**Großsachsen**	
	Hirschberg	**Leutershausen**	
	Laudenbach	–	
	Schriesheim	–	
	Weinheim	–	
	Weinheim	**Hohensachsen**	
	Weinheim	**Lützelsachsen**	
	Weinheim	**Sulzbach**	
Rochusfels	Nittel	–	MSR 511 T
	Nittel	Köllig	
Rödchen	Eltville	Martinsthal	Rhg 85
Römerberg	Alsheim	–	Rhh 329
Römerberg	Alzey	–	Rhh 348
Römerberg	Badenheim	–	Rhh 24
Römerberg	Badenweiler	–	B 301 T
	Müllheim	Niederweiler	
Römerberg	Bingen	Bingerbrück	N 4 T
	Weiler		
Römerberg	Burgen	–	MSR 272
Römerberg	Dorn-Dürkheim	–	Rhh 332
Römerberg	Engelstadt	–	Rhh 135
Römerberg	Essenheim	–	Rhh 195
Römerberg	Gutenberg	–	N 94
Römerberg	Merxheim	–	N 188
Römerberg	Münster-Sarmsheim	–	N 4 a
Römerberg	Nehren	–	MSR 106
Römerberg	Oberbillig	–	MSR 503

Site	Town	Ortsteil	Region & Site No.
Römerberg	Oberheimbach	–	Mrh 104
Römerberg	Perl	Nennig	MSR 521
Römerberg	Rheinbrohl	–	Mrh 17
Römerberg	Riol	–	MSR 346
Römerberg	Senheim	Senhals	MSR 73
Römerberg	Waldböckelheim	–	N 311
Römerberg	Windesheim	–	N 36
Römerbrunnen	Neustadt an der Weinstraße	Hambach an der Weinstraße	Rhpf 210
Römergarten	Briedern	–	MSR 95
Römerhalde	Bad Kreuznach	Planig	N 131
Römerhang	Kinheim	–	MSR 199 a
Römerkrug	Oberwesel	–	Mrh 73
Römerkrug	Oberwesel	Dellhofen	Mrh 74
Römerlay	**Franzenheim**	**–**	**MSR 355–**
	Hockweiler	**–**	**415**
	Kasel	**–**	
	Mertesdorf	**–**	
	Mertesdorf	**Lorenzhof**	
	Mertesdorf	**Maximin Grünhaus**	
	Morscheid	**–**	
	Plowig	**–**	
	Riveris	**–**	
	Sommerau	**–**	
	Trier	**–**	
	Trier	**Biewer**	
	Trier	**Eitelsbach**	
	Trier	**Filsch**	
	Trier	**Irsch**	
	Trier	**Kernscheid**	
	Trier	**Korlingen**	
	Trier	**Kürenz**	
	Trier	**Matthias**	
	Trier	**Olewig**	
	Trier	**Ruwer**	
	Trier	**Tarforst**	
	Waldrach	**–**	
Römerpfad	Maring-Noviand	–	MSR 269
Römerpfad	Unkenbach	–	N 229
Römerquelle	Zell	Kaimt	MSR 155
Römerschanze	Eimsheim	–	Rhh 299
Römersteg	Worms	Herrnsheim	Rhh 428
Römerstich	Auen	–	N 183
Römerstraße	Kirchheim an der Weinstraße	–	Rhpf 72
Römerweg	Kirrweiler	–	Rhpf 222
Röth	Grünstadt	–	Rhpf 38
Röthen	Schliengen	Niedereggenen	B 310 T
	Schliengen	Obereggenen	
Rosenberg	Bad Kreuznach	–	N 102
Rosenberg	Bad Neuenahr-Ahrweiler	Marienthal	A 23
Rosenberg	Bad Windsheim	Oberntief	F 128 g
Rosenberg	Bernkastel-Kues	Kues	MSR 254
Rosenberg	Bernkastel-Kues	Wehlen	MSR 133 a
Rosenberg	Biebelnheim	–	Rhh 325
Rosenberg	Billigheim-Ingenheim	Billigheim	Rhpf 313 T
	Billigheim-Ingenheim	Mühlhofen	
	Steinweiler	–	
Rosenberg	Birkweiler	–	Rhpf 292 T
	Landau in der Pfalz	Arzheim	
	Siebeldingen	–	
Rosenberg	Bruttig-Fankel	Fankel	MSR 88
Rosenberg	Cochem	Cond	MSR 78
Rosenberg	Dielheim	–	B 54 T
	Mühlhausen	Tairnbach	

Site	Town	Ortsteil	Region & Site No.
Rosenberg	Ehrenkirchen	Ehrenstetten	B 280
Rosenberg	Frankenwinheim	–	F 102 a
Rosenberg	Hardthausen	Kochersteinsfeld	W 17 a
Rosenberg	Kinheim	–	MSR 199
Rosenberg	Klotten	–	MSR 55 a
Rosenberg	Konz	Oberemmel	MSR 443
Rosenberg	Leutesdorf	–	Mrh 23
Rosenberg	Lorch	Lorchhausen	Rhg 1
Rosenberg	Mannweiler-Cölln	–	N 254
Rosenberg	Minheim	–	MSR 295
Rosenberg	Monzingen	–	N 191
Rosenberg	Moselkern	–	MSR 41
Rosenberg	Müllheim	Britzingen	B 294 T
	Müllheim	Dattingen	
	Müllheim	Zunzingen	
Rosenberg	Neef	–	MSR 123
Rosenberg	Niederhausen an der Nahe	–	N 292
Rosenberg	Nierstein	–	Rhh 246
Rosenberg	Oberfell	–	MSR 28
Rosenberg	Osann-Monzel	Osann	MSR 284
Rosenberg	Palzem	Wehr	MSR 515
Rosenberg	Pommern	–	MSR 55
Rosenberg	Pünderich	–	MSR 162
Rosenberg	Rivenich	–	MSR 320
Rosenberg	Sehnheim	–	MSR 102
Rosenberg	Sommerach	–	F 90 T
	Volkach	Hallburg	
Rosenberg	St. Goar	Werlau	Mrh 50
Rosenberg	Windesheim	–	N 32
Rosenberg	Wiltingen	–	MSR 443 a
Rosenberg	Wittlich	–	MSR 216
Rosenborn	Zell	Kaimt	MSR 154
Rosenbühl	**Erpolzheim**	**–**	**Rhpf 75–**
	Freinsheim	**–**	**81**
	Lambsheim	**–**	
	Weisenheim am Sand	**–**	
Rosengärtchen	Neumagen-Dhron	Neumagen	MSR 312
Rosengarten	Bechtheim	–	Rhh 389
Rosengarten	Bingen	Gaulsheim	Rhh 7
Rosengarten	Edesheim	–	Rhpf 248
Rosengarten	Friedelsheim	–	Rhpf 164
Rosengarten	Gabsheim	–	Rhh 215
Rosengarten	Kapellen-Drusweiler	–	Rhpf 322
Rosengarten	Karlsruhe	Hohenwettersbach	B 111
Rosengarten	Monsheim	Kriegsheim	Rhh 410
Rosengarten	Obrigheim	–	Rhpf 30
Rosengarten	Rhodt unter Rietburg	–	Rhpf 239
Rosengarten	Rüdesheim	–	Rhg 21
Rosengarten	Starkenburg	–	MSR 182
Rosengarten	**Bockenau**	**–**	**N 144–**
	Braunweiler	**–**	**181**
	Burgsponheim	**–**	
	Hüffelsheim	**–**	
	Mandel	**–**	
	Roxheim	**–**	
	Rüdesheim	**–**	
	Sponheim	**–**	
	St. Katharinen	**–**	
	Weinsheim	**–**	

Site	Town	Ortsteil	Region & Site No.
Rosenhang	**Beilstein**	**—**	**MSR 74–**
	Bremm	**—**	**104**
	Briedern	**—**	
	Bruttig-Fankel	**Bruttig**	
	Bruttig-Fankel	**Fankel**	
	Cochem	**Cond**	
	Ediger-Eller	**Eller**	
	Ellenz-Poltersdorf		
	Mesenich	**—**	
	Senheim	**—**	
	Treis-Karden	**Treis**	
	Valwig	**—**	
Rosenheck	Bad Kreuznach	Winzenheim	N 128
Rosenheck	Niederhausen an der Nahe	—	N 293
Rosenhügel	Königswinter	Oberdollendorf	Mrh 1
Rosenkränzel	Roschbach	—	Rhpf 280
Rosenkranz	Böchingen	—	Rhpf 273
Rosenkranz	Vogtsburg im Kaiserstuhl	Bischoffingen	B 235
Rosenkranzweg	Östringen	—	B 63
Rosenlay	Lieser	—	MSR 250
Rosental	Perscheid	—	Mrh 77
Rosenteich	Guldental	Heddesheim und Waldhilbersheim	N 45
Rosenthal	Bad Neuenahr-Ahrweiler	Ahrweiler	A 13
Roßberg	Essingen	—	Rhpf 255
Roßberg	Roßdorf	—	HB 2
Roßberg	Winnenden	—	W 166
Rossel	Waldalgesheim	Genheim	N 24
Roßstein	Kaub	—	Mrh 80
Roßtal	**Arnstein**	**—**	**F 33–43**
	Eußenheim	**—**	
	Gössenheim	**—**	
	Himmelstadt	**—**	
	Karlstadt	**—**	
	Karlstadt	**Gambach**	
	Karlstadt	**Karlburg**	
	Karlstadt	**Stetten**	
	Laudenbach	**—**	
	Mühlbach	**—**	
	Retzstadt	**—**	
Rote Halde	Sasbach	—	B 245
Rotenberg	Altenbamberg	—	N 265
Rotenberg	Oberhausen an der Nahe	—	N 319
Rotenberg	Sugenheim	Ingolstadt	F 127 a
Rotenberg	Wachenheim	—	Rhh 408
Rotenbusch	Pfinztal	Söllingen	B 109
Rotenfels	Alzey	—	Rhh 347 T
	Alzey	Heimersheim	
Rotenfels	Traisen	—	N 280
Rotenfelser im Winkel	Bad Münster am Stein-Ebernburg	Münster	N 276
Rotenpfad	Flonheim	—	Rhh 100
Rotenstein	Westhofen	—	Rhh 365
Roter Berg	Hochstadt	—	Rhpf 262
Roter Berg	Ilsfeld	Schozach	W 77
Roter Berg	Ipsheim	Weimersheim	F 127 a
Roter Berg	Kenzingen	—	B 193
Roter Bur	Glottertal	—	B 205
Roterd	Neumagen-Dhron	Dhron	MSR 306
Rotes Kreuz	Ingelheim	Groß-Winternheim	Rhh 155
Rotfeld	Nußbaum	—	N 195
Rotgrund	Breisach	Niederrimsingen	B 261
Rothenack	Bornich	—	Mrh 62

Site	Town	Ortsteil	Region & Site No.
Rothenberg	Duchroth	—	N 319 a
Rothenberg	Eltville	Rauenthal	Rhg 80
Rothenberg	Gau-Algesheim	—	Rhh 40
Rothenberg	Geisenheim	—	Rhg 22
Rothenberg	Langenlonsheim	—	N 66
Rothenberg	Nackenheim	—	Rhh 245
Rothenberg	Rümmelsheim mit Ortsteil Burg Layen	—	N 16
Rotlay	Platten	—	MSR 222
Rotlay	Sehlem	—	MSR 322
Rotlay	Trier	Kürenz	MSR 368
Rotsteig	Malsch	—	B 59
Rott	**Alsbach**	**—**	**HB 1–5**
	Bensheim-Auerbach	**—**	
	Bensheim-Schönberg	**—**	
	Zwingenberg	**—**	
Rozenberg	Mundelsheim	—	W 124
Rüberberger Domherrenberg	Briedern	—	MSR 71 T
	Ellenz-Polterberg	—	
	Senheim	Senhals	
Ruthe	Nordheim	—	W 84 a T
	Schwaigern	—	

Site	Town	Ortsteil	Region & Site No.
Saarfeilser Marienberg	Schoden	–	MSR 459
Sackträger	Oppenheim	–	Rhh 271
Sängerhalde	Markdorf	–	B 337 T
	Meersburg	–	
	Stetten	–	
Sätzler	Baden-Baden	–	B 117 T
	Sinzheim	–	
Salzberg	**Eberstadt**	**–**	**W 39–52**
	Ellhofen	**–**	
	Lehrensteinsfeld	**–**	
	Löwenstein	**–**	
	Löwenstein	**Hößlinsülz**	
	Obersulm	**Affaltrach**	
	Obersulm	**Eichelberg**	
	Obersulm	**Eschenau**	
	Obersulm	**Sülzbach**	
	Obersulm	**Weiler**	
	Obersulm	**Willsbach**	
	Weinsberg	**–**	
	Weinsberg	**Grantschen**	
	Weinsberg	**Wimmental**	
Sand	Mainz	Ebersheim	Rhh 167
Sandberg	Wiltingen	–	MSR 446
Sanderberg	Obernau	–	F 7
Sandgrub	Eltville	–	Rhg 71 T
	Kiedrich	–	
Sandrocken	Hirschberg	Großsachsen	B 34
Sankt Alban	**Bodenheim**	**–**	**Rhh 163–189**
	Gau-Bischofsheim	**–**	
	Harxheim	**–**	
	Lörzweiler		
	Mainz	**Ebersheim**	
	Mainz	**Hechtsheim**	
	Mainz	**Laubenheim**	
Sankt Annaberg	Burrweiler	–	Rhpf 266
Sankt Annaberg	Worms	Herrnsheim	Rhh 424
Sankt Anna Kapelle	Flörsheim	–	Rhg 110 a
Sankt Antoniusweg	Langenlonsheim	–	N 68
Sankt Castorhöhle	Müden	–	MSR 47
Sankt Cyriakusstift	Worms	–	Rhh 420
Sankt Georgen	Partenheim	–	Rhh 60
Sankt Georgenberg	Jugenheim	–	Rhh 130
Sankt Georgenberg	Worms	Pfeddersheim	Rhh 426
Sankt Georgshof	Temmels	–	MSR 505
Sankt Jakobsberg	Ockenheim	–	Rhh 33
Sankt Johännser	Markgröningen	–	W 129 T
	Vaihingen	Enzweihingen	
Sankt Jost	Bacharach	Steeg	Mrh 88
Sankt Julianenbrunnen	Guntersblum	–	Rhh 288
Sankt Kathrin	Wolfsheim	–	Rhh 59
Sankt Kiliansberg	Mainz	Kostheim	Rhg 100 a
Sankt Klausen	Ramsthal	–	F 31
Sankt Laurenzikapelle	Gau-Algesheim	Laurenziberg	Rhh 41
Sankt Martin	Bad Kreuznach	–	N 118
Sankt Martin	Ensch	–	MSR 334
Sankt Martin	Guldental	Heddesheim und Waldhilbersheim	N 40
Sankt Martiner Hofberg	Trier	Irsch	MSR 371 T
	Trier	Tarforst	
Sankt Martiner Klosterberg	Trier	Irsch	MSR 372 T
	Trier	Tarforst	

Site	Town	Ortsteil	Region & Site No.
Sankt Martinsberg	Oberwesel	–	Mrh 71
Sankt Martinskreuz	Mertesheim	–	Rhpf 33
Sankt Matheiser	Trier	Matthias	MSR 383
Sankt Maximiner Kreuzberg	Trier	–	MSR 377 T
	Trier	Kürenz	
Sankt Michael	**Bekond**	**–**	**MSR 323–344**
	Detzem	**–**	
	Ensch	**–**	
	Klüsserath	**–**	
	Köwerich	**–**	
	Leiwen	**–**	
	Longen	**–**	
	Mehring	**–**	
	Mehring	**Lörsch**	
	Pölich	**–**	
	Schleich	**–**	
	Thörnich	**–**	
Sankt Michaelsberg	Riegel	–	B 211
Sankt Nikolaus	Oestrich-Winkel	Mittelheim	Rhg 42
Sankt Oswald	Manubach	–	Mrh 97
Sankt Petrusberg	Trier	Kernscheid	MSR 378
Sankt Quirinusberg	Perl	–	MSR 524
Sankt Rochuskapelle	**Aspisheim**	**–**	**Rhh 1–36**
	Badenheim	**–**	
	Biebelsheim	**–**	
	Bingen	**Büdesheim**	
	Bingen	**Dietersheim**	
	Bingen	**Dromersheim**	
	Bingen	**Gaulsheim**	
	Bingen	**Kempten**	
	Bingen	**Sponsheim**	
	Gensingen	**–**	
	Grolsheim	**–**	
	Horrweiler	**–**	
	Ockenheim	**–**	
	Pfaffen-Schwabenheim	**–**	
	Welgesheim	**–**	
	Zotzenheim	**–**	
Sankt Ruppertsberg	Gutenberg	–	N 93
Sankt Remigiusberg	Laubenheim	–	N 57
Sankt Stephan	Grünstadt	Asselheim	Rhpf 35
Sankt Werner-Berg	Oberwesel	Dellhofen	Mrh 75
Satzenberg	Wertheim	Reichholzheim	B 7
Sauberg	Ötisheim	–	W 104
Saukopf	Gau-Bickelheim	–	Rhh 121
Saukopf	Windesheim	–	N 29
Sauloch	Flörsheim-Dalsheim	Dalsheim	Rhh 399
Saumagen	Kallstadt	–	Rhpf 98 a
Sauschwänzel	Billigheim-Ingenheim	Billigheim	Rhpf 310
Schäf	Auggen	–	B 306 T
	Neuenburg am Rhein	Steinenstadt	
Schäfergarten	Insheim	–	Rhpf 303 T
	Rohrbach	–	
Schäferlay	Briedel	–	MSR 157
Schäfersberg	Schöneberg	–	N 69
Schäwer	Burrweiler	–	Rhpf 267
Schafberg	Großniedesheim	–	Rhpf 53
Schafsteige	Niederstetten	–	W 6 T
	Niederstetten	Oberstetten	
	Niederstetten	Vorbachzimmern	
	Niederstetten	Wermutshausen	
	Weikersheim	Laudenbach	
	Weikersheim	Haagen	
Schalk	Elsenfeld	Rück	F 11 a

Site	Town	Ortsteil	Region & Site No.
Schalkstein	**Affalterbach**	—	**W 120–133**
	Aspach	**Allermsbach**	
	Aspach	**Kleinaspach**	
	Aspach	**Rietenau**	
	Asperg	—	
	Benningen	—	
	Besigheim	—	
	Bietigheim-Bissingen	**Bietigheim**	
	Beitigheim-Bissingen	**Bissingen**	
	Erdmannhausen	—	
	Freiburg/Neckar	**Beihingen**	
	Gemmrigheim	—	
	Hessigheim		
	Ingersheim	**Kleiningersheim**	
	Ingersheim	**Großingersheim**	
	Kirchberg/Murr	—	
	Löchgau	—	
	Ludwigsburg	**Hoheneck**	
	Ludwigsburg	**Neckarweihingen**	
	Ludwigsburg	**Poppenweiler**	
	Marbach/Neckar	—	
	Marbach/Neckar	**Rielingshausen**	
	Markgröningen	—	
	Mundelsheim	—	
	Murr	—	
	Steinheim	—	
	Steinheim	**Höpfigheim**	
	Vaihingen	**Enzweihingen**	
	Walheim	—	
Schanzreiter	Illingen	—	W 112 T
	Vaihingen	Ensingen	
Scharlachberg	Bingen	Gaulsheim	Rhh 8
Scharlachberg	Thüngersheim	—	F 46
Scharrenberg	Stuttgart	Degerloch	W 138
Scharzberg	**Ayl**	**Biebelhausen**	**MSR 416–495**
	Irsch	—	
	Kanzem	—	
	Kastel-Staadt	—	
	Konz	—	
	Konz	**Falkenstein**	
	Konz	**Filzen**	
	Konz	**Hamm**	
	Konz	**Krettnach**	
	Konz	**Kommlingen**	
	Konz	**Könen**	
	Konz	**Niedermennig**	
	Konz	**Oberemmel**	
	Konz	**Obermennig**	
	Ockfen	—	
	Pellingen	—	
	Saarburg	—	
	Saarburg	**Krutweiler**	
	Schoden	—	
	Serrig	—	
	Wawern	—	
	Wiltingen	—	
	Wiltingen	**Scharzhofberg**	
Schatzgarten	Traben-Trarbach	Wolf	MSR 194
Scheibenbuck	Sasbach	—	B 243
Scheidterberg	Ayl mit Ortsteil Biebelhausen		MSR 471
Scheinberg	Euerdorf	Wirmsthal	F 32
Schellenbrunnen	Östringen	Tiefenbach	B 90
Schelm	Briedel	—	MSR 160
Schelmen	Wahlheim	—	Rhh 352
Schelmenklinge	Ilsfeld	Schozach	W 76
Schelmenstück	Bingen	Bündesheim	Rhh 9 T
	Bingen	Dietersheim	
Schemelsberg	Weinsberg	—	W 25
Schenkenberg	Eßlingen	—	W 158 T
	Eßlingen	Mettingen	
Schenkenböhl	**Bad Dürkheim**	—	**Rhpf 124–130**
	Wachenheim	—	

Site	Town	Ortsteil	Region & Site No.
Scheuerberg	Neckarsulm	—	W 23
Schieferlay	Bad Neuenahr-Ahrweiler	Neuenahr	A 6
Schieferlay	Dernau	—	A 30
Schieferlay	Mayschoß	—	A 37
Schießlay	Thörnich	—	MSR 332
Schikanenbuckel	Rehborn	—	N 218
Schild	**Abtswind**	—	**F 105–106, 108**
	Castell	—	
	Castell	**Greuth**	
	Prichsenstadt	**Kirchschönbach**	
Schildberg	Sulzheim	—	Rhh 118
Schlangengraben	Wiltingen	—	MSR 453
Schleidberg	Tawern	Fellerich	MSR 504
Schlemmertröpfchen	Bremm	—	MSR 119
Schlierbach	Obersulm	Weiler	W 50
Schlipf	Weil am Rhein	—	B 325
Schlittberg	Römerberg (bei Speyer)	Mechtersheim	Rhpf 264 b
Schlössel	Neustadt an der Weinstraße	Gimmeldingen an der Weinstraße	Rhpf 188
Schloß	Dienheim	—	Rhh 280 T
	Oppenheim	—	
Schloß	Edesheim	—	Rhpf 247
Schloß	Grünstadt	Asselheim	Rhpf 36
Schloß	Obrigheim	Mühlheim	Rhpf 32
Schloß	Schonungen	Mainberg	F 103 e
Schloß	Uelversheim	—	Rhh 301
Schloßberg	Altenbamberg	—	N 264
Schloßberg	Alzenau	Wasserlos	F 3
Schloßberg	Appenweier	Nesselried	B 155 T
	Durbach	—	
Schloßberg	Baden-Baden	Neuweier	B 125
Schloßberg	Bad Hönningen	—	Mrh 15
Schloßberg	Bad Münster am Stein-Ebernburg	Ebernburg	N 266
Schloßberg	Battenberg	—	Rhpf 50
Schloßberg	Beilstein	—	MSR 91
Schloßberg	Bekond	—	MSR 328
Schloßberg	Bernkastel-Kues	Andel	MSR 252 T
	Bernkastel-Kues	Bernkastel	
	Lieser	—	
Schloßberg	Bockenheim an der Weinstraße	—	Rhpf 18
Schloßberg	Bolanden	—	Rhpf 3
Schloßberg	Brackenheim	—	W 82 T
	Brackenheim	Neipperg	
	Heilbronn	Klingenberg	
Schloßberg	Braunweiler	—	N 147
Schloßberg	Burg	—	MSR 173
Schloßberg	Burgsponheim	—	N 172 T
	Sponheim	—	
Schloßberg	Castell	—	F 112
Schloßberg	Cochem	—	MSR 61
Schloßberg	Dalberg	—	N 72
Schloßberg	Elfershausen	Engenthal	F 30 c T
	Elfershausen	Trimberg	
Schloßberg	Eltville	Erbach	Rhg 61
Schloßberg	Freiburg	—	B 208
Schloßberg	Gau-Heppenheim	—	Rhh 319
Schloßberg	Gutenberg	—	N 95
Schloßberg	Hammelburg	Saaleck	F 28

Site	Town	Ortsteil	Region & Site No.
Schloßberg	Hammerstein	–	Mrh 20
Schloßberg	Harxheim	–	Rhh 186
Schloßberg	Hohberg	Diersburg	B 181
Schloßberg	Ihringen	–	B 221 T
	Vogtsburg im Kaiserstuhl	Achkarren	
	Vogtsburg im Kaiserstuhl	Oberrotweil	
Schloßberg	Ilsfeld	Auenstein	W 57 T
	Ilsfeld	Helfenberg	
Schloßberg	Ingelheim	Groß-Winternheim	Rhh 139
Schloßberg	Ingersheim	Großingersheim	W 127 T
	Ingersheim	Kleiningersheim	
Schloßberg	Kanzem	–	MSR 432
Schloßberg	Kenzingen	Hecklingen	B 196
Schloßberg	Klingenberg am Main	–	F 15
Schloßberg	Kobern-Gondorf	Gondorf	MSR 14 T
	Kobern-Gondorf	Kobern	
Schloßberg	Knetzgau	Zell am Ebersberg	F 133 a
Schloßberg	Lorch	–	Rhg 3
Schloßberg	Mandel	–	N 152
Schloßberg	Martinstein	–	N 184
Schloßberg	Mettenheim	–	Rhh 334
Schloßberg	Nassau	–	Mrh 26
Schloßberg	Neuleiningen	–	Rhpf 44
Schloßberg	Neustadt an der Weinstraße	Hambach an der Weinstraße	Rhpf 205
Schloßberg	Niederkirchen	–	Rhpf 170
Schloßberg	Obermoschel	–	N 231
Schloßberg	Oestrich-Winkel	Winkel	Rhg 38
Schloßberg	Oppenheim	–	Rhh 279
Schloßberg	Ortenberg	–	B 172
Schloßberg	Perl	Nennig	MSR 520
Schloßberg	Pleisweiler-Oberhofen	–	Rhpf 320
Schloßberg	Raumbach/Glan	–	N 221
Schloßberg	Rauenberg	Rotenberg	B 56
Schloßberg	Rhodt unter Rietburg	–	Rhpf 238
Schloßberg	Rümmelsheim mit Ortsteil Burg Layen	–	N 14
Schloßberg	Saarburg	–	MSR 476
Schloßberg	Salem	Kirchberg	B 339
Schloßberg	Saulheim	–	Rhh 202
Schloßberg	Schriesheim	–	B 40
Schloßberg	Schwabenheim	–	Rhh 139 a
Schloßberg	Sommerau	–	MSR 386
Schloßberg	Staufen im Breisgau	–	B 282 T
	Staufen im Breisgau	Grunern	
Schloßberg	Stuttgart	Rotenberg	W 147 T
	Stuttgart	Uhlbach	
	Stuttgart	Untertürkheim	
Schloßberg	Talheim	–	W 70 a
Schloßberg	Traben-Trarbach	Trarbach	MSR 186
Schloßberg	Untergruppenbach	–	W 70
Schloßberg	Volkach	Hallburg	F 103
Schloßberg	Wachenheim	–	Rhpf 130
Schloßberg	Weingarten	–	Rhpf 264
Schloßberg	Wertheim	–	B 5
Schloßberg	Wiltingen	–	MSR 432 a
Schloßberg	Winnenden	Bürg	W 167
Schloßberg	Würzburg	–	F 56
Schloßberg	Zeltingen-Rachtig	–	MSR 231

Site	Town	Ortsteil	Region & Site No.
Schloßberg	**Heppenheim (einschließlich Erbach und Hambach)**		**HB 11–16**
Schloßberg	**Großlangheim**	–	**F 114–120**
	Iphofen	–	
	Kitzingen	**Sickershausen**	
	Kleinlangheim	–	
	Rödelsee	–	
	Wiesenbronn	–	
Schloßberg Schwätzerchen	Bingen	Büdesheim	Rhh 1 T
	Bingen	Kempten	
Schloßblick	Stuttgart	Hohenheim	W 138 a
Schloß Bübinger	**Besch**	–	**MSR 520–525**
	Perl	–	
	Perl	**Nennig**	
	Perl	**Sehndorf**	
	Tettingen	–	
	Wochern	–	
Schloßgarten	Bretzenheim	–	N 141
Schloßgarten	Burrweiler	–	Rhpf 268
Schloßgarten	Friedelsheim	–	Rhpf 132
Schloßgarten	Geisenheim	–	Rhg 28
Schloßgarten	Hochheim	Massenheim	Rhg 114 a
Schloßgarten	Kirchheimbolanden	–	Rhpf 2
Schloßgarten	Kleinniedesheim	–	Rhpf 51
Schloßgarten	Müllheim	Hügelheim	B 297
Schloßgarten	Offstein	–	Rhh 414
Schloßgarten	Schweppenhausen	–	N 28
Schloßgarten	Vogtsburg im Kaiserstuhl	Burkheim	B 238
Schloß Grohl	Durbach	–	B 164
Schloß Gutenburg	Gutenberg	–	N 96
Schloß Hammerstein	Albig	–	Rhh 321 T
	Alzey	–	
Schloßhölle	Gumbsheim	–	Rhh 119 T
	Wöllstein	–	
Schloß Hohenrechen	Nierstein	–	Rhh 250
Schloß Hohneck	Niederheimbach	–	Mrh 109
Schloß Johannisberg	Geisenheim	Johannisberg	Rhg Ortst. A
Schloßkapelle	**Bingen**	**Bingerbrück**	**N 1–61**
	Dorsheim	–	
	Eckenroth	–	
	Guldental	**Heddesheim und Waldhilbersheim**	
	Laubenheim	–	
	Münster-Sarmsheim	–	
	Rümmelsheim	–	
	Schweppenhausen	–	
	Waldalgesheim	**Genheim**	
	Waldlaubersheim	–	
	Weiler	–	
	Windesheim	–	
Schloßleite	Eltmann	–	F 135
Schloß Ludwigshöhe	**Edenkoben**	–	**Rhpf 225–236**
	St. Martin	–	
Schloßpark	Volkach	Gaibach	F 103 a
Schloß Randeck	Mannweiler-Cölln	–	N 252
Schloß Reichenstein	**Niederheimbach**	–	**Mrh 101 a, 104–112**
	Oberheimbach	–	
	Oberheimbach	**Schloß Fürstenberg**	
	Trechtingshausen	–	
Schloß Reichhartshausen	Oestrich-Winkel	Oestrich	Rhg Ortst. C
Schloß Rheinburg	Gailingen	–	B 350

Site	Town	Ortsteil	Region & Site No.
Schloß Rodeck	**Achern**	**Mösbach**	**B 116—150**
	Achern	**Oberachern**	
	Baden-Baden	—	
	Baden-Baden	**Neuweier**	
	Baden-Baden	**Steinbach**	
	Baden-Baden	**Varnhalt**	
	Bühl	**Altschweier**	
	Bühl	**Eisental**	
	Bühl	**Neusatz**	
	Bühlertal	—	
	Gernsbach	**Obertsrot**	
	Gernsbach	**Staufenberg**	
	Kappelrodeck	—	
	Kappelrodeck	**Waldulm**	
	Lauf	—	
	Ottersweier	—	
	Renchen	—	
	Sasbach	**Obersasbach**	
	Sasbachwalden	—	
	Sinzheim	—	
	Weisenbach	—	
Schloß Saarfelser Schloßberg	Serrig	—	MSR 487
Schloß Saarsteiner	Serrig	—	MSR 486
Schloß Schönburg	**Damscheid**	—	**Mrh 63—77**
	Niederburg	—	
	Oberwesel	—	
	Oberwesel	**Dellhofen**	
	Oberwesel	**Engehöll**	
	Oberwesel	**Langscheid**	
	Oberwesel	**Urbar**	
	Perscheid	—	
Schloß Schwabsburg	Nierstein	—	Rhh 267 T
	Nierstein	Schwabsburg	
Schloß Stahlberg	Bacharach	Breitscheid	Mrh 86 T
	Bacharach	Steeg	
Schloß Stahleck	**Bacharach**	—	**Mrh 86—103**
	Bacharach	**Breitscheid**	
	Bacharach	**Medenscheid und Neurath**	
	Bacharach	**Steeg**	
	Manubach	—	
	Oberdiebach	—	
	Oberdiebach	**Rheindiebach**	
	Oberheimbach	**Schloß Fürstenberg**	
Schloßsteige	Beuren	—	W 197 T
	Frickenhausen	—	
	Frickenhausen	Linsenhofen	
	Kohlberg	—	
	Metzingen	—	
	Neuffen	—	
	Neuffen	Kappishäusern	
	Weilheim	—	
Schloß Stolzenberg	Bayerfeld-Steckweiler	—	N 256
Schloßstück	**Bad Windsheim**	**Humprechtsau**	**F 123—128**
	Bad Windsheim	**Ickelheim**	
	Bad Windsheim	**Külsheim**	
	Bad Windsheim	**Rüdisbronn**	
	Dietersheim	**Dottenheim**	
	Dietersheim	**Walddachsbach**	
	Ergersheim	—	
	Ippesheim	—	
	Ippesheim	**Bullenheim**	
	Ipsheim	—	
	Ipsheim	**Kaubenheim**	
	Ipsheim	**Weimersheim**	
	Seinsheim	—	
	Sugenheim	**Ingolstadt**	
	Sugenheim	**Krassolzheim**	
	Weigenheim	—	
	Weigenheim	**Reusch**	
	Willanzheim	**Hüttenheim**	
	Windsheim	**Humprechtsau**	
Schloß Thorner Kupp	Palzem	Kreuzweiler	MSR 519
Schloß Vollrads	Oestrich-Winkel	Winkel	Rhg Ortst. B

Site	Town	Ortsteil	Region & Site No.
Schloßwengert	Beilstein	Hohenbeilstein	W 60
Schloß Westerhaus	Ingelheim	—	Rhh 144 T
	Ingelheim	Groß-Winternheim	
Schlüsselberg	Schöntal	Bieringen	W 15
Schmecker	Weikersheim	—	W 4
Schmittskapellchen	Nackenheim	—	Rhh 220
Schneckenberg	Worms	Heppenheim	Rhh 434
Schneckenhof	Bretzfeld	Adolzfurt	W 36 T
	Bretzfeld	Geddelsbach	
	Bretzfeld	Unterheimbach	
	Wüstenrot	Maienfels	
Schnepfenflug an der Weinstraße	**Deidesheim**	—	**Rhpf 131—137**
	Forst an der Weinstraße	—	
	Friedelsheim	—	
	Wachenheim	—	
Schnepfenflug vom Zellertal	**Albisheim**	—	**Rhpf 1—17**
	Bolanden	—	
	Bubenheim	—	
	Einselthum	—	
	Gauersheim	—	
	Immesheim	—	
	Kerzenheim	—	
	Kirchheimbolanden	—	
	Morschheim	—	
	Ottersheim/ Zellertal	—	
	Rittersheim	—	
	Rüssingen	—	
	Stetten	—	
	Zellertal	**Harxheim**	
	Zellertal	**Niefernheim**	
	Zellertal	**Zell**	
Schnepp	Obersülzen	—	Rhpf 58
Schnorbach Brückstück	Koblenz	—	Mrh 32
Schön	Bad Friedrichshall	Duttenberg	W 19 T
	Bad Friedrichshall	Offenau	
Schönberg	Bornheim	—	Rhh 107 T
	Lonsheim	—	
Schönhell	Oestrich-Winkel	Hallgarten	Rhg 56
Schönhölle	Ockenheim	—	Rhh 36
Schöntal	Alsbach	—	HB 7
Schollerbuckel	Eberbach	—	B 74
Schozachtal	**Abstatt**	—	**W 53—57**
	Ilsfeld	—	
	Ilsfeld	**Auenstein**	
	Ilsfeld	**Helfenberg**	
	Löwenstein	—	
	Untergruppenbach	**Unterheinriet**	
Schubertslay	Piesport	—	MSR 303
Schützenhaus	Eltville	Hattenheim	Rhg 53
Schützenhütte	Dolgesheim	—	Rhh 296
Schützenhütte	Oppenheim	—	Rhh 272
Schützenlay	Ediger-Eller	Eller	MSR 117
Schutterlindenberg	**Ettenheim**	**Münchweier**	**B 183—186**
	Ettenheim	**Wallburg**	
	Friesenheim	—	
	Friesenheim	**Heiligenzell**	
	Friesenheim	**Oberschopfheim**	
	Friesenheim	**Oberweier**	
	Kippenheim	—	
	Kippenheim	**Mahlberg**	
	Kippenheim	**Schmieheim**	
	Lahr	—	
	Lahr	**Hugsweier**	
	Lahr	**Kippenheimweiler**	
	Lahr	**Mietersheim**	
	Lahr	**Sulz**	
Schwalben	Wackernheim	—	Rhh 158
Schwalbennest	Raumbach/Glan	—	N 220

Site	Town	Ortsteil	Region & Site No.
Schwanleite	Rödelsee	–	F 117
Schwarze Katz	**Zell**	–	**MSR 139–**
	Zell	**Kaimt**	**155**
	Zell	**Merl**	
Schwarzenberg	Bingen	Büdesheim	Rhh 10
Schwarzenberg	Valwig	–	MSR 80
Schwarzenstein	Geisenheim	Johannisberg	Rhg 30
Schwarzerde	**Bissersheim**	–	**Rhpf 51–**
	Dirmstein	–	**74**
	Gerolsheim	–	
	Großkarlbach	–	
	Großniedesheim	–	
	Grünstadt Land	**Heuchelheim bei Frankenthal**	
	Heßheim	–	
	Kirchheim an der Weinstraße		
	Kleinniedesheim	–	
	Laumersheim	–	
	Obersülzen	–	
Schwarzer Herrgott	Zellertal	Zell	Rhpf 11
Schwarzer Letten	Edenkoben	–	Rhpf 235
Schwarzes Kreuz	Freinsheim	–	Rhpf 93
Schwarzlay	**Bausendorf**	**Olkenbach**	**MSR 169–**
	Bengel	–	**222**
	Burg	–	
	Dreis	–	
	Enkirch	–	
	Erden	–	
	Flußbach	–	
	Hupperath	–	
	Kinheim	–	
	Lösnich	–	
	Platten	–	
	Starkenburg	–	
	Traben-Trarbach	**Traben**	
	Traben-Trarbach	**Trarbach**	
	Traben-Trarbach	**Wolf**	
	Ürzig	–	
	Wittlich	–	
Schwobajörgle	Neuenstein	Eschelbach	W 30 T
	Neuenstein	Kesselfeld	
Seehalde	Nonnenhorn	–	W 202
Seidenberg	Mannweiler-Cölln	–	N 253
Seilgarten	Bermersheim	–	Rhh 397
Seligmacher	Landau in der Pfalz	Arzheim	Rhpf 295 T
	Ranschbach	–	
Seligmacher	Lorch	Lorchhausen	Rhg 2
Senn	Kleinkarlbach	–	Rhpf 47
Servatiusberg	Briedern	–	MSR 94
Sieben Jungfrauen	Oberwesel	–	Mrh 69
Siegelsberg	Eltville	Erbach	Rhg 62
Silberberg	Bad Neuenahr-Ahrweiler	Ahrweiler	A 14
Silberberg	Bahlingen	–	B 212
Silberberg	Bodenheim	–	Rhh 179
Silberberg	Ellenz-Poltersdorf	–	MSR 90
Silberberg	Kraichtal	Menzingen, Münzesheim und Neuenbürg	B 95
Silberberg	Mayschoß	–	A 39
Silberberg	Mölsheim	–	Rhh 407
Silberberg	Monsheim	–	Rhh 407 a
Silberberg	Niederhorbach	–	Rhpf 317
Silberberg	Niedermoschel	–	N 234 T
	Obermoschel	–	
Silberberg	Walsheim	–	Rhpf 278
Silbergrube	Mommenheim	–	Rhh 242

Site	Town	Ortsteil	Region & Site No.
Silberquell	Tauberbischofsheim	Impfingen	B 13
Siliusbrunnen	Dienheim	–	Rhh 276
Simonsgarten	Roschbach	–	Rhpf 279
Sioner Klosterberg	Mauchenheim	–	Rhh 339
Söhrenberg	Waiblingen	Neustadt	W 163
Sommerberg	Abstatt	–	W 53 T
	Löwenstein		
	Untergruppenbach	Unterheinriet	
Sommerberg	Ebringen	–	B 275
Sommerhalde	Eberstadt	–	W 39
Sommerhalde	Kenzingen	Bombach	B 195
Sommerhalde	Korb	–	W 159
Sommerhalde	Reutlingen	–	W 199 a
Sommerheil	Hochheim	–	Rhg 105
Sommerleite	Elfershausen	Machtilshausen	F 30 d
Sommerstuhl	Güntersleben	–	F 47
Sommertal	Knetzgau	Oberschwappach	F 133
Sommerwende	Hangen-Weisheim	–	Rhh 358
Sonnberg	Laudenbach	–	B 29
Sonne	Oberheimbach	–	Mrh 107
Sonneberg	Sugenheim	Neundorf	F 128 e
Sonneck	Bullay	–	MSR 138
Sonneck	Zell	Merl	MSR 139
Sonnenberg	Alsheim	–	Rhh 330
Sonnenberg	Alzey	Heimersheim	Rhh 345
Sonnenberg	Angelbachtal	Eichtersheim	B 81 T
	Angelbachtal	Michelfeld	
	Sinsheim	Eschelbach	
	Sinsheim	Waldangelloch	
Sonnenberg	Aspisheim	–	Rhh 26
Sonnenberg	Baden-Baden	Varnhalt	B 119 T
	Sinzheim	–	
Sonnenberg	Bad Neuenahr-Ahrweiler	Neuenahr	A 5
Sonnenberg	Bechtolsheim	–	Rhh 309
Sonnenberg	Bönnigheim	–	W 119
Sonnenberg	Bockenheim an der Weinstraße	–	Rhpf 23 T
	Kindenheim	–	
Sonnenberg	Cochem	Sehl (Ebernach)	MSR 64
Sonnenberg	Dalberg	–	N 74
Sonnenberg	Ellerstadt	–	Rhpf 110
Sonnenberg	Eltville	–	Rhg 74
Sonnenberg	Essingen	–	Rhpf 256
Sonnenberg	Flein	–	W 67 T
	Heilbronn	–	
	Talheim	–	
Sonnenberg	Freiburg	Opfingen	B 260
Sonnenberg	Gönnheim	–	Rhpf 161
Sonnenberg	Guldental	Heddersheim und Waldhilbersheim	N 41
Sonnenberg	Gundheim	–	Rhh 361
Sonnenberg	Guntersblum	–	Rhh 286
Sonnenberg	Hackenheim	–	Rhh 67
Sonnenberg	Hergenfeld	–	N 76
Sonnenberg	Hohen-Sülzen	–	Rhh 411
Sonnenberg	Ilbesheim	–	Rhpf 296 T
	Leinsweiler	–	
Sonnenberg	Ingelheim	Groß-Winternheim	Rhh 147
Sonnenberg	Irsch	–	MSR 481
Sonnenberg	Kanzem	–	MSR 433
Sonnenberg	Konz	Niedermennig	MSR 435

Site	Town	Ortsteil	Region & Site No.
Sonnenberg	Korb	Kleinheppach	W 176 a
Sonnenberg	Marktbreit Marktsteft	— —	F 75 T
Sonnenberg	Neuleiningen	—	Rhpf 43
Sonnenberg	Nieder-Olm	—	Rhh 217
Sonnenberg	Norheim	—	N 283
Sonnenberg	Nußbaum	—	N 193
Sonnenberg	Oberotterbach Schweigen-Rechtenbach Schweighofen	— — —	Rhpf 324 T
Sonnenberg	Pfaffen-Schwabenheim	—	Rhh 20
Sonnenberg	Pfinztal	Berghausen	B 107
Sonnenberg	Remshalden Weinstadt Weinstadt	Geradstetten Beutelsbach Schnait	W 176 T
Sonnenberg	Roxheim	—	N 158
Sonnenberg	Schleich	—	MSR 338
Sonnenberg	Schöneberg	—	N 70
Sonnenberg	Schwabenheim	—	Rhh 138
Sonnenberg	Schwaigern Schwaigern	— Stetten	W 96 T
Sonnenberg	Sommerloch	—	N 91
Sonnenberg	Sprendlingen	—	Rhh 52
Sonnenberg	Stein-Bockenheim	—	Rhh 78
Sonnenberg	Trier	Ruwer	MSR 355
Sonnenberg	Udenheim	—	Rhh 208
Sonnenberg	Unkel	—	Mrh 10
Sonnenberg	Vendersheim	—	Rhh 128
Sonnenberg	Waldrach	—	MSR 393
Sonnenberg	Weisenheim am Berg	—	Rhpf 87
Sonnenberg	Wertheim Wertheim	Dertingen Kembach	B 2 T
Sonnenberg	Wonsheim	—	Rhh 78 a
Sonnenborn	**Langenlonsheim**	**—**	**N 62–68**
Sonnenbrunnen	Lörrach	—	B 320
Sonnenbüchel	Nonnenhorn	—	W 203
Sonnenbühl	**Kernen** **Kernen** **Weinstadt** **Weinstadt** **Weinstadt** **Weinstadt**	**Rommelshausen** **Stetten** **Beutelsbach** **Endersbach** **Schnait** **Strümpfelbach**	**W 192–195**
Sonnengold	Klotten	—	MSR 57
Sonnenhain	Remlingen	—	F 27 b
Sonnenhalden	Tübingen	Stadt und Ortsteile Hirschau und Unterjesingen	W 198
Sonnenhang	Eimsheim	—	Rhh 298
Sonnenhang	Guntersblum	—	Rhh 285
Sonnenhang	Ingelheim	Groß-Winternheim	Rhh 145
Sonnenhang	Schornsheim	—	Rhh 212
Sonnenhof	Gundelfingen	Wildtal	B 207
Sonnenköpfchen	Eckelsheim	—	Rhh 92
Sonnenlauf	Gutenberg	—	N 97
Sonnenlay	Ensch	—	MSR 335
Sonnenlay	Mülheim	—	MSR 260
Sonnenlay	Rhens	—	Mrh 40
Sonnenlay	Traben-Trarbach	Wolf	MSR 195
Sonnenleite	Dettelbach Dettelbach Dettelbach Volkach	— Brück Schnepfenbach Krautheim	F 83 T

Site	Town	Ortsteil	Region & Site No.
Sonnenmorgen	Windesheim	—	N 30
Sonnenplätzchen	Obermoschel	—	N 230
Sonnenring	Löf	—	MSR 36
Sonnenring	Müden	—	MSR 46
Sonnenschein	Bad Neuenahr-Ahrweiler	Bachem	A 9
Sonnenschein	Veitshöchheim	—	F 51
Sonnenseite ob der Bruck	Heidelberg	—	B 43
Sonnenstock	Damscheid	—	Mrh 67
Sonnenstück	Immesheim	—	Rhpf 14
Sonnenstück	Bad Bellingen Neuenburg am Rhein Schliengen Schliengen Schliengen Schliengen	— Steinenstadt — Liel Mauchen Niedereggenen	B 308 T
Sonnenstuhl	Randersacker	—	F 61
Sonnenufer	**Bermatingen** **Bodman** **Hagnau** **Hilzingen** **Immenstaad** **Immenstaad** **Konstanz** **Markdorf** **Meersburg** **Reichenau** **Salem** **Singen (Hohentwiel)** **Stetten** **Überlingen** **Uhldingen-Mühlhofen**	**—** **—** **—** **—** **—** **Kippenhausen** **—** **—** **—** **—** **Kirchberg** **—** **—** **—** **Oberuhldingen**	**B 328–334, 347, 348**
Sonnenuhr	Bernkastel-Kues	Wehlen	MSR 233
Sonnenuhr	Maring-Noviand	—	MSR 271
Sonnenuhr	Neumagen-Dhron	Neumagen	MSR 313
Sonnenuhr	Pommern	—	MSR 54
Sonnenuhr	Zeltingen-Rachtig	—	MSR 232
Sonnenweg	Gimbsheim	—	Rhh 289
Sonnenweg	Wallhausen	—	N 87
Sonnenwinkel	Michelau	Altmannsdorf	F 136
Sonnhalde	Denzlingen Sexau Waldkirch	— — Buchholz	B 200 T
Sonnhalde	Heitersheim	—	B 286
Sonnhalde	Konstanz	—	B 344
Sonnhalde	Müllheim Müllheim	— Vögisheim	B 298 T
Sonnheil	Hillesheim	—	Rhh 293
Sonnhohle	Bad Bellingen Binzen Efringen-Kirchen Efringen-Kirchen Eimeldingen Fischingen Rümmingen Schallbach Weil am Rhein	Hertingen — — Egringen — — — — Ötlingen	B 322 T
Sonnhole	Müllheim Müllheim	Britzingen Dattingen	B 293 T
Sonnleite	Zellingen	—	F 44 a
Sonntagsberg	Heilbronn Nordheim Nordheim	Klingenberg — Nordhausen	W 83 T
Soonecker Schloßberg	Niederheimbach	—	Mrh 111
Sorentberg	Reil	—	MSR 168
Spiegel	Neustadt an der Weinstraße	Mußbach an der Weinstraße	Rhpf 192

Site	Town	Ortsteil	Region & Site No.
Spiegelberg	Eppingen	Elsenz	B 91 T
	Kraichtal	Landshausen und Menzingen	
	Östringen	Tiefenbach	
Spiegelberg	**Nackenheim**	**–**	**Rhh 244–**
	Nierstein	**–**	**255**
	Nierstein	**Schwabsburg**	
Spielberg	Bad Dürkheim	–	Rhpf 121
Spielberg	Meckenheim	–	Rhpf 179
Spieß	Ruppertsberg	–	Rhpf 176
Spitalberg	Sobernheim	Steinhard	N 206
Spitalhalde	Lindau	–	W 204 T
	Wasserburg	–	
Spitzberg	Stadecken-Elsheim	Stadecken	Rhh 200
Spitzenberg	Wiesloch	–	B 50
St. siehe Sankt			
Stachelberg	Groß-Umstadt	Klein-Umstadt	HB 3
Stahlberg	Kühlsheim	Uissigheim	B 9
Stahlbühl	Heilbronn	–	W 29
Staig	Brackenheim	Hausen	W 89
Staudenberg	Hirschberg	Leutershausen	B 36 T
	Schriesheim	–	
Staufenberg	**Bad Friedrichshall**	**Duttenberg**	**W 18–**
	Bad Friedrichshall	**Offenau**	**27**
	Eberstadt	**–**	
	Ellhofen	**–**	
	Erlenbach-Binswangen	**Binswangen**	
	Erlenbach-Binswangen	**Erlenbach**	
	Gundelsheim	**–**	
	Heilbronn	**–**	
	Heilbronn	**Horkheim**	
	Langenbrettach	**Brettach**	
	Neckarsulm	**–**	
	Neckarsulm	**Untereisesheim**	
	Oedheim	**–**	
	Talheim	**–**	
	Weinsberg	**–**	
	Weinsberg	**Gellmersbach**	
Stefansberg	Zell	Merl	MSR 142
Stefanslay	Wintrich	–	MSR 288
Steffensberg	Enkirch	–	MSR 176
Steffensberg	Kröv	–	MSR 225
Stehlerberg	Kasbach-Ohlenberg	Kasbach	Mrh 11
Steig	Bissersheim	–	Rhpf 68
Steig	Eisingen	–	B 113
Steig	Flörsheim-Dalsheim	Dalsheim	Rhh 400 T
	Flörsheim-Dalsheim	Niederflörsheim	
Steig	Mainz	Kostheim	Rhg 100
Steige	Fürfeld	–	Rhh 77
Steigerberg	Wendelsheim	–	Rhh 96
Steigerdell	Bad Münster am Stein-Ebernburg	Münster	N 274
Steig-Terrassen	Guntersblum	–	Rhh 304
Steil	**Rüdesheim**	**Assmannshausen**	**Rhg 8–10**
	Rüdesheim	**Aulhausen**	
Stein	Bechtheim	–	Rhh 391
Stein	Flörsheim	Wicker	Rhg 111
Stein	Hochheim	–	Rhg 109
Stein	Karlstadt	Stetten	F 39
Stein	Würzburg	–	F 54
Stein/Harfe	Würzburg	–	F 55
Steinacker	Ellhofen	–	W 44 T
	Lehrensteinsfeld	–	
	Weinsberg	–	
Steinacker	Heidesheim	–	Rhh 161

Site	Town	Ortsteil	Region & Site No.
Steinacker	Ingelheim	Groß-Winternheim	Rhh 153
Steinacker	Kallstadt	–	Rhpf 98
Steinacker	Kirchheim an der Weinstraße	–	Rhpf 73
Steinacker	Nieder-Hilbersheim	–	Rhh 47
Steinacker	Rheinfelden	Herten	B 327
Steinbach	Sommerhausen	–	F 64 T
	Eibelstadt	–	
Steinbachhof	Vaihingen	Gündelbach	W 111
Steinberg	Alzenau	Michelbach	F 4
Steinberg	Bad Dürkheim	–	Rhpf 108
Steinberg	Bad Kreuznach	–	N 123
Steinberg	Beilstein	–	W 59
Steinberg	Bollschweil	–	B 281
Steinberg	Dalheim	–	Rhh 223
Steinberg	Durbach	–	B 159
Steinberg	Eltville	Hattenheim	Rhg Ortst. D
Steinberg	Guntersblum	–	Rhh 284
Steinberg	Niederhausen an der Nahe	–	N 301
Steinberg	Partenheim	–	Rhh 61
Steinberg	Sankt Johann	–	Rhh 55
Steinberg	Wackernheim	–	Rhh 159
Steinberger	Konz	Filzen	MSR 429
Steinbiß	Billigheim-Ingenheim	Appenhofen	Rhpf 311
Steinbuck	Vogtsburg im Kaiserstuhl	Bischoffingen	B 236
Steinchen	Löf	Kattenes	MSR 30
Steinchen	Langenlonsheim	–	N 67
Steinert	Gau-Algesheim	–	Rhh 37
Steinfelsen	Ihringen	–	B 223 T
	Vogtsburg im Kaiserstuhl	Bickensohl	
Steingässle	Efringen-Kirchen	–	B 311 T
	Efringen-Kirchen	Welmlingen	
	Efringen-Kirchen	Wintersweiler	
	Kandern	Feuerbach	
	Kandern	Holzen	
	Kandern	Riedlingen	
	Kandern	Tannenkirch	
	Kandern	Wollbach	
Steingebiß	Billigheim-Ingenheim	Appenhofen	Rhpf 311
Steingeröll	Zwingenberg	–	HB 8
Steingerück	Groß Umstadt	–	HB 4
Steingrube	Brackenheim	Neipperg	W 88
Steingrube	Endingen	–	B 253
Steingrube	March	Neuershausen	B 210 T
	Teningen	Nimburg	
Steingrube	Sasbach	Jechtingen	B 239
Steingrube	Stuttgart	Uhlbach	W 148
Steingrube	Westhofen	–	Rhh 366
Steingrüble	Bad Krozingen	–	B 271 T
	Bad Krozingen	Schlatt	
Steingrüble	Endingen	Königschaffhausen	B 250
Steingrüble	Korb	–	W 175 T
	Korb	Kleinheppach	
	Weinstadt	Großheppach	
Steingrübler	Baden-Baden	Varnhalt	B 121
Steingrübler	Miltenberg	–	F 18
Steinhalde	Edingen	Amoltern	B 251

Site	Town	Ortsteil	Region & Site No.
Steinhalde	Stuttgart	Bad Cannstatt	W 139 T
	Stuttgart	Mühlhausen	
	Stuttgart	Münster	
Steinhöhl	Monzernheim	–	Rhh 382
Steinkaul	Bad Neuenahr-Ahrweiler	Bachem	A 10
Steinkaut	Weinsheim	–	N 167
Steinklinge	Lauda-Königshofen	Oberlauda	B 17
Steinköpfchen	Rümmelsheim mit Ortsteil Burg Layen		N 13
Steinkopf	Heppenheim	–	HB 20 T
	Heppenheim	Hambach	
Steinkopf	Grünstadt Land	Heuchelheim bei Frankenthal	Rhpf 54
Steinkopf	Münster-Sarmsheim	–	N 11
Steinkreuz	Sankt Katharinen	–	N 150
Steinler	Freiburg	–	B 265
Steinler	Lottstetten	Nack	B 348
Steinmauer	Freiburg	Waltershofen	B 259
Steinmächer	**Eltville**	**–**	**Rhg 66,**
	Eltville	**Martinsthal**	**71–90,**
	Eltville	**Rauenthal**	**92–97**
	Walluf	**Nieferwalluf**	
	Walluf	**Oberwalluf**	
	Wiesbaden	**Dotzheim**	
	Wiesbaden	**Frauenstein**	
	Wiesbaden	**Schierstein**	
Steinmorgen	Eltville	–	Rhg 66 T
	Eltville	Erbach	
Steinrossel	Sommerloch	–	N 90
Steinsberg	Sinsheim	Steinsfurt	B 84 T
	Sinsheim	Weiler	
Steinschmetzer	Tauberbischofsheim	Dittigheim	B 14 b
Steinwengert	Pfinztal	Wöschbach	B 108
Steinwingert	Niederhausen an der Nahe	–	N 295
Stemmler	Heppenheim	–	HB 18 T
	Heppenheim	Hambach	
Stephansberg	Bad Münster am Stein-Ebernburg	Ebernburg	N 269
Stephansberg	Weinheim	Hohensachsen	B 33 T
	Weinheim	Lützelsachsen	
Stephanus-Rosengärtchen	Bernkastel-Kues	Bernkastel	MSR 253
Sternberg	Pleitersheim	–	Rhh 62
Sternenberg	Bühl	Altschweier	B 132 T
	Bühl	Neusatz	
Steyer	Hüffelsheim	–	N 180
Steyerberg	Schweppenhausen	–	N 27
Stich den Buben	Baden-Baden	Steinbach	B 122
Stiefel	Seinsheim	Tiefenstockheim	F 128 a
Stiege	Weil am Rhein	–	B 324 T
	Weil am Rhein	Haltingen	
	Weil am Rhein	Ötlingen	
Stielweg	Hochheim	–	Rhg 104
Stift	Forst an der Weinstraße	–	Rhpf 136
Stiftsberg	Bad Neuenahr-Ahrweiler	Marienthal	A 27
Stiftsberg	Heilbronn	–	W 27 T
	Heilbronn	Horkheim	
	Talheim	–	

Site	Town	Ortsteil	Region & Site No.
Stiftsberg	Angelbachtal	Eichtersheim	B 73–
	Angelbachtal	Michelfeld	100
	Bad Rappenau	Heinsheim	
	Binau	–	
	Bretten	Bauerbach	
	Eberbach	–	
	Eppingen	–	
	Eppingen	Elsenz	
	Eppingen	Mühlbach	
	Eppingen	Rohrbach a. G.	
	Gemmingen	–	
	Haßmersheim	–	
	Haßmersheim	Neckarmühlbach	
	Kirchardt	Berwangen	
	Kraichtal	Bahnbrücken, Gochsheim und Oberacker	
	Kraichtal	Landshausen und Menzingen	
	Kraichtal	Menzingen, Münzesheim und Neuenbürg	
	Kürnbach	–	
	Mosbach	Diedesheim	
	Neckarzimmern	–	
	Neudenau	–	
	Neudenau	Herbolzheim	
	Oberderdingen	Flehingen	
	Östringen	Eichelberg	
	Östringen	Odenheim	
	Östringen	Tiefenbach	
	Sinsheim	Eschelbach	
	Sinsheim	Hilsbach	
	Sinsheim	Steinsfurt	
	Sinsheim	Waldangelloch	
	Sinsheim	Weiler	
	Sulzfeld	–	
	Zaisenhausen	–	
Stirn	Saarburg mit Ortsteil Niederleuken		MSR 474
Stollberg	Oberschwarzach	Handthal	F 139
Stollenberg	Niederhausen an der Nahe	–	N 296
Stolzenberg	Löf	Hatzenport	MSR 37
Storchenbrünnle	Kitzingen	Sickershausen	F 119
Straußberg	Hargesheim	–	N 142
Streichling	Bensheim	–	HB 15 T
	Bensheim	Zell	
Stromberg	Bockenau	–	N 176
Stromberg	**Bönnigheim**	**–**	**W 99–**
	Bönnigheim	**Hofen**	**119**
	Bönnigheim	**Hohenstein**	
	Erligheim	**–**	
	Freudental	**–**	
	Illingen	**–**	
	Illingen	**Schützingen**	
	Kirchheim	**–**	
	Knittlingen	**–**	
	Knittlingen	**Freudenstein**	
	Maulbronn	**–**	
	Mühlacker	**Lienzingen**	
	Mühlacker	**Lomersheim**	
	Mühlacker	**Mühlhausen**	
	Oberderdingen	**Drifenbach**	
	Oberderdingen	**Großvillars**	
	Oberdingen	**–**	
	Ötisheim	**–**	
	Sachsenheim	**Häfnerhaslach**	
	Sachsenheim	**Hohenhaslach**	
	Sachsenheim	**Kleinsachsenheim**	
	Sachsenheim	**Ochsenbach**	
	Sachsenheim	**Spielberg**	
	Sternenfels	**–**	
	Sternenfels	**Diefenbach**	
	Vaihingen	**–**	
	Vaihingen	**Ensingen**	
	Vaihingen	**Gündelbach**	
	Vaihingen	**Horrheim**	
	Vaihingen	**Riet**	
	Vaihingen	**Roßweg**	

Site	Town	Ortsteil	Region & Site No.
Stubener Klostersegen	Ediger-Eller	Eller	MSR 104
Südlay	Pölich	—	MSR 341
Sülzenberg	Königswinter	Oberdollendorf	Mrh 3
Süßenberg	Lieser	—	MSR 248
Süßkopf	Forst an der Weinstraße	—	Rhpf 135
Süßmund	Steinheim	Kleinbottwar	W 65
Sybillenstein	**Alzey**	**—**	**Rhh 337—353**
	Alzey	**Dautenheim**	
	Alzey	**Heimersheim**	
	Alzey	**Schafhausen**	
	Alzey	**Weinheim**	
	Bechenheim	**—**	
	Freimersheim	**—**	
	Mauchenheim	**—**	
	Offenheim	**—**	
	Wahlheim	**—**	

Site	Town	Ortsteil	Region & Site No.
Täuscherspfad	Ingelheim	Groß-Winternheim	Rhh 150
Tafelstein	Dienheim	—	Rhh 278 T
	Uelversheim	—	
Tannacker	Endingen	—	B 254
Tannenberg	Willianzheim	Hüttenheim	F 123
Taubenberg	Eltville	—	Rhg 72
Taubenhaus	Traben-Trarbach	Trarbach	MSR 190
Tauberberg	**Bad Mergentheim**	**Markelsheim**	**W 1—6**
	Niederstetten	**—**	
	Niederstetten	**Oberstetten**	
	Niederstetten	**Vorbachzimmern**	
	Niederstetten	**Wermutshausen**	
	Weikersheim	**—**	
	Weikersheim	**Elpersheim**	
	Weikersheim	**Haagen**	
	Weikersheim	**Laudenbach**	
	Weikersheim	**Schäftersheim**	
Tauberklinge	**Bad Mergentheim**	**Dainbach**	**B 1—28 a**
	Boxberg	**Oberschüpf**	
	Boxberg	**Unterschüpf**	
	Großrinderfeld	**—**	
	Königheim	**—**	
	Königheim	**Gissigheim**	
	Krautheim	**—**	
	Krautheim	**Klepsau**	
	Külsheim	**—**	
	Külsheim	**Uissigheim**	
	Lauda-Königshofen	**Beckstein**	
	Lauda-Königshofen	**Gerlachsheim**	
	Lauda-Königshofen	**Königshofen**	
	Lauda-Königshofen	**Lauda**	
	Lauda-Königshofen	**Marbach**	
	Lauda-Königshofen	**Oberlauda**	
	Lauda-Königshofen	**Oberbalbach**	
	Lauda-Königshofen	**Sachsenflur**	
	Lauda-Königshofen	**Unterbalbach**	
	Tauberbischofsheim	**—**	
	Tauberbischofsheim	**Distelhausen**	
	Tauberbischofsheim	**Dittigheim**	
	Tauberbischofsheim	**Impfingen**	
	Werbach	**—**	
	Wertheim	**—**	
	Wertheim	**Bronnbach**	
	Wertheim	**Dertingen**	
	Wertheim	**Höhefeld**	
	Wertheim	**Kembach**	
	Wertheim	**Lindelbach**	
	Wertheim	**Reichholzheim**	
Tempelchen	Stadecken-Elsheim	Elsheim	Rhh 197
Teufel	Oberschwarzach	Kammerforst	F 140
Teufelsburg	Endingen	Kiechlinsbergen	B 247
Teufelskeller	Randersacker	—	F 60
Teufelskopf	Dielheim	—	B 53
Teufelskopf	Ludwigshöhe	—	Rhh 302
Teufelsküche	Guldental	Heddesheim und Waldhilbersheim	
Teufelspfad	Essenheim	—	Rhh 194
Teufelstein	Patersberg	—	Mrh 57
Teufelstor	**Eibelstadt**	**—**	**F 66—68**
	Randersacker	**—**	
	Randersacker	**Lindelbach**	
Thiergarten Felsköpfchen	Trier	Olewig	MSR 380
Thiergarten Unterm Kreuz	Trier	Olewig	MSR 379
Thomasberg	Burg	—	MSR 171
Tilgesbrunnen	Bad Kreuznach	—	N 101
Timpert	Kasel	—	MSR 409

Site	Town	Ortsteil	Region & Site No.
Trappenberg	**Altdorf**	–	**Rhpf 249–**
	Bellheim	–	**264 d**
	Böbingen	–	
	Bornheim	–	
	Essingen	–	
	Freimersheim	–	
	Groß- und Kleinfischlingen	–	
	Hochstadt	–	
	Knittelsheim	–	
	Lustadt	–	
	Ottersheim	–	
	Römerberg (bei Speyer)	**Berghausen**	
	Römerberg (bei Speyer)	**Mechtersheim**	
	Römerberg (bei Speyer)	**Heiligenstein**	
	Schwegenheim	–	
	Venningen	–	
	Weingarten	–	
	Zeiskam	–	
Trautberg	Castell	–	F 113
Trautlestal	Hammelburg	–	F 30
Treppchen	Erden	–	MSR 205
Treppchen	Piesport	–	MSR 296 T
	Piesport	Niederemmel	
Treppchen	Treis-Karden	Treis	MSR 76
Treuenfels	Altenbamberg	–	N 262
Trollberg	Dorsheim	–	N 54
Trollberg	Münster-Sarmsheim	–	N 8
Trotzenberg	Bad Neuenahr-Ahrweiler	Marienthal	A 25
Turmberg	Karlsruhe	Durlach	B 106 T
	Karlsruhe	Grötzingen	
Turmberg	Landau-Königshofen	Königshofen	B 23

Site	Town	Ortsteil	Region & Site No.
Übereltzer	Moselkern	–	MSR 43
Übigberg	Altenahr	–	A 43 T
	Altenahr	Kreuzberg	
	Ahrbrück	Pützfeld	
Uhlen	Kobern-Gondorf	Kobern	MSR 11 a
Uhlen	Winningen	–	MSR 11
Ulrichsberg	Östringen	–	B 61
Ungeheuer	Forst an der Weinstraße	–	Rhpf 149
Ungsberg	Traben-Trarbach	Trarbach	MSR 187
Unterberg	Konz	Filzen	MSR 427
Urbelt	Konz	Filzen	MSR 425
Ursulinengarten	Bad Neuenahr-Ahrweiler	Ahrweiler	A 16

Site	Town	Ortsteil	Region & Site No.
Venusbuckel	Billigheim-Ingenheim	Billigheim	Rhpf 309
Verrenberg	Öhringen	Verrenberg	W 35
Villenkeller	Klein-Winternheim	–	Rhh 191
Vitusberg	Walluf	Oberwalluf	Rhg 89
Vögelein	Nordheim	–	F 91
Vogelsang	Bad Kreuznach	–	N 113
Vogelsang	Bockenheim an der Weinstraße	–	Rhpf 19 T
	Kindenheim	–	
Vogelsang	Brackenheim	Hausen	W 79 a
Vogelsang	Bretzenheim	–	N 138
Vogelsang	Erbes-Büdesheim	–	Rhh 103
Vogelsang	Gau-Odernheim	–	Rhh 315
Vogelsang	Geisenheim	Johannisberg	Rhg 31
Vogelsang	Gemmingen	–	B 92 T
	Kirchardt	Berwangen	
Vogelsang	Iphofen	Possenheim	F 122 T
	Markt Einersheim	–	
Vogelsang	Laubenheim	–	N 55
Vogelsang	Merxheim	–	N 187
Vogelsang	Serrig	–	MSR 489
Vogelsang	Untereisesheim	–	W 21
Vogelsang	Wallertheim	–	Rhh 123
Vogelsang	Weisenheim am Berg	–	Rhpf 104
Vogelsang	Zornheim	–	Rhh 237
Vogelsberg	Lauda-Königshofen	Unterbalbach	B 23 a
Vogelschlag	Duchroth	–	N 322
Vogelsgärten	**Guntersblum**	**–**	**Rhh 302–307**
	Ludwigshöhe	**–**	
Vogelsprung	Flemlingen	–	Rhpf 271
Vogteiberg	Senheim	–	MSR 101
Vogtei Rötteln	**Bad Bellingen**	**Bamberg**	**B 311–327**
	Bad Bellingen	**Hertingen**	
	Bad Bellingen	**Rheinweiler**	
	Binzen	**–**	
	Efringen-Kirchen	**–**	
	Efringen-Kirchen	**Blansingen**	
	Efringen-Kirchen	**Egringen**	
	Efringen-Kirchen	**Huttingen**	
	Efringen-Kirchen	**Istein**	
	Efringen-Kirchen	**Kleinkems**	
	Efringen-Kirchen	**Welmlingen**	
	Efringen-Kirchen	**Wintersweiler**	
	Eimeldingen	**–**	
	Fischingen	**–**	
	Grenzach-Whylen	**Grenzach**	
	Kandern	**Feuerbach**	
	Kandern	**Holzen**	
	Kandern	**Riedlingen**	
	Kandern	**Tannenkirch**	
	Kandern	**Wollbach**	
	Lörrach	**–**	
	Rheinfelden	**Herten**	
	Rümmingen	**–**	
	Schallbach	**–**	
	Weil am Rhein	**–**	
	Weil am Rhein	**Haltingen**	
	Weil am Rhein	**Ötlingen**	
Vollburg	Michelau	–	F 137
Vom heißen Stein	**Briedel**	**–**	**MSR 156–168**
	Pünderich	**–**	
	Reil	**–**	
Vorderberg	Kleinniedesheim	–	Rhpf 52
Vor der Hölle	Desloch	–	N 223

Site	Town	Ortsteil	Region & Site No.
Vulkanfelsen	**Bahlingen**	**–**	**B 210–256**
	Bötzingen	**–**	
	Breisach	**–**	
	Eichstetten	**–**	
	Endingen	**–**	
	Endingen	**Amoltern**	
	Endingen	**Kiechlinsbergen**	
	Endingen	**Königschaffhausen**	
	Ihringen	**–**	
	Ihringen	**Blankenhornberg**	
	Ihringen	**Wasenweiler**	
	March	**Neuershausen**	
	Riegel	**–**	
	Sasbach	**–**	
	Sasbach	**Jechtingen**	
	Sasbach	**Leiselheim**	
	Teningen	**Nimburg**	
	Vogtsburg im Kaiserstuhl	**Achkarren**	
	Vogtsburg im Kaiserstuhl	**Bickensohl**	
	Vogtsburg im Kaiserstuhl	**Bischoffingen**	
	Vogtsburg im Kaiserstuhl	**Burkheim**	
	Vogtsburg im Kaiserstuhl	**Oberbergen**	
	Vogtsburg im Kaiserstuhl	**Oberrotweil**	
	Vogtsburg im Kaiserstuhl	**Schelingen**	

Site	Town	Ortsteil	Region & Site No.
Wachhügel	Wiesenbronn	–	F 115
Wachtkopf	Vaihingen	Gündelbach	W 110
Wahrheit	Oberheimbach	–	Mrh 106
Wahrsager	Senheim	–	MSR 99
Walkenberg	Walluf	Niederwalluf	Rhg 87
Wallmauer	Neckarzimmern	–	B 75
Walterstal	Lauda-Königshofen	Königshofen	B 22 T
	Lauda-Königshofen	Sachsenflur	
Wanne	Weinstadt	Großheppach	W 168
Wartberg	Alzey	–	Rhh 350
Wartberg	Beilstein	–	W 58
Wartbühl	**Aichwald**	**Aichelberg**	**W 172–**
	Kernen	**Rommelshausen**	**190**
	Kernen	**Stetten**	
	Korb	**–**	
	Korb	**Kleinheppach**	
	Remshalden	**Geradstetten**	
	Remshalden	**Grunbach**	
	Remshalden	**Hebsack**	
	Weinstadt	**Beutelsbach**	
	Weinstadt	**Endersbach**	
	Weinstadt	**Großheppach**	
	Weinstadt	**Schnait**	
	Weinstadt	**Strümpelbach**	
	Winnenden	**–**	
	Winnenden	**Baach**	
	Winnenden	**Breuningsweiler**	
	Winnenden	**Hahnweiler**	
	Winnenden	**Hertmannsweiler**	
Wasseros	Kiedrich	–	Rhg 70
Weilberg	Bad Dürkheim	Ungstein	Rhpf 117
Weinberge	Viereth	Weiher	F 135 a
Weingarten	Fischingen	–	B 323
Weingrube	Boppard	Boppader Hamm	Mrh 46
Weinhecke	Bruchsal	–	B 65 T
	Ubstadt-Weiher	Ubstadt	
Weinhex	**Alken**	**–**	**MSR 1–**
	Brodenbach	**–**	**40**
	Burgen	**–**	
	Dieblich	**–**	
	Kobern-Gondorf	**Gondorf**	
	Kobern-Gondorf	**Kobern**	
	Koblenz	**Güls und**	
		Metternich	
	Koblenz	**Lay**	
	Koblenz	**Moselweiß**	
	Lehmen	**–**	
	Löf	**–**	
	Löf	**Hatzenport**	
	Löf	**Kattenes**	
	Moselsürsch	**–**	
	Niederfell	**–**	
	Oberfell	**–**	
	Winningen	**–**	
Weinkammer	Enkirch	–	MSR 177
Weinkeller	Mainz	Ebersheim	Rhh 169
Weinsack	Odernheim am Glan	–	N 215
Weinsteig	Erlabrunn	–	F 48 T
	Leinach	Oberleinach	

Site	Town	Ortsteil	Region & Site No.
Weinsteige	**Eßlingen**	**–**	**W 134–**
	Fellbach	**–**	**158**
	Gerlingen	**–**	
	Stuttgart		
	Stuttgart	**Bad Cannstatt**	
	Stuttgart	**Degerloch**	
	Stuttgart	**Feuerbach**	
	Stuttgart	**Gaisburg**	
	Stuttgart	**Hedelfingen**	
	Stuttgart	**Hofen**	
	Stuttgart	**Hohenheim**	
	Stuttgart	**Mühlhausen**	
	Stuttgart	**Münster**	
	Stuttgart	**Obertürkheim**	
	Stuttgart	**Rohracker**	
	Stuttgart	**Rotenberg**	
	Stuttgart	**Uhlbach**	
	Stuttgart	**Untertürkheim**	
	Stuttgart	**Wangen**	
	Stuttgart	**Zuffenhausen**	
Weisenstein	Bernkastel-Kues	Kues	MSR 256
Weißenberg	Kobern-Gondorf	Kobern	MSR 13
Weißenstein	Mannweiler-Cölln	–	N 248 a
Weißenstein	Oberndorf	–	N 248
Weißerberg	Briedel	–	MSR 156
Weiß Erd	Mainz	Kostheim	Rhg 99
Weißes Kreuz	Leubsdorf	–	Mrh 14
Wendelstück	Burg	–	MSR 169
Wernleite	Gemünden	Adelsberg	F 68 a
Westrum	Bodenheim	–	Rhh 175
Wetterkreuz	Braunweiler	–	N 145
Wetzstein	Fellbach	–	W 146 T
	Stuttgart	Untertürkheim	
Wetzstein	Weinstadt	Endersbach	W 180
Wiesberg	Rüdesheim	–	N 162
Wildenberg	Ellhofen	–	W 42 T
	Weinsberg	Grantschen	
Wildgrafenberg	Kirschroth	–	N 196
Wildsau	Eltville	Martinstal	Rhg 83
Wilhelmsberg	Kitzingen	–	F 78
Wilhelmsberg	Nußloch	–	B 48
Wingertsberg	Dietzenbach	–	HB 1
Wingertsberg	Nieder-Wiesen	–	Rhh 93
Wingertstor	Bechtolsheim	–	Rhh 308
Winklerberg	Ihringen	–	B 220
Wißberg	Gau-Weinheim	–	Rhh 125
Wißberg	Sprendlingen	–	Rhh 53
Wisselbrunnen	Eltville	Hattenheim	Rhg 50
Wölflein	Veitshöchheim	–	F 50
Wohlfahrtsberg	Löwenstein	–	W 52
Wolfer	Efringen-Kirchen	Blansingen	B 317 T
	Efringen-Kirchen	Kleinkems	
Wolfhag	Bühl	Neusatz	B 135 T
	Ottersweier		
Wolfsaugen	Brackenheim	–	W 85
Wolfsberg	Schweighofen	–	Rhpf 325
Wolfshöhle	Bacharach	–	Mrh 92
Wolfsmagen	**Bensheim einschließlich**		**HB 6–10**
	Zell und Gronau		
Wolfsnach	Dörscheid	–	Mrh 78
Wonne	Neundorf	Sugenheim	F 128 f
Wonneberg	Bad Bergzabern	–	Rhpf 323 T
	Dörrenbach	–	
Woogberg	Ellenz-Poltersdorf	–	MSR 89
Wülfen	Eltville	Rauenthal	Rhg 79
Würtzberg	Serrig	–	MSR 492

Site	Town	Ortsteil	Region & Site No.
Würzgarten	Detzem	–	MSR 336
Würzgarten	Oestrich-Winkel	Hallgarten	Rhg 57
Würzgarten	Traben-Trarbach	Traben	MSR 193
Würzgarten	Ürzig	–	MSR 207
Würzhölle	Unkenbach	–	N 228
Würzlay	Lehmen	–	MSR 24
Wüstberg	Weinheim	–	B 32
Wunnenstein	**Beilstein**	**–**	**W 58–**
	Beilstein	**Hohenbeilstein**	**66**
	Großbottwar	**–**	
	Großbottwar	**Hof und Lembach**	
	Großbottwar	**Winzerhausen**	
	Ilsfeld	**–**	
	Ludwigsburg	**Hoheneck**	
	Oberstenfeld	**–**	
	Oberstenfeld	**Gronau**	
	Steinheim	**–**	
	Steinheim	**Kleinbottwar**	
Wurmberg	Besigheim	–	W 120 T
	Bietigheim-Bissingen	Bietigheim	
	Gemmrigheim	–	
	Hessigheim	–	
	Walheim	–	
Wurmberg	Neubrunn	Böttigheim	F 52 a
Wutschenberg	Kleinlangheim	–	F 114
Yburgberg	Baden-Baden	Steinbach	B 123

Site	Town	Ortsteil	Region & Site No.
Zechberg	Framersheim	–	Rhh 316
Zechpeter	Flemlingen	–	Rhpf 272
Zehmorgen	Nierstein	–	Rhh 261
Zehntgraf	Wipfeld	–	F 102
Zeilberg	Löwenstein	Hößlinsülz	W 47 T
	Obersulm	Affaltrach	
	Obersulm	Willsbach	
Zeisel	Pommern	–	MSR 52
Zellerberg	Longen	–	MSR 344 T
	Mehring	–	
	Mehring	Lörsch	
Zellerweg am schwarzen Herrgott	Mölsheim	–	Rhh 406
Zeppwingert	Enkirch	–	MSR 179
Zickelgarten	Ockfen	–	MSR 466
Zitadelle	Sankt Martin	–	Rhpf 227
Zobelsberg	Segnitz	–	F 73
Zollturm	Traben-Trarbach	Traben	MSR 184
Zuckerberg	Oppenheim	–	Rhh 269
Zuckerle	Stuttgart	Bad Cannstatt	W 140 T
	Stuttgart	Mühlhausen	
	Stuttgart	Münster	
Zügernberg	Weinstadt	Großheppach	W 177
Zweifelberg	Brackenheim	–	W 84

INDEX

This index contains both the names of wine producers and the placenames connected with the vineyard maps. The Bereiche are also shown; Großlagen and Einzellagen are listed in the Vineyard Register (see p184). Abbreviations are explained on p184.

ILLUSTRATIONS
Jonathan Field

KEY MAPS
John Laing

PHOTOGRAPHS
Bildagentur Mauritius,
Frankfurt: pages 36, 40,
41, 44L, 44/5, 49R, 58,
59, 62T, 63BL, 63TR,
84B, 102/3, 103CR,
114, 128, 129, 140,
153L, 153R, 168T,
168B, 169; Jon Wyand:
pages 39, 41TL, 49L,
63BR, 75, 84T, 85,
92L, 92R, 93, 103BL,
103TL, 103CL; ZEFA,
London: pages 37, 141,
153C.